ALTRUISM IN INTERNATIONAL LAW

Much emphasis has been placed on the role that individualism, self-interest and reciprocity have in the formation and function of international legal rules. Rarely has attention been given to the presence of altruism in legal systems, let alone the international legal system. In a study that is the first of its kind in international legal scholarship, *Altruism in International Law* explores and analyses the emergence of altruistic legal relationships between states and people in other countries. The book also argues that the impulse for the emergence of these relationships is a cosmopolitan ideology which co-exists with a persisting statist ideology, among the major actors in international law-making processes. Further still, the book reveals that individualistic legal norms are more often manifested as strict rules, while altruistic legal norms find expression in flexible standards. This suggests that there is a connection between substance and form in international law.

JASON RUDALL is Assistant Professor of Public International Law at the Grotius Centre for International Legal Studies, Leiden University. His other books include *Compensation for Environmental Damage under International Law* (2020) and *The UN Convention on the Law of the Non-Navigational Uses of International Watercourses: A Commentary* (2018). He has worked with international organisations, NGOs, law firms and in litigation.

ALTRUISM IN INTERNATIONAL LAW

JASON RUDALL
Leiden University

CAMBRIDGE
UNIVERSITY PRESS

CAMBRIDGE
UNIVERSITY PRESS

Shaftesbury Road, Cambridge CB2 8EA, United Kingdom

One Liberty Plaza, 20th Floor, New York, NY 10006, USA

477 Williamstown Road, Port Melbourne, VIC 3207, Australia

314–321, 3rd Floor, Plot 3, Splendor Forum, Jasola District Centre, New Delhi – 110025, India

103 Penang Road, #05–06/07, Visioncrest Commercial, Singapore 238467

Cambridge University Press is part of Cambridge University Press & Assessment, a department of the University of Cambridge.

We share the University's mission to contribute to society through the pursuit of education, learning and research at the highest international levels of excellence.

www.cambridge.org
Information on this title: www.cambridge.org/9781108799867

DOI: 10.1017/9781108892018

First published 2021
First paperback edition 2026

A catalogue record for this publication is available from the British Library

Library of Congress Cataloging-in-Publication data
Names: Rudall, Jason, author.
Title: Altruism in international law / Jason Rudall.
Description: New York : Cambridge University Press, 2021. | Includes bibliographical references and index.
Identifiers: LCCN 2021009531 (print) | LCCN 2021009532 (ebook) | ISBN 9781108835251 (hardback) | ISBN 9781108892018 (ebook)
Subjects: LCSH: Responsibility to protect (International law) | International cooperation. | Environmental law, International. | Environmental justice – International cooperation. | Altruism. | Helping behavior. | Altruism – Social aspects. | Human rights. | BISAC: LAW / International | LAW / International
Classification: LCC KZ4082 .R83 2021 (print) | LCC KZ4082 (ebook) | DDC 341/.011–dc23
LC record available at https://lccn.loc.gov/2021009531
LC ebook record available at https://lccn.loc.gov/2021009532

ISBN 978-1-108-83525-1 Hardback
ISBN 978-1-108-79986-7 Paperback

Carolyn, Nigel and Amy

CONTENTS

PREFACE AND ACKNOWLEDGEMENTS

In a project that has spanned eight years, much changed in the world around me, and there were reasons to doubt the existence of altruism in our species. It is often easy to overlook the quiet but constant altruism in our communities when we are confronted every so often with selfish acts that shock our conscience. But that such things shock us says something about our natural predisposition. In this study, relying as it does on empirical research, I have had the opportunity to inquire into the true nature of human behaviour, to consider how this shapes our social structures and whether it is manifested in the law. Writing this book has allowed me to explore other cultures, conduct research in different countries and cross disciplinary boundaries. In doing so, the project has led me to take a long evidence-based view and, ultimately, affirmed my faith in both the international legal system and humanity at large. That is, of course, not to suggest that there exist fundamental deficiencies nor that we should be in any way complacent because, as will be seen, the altruism in international law – as in our society – is fragile and vulnerable to abuse. However, I hope that the readers of this book will take away a similar optimism about the future of international law and, more generally, our world.

This is a book about altruism. While writing it, I have been the beneficiary of many individual acts of altruism, and I am indebted to those who accompanied me on this academic journey. The book's origins lie in my PhD on the topic, and I owe a particular debt of gratitude to my international law teachers who have allowed me to acquire the knowledge, skills and perspectives to write it. I am especially grateful to my PhD supervisor Andrea Bianchi at the Graduate Institute of International and Development Studies, Geneva. He helped me to approach legal study from different perspectives, to question dogmas and gave me the discretion to think creatively about the law. I am also thankful to Andrew Clapham at the Graduate Institute and Tom Ruys at Ghent University, who both served on my PhD jury and offered valuable feedback that has improved this book immeasurably. I would similarly like to express my gratitude to Laurence Boisson de Chazournes at the University of Geneva, who has been a source of precious guidance for many years.

The wider communities at the International Law Department of the Graduate Institute, the *Département de droit international public et organisation internationale* at the University of Geneva and the Grotius Centre for International Legal Studies at Leiden University have all been incredibly supportive environments out of which I have taken much inspiration and that allowed work on this book to be completed.

The encouragement I received from my close friends and wider family throughout this project has been a powerful motivating force, and they have all helped me to keep perspective while writing the book. I am particularly grateful to my parents and sister for their unconditional love and support. They have taught me the importance of education, hard work, and persistence, which have all been critical in seeing this book to fruition. Most importantly of all, however, they taught me everything I really needed to know about altruism. This book is for them.

Introduction

The Problématique

There is a widely shared assumption that law is primarily characterised by individualism.[1] International law is no different. Much emphasis has been placed on the role that self-interest and reciprocity have in the formation and ultimate function of international legal rules. Rarely has attention been given to the presence of altruism in legal systems, let alone the international legal system. However, altruistic legal relationships between states and individuals in other countries or future generations are apparent in international law. This observation about the nature of some legal relationships is the point of departure for the present book. These legal relationships defy characterisation as individualistic or primarily self-interested and pose an analytical problem for statist and realist theory.

This book challenges the view that international law can be reduced to the maximisation of individual state interests. It does not deny that states often act in self-interested ways, and that international legal rules reflect or permit such behaviour. Neither does it aim to suggest that this is, in and of itself, wrong. Instead, the book is a humble reminder that people are capable of acting, and perhaps even predisposed to act, in altruistic ways. The altruism that exists in international society is also reflected in and often encouraged by international legal rules. This book's basic premise is that the normative system of international law is a complex one where altruistic tendencies go hand-in-hand with other, often opposite, tendencies. It aims to show that cosmopolitan altruism is more omnipresent in the fabric of international law than commonly thought. The book also serves as a warning that the altruistic behaviour of states can wax and wane at different points in time, and illustrates that altruistic promises made in

[1] Duncan Kennedy, 'Form and Substance in Private Law Adjudication' (1976) 89 *Harvard Law Review* 1685, 1718–1719.

the substance of international law can be vulnerable because of the form they take, not least as flexible legal standards. But promises should be kept and this book suggests several ways to help ensure they are.

The Evolution of International Legal Relationships

Understanding the nature of legal relationships is central to this inquiry. I argue that there have been several major turns in the evolution of international legal obligations. Traditionally, obligations existed horizontally between states at the international level,[2] and the Westphalian order came to require that international law regulated state-to-state relations.[3] The well-known *Lotus* case of 1927 is symbolic of this traditional approach, and the following passage from that case brings this nature of legal relationships into sharp focus:

> International law governs relations between independent States. The rules of law binding upon States therefore emanate from their own free will as expressed in conventions or by usages of law and established in order to regulate the relations between these co-existing independent communities or with a view to the achievement of common aims. Restrictions upon the independence of States cannot therefore be presumed.[4]

[2] Wolfgang Friedmann, *The Changing Structure of International Law* (Stevens, 1964). In this book Friedmann highlights a variety of changes to the structure and content of international law, from its reach over new subject matter like economic co-operation and its inclusion of all civilisations around the world to its adaptation to different ideologies and new technologies. Moreover, Friedmann argued that there were three main levels of international law: (i) the law of co-existence; (ii) the law of co-operation at the universal level; and (iii) the law of co-operation at the regional level; on the centrality of sovereignty to the international legal order, see Steve Smith, 'Reasons of State' in David Held and Christopher Pollitt (eds.), *New Forms of Democracy* (Sage, 1987), 192–217; Kalevi J. Holsti, *International Politics: A Framework of Analysis* (5th ed., Prentice Hall, 1988). Arguing that the inter-state model preceded the human rights model, see Daniel Levy and Natan Sznaider, 'The Institutionalization of Cosmopolitan Morality' (2004) 3(2) *Journal of Human Rights* 143, 144; Bruno Simma, 'From Bilateralism to Community Interest in International Law' (1994-VI) *Collected Courses of the Hague Academy of International Law* 234 (noting the shift from bilateral legal relations between states which characterised classical international law to a system becoming more oriented towards the community interests of all human beings); Georges Abi-Saab, 'Cours general de droit international public' (1987-VII) *Collected Courses of the Hague Academy of International Law* 207, 460 (describing the change in the structure of international law as an evolutionary process).

[3] Sigrun Skogly, *Beyond National Borders: States' Human Rights Obligations in International Cooperation* (Intersentia, 2006), 23.

[4] *The Case of the S.S. Lotus (France* v. *Turkey)*, PCIJ Series A, no. 10 (1927), 18.

That international legal obligations would be almost exclusively of a horizontal character would change after the atrocities of the interwar period. With the development of international human rights in the last century,[5] vertical obligations between states and their own peoples became a cause for international concern.[6] Following the horrors perpetrated by the authoritarian regimes of the 1930s and 1940s, the need for national human rights protection with international oversight became apparent and there was a growing consensus that traditional conceptions of absolute sovereignty had to be reconsidered.[7] Since then human rights protection has broadened and deepened, particularly in terms of the types of obligations and mechanisms of supervision. The universalisation of international human rights protection in the post-war period is symbolised not least by Article 28 of the Universal Declaration of Human Rights of 1948, which provides that '[e]veryone is entitled to a social and international order in which the rights and freedoms set forth in the

[5] This includes the emergence of a myriad of human rights treaties, many of which will be referred to in this project. For example, European Convention for the Protection of Human Rights and Fundamental Freedoms, 4 November 1950, 213 UNTS 221; Convention on the Prevention and Punishment of Genocide, 9 December 1948, 78 UNTS 277; Convention on the Abolition of Slavery, the Slave Trade, and Institutions and Practices Similar to Slavery, Supplementary to the International Convention signed at Geneva on 25 September 1926, 7 September 1956, 266 UNTS 3; International Covenant on Economic, Social and Cultural Rights, 16 December 1966, 993 UNTS 3; International Covenant on Civil and Political Rights, 16 December 1966, 999 UNTS 171; American Convention on Human Rights, 22 November 1969, 1144 UNTS 123; International Convention on the Elimination of All Forms of Racial Discrimination, 21 December 1965, 660 UNTS 195; International Convention on the Elimination of All Forms of Discrimination Against Women, 18 December 1979, 1249 UNTS 13; African Charter on Human and Peoples' Rights, 27 June 1981, OAU Doc. CAB/LEG/67/3 rev.5; Convention on the Rights of the Child, 20 November 1989, 1577 UNTS 3; Convention against Torture and Other Cruel, Inhuman or Degrading Treatment or Punishment, 10 December 1984, 1465 UNTS 85.

[6] Malcolm Shaw, *International Law* (5th ed., Cambridge University Press, 2003), 232: 'individuals have become increasingly recognized as participants and subjects of international law ... primarily but not exclusively through human rights law'. See also Giorgio Gaja, 'The Position of Individuals in International Law: An ILC Perspective' (2010) 21 *European Journal of International Law* 11–14; Andrea Bianchi, '*Ad-Hocism* and the Rule of Law' (2002) 13(1) *European Journal of International Law* 263, 269 (noting the 'complexity and emerging vertical structure' of the international legal order pointing 'to an evolutionary process, which, though far from being fully achieved, is well under way').

[7] See Christian Tomuschat, *Human Rights: Between Idealism and Realism* (2nd ed., Oxford University Press, 2008), 22.

Declaration can be fully realized'.[8] States committed to creating the international conditions that would allow all people to enjoy the basic rights and freedoms to which they were entitled.

In fact, the international legal framework has been humanised in various dimensions.[9] Alongside the emergence of international human rights law, since the Nuremburg military tribunals the individuation of punishment has become a feature of international justice through the definition of international crimes, the increasing acceptance of universal criminal jurisdiction and the proliferation of international criminal courts. This development is in contrast to the approach taken in the aftermath of World War I when there had been a focus on state aggression and collective sanctions.

This evolution in the protection of human beings at the international level after World War II was characterised by the International Tribunal for the Prosecution of Persons Responsible for Serious Violations of International Humanitarian Law Committed in the Territory of the former Yugoslavia since 1991 (ICTY) as a 'trend towards the so-called "humanisation" of international legal obligations', which could also be evidenced by a retreat from reciprocity in recent years.[10] The Tribunal went on to observe that this 'trend marks the translation into legal norms of the "categorical imperative" formulated by Kant in the field of morals: one ought to fulfil an obligation regardless of whether others comply with it or disregard it'.[11] Similarly, in a different case the ICTY observed that:

[8] Universal Declaration of Human Rights, 10 December 1948, 999 UNTS 302; see also, for example, Jonathan Charney, 'Universal International Law' (1993) 87 *American Journal of International Law* 529.

[9] See, for example, Bruno Simma and Philip Alston, 'The Sources of Human Rights Law: Custom, Jus Cogens, and General Principles' (1988) 12 *Australian Yearbook of International Law* 82, (noting in 1988 in particular that '[t]he last few years have witnessed an ever-expanding number of contexts in which those norms are being invoked. International development assistance has become far more human rights-conscious than was the case a decade ago, labour rights issues are intruding further and further into the international trade regime, and the very legitimacy of governments is being regularly assessed on the basis of their compliance with international human rights norms'); Ruti Teitel, *Humanity's Law* (Oxford University Press, 2013); Steven Ratner, *The Thin Justice of International Law: A Moral Reckoning of the Law of Nations* (Oxford University Press, 2015); Antônio Augusto Cançado Trindade, *International Law for Humankind: Towards a New Jus Gentium* (Brill, 2010).

[10] Case no. IT-95-16-T, *The Prosecutor* v. *Kupreskic et al.*, International Tribunal for the Prosecution of Persons Responsible for Serious Violations of International Humanitarian Law Committed in the Territory of the former Yugoslavia since 1991, 14 January 2000, para 518.

[11] *Ibid.*

> [T]he impetuous development and propagation in the international community of human rights doctrines, particularly after the adoption of the Universal Declaration of Human Rights in 1948, has brought about significant changes in international law. . . . A State-sovereignty-oriented approach has gradually been supplanted by a human-being-oriented approach. Gradually the maxim of Roman law *hominum causa omne jus constitutum est* (all law is created for the benefit of human beings) has gained a firm foothold in the international community as well.[12]

But another turn in the normative orientation of international legal rules is also apparent in the aftermath of World War II, namely a concern for the other. A number of significant conventions that are fundamental to the universal humanisation of international law were adopted throughout this period, including the Convention on the Prevention and Punishment of the Crime of Genocide 1948,[13] the International Covenant on Civil and Political Rights 1966[14] and the International Covenant on Economic, Social and Cultural Rights 1966.[15] Moreover, the scope of the Geneva Conventions was expanded.[16] Further still, the emergence of *jus cogens* and *erga omnes* obligations was made possible by a culture of widely shared values in the international community. There was, generally speaking, a crystallisation of certain universal norms.

Early in the second half of the twentieth century there were signs of an emerging solidarity with people of third states through the emergence of, for example, the principle of non-refoulement in the Convention Relating to the Status of Refugees 1951[17] or the various legal and political measures crafted to catalyse development, including the creation of the New International Economic Order and a legal framework around the right to development.[18] An early (if controversial) example

[12] Case no. IT-94-1-I, *The Prosecutor* v. *Tadić*, International Tribunal for the Prosecution of Persons Responsible for Serious Violations of International Humanitarian Law Committed in the Territory of the former Yugoslavia since 1991, Defence Motion for Interlocutory Appeal on Jurisdiction, 2 October 1995, para 97.

[13] Convention on the Prevention and Punishment of the Crime of Genocide, 9 December 1948, 78 UNTS 277.

[14] International Covenant on Civil and Political Rights, 16 December 1966, 999 UNTS 171.

[15] International Covenant on Economic, Social and Cultural Rights, 16 December 1966, 993 UNTS 3.

[16] Protocols I and II additional to the Geneva Conventions, 8 June 1977, 1125 UNTS 3.

[17] Convention Relating to the Status of Refugees, 28 July 1951, 189 UNTS 137.

[18] See, for example, Declaration on the Establishment of a New International Economic Order, UN General Assembly Resolution 3201, 1 May 1974, UN Doc. A/RES/3201 (S-VI); Charter of Economic Rights and Duties of States, UN General Assembly Resolution 3281 (XXIX), 12 December 1974, UN Doc. A/RES/3281 (XXIX); Declaration on the Right to

of this solidarity may be found in Article 73 of the UN Charter,[19] which provides that

> [m]embers of the United Nations which have or assume responsibility for . . . territories whose people have not yet attained a full measure of self-government . . . accept as a sacred trust the obligation to promote to the utmost . . . the well-being of inhabitants of the territories.

It has been argued that this provision in particular shows how states may be under a moral obligation towards people in other states or even communities that do not belong to a state as such.[20] Indeed, these types of obligations are also evident in the context of the right to food, the legal provision for which envisages a role for third states in its implementation.[21] Similarly, legal commitments made to people in other countries are also evident in the interpretations of major multilateral treaties and principles, including the prevention of genocide, torture and breaches of international humanitarian law, as well as expanding notions of solidarity, which will all be explored in the chapters to follow. Moreover, the law of state responsibility is evolving, particularly with respect to obligations on bystanders. In this context, some international legal scholars have observed that international law now has a framework for the protection of populations through the shared responsibility of bystanders.[22]

The atrocities that took place in the Balkans and Rwanda in the 1990s prompted a change in the international community's attitude to the internal conflicts of states, particularly that they came to be perceived as a threat to international peace and security.[23] Subsequently, judicial mechanisms were set up by the Security Council to prosecute those who committed international crimes in those internal conflicts. As such, law

Development, General Assembly Resolution 41/128, 4 December 1986, UN Doc. A/RES/41/128.

19 Charter of the United Nations, 26 June 1945, 1 UNTS XVI.

20 John Philippe Rushton, *Altruism, Socialization, and Society* (Prentice Hall, 1980), 2.

21 See, for example, Food Assistance Convention, 25 April 2012, 2884 UNTS 3.

22 André Nollkaemper, '"Failures to Protect" in International Law' in Marc Weller (ed.), *The Oxford Handbook of the Use of Force in International Law* (Oxford University Press, 2015), 439. See also, André Nollkaemper and Dov Jacobs, 'Shared Responsibility in International Law: A Conceptual Framework' (2013) 34 *Michigan Journal of International Law* 359. For an earlier example of a diagonal obligation upon states to protect foreign nations from injury by private actors, see FV Garcia Amador, Louis Bruno Sohn, and Richard R. Baxter, *Recent Codification of the Law of State Responsibility for Injuries to Aliens* (Martinus Nijhoff Publishers, 1974), 28.

23 See, for example, UN Security Council Resolution 713, 25 September 1991 (Socialist Federal Republic of Yugoslavia) and UN Security Council Resolution 836, 4 June 1993 (Bosnia and Herzegovina); UN Security Council Resolution 918, 17 May 1994 (Rwanda).

was used as a tool for both deterrence and reconciliation. Moreover, after the North Atlantic Treaty Organization's (NATO) intervention in Kosovo, the responsibility to protect (R2P) doctrine emerged. The conceptual development of this doctrine helped to fundamentally recharacterise the notion of sovereignty as responsibility and placed a moral obligation on the international community to intervene where a state fails to discharge its responsibility to its population.[24] According to the rhetoric of R2P, states have a fallback responsibility to ensure the most fundamental human rights are guaranteed to people in other countries. The emergence of R2P is an important aspect of a broader normative turn to human security in international law's response to the most serious human crises.[25]

The concept of international cooperation has played a role in urging states to assist with the proliferation of peace, human rights, development and environmental protection in third states. The importance of cooperation and its implications for ensuring the needs of others are taken into account was underlined in 2005 by the Secretary-General of the United Nations, who wrote in his report *In Larger Freedom* that:

> the cause of larger freedom can only be advanced by broad, deep and sustained global cooperation among States. Such cooperation is possible if every country's policies take into account not only the needs of its own citizens but also the needs of others. This kind of cooperation not only advances everyone's interests but also recognizes our common humanity.[26]

Increasing interdependence, the need for cooperation and the erosion of traditionally conceived sovereignty is also evident in various aspects of the evolving architecture of the world order. One example is the creation of various international mechanisms for monitoring the domestic implementation of international human rights norms, such as expert committees and special rapporteurs, which have also become more numerous and prominent over time.[27] Indeed, this development is part of a phenomenon

[24] See, for example, 2005 World Summit Outcome, UN General Assembly Resolution 60/1, 24 October 2005, UN Doc. A/RES/60/1, paras 138 and 139.

[25] See, for example, Grant Marlier and Neta C. Crawford, 'Incomplete and Imperfect Institutionalisation of Empathy and Altruism in the "Responsibility to Protect" Doctrine' (2013) 5 *Global Responsibility to Protect* 397.

[26] UN Secretary General's Report, *In Larger Freedom: Towards Development, Security and Human Rights For All*, 21 March 2005, UN Doc. A/59/2005, 6 (para 18).

[27] Jack Donnelly, *Universal Human Rights in Theory and Practice* (3rd ed., Cornell University Press, 2013), 3 4.

that may be characterised as 'international proceduralization'.[28] In this way, states are held accountable at the international level for their internal human rights protection in a way they had not been before through bodies like the Human Rights Council, the Human Rights Committee and the Committee on Economic, Social and Cultural Rights. As will be seen, these mechanisms have played an important role in the institutionalisation of altruism.[29] They help to expand our circle of empathy such that we can better relate to the experience of those in far-away places and assist with triggering an altruistic response to others who are in need.

In the context of development, many initiatives that followed the 1969 UN General Assembly Declaration on Social Progress and Development illustrate a growing solidarity with the cause of development for all peoples.[30] This can be seen with the creation of Official Development Assistance (ODA), which states have committed to providing in an amount of 0.7 per cent of their gross national product (GNP). Furthermore, the 1986 Declaration on the Right to Development illustrates that states were willing to commit to creating the conditions for the emergence of the right to development for all to enjoy.[31] The most recent evolution in this area is the Sustainable Development Goals of 2015, which aim to 'end poverty in all its forms everywhere'.[32] These goals are universal in their application, both in terms of their beneficiaries and of the states required to take action or commit resources to ensure they are realised.

A variety of developments that show an increasing solidarity among nations are also notable in the area of environmental protection.[33] The *Trail Smelter* case,[34] the Stockholm Conference of 1972, the Rio

[28] Joseph Weiler and Iulia Motoc, 'Taking Democracy Seriously: The Normative Challenges to the International Legal System' in Stefan Griller (ed.), *International Economic Governance and Non-Economic Concerns – New Challenges for the International Legal Order* (Springer, 2003), 68–69.

[29] Marlier and Crawford, 'Incomplete and Imperfect Institutionalisation of Empathy and Altruism in the "Responsibility to Protect" Doctrine'.

[30] Declaration on Social Progress and Development, UN General Assembly Resolution 2542 (XXIV), 11 December 1969, UN Doc. A/RES/2542 (XXIV).

[31] Declaration on the Right to Development, General Assembly Resolution 41/128, 4 December 1986, UN Doc. A/RES/41/128.

[32] Transforming Our World: The 2030 Agenda for Sustainable Development, UN General Assembly Resolution 70/1, 25 September 2015, UN Doc. A/RES/70/1, para 59.

[33] See, for a more detailed presentation of developments, Benedict Kingsbury, 'The International Legal Order' in Peter Cane and Mark Tushnet (eds.), *Oxford Handbook of Legal Studies* (Oxford University Press, 2003), 271.

[34] *Trail Smelter Case (United States, Canada)*, Arbitral Tribunal, 3 UN Rep. Int'l Arb. Awards 1905 (1941).

Conference of 1992, the UN Framework Convention on Climate Change of 1992 and the Convention on Biological Diversity of 1992[35] all represented important normative milestones for the international community in the pursuit of global environmental governance, and required profound international cooperation. In a similar way, international courts and tribunals have been assertive in protecting common environmental interests.[36] At the heart of the protection of the environment are the principles of preventing transboundary harm, sustainable development, the common heritage of humankind and the responsibility to future generations. All are inherently other-oriented concepts. Today, a greater emphasis is placed on facilitating universal compliance with global environmental objectives, in the context of which financial support and technology transfer – particularly from the developed to the developing world – have an important role to play. Indeed, the principle of common but differentiated responsibility has become a cornerstone of contemporary international environmental law. As such, environmental obligations include commitments by states to other states or to individuals outside of their traditional polity of interest.

This brief survey of the major turns in the international legal order – from state coexistence to humanisation to concern for those in other countries – helps to frame the subject matter of this book. I also hasten to add that these turns do not represent wholescale change in the nature of the international legal order, they are not mutually exclusive but rather new dimensions added to an increasingly complex corpus of legal rules that cannot solely be characterised as reflecting self-interest. We will explore this further in the next section.

The Dimensions of Altruism in International Law

As is becoming evident from this overview of the evolving character of international legal norms, there has been a turn towards human

[35] United Nations Framework Convention on Climate Change, 9 May 1992, 1771 UNTS 107; Convention on Biological Diversity, 5 June 1992, 1760 UNTS 69.

[36] See, for example, cases such as *Gabčíkovo-Nagymaros Project (Hungary/Slovakia)*, Judgment (1997) ICJ Rep. 7; *Southern Bluefish Tuna (New Zealand* v. *Japan; Australia* v. *Japan)*, Provisional Measures, ITLOS Case Nos. 3 and 4 (27 August 1999); *Iron Rhine Arbitration (Belgium/Netherlands)*, XXVII (2005) Reports of International Arbitral Awards 35; *Whaling in the Antarctic (Australia* v. *Japan: New Zealand intervening)*, Judgment (2014) ICJ Rep. 226; see also, Markus Benzing, 'Community Interests in the Procedure of International Courts and Tribunals' (2006) 5 *Law and Practice of International Courts and Tribunals* 369.

protection and a more acute concern for the plight of individuals in all countries. My proposition is that norms with an altruistic orientation are increasingly apparent in positive international law and its interpretation, and this presence reveals an ethical substratum in international law that has cosmopolitan features. Cosmopolitan ideology can help to explain the evolving anthropocentrism in international law.[37] This anthropocentrism is manifested both in the way states guarantee a growing corpus of rights to their own people and the way in which states are increasingly concerned for the rights and welfare of people in other states or future generations. The former is the dominant trend whereas the latter has been less prominent, more nuanced and subject to resistance.[38] Altruistic commitments to the other are nevertheless present in the fabric of international law and it will be the task of this book to ask why, how and what: why they have emerged, how they have infiltrated international law, and what their content and form are.

Such altruistic legal relationships have received some attention in the legal literature,[39] but have often been ascribed different labels and analysed in a wide variety of ways. For example, distinctions have been made between so-called 'state by-stander responsibility', which involves a responsibility (including positive obligations) to protect people from

[37] See Richard Shapcott, *International Ethics: A Critical Introduction* (Wiley, 2010), 1794–1795. See also, Jason Rudall, 'A Cartography of Cosmopolitanism: Particularising the Universal' (2014) 3(3) *Cambridge Journal of International and Comparative Law* 747.

[38] This is consistent with claims made by Kantian cosmopolitan theory about the centrality of states and state interests in the international order more generally. See Hedley Bull, *The Anarchical Society: A Study of Order in World Politics* (2nd ed., Columbia University Press, 1977), Chapter 2 (presenting the Kantian view).

[39] See, for examples of scholarship on altruistic-type legal relationships, Lea Brilmayer and Isaias Yemane Tesfalidet, 'Third State Obligations and the Enforcement of International Law' (2011) 44(1) *International Law and Politics* 1; Monica Hakimi, 'State Bystander Responsibility' (2010) 21(2) *European Journal of International Law* 341; Luke Glanville, 'The Responsibility to Protect Beyond Borders' (2012) 12(1) *Human Rights Law Review* 1; Carla Bagnoli, 'Humanitarian Intervention as a Perfect Duty: A Kantian Argument' in Terry Nardin and Melissa Williams (eds.), *Humanitarian Intervention* (New York University Press, 2006); Kok Chor Tan, 'The Duty to Protect' in Nardin and Williams (eds.), *Humanitarian Intervention*; Jennifer Welsh and Maria Banda, 'International Law and the Responsibility to Protect: Clarifying or Expanding States' Responsibilities?' (2010) 2 *Global Responsibility to Protect* 213; Nollkaemper, 'Failures to Protect in International Law' in Weller (ed.), *The Oxford Handbook of the Use of Force in International Law*; John H. Knox, 'Diagonal Environmental Rights' in Mark Gibney and Sigrun Skogly (eds.), *Universal Human Rights and Territorial Obligations* (University of Pennsylvania Press, 2010). For a fuller consideration of this literature and for examples of practice, see *infra*.

third-party harm,[40] and 'third state obligations', which involve a purely negative obligation not to contribute to the illegal activity, and are described as analogous to laws concerning accessories or accomplices.[41] Notably, some have observed that there can be a 'diagonal' aspect to international human rights, which is supplementary to their horizontal and vertical operation, and this aspect is concerned with the obligation that states are under to people in third states who have had their human rights denied.[42] For others, 'diagonal' obligations are similarly conceived as obligations towards people in third countries, and these types of obligations involve a form of positive action to ensure the rights and welfare of those people.[43]

I reiterate that my claim is not that there has been a total change in the behaviour of states or the character of all international legal rules. It is important to underline that sovereignty, consent and reciprocity remain cornerstones of the international legal order, as they have been since the Peace of Westphalia in 1648.[44] International law continues to regulate horizontal state-to-state relations. Indeed, the ideologies of realism, statism, and liberalism continue to shape the law[45] and all are evident in the normative content of international

[40] Hakimi, 'State Bystander Responsibility'.

[41] Brilmayer and Tesfalidet, 'Third State Obligations and the Enforcement of International Law'.

[42] Skogly, *Beyond National Borders: States' Human Rights Obligations in International Cooperation*, 48.

[43] Michael Wabwile, 'Re-examining States' External Obligations to Implement Economic and Social Rights of Children' (2009) 22(2) *Canadian Journal of Law and Jurisprudence* 407, 414.

[44] José E. Alvarez, 'State Sovereignty is Not Withering Away: A Few Lessons for the Future' in Antonio Cassese (ed.), *Realizing Utopia: The Future of International Law* (Oxford University Press, 2012); Skogly, *Beyond National Borders: States' Human Rights Obligations in International Cooperation*, 23; David Held, 'Law of States, Law of Peoples: Three Models of Sovereignty' (2002) 8(1) *Legal Theory* 1 (presenting three models of international legal regulation: classic sovereignty (the law of states), liberal international sovereignty (the law of states and the law of peoples), and cosmopolitan sovereignty (the law of peoples)).

[45] See, for example, Bull, *The Anarchical Society: A Study of Order in World Politics*, Chapter 2 (noting '[t]hroughout the history of the modern states system there have been three competing traditions of thought: the Hobbesian or realist tradition, which views international politics as a state of war; the Kantian or universalist tradition, which sees at work in international politics a potential community of mankind; and the Grotian or internationalist tradition, which views international politics as taking place within an international society'); Martin Wight, 'Western Values in International Relations' in Butterfield and Wight (eds), *Diplomatic Investigations*; Held, 'Law of States, Law of Peoples: Three Models of Sovereignty'.

law.[46] In the international context, these explain individualistic approaches that can be seen in abundance. However, we must now recognise at least several exceptions and that sovereignty has been reconceptualised.[47] Further, some scholars argue that there may even exist a 'dual foundation of international law' rooted in human rights[48] and several scholars have shown how solidarity has helped to shape legal obligations.[49] All of this said, I do not claim there is a general obligation to assist people in other countries. Indeed, the International Law Commission (ILC) has been reticent about the existence of general obligations to cooperate for the realisation of certain ends.[50] Moreover, only certain norms generate altruistic legal

[46] A detailed consideration of the substantive influence that these other ideologies have on international law is beyond the scope of this project, as is providing an exhaustive list of all the ideologies at play.

[47] See, for good analyses of these exceptions, Anne-Marie Slaughter, *A New World Order* (Princeton University Press, 2005); Eyal Benvenisti, 'Sovereigns as Trustees of Humanity: On the Accountability of States to Foreign Stakeholders' (2013) 107(2) *American Journal of International Law* 295.

[48] Itamar Mann, *Humanity at Sea: Maritime Migration and the Foundations of International Law* (Cambridge University Press, 2016), 211–215. Mann argues that '[i]nternational law – the law of international rights and duties – is founded neither solely on sovereignty, nor on its ever-growing parade of transnational and global governance-based alternatives or reconceptualisations. The second basis for law – alongside sovereignty as the projection of collective political will, and the source of positive law – is a distinct and independent source: human rights' (at 215).

[49] Ronald St. J. Macdonald, 'Solidarity in the Practice and Discourse of Public International Law' (1996) 8 *Pace International Law Review* 259; Karel Wellens, 'Revisiting Solidarity as a (Re-)Emerging Constitutional Principle: Some Further Reflections' in Wolfrum and Kojima (eds.), *Solidarity: A Structural Principle of International Law*; Rüdiger Wolfrum, 'Solidarity amongst States: An Emerging Structural Principle of International Law' in Pierre-Marie Dupuy (ed.), *Völkerrecht als Weltordnung. Festschrift für Christian Tomuschat* (NP Engel, Kehl, 2006), 1087–1102; Rüdiger Wolfrum and Chie Kojima (eds.), *Solidarity: A Structural Principle of International Law* (Springer, 2010).

[50] Chapter IV of the Draft Articles on Responsibility of States for Internationally Wrongful Acts, with Commentaries, II(2) (2001) *Yearbook of the International Law Commission* 31, (Responsibility of a State in Connection with the Act of Another State), para 9:

> It seems there is no general obligation on the part of third States to cooperate in suppressing internationally wrongful conduct of another State which may already have occurred. Again it is a matter for specific treaty obligations to establish any such obligation of suppression after the event. There are, however, two important qualifications here. First, in some circumstances assistance given by one State to another after the latter has committed an internationally wrongful act may amount to the adoption of that act by the former State ... secondly, special obligations of cooperation in putting an end to an unlawful situation arise in the case of serious breaches of obligations under peremptory norms of general international law. By definition, in such cases States will have

relationships while many others do not (such as territorial rights or diplomatic rights, for example).[51]

There is good reason for being cautious about taking into account the interests of those in third countries. If we accept that the state is a vehicle for the self-determination of a particular group of people, it acts primarily as a vehicle for the rights and interests of those people.[52] Self-determination is concerned with the freedom to develop and govern without interference from other nations. Indeed, international law has often been critiqued for its imperialistic nature and there can be a fine line between assistance, interference and imperialism.[53] One of the aims of this book is to reveal more clearly the dichotomies and contradictions that exist in the nature of international legal rules.

A Roadmap for This Study

This book seeks to examine manifestations of altruism in international law. Inspired by the approach of Duncan Kennedy in his 1976 article on 'Form and Substance in Private Law Adjudication',[54] the present inquiry exposes two main dichotomies: that between individualism and altruism, and that between rules and standards. In doing so, it develops an understanding of altruism before analysing the presence of altruism in the substance of international law. It then turns to consider whether the substantive norms of altruism are contingently related to the form of the law. More particularly, whether standards are used as vehicles for altruism.

By way of overview, the book will show that legal relationships between states and people in other countries are evident in the substance of

agreed that no derogation from such obligations is to be permitted and, faced with a serious breach of such an obligation, certain obligations of cooperation arise. These are dealt with in article 41.

51 Brilmayer and Tesfalidet, 'Third State Obligations and the Enforcement of International Law'.

52 For a detailed elaboration of sovereignty as a trust, see Benvenisti, 'Sovereigns as Trustees of Humanity: On the Accountability of States to Foreign Stakeholders'.

53 See, for example, B. S. Chimni, 'Third World Approaches to International Law: A Manifesto' (2006) 8(1) *International Community Law Review* 27; James T. Gathii, 'TWAIL: A Brief History of its Origins, its Decentralized Network and a Tentative Bibliography' (2011) 3(1) *Trade, Law and Development* 26; Antony Anghie, *Imperialism, Sovereignty and the Making of International Law* (Cambridge University Press, 2012).

54 Kennedy, 'Form and Substance in Private Law Adjudication'.

contemporary international law in many of its specialised areas from the law of cooperation, human rights law, international humanitarian law, refugee law, international development law, international economic law and international environmental law. These legal relationships have an altruistic nature. Further, the impulse for the emergence of these legal relationships is a strain of cosmopolitan ideology. More particularly, I will argue that a strand of cosmopolitan altruism is responsible for the emergence of other-oriented legal standards in the contemporary international legal order, as well as for the interpretation of existing law in an altruistic way. That said, various manifestations of state-centric individualist ideology continue to influence the formation and interpretation of international law. This results in an observable dialectic between individualistic and altruistic norms in the architecture of international law that is reminiscent of Duncan Kennedy's portrayal of domestic private law.[55] As a result, there is an unresolvable contradiction in the values that inform the law, the substance of the law, as well as the choice of form the law takes.

Following this introduction, Chapter 1 turns to altruism. Drawing on definitions, concepts and studies from a wide range of disciplines, the chapter sets out to identify common themes in altruistic theory. The concept of altruism is first considered in a non-legal context. In so doing, this investigation reaches out to the fields of philosophy, sociology, biology and behavioural science to define and elaborate the contours of altruism. Next the chapter reveals the role that cosmopolitanism plays in expanding the circle of altruism in international society. As such, the connection with cosmopolitanism becomes apparent and evidence for the role that cosmopolitan ideology has in driving an expanding circle of altruism is highlighted. The catalysing factors of globalisation and increasing interconnectedness between peoples across borders is also emphasised in this context. In the final part of Chapter 1, an appraisal is made of the current state of the literature in legal scholarship, both national and international, that

[55] *Ibid.*, 1712 and 1722, arguing that there has always been a 'substantive dichotomy of individualism and altruism' and '[i]f the concepts of individualism and altruism turn out to be useful, it is because they capture something of this struggle of contradictory utopian visions'. This is particularly evident in a variety of 'clashes' of norms in international law, not least the law of human rights and the law of jurisdictional immunities. See, for example, Andrea Bianchi, 'Immunity versus Human Rights: The Pinochet Case' (1999) 10(2) *European Journal of International Law* 237.

draws on altruism or related concepts. This comprehensive consideration of the literature on altruism will be with the aim of identifying tools that help to understand whether it may have a presence in the architecture of international law.

Chapter 2 considers the modalities by which altruistic norms become imbued in the substance of international law. In doing so, the processes and actors involved are identified. It is important to understand how values like altruism can infiltrate the law and manifest themselves as commitments to 'the other'. In this way, the book will evaluate the way in which law is used to structure or restructure the social relations between human beings in a manner consistent with a given moral or political philosophy.[56]

Next, a detailed appraisal of the existence of altruism in international law will ensue. Chapters 3–6 examine in detail the substantive elements of positive international law that are altruistic in nature. It considers legal norms that promote altruistic behaviour as well as regulatory spaces that allow states to act altruistically. These chapters deal with four broad categories of international law norms, namely cooperation for the other, protection for the other, development for the other and environmental justice for the other. These are intended to give an insight into the substance of altruistic legal relationships in different areas of international law.

Finally, the focus of the book turns to form. It assesses whether there is a relationship between the substance of international law and the form of international law. In particular, it asks whether altruistic legal norms may be characterised more accurately as flexible standards rather than strict rules. Using the preceding chapters on substance as a springboard, Chapter 7 investigates Duncan Kennedy's observation about the relationship between individualism and a preference for rules and altruism and a preference for standards in the context of international law.[57]

The final chapter concludes and reflects on the future of altruism in international law. It does so at a critical juncture for the world when global crises, democratic backsliding and nationalism appear to threaten the altruism in international law. Such turning points have been

[56] Patrick Capps, *Human Dignity and the Foundations of International Law* (Hart, 2009), 27. See also, Philip Allott, *Eunomia: A New Order for A New World* (2nd ed., Oxford University Press, 2001); Roscoe Pound, *A Theory of Judicial Decision for Today* (Harvard Law Review Association, 1923), 954.

[57] Kennedy, 'Form and Substance in Private Law Adjudication', 1776.

encountered before but that does not mean the outcome should be taken for granted. As we face these contemporary challenges, we should recall that '[a]lone we can do so little; together we can do so much'.[58]

[58] Attributed to the American author and political activist Helen Keller. See Joseph P. Lash, *Helen and Teacher: The Story of Helen Keller and Anne Sullivan Macy* (Da Capo Press, 1980), 489.

1

Altruism

1.1 Introduction

This chapter seeks to uncover the meaning of altruism. First, an understanding of the essence of altruism is garnered from the consideration of a wide range of scholarship from different disciplines. Certain common themes of the concept will be identified. Second, the connection between altruism and cosmopolitanism is revealed in an effort to show how altruistic behaviour between people from different countries can develop. Third, the influence of altruism in legal systems at the domestic level is considered by having reference to major studies that have analysed manifestations of altruism in European and US private law regimes. Other references to altruism or related concepts in international legal scholarship will also be considered.

1.2 The Essence of Altruism

1.2.1 Alteri Huic

Altruism is derived from the Latin *alteri huic*, meaning 'to this other',[1] which underlines that altruism is essentially concerned with a form of action for 'the other'. It was the French philosopher Auguste Comte who is believed to have coined the word.[2] Altruism is popularly defined as the '[d]isinterested or selfless concern for the well-being of others'.[3] However, a closer examination of the scholarship on altruism in moral philosophy, sociobiology, psychology, behavioural economics and other

[1] 'Altruism', *Oxford Dictionaries*, www.oxforddictionaries.com/definition/english/altruism.

[2] Robert L. Campbell, 'Altruism in Auguste Comte and Ayn Rand' (2006) 7(2) *The Journal of Ayn Rand Studies* 357. Auguste Comte, *System of Positive Polity, Volume 1: Containing the General View of Positivism & Introductory Principles* (John Henry Bridges trans., Burt Franklin, 1973).

[3] 'Altruism', *English Oxford Living Dictionary*, https://en.oxforddictionaries.com/definition/altruism.

disciplines reveals a much more textured concept. There is in fact a lack of common consensus around the concept of altruism, and it is regularly employed as a synonym for giving, sharing, cooperating, helping or other types of selfless or pro-social behaviour.[4] It may operate in situations that involve rescue from imminent danger or in charitable endeavours that seek to improve the welfare of another over time. A survey of scholarship across various fields reveals important contours in the concept of altruism.

One of the most consequential studies into altruistic behaviour has been conducted by political psychologist Kristen Renwick Monroe in which she makes several helpful insights about the 'heart of altruism'.[5] Her work challenges the view, propounded by scholars like Gary Becker and Richard Dawkins,[6] that human beings are essentially selfish. Monroe's study involved interviews with those who rescued Jewish people in Nazi Germany. Her results give an overview of the principal characteristics of altruistic behaviour, and she summarises the key precepts of altruism as follows:

(1) Altruism must entail action. It cannot merely be good intentions or well-meaning thoughts.
(2) The action must be goal-directed, although this may be either conscious or reflexive.
(3) The goal of the act must be to further the welfare of another. If another's welfare is treated as an unintended or secondary consequence of behaviour designed primarily to further my own welfare, the act is not altruistic.
(4) Intentions count more than consequences. If I try to do something nice for you, and it ends up badly or with long-term consequences for you, this does not diminish the altruism of any initial action. Most analysts now consider motivation and intent critical, even though motives and intent are difficult to establish, observe and measure objectively.
(5) The act must carry some possibility of diminution in my own welfare. An act that improves both my own welfare and that of

[4] *Ibid.*
[5] Kristin Renwick Monroe, *The Heart of Compassion: Portraits of Moral Choice during the Holocaust* (Princeton University Press, 2004).
[6] Gary Becker, 'Nobel Prize Lecture: The Economic Way of Looking at Life' (9 December 1992), www.nobelprize.org/uploads/2018/06/becker-lecture.pdf; Richard Dawkins, *The Selfish Gene* (2nd ed., Oxford University Press, 1989).

another person would not be altruistic but would fall instead into the category of collective welfare.

(6) Altruism sets no conditions; its purpose is to further the welfare of another person or group, without anticipation of reward for the altruist.[7]

These elements offer us an insight into the anatomy of altruistic behaviour. As such, for Monroe, unconditional action intended to improve the welfare of another at a cost to the actor is the essence of altruism.

Others have homed in on the importance of intention in altruistic behaviour. In his seminal work on altruism, Thomas Nagel describes altruism as involving a 'direct reason to promote the interests of others – a reason which does not depend on intermediate factors such as one's own interests or on antecedent sentiments of sympathy and benevolence'.[8] Nagel argues that the concept does not mean 'abject self-sacrifice, but merely a willingness to act in consideration of the interests of other persons, without the need of ulterior motives'.[9] A psychologist – C. Daniel Batson – has observed that altruism is a state of motivation which is concerned with increasing some other's welfare.[10] Vincent Jeffries has asserted that the general idea of altruism is to intend and act in a way that is beneficial to some other person. He specifies that generosity, benevolence, forgiveness, volunteering, unlimited love, virtue, philanthropy and altruistic love are all manifestations of this idea.[11] Jacqueline Macaulay and Leonard Berkowitz define altruism as behaviour carried out with the intention of benefiting someone else[12] whereas John Philippe Rushton argues that altruism is a form of social behaviour intended to achieve positive outcomes.[13]

[7] *Ibid.*, 6–7.

[8] Thomas Nagel, *The Possibility of Altruism* (Princeton University Press, 1979), 16.

[9] *Ibid.*, 79.

[10] C. Daniel Batson, *The Altruism Question: Toward a Social Psychological Answer* (Lawrence Erlbaum Associates, 1991), 6; Andrew Michael Flescher and Daniel Worthen, *The Altruistic Species: Scientific, Philosophical, and Religious Perspectives of Human Benevolence* (Templeton Foundation Press, 2007), 35.

[11] Vincent Jeffries, 'Altruism, Morality, and Social Solidarity as a Field of Study' in Vincent Jeffries (ed.), *The Palgrave Handbook of Altruism, Morality, and Social Solidarity: Formulating a Field of Study* (Palgrave Macmillan, 2014), 6; Vincent Jeffries, 'Virtue and the Altruistic Personality' (1998) 41 *Sociological Perspectives* 151.

[12] Jacqueline Macaulay and Leonard Berkowitz, *Altruism and Helping Behavior* (Academic Press, 1970), 3.

[13] John Philippe Rushton, *Altruism, Socialization, and Society* (Prentice Hall, 1980), 8.

After reflecting on a variety of definitions from different fields, Andrew Michael Flescher and Daniel L. Worthen consider that altruism means acting in the interests or well-being of another. Moreover, they similarly place an emphasis on the fact that the intention should be to bring a benefit to another. They also observe that altruistic behaviour can result from a moral duty or may be supererogatory, and everyone is capable of acting altruistically.[14] Interestingly, as Kristen Renwick Monroe also highlighted, they note that altruism should involve a diminution in the welfare of the actor and an amelioration in the welfare of the beneficiary. This is in fact a recurring element in the scholarship on altruism across a variety of disciplines, to which we turn now.

1.2.2 Altruism Is Action for the Other at a Cost

Altruism implies action or an intention to take action at some cost to the actor.[15] In the literature on moral philosophy, Peter Singer defines altruism as 'behaviour which benefits others at some initial cost to oneself, and is motivated by the desire to benefit others'[16] while Kristen Renwick Monroe has elaborated that altruism occurs when action is taken at a cost to ourselves and which is not in our short-term interest in order to help someone else.[17] In the area of political science, James Ozinga notes that altruism is 'behaviour benefiting someone else at some cost to oneself'[18] while in bioethics, Stephen Post perceives that altruism is 'acting for the other's sake as an end in itself rather than a means to public recognition or internal well-being, although such benefits to the self need not be resisted'.[19] Biologist Richard Dawkins describes behaviour as altruistic if

[14] Flescher and Worthen, *The Altruistic Species: Scientific, Philosophical, and Religious Perspectives of Human Benevolence*, 53.

[15] See, for example, Patrick Kennedy, Andrew D. Higginson, Andrew N. Radford and Seirian Sumner, 'Altruism in a Volatile World' (2018) 555 *Nature* 359.

[16] Peter Singer, *The Expanding Circle: Ethics, Evolution, and Moral Progress* (Princeton University Press, 1981), 43.

[17] Monroe, *The Heart of Compassion: Portraits of Moral Choice during the Holocaust*; and Kristin Renwick Monroe, *Ethics in an Age of Terror and Genocide* (Princeton University Press, 2012).

[18] James R. Ozinga, *Altruism* (Praeger, 1999), xvi; Flescher and Worthen, *The Altruistic Species: Scientific, Philosophical, and Religious Perspectives of Human Benevolence*, 35.

[19] Stephen G. Post *et al.*, 'General Introduction' in *Altruism and Altruistic Love: Science, Philosophy, and Religion in Dialogue* (Oxford University Press, 2002), 3; Flescher and Worthen, *The Altruistic Species: Scientific, Philosophical, and Religious Perspectives of Human Benevolence*, 35.

it 'increase[s] another such entity's welfare at the expense of its own'.[20] Ernst Fehr and Urs Fischbacher define altruism in a behavioural rather than a psychological way as 'costly acts that confer economic benefits on other individuals'.[21]

Through this exploration of leading scholarship on the concept of altruism, it is evident that a consensus exists among scholars to the extent that altruism involves action for another at a cost to the actor. These formulations of altruism also begin to reveal that the existence of self-regarding pay-offs (i.e. some benefit may also be derived by the actor) does not necessarily strip action of its altruistic character, an aspect which we explore in greater depth next.

1.2.3 Self-regarding Pay-offs

Whether altruism can involve a self-regarding pay-off to the actor is a persistent question across different fields of study. An early division among moral philosophers can be detected in the proposition of Immanuel Kant that a pure motive in acting is critical while John Stuart Mill argued that it is the outcome of an action that is most important.[22] The better school of thought is that altruism need not be free of any self-regarding pay-off.[23] Even Immanuel Kant, who placed an emphasis on intention, did not deny that self-benefit may flow from altruistic acts. However, he cautioned that we should be reflexively aware of these benefits (including emotional benefits such as a feeling of joy or satisfaction that may flow from altruistic behaviour) as they have the potential to override our pure motivation to benefit the other.[24]

Others have argued that self-benefit is in fact inevitable in the execution of altruistic acts. This might simply be because they relieve our anxiety, guilt or shame, or because they make us feel proud, satisfied or honourable.[25] Moreover, some have suggested that behaviour may be altruistic if any self-interested aspect is (1) accidental, (2) secondary or (3) undetermining.[26] As such, a primary motivation to help another is

[20] Dawkins, *The Selfish Gene*, 4; Flescher and Worthen, *Altruistic Species*, 36.

[21] Ernst Fehr and Urs Fischbacher, 'The Nature of Human Altruism' (2003) 425 *Nature* 785.

[22] Flescher and Worthen, *The Altruistic Species: Scientific, Philosophical, and Religious Perspectives of Human Benevolence*, 23.

[23] *Ibid.*, 24.

[24] *Ibid.*, 29.

[25] Neel Burton, 'Does True Altruism Exist', *Psychology Today* (27 March 2012), www.psychologytoday.com/blog/hide-and-seek/201203/does-true-altruism-exist.

[26] *Ibid.*

central to conceptions of altruism, and the presence of a self-interested benefit does not preclude an act or intention being characterised as altruistic.

Interestingly, the literature also refers to a class of altruism known as 'reciprocal altruism'.[27] Peter Singer describes reciprocal altruism as those acts that are not directed at relatives but that is a practice done for another which you would expect done for you, and he contrasts this with 'kin' and 'group' altruism.[28] However, it is important to note that reciprocal altruism involves no expectation of immediate reciprocity. This category of altruism is common in mammals and birds because they are highly intelligent social animals.[29] Singer explains that in the typical meaning of altruism 'an act may benefit me in the long run, and yet – perhaps because I didn't foresee that the act would redound to my advantage – still be altruistic because my intention was to benefit someone else'.[30]

Others have similarly referred to this category of reciprocal altruism and have defined this as implying the exchange of altruistic behaviour between people who are not related.[31] Where the benefits of altruistic behaviour to the beneficiary exceed the cost of that behaviour to the altruist, and the initial beneficiary reciprocates at a later time, there are cumulative benefits for both actors.[32] Evolutionary biologists have shown how this behaviour can be promoted through natural selection in species because, over time, those that engage in altruism are favoured by others who are likely to be the beneficiaries of reciprocal altruism and thus fair better in the survival race.[33]

It is submitted that there are rarely situations devoid of any pay-off at all for actors who behave altruistically.[34] We need only consider some of the archetypal acts of altruism in everyday life to show that altruism

[27] Singer, *The Expanding Circle: Ethics, Evolution, and Moral Progress*; Robert Trivers, 'The Evolution of Reciprocal Altruism' (1971) 46(1) *The Quarterly Review of Biology* 35; Robert Axelrod and William Hamilton, 'The Evolution of Cooperation' (1981) 211 *Science* 1390.

[28] Singer, *The Expanding Circle: Ethics, Evolution, and Moral Progress*, 17.

[29] See *ibid.*; Trivers, 'The Evolution of Reciprocal Altruism'.

[30] Singer, *The Expanding Circle: Ethics, Evolution, and Moral Progress*, 43.

[31] C. Packer, 'Reciprocal Altruism in Papio Anubis' (1977) 265 *Nature* 441.

[32] *Ibid.*

[33] *Ibid.*

[34] Offering a sociobiological justification for the moral preference for altruism, Robert Trivers suggests that there is a perception that those who are more altruistic make better partners than those who are more self-interested. See Trivers 'The Evolution of Reciprocal Altruism', 48.

generally does involve some benefit, however abstract, to the actor. For example, giving a gift helps to consolidate a friendship or serves as a gesture of goodwill that may materialise into some return in the future,[35] and giving to charity is often done under the auspices of religion, for some personal satisfaction or as a way of conforming with social morals, in addition to being motivated by the plight of the beneficiary.[36] As such, it is usually the case that altruistic acts have some reciprocal payoff for the actor. Consequently, analysing behaviour should not be reduced to binary conclusions about the presence of reciprocity. Behaviour is complex and can imply primary and subsidiary motives. The literature on altruism confirms that altruistic behaviour may result in a benefit to the altruist, contrary to popular belief. Another common misperception about altruism is that it is not prevalent in the behaviour of human beings, an issue to which we turn next.

1.2.4 The Prevalence of Altruism in Human Behaviour

It is commonly assumed that people act in their own interest or as *homo economicus*,[37] that is in a rational and selfish way, but empirical evidence contradicts this popular assumption and reveals that, in fact, people often

[35] See Eric Posner, *Law and Social Norms* (Harvard University Press, 2000), making an alternative rational-actor appraisal of giving gifts in the context of a relationship where benefits flow between actors. Posner argues that this is only different from contractual relationships to the extent that contractual promises are explicit and have defined legal boundaries.

[36] See, for example, James Andreoni, 'Impure Altruism and Donations to Public Goods—A Theory of Warm-Glow Giving' (1990) 100(401) *The Economic Journal* 464; Shalom Schwartz, 'Normative Influences on Altruism' (1977) 10 *Advances in Experimental Social Psychology* 221; Jeffrey Carpenter, 'When in Rome: Conformity and the Provision of Public Goods' (2004) 33 *Journal of Socio-Economics* 395.

[37] Oliver Wendell Holmes, 'The Path of Law' (1887) 10(8) *Harvard Law Review* 457, 460; John Stuart Mill, *Essays on Some Unsettled Questions of Political Economy* (London School of Economics and Political Science, 1948), 137. For example, David Hume observes that '[p]olitical writers have established it as a maxim, that, in contriving any system of government, and fixing the several checks and controls of the constitution, every man ought to be supposed a knave, and to have no other end, in all his actions, than private interest' (David Hume, 'Essay VI' in *Essays: Moral, Political and Literary* (Liberty Fund, 1987 [1777]), 42) or George Stigler: 'Much of the time, most of the time in fact, the self-interest theory ... will win' (George Stigler, 'Economics or Ethics?' in Sterling McMurrin (ed.), *Tanner Lectures on Human Values* (Cambridge University Press, 1981), 175); Becker, 'Nobel Prize Lecture: The Economic Way of Looking at Life'; Dawkins, *The Selfish Gene*.

act in altruistic ways.[38] Economic approaches to selfish human behaviour have been widely challenged with much research in various fields, suggesting that people are frequently motivated by pro-social and altruistic factors as well.[39] For example, Peter Singer argues that, based on evidence from the field of sociobiology, genuine altruism is a common occurrence in human behaviour not least because there is an evolutionary advantage to being altruistic.[40] Similarly, Lynn Stout has shown that other-regarding behaviour is much more prominent than is traditionally understood.[41] She makes reference to the empirical evidence in behavioural science that human beings do in fact behave consistently in other-regarding ways.

Empirical evidence indeed confirms that people often act altruistically rather than selfishly. A wide range of data from experimental games has shown this in particular. This evidence has been gathered over the last half century through social dilemma games, ultimatum games and dictator games. These games are generally structured in a way that incentivises selfish behaviour, such as defecting, rather than altruistic, cooperative or pro-social behaviour. The participants in these experiments were shown not to be motivated by pure self-interest, as rational choice theory would predict, but rather that other-regarding preferences were commonly exhibited.[42]

Other experimental studies using variations of games to analyse people's social behaviour conducted in this area support the conclusion that most people act altruistically.[43] In fact, as much as 97 per cent of people make sacrifices that benefit other players of

[38] Lynn Stout, 'Law and Prosocial Behaviour' in Eyal Zamir and Doron Teichman (eds.), *The Oxford Handbook of Behavioural Economics and the Law* (Oxford University Press, 2014), 209.

[39] See, for example, Herbert Gintis, Samuel Bowles, Robert Boyd and Ernst Fehr (eds.), *Moral Sentiments and Material Interests: The Foundations of Cooperation in Economic Life* (MIT Press, 2005); Simon Gächter, 'Human Prosocial Motivation and the Maintenance of Social Order' in Zamir and Teichman (eds.), *The Oxford Handbook of Behavioural Economics and the Law.*

[40] Singer, *The Expanding Circle: Ethics, Evolution, and Moral Progress*, 45–48.

[41] Lynn Stout, 'Other-Regarding Preferences and Social Norms' in John N. Drobak (ed.), *Norms and the Law* (Cambridge University Press, 2006).

[42] *Ibid.*

[43] See, for example, Christophe Engel, 'Dictator Games: A Meta Study' (2011) 14(4) *Experimental Economics* 583; Werner Güth, Rolf Schmittberger and Bernd Schwarze, 'An Experimental Analysis of Ultimatum Bargaining' (1982) 3(4) *Journal of Economic Behavior and Organization* 367; Hessel Oosterbeek, Randolph Sloof and Gijs van de Kuilen, 'Cultural Differences in Ultimatum Game Experiments: Evidence from a Meta-Analysis' (2004) 7 *Experimental Economics* 171; Ananish Chaudhuri, 'Sustaining

these games.[44] Cross-cultural studies have indicated that most people who play such games choose to share around a quarter of their stakes with others in the game.[45] In some games, it can be significantly more than this.[46]

Even in games where participants are given a free choice to contribute to the public good and then, with the knowledge of what each has contributed, may spend money to penalise other participants for free riding, the majority of participants opt to punish those deserving of punishment.[47] In experiments based on this public goods game with punishment, 80 per cent of people punished the free riders.[48] Such behaviour has been described as altruistic as those who punish the free riders incur the cost but the punishment generally benefits others.[49] Other games have similarly shown that most players will punish unfair conduct towards a third party in a way that has been characterised as 'altruistic punishment' because it is costly to the punisher.[50] In this context, it has also been shown that people are more likely to sacrifice their own self-interest to follow rules and to help others if the overall social benefit is greater.[51]

Significantly, experimental games have shown that altruistic behaviour can also depend on the perception of fellow players being part of the same 'in-group' and, in such circumstances, consideration will be given to the welfare of others.[52] As such, the more socially distant a player feels, the weaker the human connection is with the other and the less likely it is that altruistic behaviour will be exhibited. This observation correlates with the

Cooperation in Laboratory Public Goods Experiments: A Selective Survey of the Literature' (2011) 14(1) *Experimental Economics* 47.

44 David Sally, 'Conversation and Cooperation in Social Dilemmas: A Meta-analysis of Experiments from 1958 to 1992' (1995) 7(1) *Rationality and Society* 58, 62.

45 Joseph Henrich, Robert Boyd, Samuel Bowles, Colin Camerer, Ernst Fehr and Herbert Gintis, *Foundations of Human Sociality: Ethnography and Experiments in 15 Small-Scale Societies* (Oxford University Press, 2004), 27.

46 *Ibid.*

47 Ernst Fehr and Simon Gächter, 'Cooperation and Punishment in Public Goods Experiments' (2000) 90(4) *American Economic Review* 980; Ernst Fehr and Simon Gächter, 'Altruistic Punishment in Humans' (2002) 415 *Nature* 137.

48 Fehr and Gächter, 'Altruistic Punishment in Humans'.

49 Gächter, 'Human Prosocial Motivation and the Maintenance of Social Order', 8.

50 Fehr and Fischbacher, 'The Nature of Human Altruism', 786.

51 *Ibid.*

52 Stout, 'Law and Prosocial Behaviour', 202; Elizabeth Hoffman, Kevin McCabe and Vernon Smith, 'Social Distance and Other-Regarding Behavior in Dictator Games' (1996) 86 *American Economic Review* 653; Lynn Stout, *Cultivating Conscience: How Good Laws Make Good People* (Princeton University Press, 2011).

notion of the common humanity perspective that also features widely in the scholarship on altruism, to which we turn next.

1.2.5 *The Common Humanity Perspective*

It is broadly understood that altruism depends on a particular world view. Identification with the other and their plight is the perception that makes altruism possible. In other words, altruistic behaviour is motivated by the psychological state of empathy with others.[53] The feeling of empathy is, as such, the catalyst for altruistic action. When an actor takes the perspective of another person or class of persons and sympathises with their situation, altruism can be triggered.[54] This notion of identifying with the other has been characterised as 'ideal role taking', [55] 'cognitive role taking'[56] or 'perspective taking' by various scholars who have examined altruism in human societies.[57]

According to William Galston, there are three possible motives for altruism: sympathy, rationality and identity.[58] As for sympathy, humans may be motivated to act altruistically because they are sympathetic to the pain and suffering of others and are unable to keep emotional distance from it. As for rationality, this is the ability to comprehend that other people can make similarly valid claims to ourselves, and that actions are informed by this understanding. Finally, identity implies that certain individuals see themselves as at one with the universe or as part of a common humanity.

Thomas Nagel also argues that altruism has a rational characteristic insofar as people can imagine how they might feel if something that was happening to other people was happening to them.[59] Indeed, this also

[53] Simon Baron-Cohen, *Zero Degrees of Empathy: A New Theory of Human Cruelty* (Allen Lane, 2011). Interestingly, Baron-Cohen argues that empathy is something that is both learned and that there exist genes that are associated with it.

[54] Stephen Pinker, *The Better Angels of Our Nature: Why Violence has Declined* (Penguin Books, 2012), 590; Shalom Schwartz, 'Normative Influences on Altruism' (1977) 10 *Advances in Experimental Social Psychology* 221, 225.

[55] Jürgen Habermas, *Moral Consciousness and Communicative Action* (MIT Press, 1990), 182.

[56] Schwartz, 'Normative Influences on Altruism', 225.

[57] See Grant Marlier and Neta C. Crawford, 'Incomplete and Imperfect Institutionalisation of Empathy and Altruism in the "Responsibility to Protect" Doctrine' (2013) 5 *Global Responsibility to Protect* 397, 413.

[58] William A. Galston, 'Cosmopolitan Altruism' (1993) 10(1) *Social Philosophy & Policy* 118, 124.

[59] Nagel, *The Possibility of Altruism*.

implies that the notion of perspective is critical to understanding the impulse for altruistic behaviour. For Nagel, altruism is related to the ability to conceive oneself as one among others.[60] Human beings have the capacity to view themselves either subjectively or objectively, both as being at the centre of the universe and as being a part of that universe.

When identifying with 'the other', certain phenomena have strong objective value and are easier to identify with. A good example is pain. As William Galston has explained in this respect, '[b]ecause pain is objectively bad from an impersonal standpoint, my desire for the cessation of my pain at least overlaps my desire for the cessation of your pain'.[61] There are also phenomena that are not objective in nature, and these may be called 'agent-relative' interests because they are interests that certain individuals choose to exercise empathy for. Acting on these agent-relative interests is the result of personal sympathy as opposed to objective acknowledgement.[62]

In her study of altruistic actors, the perception of common humanity is of central importance for Kristen Renwick Monroe. As such, Monroe noted that identification with the beneficiary was common to all of the altruists that she interviewed.[63] The altruistic acts she investigated were motivated by a perception that the actors had in relation to others. Significantly, altruists consider themselves as part of humankind in general, rather than as exclusively part of a particular group. This perceived membership of a common humanity is critical in distinguishing the behaviour of altruists. This is at the 'heart of altruism'.[64]

Saving strangers from persecution, suffering and injustice is instinctive for altruists because they identify as being part of the same social group, namely humanity. While the means for arriving at the common humanity perspective differ, it is important to underline that this is a perception shared by altruists. It is the perspective, more than specific triggers, that is most determinant of altruistic behaviour. This common humanity perspective is therefore the best predictor of altruism.[65]

[60] *Ibid.*, 19. Hanoch Dagan, *Unjust Enrichment: A Study of Private Law and Public Values* (Cambridge University Press, 1997), 25.

[61] William A. Galston, *The Practice of Liberal Pluralism* (Cambridge University Press, 2005), 99.

[62] Galston, 'Cosmopolitan Altruism', 122. Thomas Nagel, *The View from Nowhere* (Oxford University Press, 1986), 159–162.

[63] Monroe, *The Heart of Altruism: Perceptions of a Common Humanity*, 204.

[64] *Ibid.*

[65] *Ibid.*, 216.

As for the proliferation of a common humanity perspective, the need for cooperation, society and socialisation play major roles in the propagation of altruistic behaviour in society.[66] In a study of species, John Philippe Rushton has observed that the more social the species, the more altruistic their behaviour.[67] Complex societies in fact depend on altruistic behaviour among large sections of the population.[68] This resonates with Andreas Krieg's conception of altruism, who argues that it involves 'selfless and other-oriented behaviour' and points to its fairly common and widespread practice among highly socialised species, in particular:

> birds give predator alarms, mother rats endure severe shock to save their infants, baboons help defend their troops and porpoises sustain their injured fellows. . . . It appears natural to the human species to engage in cooperative social endeavours that benefit others or the community at large, even at a cost to themselves.[69]

There is thus a widely shared view that the more interconnected a species, the greater the altruistic instinct is among that species.

It has also been observed that cooperation and division of labour is much more prominent among genetically unrelated humans than it is in any other animal species.[70] In animal species, cooperation is generally limited to significantly smaller groups. Where cooperation is more prevalent in the animal kingdom, this tends to be among creatures that have a significant genetic relatedness.[71] This characteristic that distinguishes human beings from other species has been attributed to patterns of human altruism.[72]

These are interesting observations because they correlate societal interconnectivity with altruistic behaviour. According to this logic, as there is increasing interaction between different peoples of the world, altruistic behaviour is more likely to occur between them. This phenomenon of widening altruism has also been investigated by a number of scholars. For example, Grant Marlier, Neta Crawford, Peter Singer and Stephen Pinker all use an expanding circle as a metaphor to illustrate the way in which empathy for those beyond national borders

[66] Rushton, *Altruism, Socialization, and Society.*

[67] *Ibid.*, 8.

[68] *Ibid.*, 10.

[69] Andreas Krieg, 'National Interests and Altruism in Humanitarian Intervention' in Andreas Krieg (ed.), *Motivations for Humanitarian Intervention* (Springer, 2013), 48–49.

[70] Fehr and Fischbacher, 'The Nature of Human Altruism', 785.

[71] *Ibid.*

[72] *Ibid.*

has grown.[73] As noted, the capacity to take the perspective of the other is related to the capacity for empathy and altruism. For much of human history, empathy was confined to those around us, like our families, tribes and countrymen, because these were all that we were familiar with. However, this circle has extended in recent times to peoples far away. Indeed, as Marlier and Crawford put it, 'empathy has expanded to those beyond our borders, paving the way for the growth of a more cosmopolitan identity and a more global "circle of empathy"'.[74]

The perception of common humanity suggests a relationship with the rest of humanity – that we are all, ultimately, part of the same family, group or species. An empathetic relationship with others results from a moral understanding of the others' situation, needs and challenges. Psychologists have shown that interaction and facing common challenges together builds such an empathetic relationship.[75] This helps to reduce moral and emotional distance between peoples, and to break down barriers that separate people.

In the context of our global society, the perspective of common humanity and a capacity to identify with the other give altruism a distinctly cosmopolitan character,[76] the meaning of which we will turn to next.

1.3 Cosmopolitan Altruism: The Expanding Circle

I submit that cosmopolitan culture underpins the normative developments that lead to the emergence of altruism in international law. The international law that is presented in the chapters that follow is the result

[73] Marlier and Crawford, 'Incomplete and Imperfect Institutionalisation of Empathy and Altruism in the "Responsibility to Protect" Doctrine'; Pinker, *The Better Angels of Our Nature: Why Violence has Declined*; Singer, *The Expanding Circle: Ethics, Evolution, and Moral Progress.*

[74] Marlier and Crawford, 'Incomplete and Imperfect Institutionalisation of Empathy and Altruism in the "Responsibility to Protect" Doctrine', 401.

[75] Herbert C. Kelman, 'Negotiation as Interactive Problem Solving' (1996) 1(1) *International Negotiation* 99, 100. Kelman conducted experiments with Israeli and Palestinian officials by making them work on problem solving workshops. The results of the experiments found that working on a common challenge led to a transformation in their negotiation strategies towards each other. In particular, their stance was transformed from an antagonistic to a cooperative strategy. Their relationship was ameliorated.

[76] Galston, 'Cosmopolitan Altruism'; Richard Rorty makes a similar point about greater human solidarity: Richard Rorty, *Contingency, Irony, and Solidarity* (Cambridge University Press, 1989), 192.

of an international community of shared perspectives, values and expectations. Cosmopolitanism and altruism are not the sole constituents of this international society, but neither are statism and individualism. Rather these all coexist, with many other ideologies, value systems and behavioural tendencies. This chapter seeks to understand cosmopolitanism as an ideology and world view, its role in shaping our perception of the other and how it can lead to the emergence of altruistic norms and behaviour.

1.3.1 Cosmopolitanism

Etymologically, 'cosmopolitan' derives from the Greek term 'cosmos', meaning 'universal', and 'polity', literally meaning 'city' but, more generally, meaning a way of ordering society, and *Kosmopolitêsis* from the Greek word for 'citizen of the world'.[77] Cosmopolitan theory asserts that the most fundamental unit of moral concern in international relations is the individual, not the state or any other entity.[78] It demands that no local allegiance be put ahead of allegiance to a worldwide community of human beings.[79] It has been said to motivate action to achieve a variety of different ends from the alleviation of poverty in the developing world, military intervention for humanitarian purposes to advocating the institutional structure of regional or global governance.[80] According to cosmopolitan perspectives, violations of universal human rights are a concern for all of humanity. This claim about universal concern derives from the notion of a 'common morality'.[81] Cosmopolitanism implies a more profound sense of responsibility between human beings across borders. Human beings, as rational agents, should support one another in appropriate ways in a spirit of human compassion. Conceiving of global

[77] Pauline Kleingeld and Eric Brown, 'Cosmopolitanism' in Edward Zalta (ed.), *The Stanford Encyclopedia of Philosophy* (2013), http://plato.stan-ford.edu/archives/fall2013/entries/cosmopolitanism/.

[78] *Ibid.*

[79] Kwame Anthony Appiah, *Cosmopolitanism: Ethics in a World of Strangers* (W. W. Norton & Company, 2006), xv; Noah Feldman, 'Cosmopolitan Law' (2007) 116 *Yale Law Journal* 1022, 1027; Martha Nussbaum, 'Patriotism and Cosmopolitanism' in Joshua Cohen (ed.), *For Love of Country* (Beacon Press, 1996), 4; Thomas Pogge, 'Cosmopolitanism and Sovereignty' (1992) 103 *Ethics* 48, 49.

[80] Ileana Porras, 'Liberal Cosmopolitanism or Cosmopolitan Liberalism' in M. Sellers (ed.), *Parochialism, Cosmopolitanism, and the Foundations of International Law* (Cambridge University Press, 2011), 118–199.

[81] Alan Donagan, *The Theory of Morality* (University of Chicago Press, 1979). Common morality infers that human beings have rights by virtue of being human – not as a member of any particular community – and is related to the principle of beneficence.

society as one cosmopolitan community dates back a long time. In fact, Martha Nussbaum highlights that the Stoics conceived individuals as existing within multiple 'concentric circles':

> The first one encircles the self, the next takes in the immediate family, then follows the extended family, then, in order, neighbors or local groups, fellow city-dwellers, and fellow countrymen – and we can easily add to this list groupings based on ethnic, linguistic, historical, professional, gender, or sexual identities. Outside all these circles is the largest one, humanity as a whole.[82]

Today, the cosmopolitan perspective is similarly conceived. Leading cosmopolitan scholar Kwame Anthony Appiah argues that cosmopolitans discharge a special responsibility towards the life and justice of their compatriots but, importantly, also are concerned that other states are respecting the rights and needs of their own citizens.[83]

An inquiry into the major conceptualisations of cosmopolitanism reveals that cosmopolitanism can take many forms, including as an ideology that motivates behaviour.[84] In my submission, cosmopolitan altruism is the ideology that has influenced the actors involved in the creation of international law. The propagation of this ethic is catalysed by the forces of globalisation and information exchange, which result in greater understanding and empathy between peoples.[85] We explore this further in the next section.

1.3.2 The Making of Cosmopolitan Altruism

1.3.2.1 The Role of Reason

Identifying with others is central to altruism. As revealed earlier, this perception has been characterised as the common humanity perspective.

[82] Martha Nussbaum, 'Patriotism and Cosmopolitanism' in Garrett W. Brown and David Held (eds.), *The Cosmopolitan Reader* (Wiley, 2010), 158. See also Paul Schiff Berman, 'Review Essay: "Seeing Beyond the Limits of International Law," Jack L. Goldsmith and Eric A. Posner, "The Limits of International Law"' (2006) 84 *Texas Law Review* 1265, 1293.

[83] Appiah, *Cosmopolitanism: Ethics in a World of Strangers.*

[84] See Jason Rudall, 'A Cartography of Cosmopolitanism: Particularising the Universal' (2014) 3 *Cambridge Journal of International and Comparative Law* 747.

[85] This is based on the argument about altruism made by Peter Singer. See Singer, *The Expanding Circle: Ethics, Evolution, and Moral Progress.* For a similar argument on the influence of social mobility, intellectual communication and interaction between groups of people (in this case black and white communities in the US), see Gunnar Myrdal, *An American Dilemma* (Harper & Bros, 1944).

In an international context, the common humanity perspective is cosmopolitan in nature because it knows no borders and, like cosmopolitans, those who take the common humanity perspective see the individual as the ultimate unit of moral concern rather than any artificially created group.

For William Galston, 'cosmopolitan altruism' is 'the motivationally effective desire to assist needy or endangered strangers'.[86] It is concerned with the human race in its entirety, including all those people to whom one has no particular relation.[87] Understood in a cosmopolitan way, altruism is thus concerned with assisting foreigners in need. Cosmopolitan altruism may be distinguished from kin altruism (altruism directed at relatives), from personal altruism (altruism exercised towards proximate individuals) and from communal altruism (altruism exercised in respect of a group with common characteristics (e.g. ethnicity, nationality)).[88]

Circles of altruism widen as there is greater interaction between different peoples, and therefore better identification with those other peoples. This is a process that has also been termed moral progress. Indeed, Richard Rorty has noted that 'there is such a thing as moral progress, and that this progress is indeed in the direction of greater human solidarity'.[89] For him, solidarity is the capacity to identify with and act upon the pain, suffering or humiliation of other people.[90]

To understand the process by which this occurs it is helpful to refer to the work of Peter Singer in *The Expanding Circle: Ethics, Evolution, and Moral Progress*.[91] In this work, Singer shows that the circle of altruism has been expanding from relatives to members of the tribe to the nation and race. The expanding circle symbolises the growing altruistic moral community. Singer also argues that this expanding circle means we are in the process of recognising our obligations to all human beings. The origin of altruism was a genetically motivated desire to protect our kin (kin altruism), but this has expanded to include those in the community around us (reciprocal and group altruism). However, Singer argues that the human capacity to reason explains the expansion of human ethics further still, beyond our family and immediate community:

86 Galston, 'Cosmopolitan Altruism', 118.
87 *Ibid.*
88 Singer, *The Expanding Circle: Ethics, Evolution, and Moral Progress*, 123.
89 Rorty, *Contingency, Irony, and Solidarity*, 192.
90 *Ibid.*
91 Singer, *The Expanding Circle: Ethics, Evolution, and Moral Progress*.

> The idea of a disinterested defence of one's conduct emerges because of the social nature of human beings and the requirements of group living, but in the thought of reasoning beings, it takes on a logic of its own which leads to its extension beyond the bounds of the group.[92]

Following this logic, the development of reason combined with increasing interaction led to the expanding circle of altruism. Two concrete examples help to illustrate this moral progress. The first is the abolition of inheritance laws in Europe which had prevented foreigners from inheriting property. In France, the laws were abolished by the Revolutionary French National Assembly in 1790 as it considered the law ran contrary to the notion of human brotherhood.[93] In England, foreigners were entitled to inherit property in the same way as British subjects after 1870.[94] In both cases, discrimination on the basis of nationality came to be considered morally wrong.

The second example of the expanding circle is research conducted by Gunnar Myrdal on relations between black and white communities in the United States prior to the civil rights movement.[95] Myrdal found that ethical reasoning helped to break down racist attitudes and that such reasoning was facilitated by open democratic debate, communication and interaction, which occurred at many levels from the family to the inter-community, the national and the international, while science and education similarly helped to dispel false beliefs.[96] The central thesis is that as isolated communities become exposed to other communities and ideas, their moral valuations of others change.[97] Encounter and interaction with others alter our perception of them and prompt the common humanity perspective.

A major driver of encounter and interaction between individuals and communities that had previously been isolated from each other in our contemporary global society is globalisation, which we turn to next.

1.3.2.2 The Role of Globalisation

The increasing interconnectedness of human societies through the phenomena of globalisation, commerce and technological advancement is a significant factor in the expanding circle of altruism. This

92 *Ibid.*, 114.
93 *Ibid.*
94 *Ibid.*
95 See Myrdal, *An American Dilemma*.
96 *Ibid.*, 1028.
97 *Ibid.*, 1030.

in fact resonates with the thinking of the Scottish Enlightenment, in particular that 'the social conditions that fostered sympathy were the increase in wealth, the increase in interaction, and the increase in equality – and that all of these conditions would be enhanced as the market spread'.[98] In this context, it has been observed that 'the circle of people for whom we feel sympathy has increased in scope in parallel with the development of capitalism, just as the Scottish Enlightenment said that it would'.[99] As such, the global marketplace brings people together and breaks down barriers between people. Along similar lines, Charles Beitz and Thomas Pogge have argued for responsibility across borders owing to global interconnectedness and interaction through institutional structures.[100]

In addition to commerce, the globalisation of information exchange and communication has also played a role in the way human beings interact.[101] Similarly, interaction and understanding is facilitated by technological advancement. The role that media coverage of mass atrocities can play in provoking a moral, and ultimately political, response to such events has been the subject of several major studies.[102] The media

[98] Daniel Levy and Natan Sznaider, 'The Institutionalization of Cosmopolitan Morality: The Holocaust and Human Rights' (2004) 3(2) *Journal of Human Rights* 143, 147; see also James Mittelman, 'The Dynamics of Globalization' in James Mittelman (ed.), *Globalization: Critical Reflections* (Lynne Rienner, 1996), 3 (who considers that globalization has been primarily market-induced).

[99] Levy and Sznaider, 'The Institutionalisation of Cosmopolitan Morality: The Holocaust and Human Rights', 154. Levy and Sznaider also point to the Industrial Revolution in nineteenth-century England as providing an impetus for moral reform movements and argue that 'there is every reason to presume that the same is true of modern cosmopolitanism – that economic globalization is giving rise to worldwide movements for reform in much the same way as the growth of the market in Britain gave rise to moral reform movements', 154–155.

[100] See Thomas Pogge, 'A Universalistic Approach to International Justice' in Giuseppe Zaccaria (ed.), *International Justice and Interpretation* (Lit Verlag, 2002), 57–80; Charles Beitz, *Political Theory and International Relations* (Princeton University Press, 1999).

[101] See, for example, Andrea Bianchi, 'The Role of Non-State Actors in the Globalization of Human Rights: an International Lawyer's Perspective' in Gunther Teubner (ed.), *Global Law without the State* (Dartmouth Gower, 1997), 179 (examining the universalisation of human rights through transnational civil society); Olusoji Elias, 'The Impact of Globalisation on Human Rights' (2000) 28 *Amicus Curiae* 19; Anthony Giddens, *The Consequences of Modernity* (Polity Press, 1990), 64 (defining globalisation as 'the intensification of worldwide social relations which link distant localities in such a way that local happenings are shaped by events occurring many miles away and vice versa').

[102] Nicholas Wheeler, *Saving Strangers: Humanitarian Intervention in International Society* (Oxford University Press, 2000), 165; Malcolm Shaw, *Civil Society and Media in Global Crises* (Pinter, 1996), 156; Nik Gowing, 'Real-Time Television Coverage of Armed

coverage of the first Gulf War and Kosovo provide good examples of the way support for intervention can be provoked in this respect.[103] In a similar way again, large-scale or deeply traumatic events can have an analogous effect in cultivating human solidarity, which we explore more closely in the next section.

1.3.2.3 The Role of Formative Events

A further factor in the spread of cosmopolitan altruism can be the impact of particularly significant world events.[104] The Enlightenment, industrial revolutions and the Holocaust are all examples of these. As for the Holocaust, Daniel Levy and Natan Sznaider argue that it 'functioned simultaneously as the source for a critique of Western universalism and the foundation for a cosmopolitan desire to propagate human rights universally'.[105] Further still, they claim that the Holocaust has been central to the shift from a world order characterised by absolute sovereignty towards one characterised by interconnectedness and cosmopolitanism.[106]

Identification with the suffering of others is a capacity all human beings can develop and there tends to be broad consensus around the wrongness of certain acts or events.[107] Human wrongs have an emotive force, which can be a reason to behave altruistically. A reaction to horrific events or crimes may manifest in the universalisation of victimhood. The effect of such events has also been characterised as the 'return of the

Conflicts and Diplomatic Crises: Does It Pressure or Distort Foreign Policy Decisions?', *Joan Shorenstein Barone Centre, the John F. Kennedy School of Government* (Harvard University Working Paper #1994-1, June 1994).

103 However, while there may be a correlation, there is not causation between media coverage of mass atrocities and intervention, as the examples of Rwanda and Bosnia show. See Wheeler, *Saving Strangers: Humanitarian Intervention in International Society*, 165, and Chapters 7 and 8.

104 Levy and Sznaider, 'The Institutionalisation of Cosmopolitan Morality: The Holocaust and Human Rights', 145. On the spread of philosophical ideas, see Émile Durkheim, 'Individuals and the Intellectuals' in Robert Bellah (ed.), *On Morality and Society: Selected Writings* (Chicago University Press, 1973), 44–57.

105 Levy and Sznaider, 'The Institutionalisation of Cosmopolitan Morality: The Holocaust and Human Rights', 145.

106 *Ibid.*, 155; see also Richard Rorty, 'Human Rights, Rationality and Sentimentality' in Stephen Shute and Susan Hurley (eds.), *On Human Rights: The Oxford Amnesty Lectures* (Basic Books, 1993), 111–134 (observing that negative events promote the spread of solidarity).

107 Ken Booth, 'Three Tyrannies' in Tim Dunne and Nicholas Wheeler (eds.), *Human Rights in Global Politics* (Cambridge University Press, 1999), 62.

repressed'.[108] This is illustrated, for example, by the post-Holocaust period during which crimes against the Jewish people were characterised as crimes against humanity.[109] This also expands the circle of altruism because it renders all of humanity as a victim of the horrific event or crime. As the scholarship on altruism has revealed, the perception that we are all part of a common humanity is at the heart of altruistic action.

All of the phenomena already set out create social bonds that allow people to understand, identify and empathise with each other. They are also cosmopolitan phenomena insofar as they are concerned with the social bonds that link individuals of different nationalities and across borders.[110]

The link between altruism, cosmopolitanism and the international legal system has not been explored in international law scholarship. However, there is related literature on which it will be important for this work to build. We turn to that next.

1.4 Altruism in a Legal System

1.4.1 Individualism versus Altruism

The literature on altruism in legal systems is sparse but certain related scholarly works nevertheless give an indication as to the altruistic features of and the altruism promoted by legal systems. The first major scholarly work engaging with altruism in a legal context is Duncan Kennedy's study on 'Form and Substance in Private Law Adjudication', which was published in 1976.[111] In that work, and as alluded to earlier, Kennedy contrasts individualism and altruism. Individualism is defined as 'the making of a sharp distinction between one's own interests and those of others, combined with the belief that a preference in conduct for one's own interests is legitimate, but that one should be willing to respect

[108] Itamar Mann, *Humanity at Sea: Maritime Migration and the Foundations of International Law* (Cambridge University Press, 2016), 213 (noting that this terminology is drawn from Sigmund Freud and that '[c]rises are central to international law').

[109] Levy and Sznaider, 'The Institutionalisation of Cosmopolitan Morality: The Holocaust and Human Rights', 149.

[110] Hedley Bull, *The Anarchical Society: A Study of Order in World Politics* (Columbia University Press, 2002), 24 (noting that '[t]he Kantian or universalist tradition ... takes the essential nature of international politics to lie not in conflict among states, as on the Hobbesian view, but in the transnational social bonds that link the individual human beings who are subjects or citizens of states').

[111] Duncan Kennedy, 'Form and Substance in Private Law Adjudication' (1976) 89 *Harvard Law Review* 1685.

the rules that make it possible to co-exist with others similarly self-interested'.[112] Individualism favours self-reliance. It is also characterised by the absence of sacrifice, charity and non-interference with the rights of others. Kennedy goes on to note that the individualist ethic is not pure egotism as there can be limits to the pursuit of self-interest, and self-reliance itself has moral content. But individualism is a counter-ethic to altruism.[113]

As for altruism, Kennedy observes that this does not mean total selflessness in the same way that individualism does not mean pure egoism. Indeed, despite the importance of solidarity for altruists, they do not expect that every person is responsible for the welfare of every other person.[114] The parameters of altruistic duty include the degree of communal involvement, solidarity or intimacy between the actors, the degree of moral fault or moral virtue owed by one actor to another and the magnitude of deprivation that is avoided relative to the sacrifice endured by the altruist.[115]

Kennedy thus paints a picture of coexistence and competition between the normative influences of individualism and altruism in private law. There is also a distinction in the legal form that altruistic and individualist norms take. It has been observed that an altruistic order has a preference for standards, whereas an individualist order has a preference for rules.[116] This is a point that will be elaborated upon in Chapter 7.

1.4.2 Acting in the Interests of Others

In his explanation of the norm of individualism, Kennedy notes an emphasis on the promotion of one's own interests but also an understanding that rules exist to ensure coexistence with other self-interested individuals.[117] In this context, legal norms having an individualist character are clearly defined and highly administrable rules.[118] As for the role of the judge in an individualist system, they are expected to be passive, non-interventionist and apply those clear rules in a strict fashion.

[112] *Ibid.*, 1713.
[113] *Ibid.*, 1715.
[114] *Ibid.*, 1718.
[115] *Ibid.*
[116] *Ibid.*, 1776.
[117] *Ibid.*, 1731.
[118] *Ibid.*, 1687.

In contrast, altruism encourages behaviour that is in the interests of others. When altruism is compelled by the law it requires the 'sharing or sacrifice of advantages that one might have kept for oneself' and, as such, 'the state forces the strong to behave altruistically'.[119] Kennedy points to such legal institutions as the progressive income tax, employer social security contributions, minimum wage or pure food and drug laws as having an obviously altruistic character.[120] Less obviously, laws against violence ensure that the strong respect the interests of the weak, and laws against theft ensure that thieves are punished for not having regard for the interests of property owners. In tort law, the mechanism by which compensation for injuries operates effectively means the tortfeasor must take into account the interests of the injured party, and as such they are not simply responsible for their own gains or losses. In contract, the law incorporates the losses to the promisee in any calculation the promisor makes when breaking a contract.[121]

A further contribution made by Kennedy's work is that the law can be used as an instrument to encourage or compel people to behave in the interests of others. Indeed, in response to the argument that altruistic behaviour must come from a place of voluntariness, Kennedy contends that

> [i]t is precisely the refusal to take all the advantage which one is legally, but not morally entitled that is most often offered as an example of altruism. It follows that when the law 'enforces' such conduct, it can do no more than make people behave 'as if' they had really experienced altruistic motives.[122]

In this way, he also notes that some conceptions of justice demand regulation in such a way that creates outcomes as if everyone in a given society acted altruistically.[123] This is an important idea for the argument made in this book about the presence of altruism in international law. Other scholarly works have also made explicit reference to the possibility that altruism may exist in a legal system, and we turn to that scholarship next.

[119] *Ibid.*, 1719.
[120] *Ibid.*
[121] *Ibid.*
[122] *Ibid.*
[123] *Ibid.*

1.4.3 *Duties to Render Assistance*

In the only published monograph on altruism in the law, entitled *Altruism in Private Law: Liability for Nonfeasance and Negotiorum Gestio*, Jeroen Kortmann focuses on the place of altruism in the Roman, French, German, and English legal systems.[124] In particular, Kortmann first considers whether there is a duty to assist other people and if liability follows in the event such assistance is not offered when necessary. In other words, he examines whether there might be liability for nonfeasance. Second, Kortmann asks whether there may be a claim for the intervener, in particular to recover any costs they may have incurred as a result of the intervention or even be entitled to remuneration or a reward.

In the context of English law, Kortmann answers these questions in the negative. As for the first question, after pointing to the famous extract of Lord Atkin in the English case of *Donoghue* v. *Stevenson*[125] suggesting that there may be a duty to intervene in English law where a reasonable person would do so, Kortmann ultimately concludes on the basis of subsequent case law that there is no such affirmative duty to act.[126] Furthermore, English law in fact discourages intervening to give assistance, and liability may follow for those who do intervene and make mistakes or are negligent.[127] As to the second question on the potential claim of the intervener, Kortmann confirms that English law does not reward or remunerate affirmative action to help another.[128]

Kortmann also considers these questions in the context of European legal systems.[129] In short, the French and German legal systems do make provision for the imposition of liability in cases of an omission to act. The French legal system makes a distinction between fault by commission (*faute de commission*) and fault by omission (*faute d'abstention*). In the case of fault by omission, a distinction between omissions that are part of a broader activity (*abstentions dans l'action*) and pure omissions (*abstentions pure et simples*) is made. With regard to the former, French law normally imposes liability on the basis that those who partake in risky

[124] Jeroen Kortmann, *Altruism in Private Law: Liability for Nonfeasance and Negotiorum Gestio* (Oxford University Press, 2005).
[125] *Donoghue* v. *Stevenson* [1932] AC 562.
[126] Kortmann, *Altruism in Private Law: Liability for Nonfeasance and Negotiorum Gestio.*
[127] *Ibid.*, 9.
[128] *Ibid.*, 23.
[129] *Ibid.*, 34–38.

activities should accept the possibility that liability may follow. As for the latter, while liability may follow, it is nevertheless more restricted.

The duty to render assistance remains present in the most recent French Penal Code (2020). Indeed, under French criminal law, section 3 of the Code pénal 2020 provides for '[d]e l'entrave aux mesures d'assistance et de l'omission de porter secours' or 'obstruction of assistance and the failure to provide assistance'.[130] In particular,

> Quiconque pouvant empêcher par son action immédiate, sans risque pour lui ou pour les tiers, soit un crime, soit un délit contre l'intégrité corporelle de la personne s'abstient volontairement de le faire est puni de cinq ans d'emprisonnement et de 75 000 euros d'amende.
>
> Sera puni des mêmes peines quiconque s'abstient volontairement de porter à une personne en péril l'assistance que, sans risque pour lui ou pour les tiers, il pouvait lui prêter soit par son action personnelle, soit en provoquant un secours.
>
> Les peines sont portées à sept ans d'emprisonnement et 100 000 euros d'amende lorsque le crime ou le délit contre l'intégrité corporelle de la personne mentionnée au premier alinéa est commis sur un mineur de quinze ans ou lorsque la personne en péril mentionnée au deuxième alinéa est un mineur de quinze ans.[131]

A similar provision may be found under German law in §323c(1) of the Strafgesetzbuch (or criminal code).[132] This provision is entitled 'Unterlassene Hilfeleistung' or 'Auxiliary Assistance'.[133]

> Wer bei Unglücksfällen oder gemeiner Gefahr oder Not nicht Hilfe leistet, obwohl dies erforderlich und ihm den Umständen nach zuzumuten, insbesondere ohne erhebliche eigene Gefahr und ohne Verletzung

[130] Author's translation.

[131] *Legislationonline.org*, www.legislationline.org/documents/section/criminal-codes/country/30. Author's translation:

> Any person who, by his immediate action and without danger to himself or others, could have prevented either a felonious act or misdemeanour against the person, wilfully fails to do so, shall be punished with five years of imprisonment and by a fine of 75,000 euros.
>
> Any person who wilfully fails to render or to obtain assistance to an endangered person when such was possible without danger to himself or others, shall be subject to like punishments.
>
> The penalties are increased to seven years imprisonment and a 100,000 euros fine when the crime or offense against the bodily integrity of the person mentioned in the first paragraph is committed on a minor of 15 or when the person in danger mentioned in the second paragraph is a minor of 15 years.

[132] Strafgesetzbuch (StGB), www.gesetze-im-internet.de/bundesrecht/stgb/gesamt.pdf.

[133] Author's translation.

> anderer wichtiger Pflichten möglich ist, wird mit Freiheitsstrafe bis zu einem Jahr oder mit Geldstrafe bestraft.[134]

As such, under the German legal system, there is a duty to offer assistance to another in harm where to do so would not cause harm to oneself or breach another important obligation. In addition to these examples in the French and German legal systems, we may also point to other examples in civil law systems and systems based on Sharia law, which also impose a positive legal obligation to rescue a person in danger. This is the case in the codes of Belgium, Greece, Italy, the Netherlands, Poland, Russia, Switzerland, as well as states throughout the Middle East.[135] As such, positive duties to act in the interests of others are far from alien to legal systems.

Having considered altruism in legal scholarship and practice at the domestic level, we now turn to consider altruistic themes evident in international legal scholarship.

1.5 Altruistic Themes in International Legal Scholarship

While there has not been any detailed consideration of the concept of altruism in scholarship on the international legal system, reference has been made on occasion to this concept, and several major projects adopt altruistic themes. The latter are important building blocks and it is therefore helpful to consider their contributions in this section.

Nikolaos Tsagourias provides the insight that individualistic and altruistic premises underlie the distinction between 'national egoism' and 'communitarian morality' in international law.[136] An altruistic approach emphasises the existence of common values, which may be observed as emanating from 'societal functions'.[137] Altruism is concerned with propagating community values towards the end of human

[134] §323c(1), German Criminal Code. Translated by Kortmann, *Altruism in Private Law: Liability for Nonfeasance and Negotiorum Gestio*, 42, as

> Whoever fails to render assistance in case of accident, common danger or emergency, although such assistance was needed and could have been expected from him under the circumstances, especially since he could have rendered it without placing himself in significant danger and without violating any important duties, shall be punished by up to one years' imprisonment or by fine.

[135] See The Dan Legal Network, 'The Good Samaritan Law across Europe', www.daneurope.org/c/document_library.

[136] Nikolaos Tsagourias, *Jurisprudence of International Law: The Humanitarian Dimension* (Juris Publishing, 2000), 58.

[137] *Ibid.*

solidarity. In contrast, where states act in an individualistic way, they ignore the plight of other human beings in countries where they may be subject to persecution or suffering.[138] Individualism relies on rules to set the boundaries of individual liberty and it does not favour the infiltration of values in regulatory decision-making as to do so would be subjective and arbitrary according to the individualist approach.[139] Consequently, intervention by the state is discouraged as this would likely encroach upon individual self-interest or propagate certain values.[140]

As for intervention in third states, Tsagourias offers several insights drawing upon Duncan Kennedy's theoretical premises for individualism and altruism. In the individualist perspective, non-intervention helps to consolidate the autonomy of the state and prioritises the interests of an individual state over the shared interests of a community. It also avoids 'moral paternalism' insofar as this approach tends not to spread particular values or impose those values on non-consenting members of a community.[141] However, in the altruistic perspective, non-intervention is concerned with restraining those states that might abuse a right to intervene. That said, the use of force to intervene is not ruled out by altruists. Rather, recourse to it should be compelled by moral justification.[142]

In a chapter entitled 'National Interests and Altruism in Humanitarian Intervention', Andreas Krieg considers the prevalence of altruism as a motivation for humanitarian intervention.[143] Krieg also examines national interests and defines these as the 'self-interest of a state or nation'.[144] In the context of the behaviour of states, Krieg understands altruism as

> an other-oriented action of states or policy-makers not motivated by self-interest but motivated by empathy or norms of morality with the sole purpose of helping individuals in need and who are not part of the own nation [*sic*].[145]

It is derived, Krieg argues, from cosmopolitan ideas of moral universalism and shared values across humanity. Humanity is constituted by the

[138] *Ibid.*
[139] *Ibid.*
[140] *Ibid.*
[141] *Ibid.*
[142] *Ibid.*
[143] Krieg, 'National Interests and Altruism in Humanitarian Intervention', 40.
[144] *Ibid.*, 40.
[145] *Ibid.*, 50.

connection of individuals through universal norms, and that the primary universal norms are those that may be found within law, which guarantee to individuals universal human rights that must be protected by states.[146] Where states deprive their citizens of these human rights, there is a cosmopolitan-inspired moral duty upon the international community to intervene on the basis that the violation of these universal norms are a concern for individuals and states everywhere.[147] While there are exceptions, Krieg is of the view that humanitarian intervention is primarily driven by altruism and not by national interests, although these latter interests may play a role.[148]

The pursuit of national interests is often justified by the idea that the state exists to protect the people who are its citizens. As Thomas Hobbes and John Locke argued, the very *raison d'être* of the state is arrived at through the social contract.[149] The state is the conduit through which individuals may achieve self-determination. Indeed, we might compare this perspective with the idea developed by Adam Smith that *homo economicus* pursues self-interest and, in doing so, enhances the interests of all.[150] This view challenges, for example, humanitarian intervention as such intervention may not be in the national interest of the intervening state, and the intervening state therefore violates the social contract it has with its people.[151] However, on this point it is important to bear in mind that the state has also contracted with the international community to uphold all international rights and obligations.[152]

For Grant Marlier and Neta Crawford, the responsibility to protect (R2P) doctrine represents an institutionalisation of empathy and altruism.[153] In fact, Marlier and Crawford argue that 'the adoption of a responsibility to protect was made possible, and indeed urgent, by the ... institutionalization of empathy and altruism across inter-state

[146] *Ibid.*, 51.

[147] *Ibid.*

[148] *Ibid.*, 56. For a supporting argument that humanitarian interventions have primarily involved other-regarding and altruistic motivations, see Richard Millar, 'Humanitarian Intervention, Altruism and the Limits of Casuistry' (2000) 28(1) *The Journal of Religious Ethics* 3.

[149] Thomas Hobbes, *Leviathan* [1651] (Wordsworth Editions Ltd, 2014); John Locke, *Second Treatise on Civil Government* [1690] (Prometheus, 1986).

[150] Krieg, 'National Interests and Altruism in Humanitarian Intervention'.

[151] *Ibid.*

[152] *Ibid.*

[153] Marlier and Crawford, 'Incomplete and Imperfect Institutionalisation of Empathy and Altruism in the "Responsibility to Protect" Doctrine'.

borders'.[154] Moreover, the normative turn from a right to intervene under the doctrine of humanitarian intervention to the R2P means that there is now a need to listen to, empathise with and act altruistically towards the needs of 'the other'.[155]

That said, the institutionalisation of empathy and altruism is incomplete and imperfect. In particular, the R2P doctrine is susceptible to misuse and abuse. The imperfect and incomplete nature of altruistic commitments is an important point and this can be seen in other areas of international law, as will become evident in the chapters that follow. At the same time, the process of correcting this incomplete and imperfect institutionalisation is underway. There is an expanding circle of empathy, evident for example in the practice of the Security Council, reporting on human rights abuses, and a general decline in the use of violence.[156]

Similarly conceived obligations towards peoples in third states find support in the literature.[157] There are also, of course, those who remain sceptical about the existence and application of such legal relationships,[158] as well as those who assess that this category of

[154] *Ibid.*, 398.

[155] *Ibid.*

[156] Pinker, *The Better Angels of Our Nature: Why Violence has Declined*; Singer, *The Expanding Circle: Ethics, Evolution, and Moral Progress.*

[157] See, for example, Michael Wabwile, *Legal Protection of Social and Economic Rights of Children in Developing Countries: Reassessing International Cooperation and Responsibility* (Intersentia, 2010); Rolf Künnemann, 'Extraterritorial Application of the International Covenant on Economic, Social and Cultural Rights' in Fons Coomans and Menno T. Kamminga (eds.), *Extraterritorial Application of Human Rights Treaties* (Intersentia, 2004), 210; Arjun Sengupta, 'Poverty Eradication and Human Rights' in Thomas Pogge (ed.), *Freedom from Poverty as a Human Right* (Oxford University Press, 2007), 344; Lea Brilmayer and Isaias Yemane Tesfalidet, 'Third State Obligations and the Enforcement of International Law' (2011) 44(1) *International Law and Politics* 1; Monica Hakimi, 'State Bystander Responsibility' (2010) 21(2) *European Journal of International Law* 341; Luke Glanville, 'The Responsibility to Protect Beyond Borders' (2012) 12(1) *Human Rights Law Review* 1; Kok Chor Tan, 'The Duty to Protect' in Terry Nardin and Melissa Williams (eds.), *Humanitarian Intervention* (New York University Press, 2006), 84–116; Jennifer Welsh and Maria Banda, 'International Law and the Responsibility to Protect: Clarifying or Expanding States' Responsibilities?' (2010) 2 *Global Responsibility to Protect* 213; André Nollkaemper, '"Failures to Protect" in International Law' in Marc Weller (ed.), *The Oxford Handbook of the Use of Force in International Law* (Oxford University Press, 2015), 439; John Knox, 'Diagonal Environmental Rights' in Mark Gibney and Sigrun Skogly (eds.), *Universal Human Rights and Extra-Territorial Obligations* (University of Pennsylvania Press, 2010).

[158] See, for example, M. Magdalena Sepulveda, *The Nature of Obligations under the International Covenant on Economic, Social and Cultural Rights* (Intersentia, 2003).

obligations is a work in progress.[159] That said, the literature supporting the existence of such obligations is divided and unclear on the substance of these legal relationships. For example, Monika Hakimi refers to 'state by-stander responsibility', which involves a responsibility (including positive obligations) to protect people from third-party harm,[160] while Lea Brilmayer and Isaias Yemane Tesfalidet have referred to 'third state obligations', which involve a purely negative obligation not to contribute to the illegal activity, and are described as analogous to laws concerning accessories or accomplices.[161] Alternatively, some obligations have been termed 'transnational human rights obligations',[162] 'extra-territorial human rights obligations',[163] 'external obligations'[164] or 'international obligations'.[165] For certain scholars, such legal relationships simply involve cooperation to bring to an end human rights violations in a third state,[166] while for others they imply a broader commitment to ensure the realisation of human rights in third states.[167] Some have also analysed the legal obligation that states are under to ensure that its corporations do not breach the human rights of people in third countries.[168] This is derived from the proposition that states must

[159] See, for example, Wouter Vandenhole, 'Economic, Social and Cultural Rights in the CRC: Is there a Legal Obligation to Cooperate Internationally for Development?' (2009) 17 *International Journal of Children's Rights* 23 and Fons Coomans, 'Some Remarks on the Extraterritorial Application of the International Covenant on Economic, Social and Cultural Rights' in Coomans and Kamminga (eds.), *Extraterritorial Application of Human Rights Treaties*, 183.

[160] Hakimi, 'State Bystander Responsibility'.

[161] Brilmayer and Tesfalidet, 'Third State Obligations and the Enforcement of International Law'.

[162] See, for example, Sigrun Skogly and Mark Gibney, 'Transnational Human Rights Obligations' (2002) 24 *Human Rights Quarterly* 781.

[163] See, for example, Künnemann, 'Extraterritorial Application of the International Covenant on Economic, Social and Cultural Rights'.

[164] See, for example, Matthew Craven, *The International Covenant on Economic, Social and Cultural Rights: A Perspective on Its Development* (Clarendon Press, 1995).

[165] See, for example, Coomans, 'Some Remarks on the Extraterritorial Application of the International Covenant on Economic, Social and Cultural Rights'.

[166] See, for example, Sigrun Skogly, *Beyond National Borders: States' Human Rights Obligations in International Cooperation* (Intersentia, 2006), 48.

[167] Michael Wabwile, 'Re-examining States' External Obligations to Implement Economic and Social Rights of Children' (2009) 22(2) *Canadian Journal of Law & Jurisprudence* 407.

[168] See Penelope Simons and Robert McCorquodale, 'Responsibility Beyond Borders: State Responsibility for Extraterritorial Violations by Corporations of International Human Rights law' (2007) 70 *Modern Law Review* 598.

prevent human rights violations by their citizens, even when they are acting beyond the jurisdiction of the state.[169]

The idea that sovereignty may or should imply the assumption of obligations towards people in other countries is central to the project on *Sovereigns as Trustees of Humanity* led by Eyal Benvenisti.[170] The point of departure for this project is a challenge to the proposition that sovereigns, as agents of the peoples under their jurisdiction, should have no regard to the interests of foreigners in third countries.[171] In the alternative, Benvenisti argues that sovereigns are also agents of humanity and therefore have an obligation to take the interests of all stakeholders into account and, as such, there is a principal–agent relationship that extends beyond the state. Drawing upon the administrative law tradition, Benvenisti argues that decision-making processes must be inclusive for all stakeholders and must also be accountable.[172]

This approach is between statist and globalist approaches, not least because sovereigns retain discretion to give priority to their citizens' interests. Moreover, the obligation is simply to take the interests of foreign stakeholders into account, and not to give them priority over national interests. The call is for sovereigns to consider the interests of foreign stakeholders, and even global welfare, whenever they take decisions or pursue policies that are likely to affect foreign stakeholders. In this context, foreign interests should be taken into account through the restricted Pareto criterion, where the application of the restricted Pareto criterion means accommodating the interests of others to the extent that the decision-maker (and their polity) sustains no loss.[173] Legal systems that seek to share resources in society must embrace the Pareto criterion at a minimum.[174] In this way, by being other-regarding, sovereigns can enhance global welfare and justice.[175]

[169] Wabwile, *Legal Protection of Social and Economic Rights of Children in Developing Countries: Reassessing International Cooperation and Responsibility*, 120–121.

[170] Tel Aviv University, 'GlobalTrust: Sovereigns as Trustees of Humanity Project', http://globaltrust.tau.ac.il/.

[171] Eyal Benvenisti, 'Sovereigns as Trustees of Humanity: On the Accountability of States to Foreign Stakeholders' (2013) 107(2) *American Journal of International Law* 295, 298.

[172] *Ibid.*

[173] *Ibid.*, 320.

[174] *Ibid.*, 321.

[175] *Ibid.*, 300. On the global administrative law tradition, see for example, Benedict Kingsbury, Nico Krisch and Richard Stewart, 'Global Administrative Law' (2005) 68 *Law & Contemporary Problems* 15.

To some extent, the taking into account of the interests of foreign stakeholders is reflected in certain aspects of international law and judicial decisions.[176] As for sovereignty, not only is a reconceptualisation morally required, it is in fact presently underway. In this context, Benvenisti insists on the need to retain the vehicle of sovereignty, given its particular importance for the realisation of self-determination, but it should be (and is presently being) reconceived to provide opportunities for foreign stakeholders to have their needs taken into account.[177]

As for international legal obligations that reflect the needs of the other, it is possible to point to *non-refoulement* under the Convention Relating to the Status of Refugees 1951, obligations in respect of individuals who are under the effective control of an occupying power, or obligations regarding the provision of food under the Food Aid Convention of 1999 and Food Assistance Convention of 2012. References to solidarity are also evident in the European context. Indeed, the European Court of Justice has even said that 'solidarity . . . is the basis . . . of the whole of the Community system'.[178] Moreover, Article 24(3) of the Consolidated Version of the Treaty on European Union refers to 'solidarity' and Article 222 of the Consolidated Version of the Treaty on the Functioning of the European Union provides that member states must 'act jointly in a spirit of solidarity if a member state is the object of a terrorist attack or the victim of a natural or man-made disaster'. In a similar vein, there are of course other obligations such as the duty to inform neighbouring states about hazardous activities that may cause 'significant harm' to others.[179] The Aarhus Convention Compliance Committee has said that foreigners not within the jurisdiction of a given country have a right to participate in national environmental

[176] Benvenisti, 'Sovereigns as Trustees of Humanity: On the Accountability of States to Foreign Stakeholders', 297.

[177] *Ibid.*

[178] Joined Cases 6 and 11/69, *Commission* v. *France* (1969) ECR 523, para 16, cited in Benvenisti, 'Sovereigns as Trustees of Humanity: On the Accountability of States to Foreign Stakeholders', 315.

[179] See *Corfu Channel Case (United Kingdom of Great Britain and Northern Ireland* v. *Albania),* Judgment (1949) ICJ Rep. 4; Convention on the Law of the Non-navigational Uses of International Watercourses, 21 May 1997, 2999 UNTS 1, (Article 12); International Law Commission, Draft Articles on the Prevention of Transboundary Harm from Hazardous Activities, 11 May 2001, UN Doc. A/56/10 (Article 8) cited in Benvenisti, 'Sovereigns as Trustees of Humanity: On the Accountability of States to Foreign Stakeholders', 319.

decision-making.[180] In the context of the WTO, the Appellate Body affirmed that members are under an obligation to hear foreign stakeholders who may be affected by national limitations on imports.[181]

In some areas of international law, obligations can be stronger than the restricted Pareto criterion. Examples include the obligation to prevent crimes against humanity and war crimes, and R2P. In addition, Article 3 of the European Convention on Human Rights imposes an obligation to protect foreign citizens who are at risk of ill-treatment. There are also obligations in respect of access to food under the International Covenant on Economic, Social and Cultural Rights of 1966.

Beyond explicit legal provisions where states have consented to taking the interests of foreign stakeholders into account, Benvenisti argues that states are also bound to do so by virtue of being 'agents of humanity', and he justifies this assertion on the basis of three reasons.[182] First, a sovereign entity is in principle an effective instrument for the realisation of self-determination. Second, humanity at large has vested the power of governing in peoples over certain other peoples. Third, by exercising exclusive ownership over a given portion of the world, sovereigns have certain obligations to the rest of humanity.[183]

There are criticisms of this approach, including that the behaviour of states in this way should be paid for by the beneficiaries, that sovereigns compromise their competitive advantage by heeding to other-regarding interests and that such an approach may be subject to abuse.[184] As an example of the latter, the sacred trust of civilisation was a feature of the League of Nations era and in some cases was abused insofar as it represented a veil for colonialism.[185] Further, there is the danger of imposing too many or too heavy obligations on weaker states. However, as a response to this challenge, Benvenisti suggests that other-regarding

[180] UNECE Convention on Access to Information, Public Participation in Decision-making and Access to Justice in Environmental Matters (Aarhus Convention), 25 June 1998, 2161 UNTS 447, Article 2(5) provides that those 'affected or likely to be affected by, or having an interest in, the environmental decision-making' have a right to participate in domestic decision-making on environmental matters.

[181] *United States – Measures Affecting the Cross-Border Supply of Gambling and Betting Services*, WT/DS285/AB/R, para 306, cited in Benvenisti, 'Sovereigns as Trustees of Humanity: On the Accountability of States to Foreign Stakeholders', 330.

[182] Benvenisti, 'Sovereigns as Trustees of Humanity: On the Accountability of States to Foreign Stakeholders', 300.

[183] *Ibid.*, 302.

[184] *Ibid.*, 327.

[185] *Ibid.*, 328.

obligations are shaped by the principle of common but differentiated responsibilities.[186]

Benvenisti's work may be considered part of the wider global justice debate, and the latter provides further examples at cultivating other-regardingness. As for positive obligations on states towards citizens of other states, some authors have argued that a jurisprudence of altruism encourages actors in a legal system to act affirmatively to further the interests of others, in addition to their own.[187] Moreover, states are said to be duty-bound to remedy abuses caused by other states, albeit that this duty is weaker than the duty a state is under to remedy its own abuses.[188]

Overall, this scholarship suggests a shift towards a rhetoric of common duties. This is part of the wider change in approaches to the governance of international society: from minimal norms of coexistence to more complex norms that aim at solving common challenges through the allocation of responsibility.[189]

1.6 Concluding Remarks

This chapter has inquired into the meaning of altruism. In doing so, it has considered various studies from moral and political philosophy to sociobiology, and behavioural economics and psychology to law. This exploration has revealed certain common characteristics about the nature of altruism and how it may develop in society. Bringing together these various understandings of altruism from different fields, we may summarise that altruism is concerned with action in the interests of others at a cost to the actor. There must be an intention to help 'the other' and, while there may be other reasons to act, this particular intention must be among the primary reasons. As for the action itself, this need not result in the desired outcome to be characterised as altruistic, but the action taken must nevertheless follow intention and should be directed at benefiting 'the other'. It is action

186 *Ibid.*

187 Evan J. Criddle, 'Protecting Human Rights during Emergencies: Delegation, Derogation and Deference' (2014) 45 *Netherlands Yearbook of International Law* 197.

188 David Miller, *National Responsibility and Global Justice* (Oxford University Press, 2008), 272–273.

189 Andrew Hurrell, 'Regionalism in Theoretical Perspective' in Louise Fawcett and Andrew Hurrell (eds.), *Regionalism in World Politics* (Oxford University Press, 1995), 139. See also Wolfgang Friedmann, *The Changing Structure of International Law* (Stevens, 1964).

as opposed to result-oriented. Moreover, that the action may result in some pay-off for the actor does not mitigate its altruistic character so long as this is not the primary reason for acting.

Behavioural science reveals that human beings do act in altruistic ways more often than is commonly thought to be the case. This exposes the dialectic in our moral existence. Indeed, human beings can oscillate in their behaviour between selfishness and selflessness. There is thus a 'fundamental contradiction' in our social relations. This contradiction has also been characterised as either the pursuit of individual autonomy or a sensitivity to communal force.[190] There is thus an inevitability that such a contradiction would be reflected in the substance of legal rules.

Significantly, altruists identify with the beneficiaries of their action because they perceive them to be part of the same social group. Indeed, the perception of a common humanity motivates altruistic action and is the best way of predicting altruism in any given subject. Importantly for this study, such an insight supports the proposition that the altruistic instinct to those beyond borders has a cosmopolitan origin. Cosmopolitan altruism is a phenomenon made possible by the capacity of human beings to empathise with 'the other' through an expanding common humanity perspective. It is driven by increasing interconnectedness and interaction between peoples across borders. This is the result of factors such as globalisation, capitalism, technological advancement and major events like the Holocaust.

Engaging with several major scholarly works, the features of a legal system that result from altruism or that promote altruistic behaviour among its subjects were also considered. In the domestic legal context, studies have shown that distinctions may be drawn between an individualist approach and an altruistic approach, and in turn rigid legal rules and flexible legal standards. In a legal context, altruism is concerned with acting in the interests of others. Moreover, as well as reflecting the altruism that already exists in society, the law may promote altruistic behaviour. That altruistic behaviour is prescribed by law in this way does not take away from its altruistic character. In the domestic context, various examples of altruism in the rules of legal systems around the world are evident.

[190] See Duncan Kennedy, 'The Structure of Blackstone's Commentaries' (1979) 28 *Buffalo Law Review* 209, 211–213.

As for the international legal scholarship, no detailed consideration has been given to the presence or influence of altruism in international law. However, there are a number of important studies dealing with related themes that this book will build upon to fill the gap in the literature. Before turning to examine the substance of altruism in international law, the next chapter appraises how altruistic law is made.

2

The Making of Altruism in International Law

2.1 Introduction

This study is concerned with the scope of state obligations, and in particular the legal relationships that states have with people beyond their territory. Before appraising the substance of altruistic commitments in international law, this chapter considers how certain values may come to shape the law. This will involve an exploration of the institutions, processes and actors that facilitate the emergence of altruistically oriented legal norms. In doing so, the link between ideology and law will become more apparent.

It is submitted that the evolution in international law presented in this book is the product of an underlying cosmopolitan altruistic ideology, which coexists with a statist individualistic ideology, that shapes the content of legal rules.[1] Ideologies comprise a collection of beliefs about the way in which society should be ordered and may stipulate how this will be realised. They represent widely held values, beliefs and opinions in a societal group, although they need not be unanimously shared by the entirety of the group.[2] The ideology of the societal body influences the law and the law influences the ideology of the societal body in a circular process. A legal system can be influenced by one or more philosophical ideologies,[3] and the international legal system has been and continues to

[1] By statism, I mean a state-centric vision of international order.

[2] John Jost, Christopher Federico and Jaime Napier, 'Political Ideology: Its Structure, Functions, and Elective Affinities' (2009) 60 *Annual Review of Psychology* 307; Robert S. Erikson and Kent L. Tedin, *American Public Opinion* (Longman, 2003).

[3] Rafael Domingo, *The New Global Law* (Cambridge University Press, 2010), 6. One may point to countless examples but perhaps most notably Roman law was underpinned in large part by Greek philosophy. See also Patrick Capps, *Human Dignity and the Foundations of International Law* (Hart, 2009), 273, observing that 'international law, like all forms of law, is a normative practice which is value oriented towards the respect and protection of certain rights associated with human dignity. The rights of states are, in a moral sense, corollaries of this fundamental value-orientation'. See further David Held, 'Law of States, Law of Peoples: Three Models of Sovereignty' (2002) 8 *Legal Theory* 1.

be shaped by different variations of two major ideologies. As such, cosmopolitan altruism and statist individualism have a dialectic existence in the formation of law and its interpretation. Despite the fundamental differences in the nature and effect of these ideologies, they are capable of having simultaneous normative influence on the behaviour of states and the formation of international law.[4] How the influence of ideology comes to bear on the rules of international law is examined in the following sections.

2.2 Values and the Law: Institutions, Processes and Actors

A legal system can both reflect and propagate certain social phenomena, ideologies and values. The principal means through which values infiltrate law-making and development processes are by those actors involved in these processes. In the case of international law, the relevant actors are states, international lawyers, courts and tribunals, and other international institutions. These actors may also be influenced by or have recourse to certain legal vehicles, such as human rights or general principles, that can drive the law in a given direction.[5]

To assert that the law may be shaped by values is to rebut the doctrine of formalism, which denies the susceptibility of legal norms to particular human ideals and instead holds that lawyers engaging with legal norms do so through neutral modes that allow them to reach outcomes that are wholly independent of their own values.[6] In contrast, the sections that follow illuminate several vehicles of the international legal process that in fact serve to amplify the impact of human values and ideology in international law-making.

Prior to a consideration of the specific conduits through which altruistic commitments in international law may come into being, a more general exploration of the way social phenomena, values and ideology infiltrate legal systems is helpful as it will show how such systems, by their very nature, can internalise certain external influences.

4 Jeffrey Ding, 'An Altruistic Approach to Human Rights Policy', *Iowa Center for Human Rights* (2013), 4, www.drake.edu/media/departmentsoffices/international/nelson/ding.pdf.

5 Oscar Schachter, 'The Invisible College of International Lawyers' (1977) 72(2) *Northwestern University Law Review* 217, 220.

6 David M. Trubek, 'Where the Action Is: Critical Legal Studies and Empiricism' (1984) 36 *Stanford Law Review* 575, 578.

2.2.1 *The Institutionalisation of Ideology*

Cosmopolitan altruism is an ideology. Ideologies have a functional aspect and are a socially constructed corpus of values, beliefs and opinions: an ideology is both constructed by and motivating for actors who participate in and are subject to it.[7] In other words, ideology involves both a bottom-up and top-down process of interaction.[8]

Expressions of cosmopolitan altruism orient the substance of international law through the processes of institutionalisation. Law is a 'creative social practice' that can rationalise and reflect social relationships through rights and obligations.[9] It is also, however, a 'tool of social engineering' that can propagate certain values and goals.[10] Consequently, ideologies and values can be institutionalised into the law, but the law can also be a tool by which ideologies and values are promulgated more widely in society.

By definition, the process of institutionalisation results in institutions. The law is one example of an institution. Together, individuals, states and other social groups form institutions. Institutions, understood in a broad sense, serve to coordinate the common actions of entities like individuals, social groups or states. Those entities are bound together in an institution by common ideologies, morality or a shared belief system.[11] The

[7] Jost, Federico and Napier, 'Political Ideology: Its Structure, Functions, and Elective Affinities'; Erikson and Tedin, *American Public Opinion*, 315.

[8] Erikson and Tedin, *American Public Opinion*, 315–323.

[9] Christine Sypnowich, 'Law as a Vehicle of Altruism' (1985) 5(2) *Oxford Journal of Legal Studies* 276, 284.

[10] Rosalyn Higgins, 'Ethics and International Law' (2010) 23 *Leiden Journal of International Law* 277, 279; Andrea Bianchi, '*Ad-Hocism* and the Rule of Law' (2002) 13 *European Journal of International Law* 263, 265 (observing that 'all legal systems are geared towards the accomplishment of certain goals and as such are value oriented. International law is no exception'); Grant Marlier and Neta Crawford, 'Incomplete and Imperfect Institutionalisation of Empathy and Altruism in the "Responsibility to Protect" Doctrine' (2013) 5(4) *Global Responsibility to Protect* 397; Sypnowich, 'Law as a Vehicle of Altruism', 284; Eugen Ehrlich, *Fundamental Principles of the Sociology of Law* (translated by Walker L. Moll) (Transaction, 2002); Rafael Domingo, *The New Global Law* (Cambridge University Press, 2010), 105; Capps, *Human Dignity and the Foundations of International Law*, 215 (arguing that law is a 'system of omnilateral willing which restructures international relations so that they are consistent with morality'); Steven Ratner, *The Thin Justice of International Law: A Moral Reckoning of the Law of Nations* (Oxford University Press, 2015), 1 (observing that '[l]aw and legal institutions both constrain and expand opportunities for carrying out visions to advance the cause of global justice').

[11] Marlier and Crawford, 'Incomplete and Imperfect Institutionalisation of Empathy and Altruism in the "Responsibility to Protect" Doctrine', 404.

institutionalisation of ideologies, values or emotions can also occur when those with authority within an established institution draw upon ideologies, values or emotions to structure and substantiate institutional responses to certain circumstances.[12] Over time, this process develops into a routine and the institutionalised ideologies, values or emotions come to change and characterise the behaviour of the institution itself. In other words, exceptional behaviour or responses become normalised and established practice.[13]

As mentioned in Chapter 1, the institutionalisation of values or ideologies can be catalysed by large-scale horrific events.[14] For example, it is no coincidence that the United Nations itself, the Universal Declaration of Human Rights and the two human rights covenants, which represent the foundation of contemporary international human rights, came into being in the years following the Holocaust.[15] Indeed, profound crises are often a significant impetus for institutional change in international legal structures.[16] Moreover, institutionalisation permits the collective identification of situations that require our moral attention and defines the collective response. Indeed, it has been observed that the

[12] *Ibid.*, 402.

[13] *Ibid.* Similarly, Antonio Cassese said of the influence of human rights institutions and rhetoric: '[t]he whole international ethos has gradually, if almost imperceptibly, changed, so much so that some international supervisory bodies now consider it warranted to depart from notions they themselves traditionally upheld', Antonio Cassese, *International Law* (2nd ed., Oxford University Press, 2005), 396. For examples in the European human rights context, see Cassese, *International Law*, 396–397, and footnote 21.

[14] Daniel Levy and Natan Sznaider, 'The Institutionalisation of Cosmopolitan Morality: The Holocaust and Human Rights' (2004) 3(2) *Journal of Human Rights* 143; Itamar Mann, *Humanity at Sea: Maritime Migration and the Foundations of International Law* (Cambridge University Press, 2016), 213.

[15] Levy and Sznaider, 'Institutionalisation of Cosmopolitan Morality: The Holocaust and Human Rights', 144 ('after 1945 the knowledge of the enormity of the Holocaust has come to provide the main impetus for the privileged position that human rights regimes currently enjoy in the international arena').

[16] Mann, *Humanity at Sea: Maritime Migration and the Foundations of International Law*; Ralph Wilde, '"Let Them Drown": Rescuing Migrants at Sea and the Non-Refoulement Obligation as a Case Study of International Law's Relationship to "Crisis"' *EJIL: Talk* (25 February 2017), www.ejiltalk.org/let-them-drown-rescuing-migrants-at-sea-and-the-non-refoulement-obligation-as-a-case-study-of-international-laws-relationship-to-crisis-part-i/; Benjamin Authers and Hilary Charlesworth, 'The Crisis and the Quotidian' (2013) 44 *Netherlands Yearbook of International Law* 19, 38; Hilary Charlesworth, 'International Law: A Discipline of Crisis' (2002) 64(3) *Modern Law Review* 377 (noting that 'international lawyers tend to focus on crises for the development of international law' and critiquing that 'the crisis focus impoverishes the discipline of international law').

UN Security Council institutionalised the shared value of altruism into its working practices by adopting the responsibility to protect (R2P) doctrine.[17] And there are other instances in which altruism has been institutionalised in the UN system, such as through the mechanism of collective security, which requires other member states to come to the aid of a member state that has been attacked.[18]

How law is susceptible to social developments or particular events can be illuminated further by considering it as a system. Niklas Luhmann's social systems theory is helpful to conceiving of law in this way.[19] Luhmann distinguishes between open and closed systems.[20] An open system is reactive to social change or events while a closed system is not affected by external political or ethical forces and instead is self-regenerative.[21] A legal system can, in fact, be both.[22] For Luhmann, legal systems are made up of legal communications. These communications have both structures and operations, and the structures and operations are in a circular relationship with each other. Structures are created and altered by operations and vice versa.[23] In this way, a legal system operates like a closed system and is insulated from certain externalities (like short-lived political movements).

But a legal system also has characteristics of an open system. Where it is exposed to social phenomena, it will process the information it receives in a way that it can understand, thereby translating external phenomena into legal meaning.[24] A system is successful when it creates meanings that are internally congruent and can thereby reproduce itself. A legal system evaluates new communications by reference to empirical, teleological and axiological criteria (such as the precepts of effectiveness or

[17] Marlier and Crawford, 'Incomplete and Imperfect Institutionalisation of Empathy and Altruism in the "Responsibility to Protect" Doctrine', 415.

[18] *Ibid.*

[19] Niklas Luhmann, *Law as a Social System* (Oxford University Press, 2004); Niklas Luhmann, *Social Systems* (Stanford University Press, 1995).

[20] *Ibid.*

[21] *Ibid.* See also, Vera Gowlland-Debbas, 'The Limits of Unilateral Enforcement of Community Objectives in the Framework of UN Peace Maintenance' (2000) 11 *European Journal of International Law* 361, 380.

[22] Gowlland-Debbas, 'The Limits of Unilateral Enforcement of Community Objectives in the Framework of UN Peace Maintenance', 380.

[23] Luhmann, *Social Systems*, 6.

[24] *Ibid.*, 92–96.

legitimacy, finalities, or essential values), which underlie and form implicit rules and principles of the system.[25]

An effective legal system combines 'normative closure' with 'cognitive openness', which means that the law adjusts to developments in society while at the same time having normative force.[26] As such, it ingests certain external norms but also determines its own content according to its implicit rules and principles.[27] And so a legal system is paradoxically both open, given that it relies on a society for its existence, and closed because that society, including its values and ideologies, is interpreted to fit with the structures and processes of the legal system. Political or ethical considerations are therefore selected and transformed by the constraints of the legal system before they become part of its content.[28]

Others have observed the impact of phenomena such as social, economic and cultural globalisation on international law in particular. They argue that, as a result of these influences, international law increasingly reflects shared values and the interests of a broader range of actors.[29] Indeed, as systems theory helps us to understand, where these influences are congruent with the implicit rules and principles of the system, the international legal system is cognitively open to them, and they will be integrated as the system develops.

In the sections that follow, we turn to consider the specific conduits by which ideologies and values can have an impact on the evolution of legal norms.

2.2.2 The Role of States

States play a central role in the creation of international law that is altruistic in its orientation. Indeed, it is states that have negotiated, signed and ratified treaties, elaborated soft law instruments, and been active participants in the emergence of customary international law. This

[25] Gowlland-Debbas, 'Limits of Unilateral Enforcement of Community Objectives in the Framework of UN Peace Maintenance', 381. See also François Ost, 'Between Order and Disorder: The Game of Law' in Gunther Teubner (ed.), *Autopoietic Law: A New Approach to Law and Society* (De Gruyter, 1988), 70–96.

[26] Niklas Luhmann, 'The Unity of the Legal System' in Teubner (ed.), *Autopoietic Law: A New Approach to Law and Society*, 12–35.

[27] Ost, 'Between Order and Disorder: The Game of Law', 91–92.

[28] Gowlland-Debbas, 'Limits of Unilateral Enforcement of Community Objectives in the Framework of UN Peace Maintenance', 382.

[29] Andreas L. Paulus, 'Law and Politics in the Age of Globalization' (2000) 11 *European Journal of International Law* 465, 472.

subsection brings the contribution of states to altruistic law-making, particularly following catastrophic events, into sharper focus.

Ideologies in a societal body influence state behaviour and, ultimately, law-making. It can be recalled from the studies in behavioural science and moral philosophy referred to in Chapter 1 that human beings do not act in an exclusively self-interested way and, in fact, often act altruistically. If, as has been argued, the state and its behaviour are contingent on the ideologies and values of its citizens, it follows that states do not always act in an exclusively self-interested way either.[30] This was an argument that was also made by Voltaire, who observed that state behaviour was reflective of human relations.[31] Just as individualistic and altruistic behaviour (or *amour propre* and *bienveillance* as Voltaire termed them) was evident in the relationships between human beings, so it was also in the relations between states.[32] Where individuals are organised in groups that have some form of institutionalisation, those ideologies or values that are dominant will also become institutionalised.[33] As such, for states, groupings of states, international or regional organisations, ideologies or values can be institutionalised where they are sufficiently general and widely shared.[34]

Several of what have become the cornerstones of international law evolved from responses to an outpouring of empathy and an attempt to prevent suffering to human beings in the future. The UN Charter and Universal Declaration of Human Rights have been characterised not least as responses to the Holocaust and as representing a convergence in moral consensus on human rights following World War II.[35] In particular, the delegations that drafted and adopted these instruments were acting on their revulsion at the events they had witnessed in their lives. As the Preamble to the UN Charter provides: 'We the peoples of the United Nations . . . determined to save succeeding generations from the scourge of war, which twice in our lifetime has brought untold sorrow to mankind . . .'. Similarly, the Preamble of the Universal Declaration of

30 Jack Goldsmith and Eric Posner, *The Limits of International Law* (Oxford University Press, 2007), 4.

31 Nikolaos Tsagourias, *Jurisprudence of International Law: The Humanitarian Dimension* (Manchester University Press, 2000), 59.

32 *Ibid.*

33 Marlier and Crawford, 'Incomplete and Imperfect Institutionalisation of Empathy and Altruism in the "Responsibility to Protect" Doctrine', 402.

34 *Ibid.*

35 John Torpey, 'Making Whole What Has Been Smashed: Reflections on Reparations' (2001) 73(2) *Journal of Modern History* 333.

Human Rights provides: 'whereas disregard and contempt for human rights have resulted in barbarous acts which have outraged the conscience of mankind . . .'. Clearly, delegates were motivated by the atrocities and suffering of war, which had been inflicted on particular groups but were being felt and presented as affecting the entire circle of humanity.[36] We may also observe that legal principles developed in the Nuremberg trials and the UN War Crimes Commission established in the aftermath of the Holocaust fed into the Human Rights Division of the United Nations and the Universal Declaration of Human Rights.[37] Overall, many delegations from different nations and cultures agreed upon a universal moral code.[38] It was the experience of horrific events that, to a large extent, motivated these human rights projects.[39]

States have also imbued various systems of collective security with universalist ideals. This is acutely evident in Article 5 of the North Atlantic Treaty of 1949,[40] which constitutes NATO and sets out the fundamental precept that an attack on one NATO state is an attack on all NATO states, and as such demands a collective response. It is similarly evident in the architecture of the collective security mechanism of the United Nations.[41] In this way, victimhood is universalised and, in turn, so is the response to an attack or atrocity. All states identify with the victim because all states are now said to be affected by the grievance.

Beyond catastrophic events, states have often acted with surprising speed to broaden and deepen human rights protection at the international level. For example, in the context of the Convention on the Rights of the Child,[42] some have noted the unprecedented ratification speed for a treaty on children's rights, despite that only a decade previously many had doubted the existence of the rights contained in the convention.[43] This also serves to illustrate that state behaviour often reflects prevailing social attitudes and developing trends in the

[36] Levy and Sznaider, 'The Institutionalisation of Cosmopolitan Morality: The Holocaust and Human Rights', 150.

[37] Johannes Morsink, *The Universal Declaration of Human Rights: Origins, Drafting and Intent* (University of Pennsylvania Press, 1999), chapter 2 and p 345.

[38] *Ibid.*, 36.

[39] Torpey, 'Making Whole What Has Been Smashed: Reflections on Reparations', 333–358.

[40] North Atlantic Treaty, 4 April 1949, 34 UNTS 541.

[41] Chapter VII, Charter of the United Nations, 26 June 1945, 1 UNTS XVI.

[42] Convention on the Rights of the Child, 20 November 1989, 1577 UNTS 3.

[43] Rosalyn Higgins, *Problems and Process: International Law and How We Use It* (Clarendon Press, 1994), 105.

international community can be a powerful force.[44] In this context, states – like individuals – are indeed capable of pursuing both individualistic and altruistic ends in their approach to law-making.

States have crafted the contemporary international legal system with 'a minimal ethical core'.[45] This core encompasses universalist ideals, community interests as well as standards of security and justice.[46] That the ethical core of the international legal system has evolved is well illustrated by the way in which the International Court of Justice (ICJ) has conceived the rationale of human rights regimes in its *Reservations to the Convention on the Prevention and Punishment of the Crime of Genocide* case:

> Unlike other multilateral agreements, in international human rights conventions, the contracting states do not pursue any partisan interests: instead they have one and all a common interest that is the common accomplishment of those high purposes which are the *raison d'etre* of the convention.[47]

By creating human rights regimes, states have put in place universal standards and established a framework of shared responsibility in the international community to ensure such common values are implemented for all people.[48]

2.2.3 *The Role of Individuals*

We now turn to illustrate how international legal norms can be shaped by individuals, particularly by eminent jurists who are in a position to influence the content of international law. Their values have, in the process, been reflected in the content of the norms they designed and promoted.

[44] Abram Chayes and Antonia Handler Chayes, *The New Sovereignty* (Harvard University Press, 1995), 27.

[45] Gowlland-Debbas, 'The Limits of Unilateral Enforcement of Community Objectives in the Framework of UN Peace Maintenance', 382; see also Levy and Sznaider, 'The Institutionalization of Cosmopolitan Morality: The Holocaust and Human Rights', 143, 155–156.

[46] *Ibid.*

[47] *Reservations to the Convention on the Prevention and Punishment of the Crime of Genocide*, Advisory Opinion, (1951) ICJ Rep. 14, 23.

[48] Michael Nyongesa Wabwile, *Legal Protection of Social and Economic Rights of Children in Developing Countries: Reassessing International Cooperation and Responsibility* (Intersentia, 2010), 157.

It has been suggested that international law has often been the product of '[p]eople with projects',[49] that there exists an invisible college of international lawyers who are 'dedicated to a common intellectual enterprise',[50] and that these lawyers have a 'legislative role'.[51] Indeed, Oscar Schachter observed that international lawyers play a role in the creation of new law, as well as the extension of existing law. The legislative role is mainly conducted through the part they play in conceiving, drafting or interpreting international treaties, but it may also be by shaping customary law, general principles or resolutions of international organisations.[52] Moreover, the invisible college of international lawyers extends into government, which in turn facilitates a gradual penetration of ideas into official channels, especially where international lawyers perform a *dedoublement fonctionnel.*[53] Several scholars have argued that the professional community of international lawyers has had an especially influential role in endowing the international legal order with *la conscience juridique* or concepts of justice through the formulation of general principles of law and suggesting standards for conventions, institutions or legal processes.[54] Particularly influential lawyers have included the members of the *Institut de Droit International* (for example in shaping the law of armed conflict, environmental law, or regulation concerning the seabed and outer space), the International Law Association (for example in shaping the Helsinki Rules on the Uses of the Waters of International Rivers[55]), as well as specific individuals such as Sir Hersch Lauterpacht, Gustave Rolin-Jaequemyns, Gustav Moynier and Hans Morgenthau.

[49] See Andrea Bianchi, *International Law Theories: An Inquiry into Different Ways of Thinking* (Oxford University Press, 2016), 168–169.

[50] Oscar Schachter, 'The Invisible College of International Lawyers' (1977) 72(2) *Northwestern University Law Review* 217. See also Dag Hammarskjöld, 'The International Civil Servant in Law and in Fact (1961)' in A. Cordier and W. Foote (eds.), *Public Papers of the Secretaries-General of the United Nations* (Columbia University Press, 1975), 471.

[51] Schachter, 'The Invisible College of International Lawyers', 223.

[52] *Ibid.*

[53] *Ibid.*, 217 and 225.

[54] See, for example, Wolfgang Friedmann, *The Changing Structure of International Law* (Stevens, 1964), 188–210; Hermann Mosler, 'The International Society as a Legal Community' (1974) 140 *Collected Courses of the Hague Academy of International Law* 1, 138–148; Oscar Schachter, *Sharing the World's Resources* (Columbia University Press, 1977); Schachter, 'The Invisible College of International Lawyers', 225.

[55] International Law Association, Helsinki Rules on the Uses of the Waters of International Rivers, Report of the Fifty-Second Conference, Helsinki, 14–20 August 1966 (London, 1967), 484–532.

Gustave Rolin-Jaequemyns and Gustav Moynier played a central role in founding the *Institut de Droit International* in 1873. Ten years earlier these two individuals had also been among the five founders of the International Committee of the Red Cross. Following the Franco-Prussian war of the 1870s, Rolin-Jaequemyns and Moynier assembled a group of eminent jurists to actively promote the development and rule of international law, which they believed would in turn promote peace.[56] Thus, in September 1873 these jurists met for the first time in the town hall of Ghent, Belgium.[57] On this occasion, the Statutes of the *Institut de Droit International* were adopted, and they offer an insight into the means by which this organisation exercises its influence. Article 1(2) provides that the purpose of the *Institut* is to 'promote the progress of international law'.[58] Article 5(1) of the Statutes goes on to provide that 'Associates shall be selected by the Institute from among those of various nations who have given service to international law either in thc field of theory or in that of practice'.[59] The experience of the *Institut* has shown that those chosen to be Associates are likely to be free from political pressure.[60]

Since its foundation, and despite that it lacks any official nature, the *Institut* has been perceived as an important authority on international law and has had a marked impact on international legal rules. For example, the *Institut* played a significant role in shaping the provisions on arbitration that were adopted by the Hague Congress in 1899, as well as persuading states to accept the rule of law in armed conflict. Further still, both the League of Nations and the United Nations have relied on the reports and interpretations of the *Institut* over time.

Turning to other contexts in which individuals have had a marked influence, Philippe Sands has traced the influence of two other eminent

[56] See Gustave Rolin-Jaequemyns, 'De la nécessité d'organiser une institution scientifique permanente pour favoriser l'étude et les progress du droit international' *Revue de droit international et de legislation compare* (1873).

[57] The jurists included Gustave Rolin-Jaequemyns (Belgium); Tobias Asser (The Netherlands), Wladimir Besobrasoff (Russia), J. K. Bluntschli (Germany), Carlos Calvo (Argentina), David Dudley Field (U.S.A.), Émile de Laveleye (Belgium), James Lorimer (Great Britain), P. S. Mancini (Italy), Gustave Moynier (Switzerland) and Augusto Pierantoni (Italy).

[58] Statutes of the *Institut de Droit International*, adopted by the *Conférence internationale juridique* in Ghent, 10 September 1873, www.idi-iil.org/app/uploads/2017/06/Statutes-of-the-Institute-of-International-Law.pdf.

[59] *Ibid.*

[60] See, Institute of International Law: History, *The Nobel Prize*, www.nobelprize.org/prizes/peace/1904/international-law/history/.

international lawyers on the content of international law. Indeed, Sands highlights the roles Sir Hersch Lauterpacht and Raphael Lemkin played in crafting the legal definitions of crimes against humanity and genocide.[61] Their projects led to the creation of fundamental legal standards. In fact, Raphael Lemkin coined the term 'genocide' in 1944. By 1946, the UN General Assembly adopted Resolution 96 (I) and the Convention on the Prevention and Punishment of the Crime of Genocide was approved and proposed for signature and ratification or accession by General Assembly Resolution 260 A (III) in 1948.[62] The latter Convention entered into force on 12 January 1951.

As for the role that international lawyers have played in the evolution of sovereignty, Philip Alston has noted that international lawyers have often been the 'handmaidens of the changes wrought by globalization'.[63] Indeed, the character of sovereignty has evolved in part because of the way in which international lawyers have helped ensure this concept reflects contemporary realities and certain world views or values. The changes international lawyers have facilitated in this context are in both normative and institutional directions.[64] It has been observed that those who shaped the international legal order after World War II were inspired by similar ideals. Indeed, Martti Koskenniemi has said that those who crafted international law were cosmopolitans and sought to nurture the connections between peoples.[65]

For Wilfred Jenks, international lawyers helped catalyse the evolution of international law by giving centre stage to principles of political morality, such as the unity of humankind, the need to proscribe the arbitrary use of force, limiting sovereignty under law, promoting justice administered in an impartial way by third parties as well as emphasising good faith, fair dealing, mutual aid and human dignity.[66] We have seen the consequences of this effort with the development of concepts like

[61] Philippe Sands, *East West Street: On the Origins of Genocide and Crimes Against Humanity* (Weidenfeld and Nicolson, 2016).

[62] UN General Assembly Resolution 96 (I), 11 December 1946, UN Doc. A/RES/96 (I); UN General Assembly Resolution 260 A (III), 9 December 1948, UN Doc. A/RES/260 A (III); Convention on the Prevention and Punishment of the Crime of Genocide, 9 December 1948, 78 UNTS 277.

[63] Philip Alston, 'The Myopia of the Handmaidens: International Lawyers and Globalization' (1997) 3 *European Journal of International Law* 435.

[64] *Ibid.*

[65] Martti Koskenniemi, 'Legal Cosmopolitanism: Tom Franck's Messianic World' (2002–2003) 35 *New York University Journal of International Law and Policy* 471.

[66] Bianchi, *International Law Theories: An Inquiry into Different Ways of Thinking*, 246.

R2P, to take just one example. The authors of the doctrine have spoken of their attempts to both alter perspectives and to propagate altruism.[67]

Through time, the agents of international law have been, for the most part, engaged in a purposive enterprise and directed by their own conception of international law and what international law should seek to achieve.[68] Max Weber famously argued that the rational aim of all agent action is to bring about a state of affairs consistent with an envisaged endgame and, to this extent, all action has a value-orientation.[69] Indeed, this is highly relevant to the enterprise of international law agents and, drawing upon focal analysis,[70] we can make a connection between purpose (or morality) and the value-orientation of the acts of international lawyers. However, we should not assume – as a strict focal analysis would suggest – that stable value-orientations emerge from a survey of all agents of international law.[71] Rather, we should expect deviations from the standard purposive activity of international law agents. Notwithstanding, a relatively uncontroversial claim can be made that the practice of international law is normative in nature and has a purposive orientation.[72]

But it is not simply the individual projects of international lawyers that can influence the law-making and development processes. Daniel Levy and Natan Sznaider tell the story of a journalist from Belgrade who in 1991 published an article entitled 'Nuremburg now!', which argued for the creation of a Nuremburg-like tribunal to try those responsible for atrocities in Yugoslavia.[73] Levy and Sznaider saw this specific event as catalysing the choir of voices that was ultimately successful in calling for the creation of the International Criminal Tribunal for the former Yugoslavia (ICTY).[74] Indeed, the power of individuals – whether they are lawyers or not – to influence law-making and development should

[67] See Marlier and Crawford, 'Incomplete and Imperfect Institutionalization of Empathy and Altruism in the "Responsibility to Protect" Doctrine', 399; Gareth Evans and Mohamed Sahnoun, 'The Responsibility to Protect' (2001) 81(6) *Foreign Affairs* 99; Ramesh Thakur, *The United Nations, Peace and Security: From Collective Security to the Responsibility to Protect* (Cambridge University Press, 2006); James Traub, *The Best Intentions: Kofi Annan and the UN in the Era of American World Power* (Picador, 2007).

[68] Capps, *Human Dignity and the Foundations of International Law*, 24.

[69] *Ibid.*

[70] *Ibid.*

[71] *Ibid.*, 49 (Patrick Capps refers to such surveys as 'raw data').

[72] *Ibid.*, 79.

[73] See Levy and Sznaider, 'The Institutionalisation of Cosmopolitan Morality: The Holocaust and Human Rights', 153.

[74] *Ibid.*

not be underestimated. Neither should that of international institutions, to which we turn next.

2.2.4 The Role of International Institutions

International institutions have a particularly acute influence in the operation of the law. Their structure and working practices can facilitate the application of the law in an altruistic way. We explore the modes by which they do so in this section.

International institutions play a significant role in enabling perspective-taking, promoting a sense of common humanity as well as the development of international law.[75] Generally speaking, international law-making and monitoring bodies have continually – albeit often subtly – emphasised the need for human rights to be respected, and this has had an impact on state behaviour over time.[76] The rhetoric of the UN Security Council, the Human Rights Council, the Office of the UN High Commissioner for Human Rights, the human rights treaty bodies and international courts and tribunals reinforces perspective-taking. To illustrate this point, we may observe the rhetoric around Syria and the calls to action to prevent the suffering and slaughter of the Syrian people in recent years[77] or the symbolism and rhetoric of war crimes tribunals like Nuremburg and Tokyo.[78]

75 See Bruno Simma and Philip Alston, 'The Sources of Human Rights Law: Custom, Jus Cogens, and General Principles' (1988–1989) 12 *Australian Yearbook of International Law* 82 (noting that 'treaty law on its own provides a rather unsatisfactory basis on which to ground the efforts of international institutions whose reach is truly universal, such as the General Assembly and the Commission on Human Rights').

76 Cassese, *International Law*, 396.

77 See, for example, General Assembly Resolution 71/130, The situation in the Syrian Arab Republic, 7 December 2016, UN Doc. A/71/L.39, '[e]xpressing outrage at the escalation of violence in the Syrian Arab Republic', '[e]xpressing grave concern also at the dire situation of the civilian population, in particular of the 974,080 people trapped in besieged areas, as well as the dire situation of nearly 3.9 million people in hard-to-reach areas', and '[e]xpressing alarm that the responsibility of the Security Council to ensure prompt and effective action has not been further discharged with regard to the Syrian Arab Republic'; Security Council Resolution 2328, 19 December 2016, UN Doc. S/RES/2328 (2016), 'Alarmed by the continued deterioration of the devastating humanitarian situation in Aleppo and by the fact that urgent humanitarian evacuation and assistance are now needed by a large number of Aleppo inhabitants'.

78 Levy and Sznaider, 'The Institutionalisation of Cosmopolitan Morality: The Holocaust and Human Rights', 145. On how international criminal trials can shape historical narratives, see Barrie Sander, *Doing Justice to History: The Construction of Historical*

The creation of the R2P doctrine also serves to facilitate perspective-taking.[79] Perspective-taking is a critical part of empathy. Certain mechanisms, operational practices and policies of international organisations like the UN can help their member-states bear witness to the suffering of those in other countries. This in turn helps to foster empathy. In the context of R2P, this particular framework reinforces UN procedures that already exist and rely on 'perspective-taking', such as the operations of the Office of the High Commissioner for Human Rights and the Human Rights Council.[80] Similarly, the establishment of the ICTY and the International Criminal Court (ICC) were catalysed by the 'coincidence of imagery' between mass atrocities and the Holocaust.[81]

Special Rapporteurs and Special Advisors (e.g. at the Office on Genocide Prevention and the Responsibility to Protect) are also tasked with perspective-taking. Further, reports from the Secretary-General of the United Nations or the heads of UN agencies facilitate perspective-taking. Further still, international inquiry commissions or the sending of UN observers contribute to building a picture of situations on the ground about 'the other'. The ultimate aim of these perspective-taking processes is to motivate action in response to certain crises or human rights abuses. Mechanisms like those set out above serve as the 'official eyes and ears' of the UN Security Council and help the latter take the perspective of the victims. They also give a voice to the victims in the call they make for international assistance.[82]

In a different way, the institutional response to mass atrocities can help in expanding the circle of altruism by universalising victimhood. A good example is provided by the emergence of crimes against humanity during the Nuremberg trials. In the case of the Holocaust, the crimes against the Jewish people were presented as crimes against humanity at large.[83] Justice Robert Jackson, the Chief American prosecutor in the Nuremberg trials, said at the time:

Narratives within International Criminal Courts (PhD Thesis, Graduate Institute of International and Development Studies, 2017).

[79] Marlier and Crawford, 'Incomplete and Imperfect Institutionalization of Empathy and Altruism in the "Responsibility to Protect" Doctrine', 419.

[80] *Ibid.*

[81] Samantha Power, *A Problem from Hell: America and the Age of Genocide* (Basic Books, 2002).

[82] Marlier and Crawford, 'Incomplete and Imperfect Institutionalization of Empathy and Altruism in the "Responsibility to Protect" Doctrine', 421.

[83] Levy and Sznaider, 'The Institutionalisation of Cosmopolitan Morality: The Holocaust and Human Rights', 149.

> The crime against the Jews, insofar as it is a crime against humanity and not a war crime as well, is one which we indict because of its close association with the crime against peace.[84]

The creation of a new legal category was justified through the universalisation of victimhood and associating it with the established crime against the peace. The Jewish people represented humanity at large, and the infliction upon them was also an infliction on human society. Moreover, the Nuremberg Tribunal laid down for the first time the principle that international rules providing for humanitarian protection must trump state laws where the latter are in conflict with the former, unless there is no moral choice.[85]

The response to mass atrocity is a call to action in the name of our common humanity. Responses to particular mass atrocities are often repeated in the responses to other mass atrocities. Thus, accompanying a universalisation of victimhood is the universalisation of the response. This is evident with the link between the Nuremburg trials, the ICTY, the International Criminal Tribunal for Rwanda (ICTR) and the ICC. The response is a procedural mechanism to prosecute the perpetrators and deliver justice to the victims in a process administered by the international community.

We now turn to look more closely at the role of a specific type of international institution: international courts.

2.2.5 *The Role of International Courts*

This section considers the multifaceted dimensions of influence that the international judiciary have on law-making and development. An emphasis will be placed on the specific legal vehicles that serve to shape the law in particular directions.

The rhetoric of human rights and the discretion afforded by general principles have had a powerful impact on the judicial development of the law. As for the former, a culture of human rights has developed.[86] It is

[84] IMT: 470–471. Nuremburg Trial Proceedings, cited in *ibid.*, 149.

[85] Held, 'Law of States, Law of Peoples: Three Models of Sovereignty', 7; Antonio Cassese, *Violence and the Law in a Modern Age* (Polity Press, 1988), 132. International criminal law has followed this principle and does not generally recognise a defence of obedience to superior orders.

[86] Jason Rudall, 'Not Just a Wit but a Cause of Wit in Others: The Influence of Human Rights in International Litigation' in Nikos Skoutaris, Avidan Kent and Jamie Trinidad (eds.), *The Future of International Courts and Tribunals* (Routledge, 2019) 250–269; Levy

arguable that human rights even provide a dual foundation for international law today.[87] This human rights culture drives more comprehensive and deeper human rights protection in the architecture of international law. To illustrate, the International Bill of Human Rights, which includes the Universal Declaration of Human Rights of 1948,[88] the Covenant on Civil and Political Rights of 1966[89] and the Covenant on Economic, Social and Cultural Rights of 1966,[90] has been complemented by more specific human rights initiatives over time, including the negotiation of further treaties as well as monitoring and enforcement mechanisms.[91] National and international NGOs, advocacy groups and civil society contribute particularly to the development of this human rights culture.[92] But international courts and tribunals have also played a significant role.

As early as 1907, with the establishment of the Central American Court of Justice, there have been permanent international courts with an individual complaints mechanism for violations of human rights.[93] This development had a transformative impact on the form and substance of international law. Similarly, the role of human rights courts and tribunals in the humanisation of international law has been said to represent the most significant development in international legal thinking since World War II.[94] Indeed, individual recourse to international justice had been an idea explored in various initiatives in the early

and Sznaider, 'The Institutionalisation of Cosmopolitan Morality: The Holocaust and Human Rights', 155.

87 Mann, *Humanity at Sea: Maritime Migration and the Foundations of International Law*, 216.

88 Universal Declaration of Human Rights, 10 December 1948, 999 UNTS 302.

89 International Covenant on Civil and Political Rights, 16 December 1966, 999 UNTS 171.

90 International Covenant on Economic, Social and Cultural Rights, 16 December 1966, 993 UNTS 3.

91 See Held, 'Law of States, Law of Peoples: Three Models of Sovereignty', 9.

92 *Ibid.*, 9, stating that perhaps as important in promoting human rights, if not more so [than the legal architecture and enforcement mechanisms], have been the multiplicity of political and international nongovernmental organizations that have actively sought to implement these agreements and, thereby, to reshape the ordering principles of public life.

See also David Held, Anthony McGrew, David Goldblatt and Jonathan Perraton, *Global Transformations: Politics, Economic and Culture* (Polity Press, 1999), Chapter 1.

93 Antônio Augusto Cançado Trindade, 'A Century of International Justice and Prospects for the Future' in Mads Andenas and Eirik Bjorge (eds.), *A Farewell to Fragmentation: Reassertion and Convergence in International Law* (Cambridge University Press, 2015), 57.

94 *Ibid.*, 65.

twentieth century. This included, for example, the systems of minority protection, mandates and petitions of islands, at the time of the League of Nations. Moreover, stretching back even further is the practice of mixed arbitral tribunals and compensation commissions.[95] But, international courts and tribunals of other specialisations and none have more recently begun to engage with human rights issues. In 2005, for example, 'human rights' could be seen for the first time in the *dispositif* of an ICJ decision.[96] Similarly, various international courts and tribunals have had opportunities to develop norms through what has been termed 'norm-brokering'.[97] This is concerned with the way in which courts take heed of other interpretations of human rights, including those interpretations of non-judicial bodies, and is normally aimed at extending the reach of human rights norms.[98]

To illustrate the substantive influence of specialised tribunals on international law, two notable contributions of human rights courts are the circumscription of state voluntarism[99] and the greater emphasis placed on the *ordre publique*. The human rights cases of *Belilos*,[100] *Loizidou*[101] and *Ilaşcu and others* v. *Moldova and Russia*[102] are examples of this phenomenon in the context of the European Court of Human Rights, whereas the cases *Constitutional Tribunal*,[103] *Ivtcher Bronstein* (Jurisdiction),[104] *Hilaire, Constantine and Benjamin et al.* (Preliminary Objection)[105] show a similar tendency in the practice of the Inter-American Court of

95 *Ibid.*, 57–58, footnote 9.

96 *Armed Activities on the Territory of the Congo (Democratic Republic of the Congo* v. *Uganda)*, Judgment (2005) ICJ Rep. 168; Bruno Simma, 'Human Rights before the International Court of Justice: Community Interest Coming to Life?' in Christian J. Tams and James Sloan (eds.), *The Development of International Law by the International Court of Justice* (Oxford University Press, 2013), 586.

97 Michael Hamilton and Antoine Buyse, 'Human Rights Courts as Norm-Brokers' (2018) 18(2) *Human Rights Law Review* 205.

98 *Ibid.*; Mark Beeson, 'Living with Giants: ASEAN and the Evolution of Asian Regionalism' (2013) 1(2) *TRaNS: Trans-Regional and National Studies of Southeast Asia* 303.

99 *Ibid.*, 65.

100 Case No. 20/1986/118/167, *Belilos* v. *Switzerland* [1988] ECHR 4; (1988) 10 EHRR 466.

101 Case No. 15318/89, *Loizidou* v. *Turkey* [1995] ECHR 10; (1995) 20 EHRR 99.

102 Case No. 48787/99, *Ilaşcu and others* v. *Moldova and Russia* ECHR 2004-VII; (2005) 40 EHRR 46.

103 *Case of the Constitutional Tribunal (Camba Campos et al)* v. *Ecuador*, Inter-Am. Ct. H.R. (ser. C) No. 268.

104 *Ivtcher Bronstein* v. *Peru*, Competence, Inter-Am. Ct. H. R. (ser. C) No. 54.

105 *Hilaire, Constantine and Benjamin et al* v. *Trinidad and Tobago*, Preliminary Objections, Judgment, Inter-Am. Ct. H. R. (ser. C) No. 80.

Human Rights. These are important precedents of the way in which specialised tribunals are contributing to both the dismantling of classical precepts of international law and of how they are constructing new norms. Their influence can be detected in the jurisprudence of other international courts and tribunals, between and beyond those specialised in human rights.[106]

Aside from human rights courts and tribunals, while the PCIJ and ICJ were not endowed with a mechanism for hearing individual complaints, the judges of these courts have nevertheless pronounced upon the place or plight of individuals or groups. This is particularly evident, for example, in advisory opinions of the PCIJ in *German Settlers in Poland* (1923),[107] *Jurisdiction of the Courts of Danzig* (1928),[108] *Greco-Bulgarian 'Communities'* (1930),[109] *Access to German Minority Schools in Upper Silesia* (1931),[110] *Treatment of Polish Nationals in Danzig* (1932)[111] or *Minority Schools in Albania* (1935).[112] As such, even these courts, although officially only having jurisdiction over interstate disputes, nevertheless engaged in developing international law beyond the dimension of purely interstate relations and state interests.[113]

Similarly, the advisory jurisdiction of the ICJ has provided a means through which judges can develop international law. Those advisory opinions in *Reparation for Injuries* (1949),[114] *Namibia* (1971),[115] *Immunity from Legal Process of a Special Rapporteur of the UN*

[106] See Rudall, 'Not Just a Wit but a Cause of Wit in Others: The Influence of Human Rights in International Litigation'.

[107] *Advisory opinion given by the Court on 10 September 1923 on Certain Questions relating to Settlers of German Origin in the Territory ceded by Germany to Poland*, PCIJ Series B, no. 6 (1923).

[108] *Jurisdiction of the Courts of Danzig*, PCIJ Series B, no. 15 (1928).

[109] *Greco-Bulgarian 'Communities'*, PCIJ Series B, no. 17 (1930).

[110] *Access to German Minority Schools in Upper Silesia*, PCIJ Series A/B, no. 40 (1931).

[111] *Treatment of Polish Nationals and Other Persons of Polish Origin or Speech in the Danzig Territory*, PCIJ Series A/B, no. 44 (1932).

[112] *Minority Schools in Albania*, PCIJ Series A/B, no. 64 (1935).

[113] See Trindade, 'A Century of International Justice and Prospects for the Future', 59; Catherine Brölmann, 'The PCIJ and International Rights of Groups and Individuals' in Christian J. Tams and Malgosia Fitzmaurice (eds.), *Legacies of the Permanent Court of International Justice* (Martinus Nijhoff, 2013), 123–143.

[114] *Reparation for Injuries Suffered in the Service of the United Nations*, Advisory Opinion (1949) ICJ Rep. 174.

[115] *Legal Consequences for States of the Continued Presence of South Africa in Namibia (South West Africa) notwithstanding Security Council Resolution 276 (1970)*, Advisory Opinion (1971) ICJ Rep. 16.

Commission on Human Rights (1999),[116] the *Wall Opinion* (2005)[117] and many others have clarified and developed legal rules. Similarly, other courts, tribunals and institutions with such an advisory function have contributed to the evolution of international law. Combined with these influences, it has also been suggested that international courts and tribunals perceive themselves as the guardians of international law, as opposed to simply mechanisms for the solution of legal disputes.[118]

It is pertinent to point out that, over time, judges of international courts have regularly been engaged with issues of human rights outside of the courtroom.[119] As to the ICJ, for example, Judge Rosalyn Higgins had previously been a member of the UN Human Rights Committee, Judge Pieter Kooijmans had formerly been the UN Special Rapporteur on Torture as well as President of the UN Commission on Human Rights, Judge Thomas Buergenthal had been President of the Inter-American Court of Human Rights and a member of the UN Human Rights Committee while Judge Bruno Simma previously served as a member of the UN Committee on Economic, Social and Cultural Rights. Several other judges engaged with human rights in other ways: Judges Leonid Slotnikov and Peter Tomka were diplomats, Judges Ronny Abraham and Kenneth Keith were human rights lawyers and national judges and Judge Bernardo Sepúlveda-Amor was a human rights scholar. In this context, Higgins has observed in a personal capacity that having such judges serving on the bench means there has been a 'critical mass' of judges who are well-acquainted with human rights law and, as a result, human rights has become central to the work of the Court, rather than at the periphery.[120]

This resonates with studies conducted around judicial decision-making, in particular at the ICJ, which reveal that judges can be driven more by experience, education and values than by state interests. Indeed,

[116] *Immunity from Legal Process of a Special Rapporteur of the UN Commission on Human Rights*, Advisory Opinion (1999) ICJ Rep. 62.

[117] *Legal Consequences of the Construction of a Wall in the Occupied Palestinian Territory*, Advisory Opinion (2004) ICJ Rep. 136.

[118] Eyal Benvenisti, 'Sovereigns as Trustees of Humanity: On the Accountability of States to Foreign Stakeholders' (2013) 107(2) *American Journal of International Law* 295, 331.

[119] See Ralph Wilde, 'Human Rights beyond Borders at the World Court: The Significance of the International Court of Justice's Jurisprudence on the Extraterritorial Application of International Human Rights Law Treaties' (2013) 12 *Chinese Journal of International Law* 639, 647.

[120] Rosalyn Higgins, 'Human Rights in the International Court of Justice' (2007) 20(4) *Leiden Journal of International Law* 745, 746.

commenting on their study about biases in international dispute settlement, Eric Posner and Miguel de Figueiredo confirmed this and went on to note that judges may vote in ways that reflect their psychological or philosophical biases.[121]

In the context of the European Court of Human Rights, Erik Voeten has similarly observed that judges can harbour preferences towards certain policies, and this impacts the way in which they appraise cases, just as political scientists have shown that US Supreme Court judges are motivated by political orientation.[122] Moreover, it has been asserted that judges are often policy-seekers.[123] This fits with the attitudinal model of judicial decision-making, namely that a judge decides cases by squaring their ideological values with the legal facts arising in the given case. Extending this argument further, judges have been shown to move policy in the direction of their own preferences.[124] This is amplified at the international level given that the law is usually less settled and there is greater room for discretion than in domestic decision-making.[125]

Further still, certain sections of the international judiciary are becoming part of an increasingly homogenous epistemic community. They remain different in many ways but can share common ideas and ideals.[126] They constitute a network of knowledge-based experts who have a common belief or faith in certain forms of knowledge or given truths.[127] As many international judges share similar professional backgrounds, training and commitments to the rule of law and certain universal rights, their decisions will continue to converge, regardless of the forum in which they practice. Indeed, a comprehensive study conducted by Daniel Terris, Cesare Romano and Leigh Swigart has revealed

121 Eric Posner and Miguel de Figueiredo, 'Is the International Court of Justice Biased?' (2005) 34 *Journal of Legal Studies* 599, 625.

122 Erik Voeten, 'The Impartiality of International Judges: Evidence from the European Court of Human Rights' (2008) 102(4) *The American Political Science Review* 417, 418.

123 Lawrence Baum, 'What Judges Want: Judges' Goals and Judicial Behaviour' (1994) 47 *Political Research Quarterly* 749.

124 Lee Epstein and Jack Knight, *The Choices Judges Make* (CQ Press, 1997).

125 Voeten, 'Impartiality of International Judges: Evidence from the European Court of Human Rights', 422.

126 Peter Haas, 'Introduction: Epistemic Communities and International Policy Coordination' (1992) 46(1) *International Organization* 1; Daniel Terris, Cesare Romano and Leigh Swigart, *The International Judge: An Introduction to the Men and Women Who Decide the World's Cases* (Oxford University Press, 2007), 63. That said, there are of course other sections that remain outside of this characterisation.

127 Haas, 'Introduction: Epistemic Communities and International Policy Coordination', 2–3.

that, regardless of the court, judges generally perceive their role to be for establishing a community of law, preserving the dignity of individuals, or preventing violence and war.[128]

This helps to illustrate that, among many international judges, there is some consensus on the purpose of their judging. Overall, the experience, education, values and environment of international judges contribute to the cultural context of the interpretive community in which they make their decisions and, consciously or unconsciously, they develop legal norms in particular directions.[129]

A further dimension to the role that human rights rhetoric plays in the development of international law is provided by the increasing interaction between international courts and tribunals and specialised human rights institutions.[130] These bodies influence each other in their development of the law, and courts are relying on the latter for interpretative guidance in an increasing number of cases. This is one aspect of law as an 'intersubjective enterprise' and highlights that law often relies on a discursive process for its development. There is a dialogue that occurs between courts and tribunals through what might be termed 'cross-judging'.[131] The result of this process can be 'substantive complementarity', which is where legal norms in one legal space may be affected by the legal norms of another legal space.[132] New

[128] Terris, Romano and Swigart, *The International Judge: An Introduction to the Men and Women Who Decide the World's Cases*, 229.

[129] Stanley Fish, *Is There a Text in This Class* (Harvard University Press, 1980), 147–174.

[130] See, for example, Vaughan Lowe and Antonios Tzanakopoulos, 'The Development of the Law of the Sea by the International Court of Justice' in Christian Tams and James Sloan (eds.), *The Development of International Law by the International Court of Justice* (Oxford University Press, 2013), 181; James Sloan and Gleider Hernández, 'The Role of the International Court of Justice in the Development of the Institutional Law of the United Nations', in Tams and Sloan (eds.), *The Development of International Law by the International Court of Justice*, 207; James Crawford, 'The International Court of Justice and the Law of State Responsibility' in Tams and Sloan (eds.), *The Development of International Law by the International Court of Justice*, 77; see also Laurence Boisson de Chazournes, 'The EJIL Foreword: Plurality in the Fabric of International Courts and Tribunals: The Threads of a Managerial Approach' (2017) 28(1) *European Journal of International Law* 13.

[131] Ruti Teitel and Robert Howse, 'Cross-judging: Tribunalization in a Fragmented but Interconnected Global Order' (2008–2009) 41 *New York University Journal of International Law and Politics* 959; Ruti Teitel and Robert Howse, 'Cross-judging Revisited' (2013–2014) 46 *New York University Journal of International Law and Politics* 867.

[132] Dana Burchardt, 'Intertwinement of Legal Spaces in the Transnational Sphere' (2017) 30 (2) *Leiden Journal of International Law* 305, 324.

norms can be introduced, particular norms may be given a higher status, their application may be extended to other subjects or categories of behaviour and new positive obligations may be created as a result of judicial norm development.[133] Indeed, courts at all levels are in dialogue with each other as well as with other institutions and actors that have an interpretative role to play.[134]

There are several concrete examples that help to illustrate this point. In the *Wall Opinion* and *DRC* v. *Uganda* case,[135] the Court confirmed that the International Covenant on Civil and Political Rights could apply extraterritorially. This was the position previously laid down by the Human Rights Committee,[136] which the Court in the *Wall Opinion* relied upon, and *DRC* v. *Uganda* subsequently followed.[137] The Court also confirmed the extraterritorial application of the 1989 Convention on the Rights of the Child in these cases, which meant it followed the approach of the Committee on the Rights of the Child (although the Court did not expressly refer to the Committee's position).[138] Interestingly, in the *Wall Opinion*, the Court similarly confirmed the extraterritorial application of the International Covenant on Economic, Social and Cultural Rights, albeit in a different and more creative way.[139] As such, the Court confirmed that the latter Covenant

[133] Wayne Sandholtz, 'Expanding Rights: Norm Innovation in the European and Inter-American Courts of Human Rights' in Alison Brysk and Michael Stohl (eds.), *Expanding Human Rights: 21st-Century Norms and Governance* (Edward Elgar, 2017), 158.

[134] Teitel and Howse, 'Cross-judging: Tribunalization in a Fragmented but Interconnected Global Order', 967.

[135] *Armed Activities on the Territory of the Congo (Democratic Republic of the Congo* v. *Uganda)*, Judgment (2005) ICJ Rep. 168.

[136] See Human Rights Committee, *General Comment No. 31 on The Nature of the General Legal Obligation Imposed on State Parties to the Covenant*, 29 March 2004, UN Doc. CCPR/C/21/Rev.1/Add., para 10 (noting that 'a State party must respect and ensure the rights laid down in the Covenant to anyone within the power or effective control of that State Party, even if not situated within the territory of the State Party').

[137] See *Legal Consequences of the Construction of a Wall in the Occupied Palestinian Territory*, Advisory Opinion (2004) ICJ Rep. 136, paras 109–110 and *Armed Activities on the Territory of the Congo (Democratic Republic of the Congo* v. *Uganda)*, Judgment (2005) ICJ Rep. 168, para 216.

[138] *Legal Consequences of the Construction of a Wall in the Occupied Palestinian Territory*, Advisory Opinion (2004) ICJ Rep. 136, para 113 and *Armed Activities on the Territory of the Congo (Democratic Republic of the Congo* v. *Uganda)*, Judgment (2005) ICJ Rep. 168, paras 216–217.

[139] *Legal Consequences of the Construction of a Wall in the Occupied Palestinian Territory*, Advisory Opinion (2004) ICJ Rep. 136, para 112.

applied extraterritorially by reading into it a particular concept of jurisdiction.[140]

More generally, the development of the presumptive extraterritorial applicability of human rights treaties in the jurisprudence of courts and tribunals suggests that state action beyond its borders will be regulated by human rights law. This approach follows that of the Inter-American Commission of Human Rights and the Human Rights Committee.[141]

In a different context, the ICJ in the *Diallo* case said of the Human Rights Committee's jurisprudence:

> Although the Court is in no way obliged, in the exercise of its judicial functions, to model its own interpretation of the Covenant on that of the Committee, it believes that it should ascribe great weight to the interpretation adopted by this independent body that was established specifically to supervise the application of that treaty. The point here is to achieve the necessary clarity and the essential consistency of international law, as well as legal security, to which both the individuals with guaranteed rights and the States obliged to comply with treaty obligations are entitled.[142]

As such, the *Diallo* case evidences the increasing importance accorded to the views and opinions expressed by the Human Rights Committee. In doing so, it recognises that in extending human rights protection, it should be consistent with the more specialised jurisprudence on the matter. At the same time, the Court was cautious in acknowledging the influence of this body on its decision-making.

The impact of human rights mechanisms on the case law of courts and tribunals can have the effect of elevating human rights norms to a new level of bindingness. Unlike the human rights treaty bodies, for example, the judgments of the ICJ are binding. This is significant for the propagation and enforcement of human rights more generally.

Turning to a different example again, the ICJ has followed the lead of the International Law Commission (ILC) as regards the development of the law of state responsibility. This was evident in the *Barcelona Traction* case,[143] in which the approach to state responsibility reflected the views of former Special Rapporteur on State Responsibility, Roberto Ago. In

140 Wilde, 'Human Rights beyond Borders at the World Court: The Significance of the International Court of Justice's Jurisprudence on the Extraterritorial Application of International Human Rights Law Treaties', 667.

141 *Ibid.*, 670.

142 *Ahmadou Sadio Diallo (Republic of Guinea* v. *Democratic Republic of the Congo)*, Merits, Judgment (2010) ICJ Rep. 639, 663.

143 *Barcelona Traction, Light & Power Co.*, Judgment (1970) ICJ Rep. 3.

particular, the approach is a comprehensive one that encompasses breaches of public interest obligations in the areas of human rights, as well as environmental law and decolonisation. The classical conception of state responsibility had simply encompassed violations of bilateral obligations, such as those existing in the context of diplomatic relations.[144] In the *Wall Opinion*, the ICJ also followed the approach of the ILC when the Court used the same language as Article 41 of the Draft Articles on State Responsibility, even though it did not formally cite the Articles.[145] This signified a departure from the traditional concept of state crimes.

As for international tribunals in other fields, certain cases show a human rights approach being adopted through the amendment of traditionally established concepts. In the field of investor–state arbitration, for instance, the *Urbaser* v. *Argentina*[146] case is the first investment tribunal to accept jurisdiction over a counterclaim on human rights.[147] The tribunal rejected the argument that it could not accept jurisdiction for a human rights claim.[148] Further still, the tribunal lowered the procedural burden by only requiring the host state to establish a *prima facie* case for jurisdiction.[149] During the merits, the tribunal was of the view that the bilateral investment treaty at issue did not constitute a 'closed system'.[150] As a result, the state was entitled to invoke legal obligations beyond the treaty. The tribunal also rejected the argument that the claimant, being a non-state entity, could not be bound by human rights obligations.[151]

Similarly, principles shape and structure international law's rules and norms. According to Antônio Augusto Cançado Trindade, they are 'a manifestation of the universal juridical conscience', and in the evolution of contemporary international law 'basic considerations of humanity play a role of the utmost importance'.[152] General principles of law have

[144] Crawford, 'International Court of Justice and the Law of State Responsibility', 77.
[145] *Ibid.*, 82.
[146] *Urbaser SA and Consorcio de Aguas Bilbao Bizkaia, Bilbao Biskaia Ur Partzuergoa* v. *The Argentine Republic*, ICSID Case No. ARB/07/26, 8 December 2016.
[147] *Ibid.*, para 1151.
[148] *Ibid.*, para 1154.
[149] *Ibid.*, para 1153.
[150] *Ibid.*, para 1191.
[151] *Ibid.*, para 1195. For an insightful analysis of the Tribunal's reasoning, see Eric de Brabandere, 'Human Rights and Foreign Direct Investment' in Markus Krajewski and Rhea Tamara Hoffmann (eds.), *Research Handbook on Foreign Direct Investment* (Edward Elgar, 2018), 619–645.
[152] Trindade, 'A Century of International Justice and Prospects for the Future', 73.

long featured in international dispute settlement.[153] Principles have helped to propagate a conception of objective justice and facilitate the emergence of a '*universal* international law, the new *jus gentium* of our times'.[154] Emphasising the discretion inherent in the judicial function and the role that principles can play in this respect, Judge *Ad Hoc* Dugard has said:

> Where authorities are divided, or different general principles compete for priority, or different rules of interpretation lead to different conclusions, or State practices conflict, the judge is required to make a choice. In exercising this choice, the judge will be guided by principles (propositions that describe rights) and policies (propositions that describe goals) in order to arrive at a coherent conclusion that most effectively furthers the integrity of the international legal order.[155]

The importance of recourse to principles is particularly acute in the area of peremptory human rights. Here, it is interesting to observe that principles have been resorted to for the development of the law by judicial actors, rather than any attempt to identify custom.[156] In this context, there is a similarity in the processes that lead to general principles and custom respectively, although general principles do not rely as squarely on traditionally understood notions of state practice but rather on legal expressions of widely held moral and humanitarian considerations.[157]

The recourse to principles suggests that certain norms may find their place in the corpus of international law without stringent reliance on the settled will of states.[158] Moreover, the drafters of the ICJ Statute

[153] *Ibid.*, 73; see also, Katarzyna Grabarczyk, *Les principes généraux dans la jurisprudence de la Cour Européenne des Droits de l'Homme* (Presses Universitaires d'Aix Marseille, 2008), 375–473; Mohamed Shahabuddeen, *International Criminal Justice at the Yugoslav Tribunal – A Judge's Recollection* (Oxford University Press, 2012), 55, 57, 86, 88–89, 185 and 203.

[154] Trindade, 'A Century of International Justice and Prospects for the Future', 73–74.

[155] *Case Concerning Armed Activities on the Territory of the Congo (Democratic Republic of the Congo* v. *Rwanda)* (New application: 2002), Jurisdiction and Admissibility (2006) ICJ Rep. 1, Separate Opinion of Judge *Ad Hoc* Dugard.

[156] Simma and Alston, 'Sources of Human Rights Law: Custom, Jus Cogens and General Principles', 82; see also, Andrea Bianchi, 'Human Rights and the Magic of Jus Cogens' (2008) 19(3) *European Journal of International Law* 491, 493.

[157] Bianchi, 'Human Rights and the Magic of Jus Cogens', 493, quoting Simma and Alston, 'Sources of Human Rights Law: Custom, Jus Cogens and General Principles', 105.

[158] For a detailed consideration of the ways in which international law is created other than by states, see in particular Christian Tomuschat, 'Obligations Arising for States without or against Their Will' 241 (1994-VI) *Collected Courses of the Hague Academy of*

envisaged that general principles of law would not simply be those existing *in foro domestico*, but that they could also be created at the international level. While principles do ultimately require general acceptance and recognition by states, to find application they do not require conclusive evidence of widespread state practice and *opinio juris*.[159] In this way, the evolution of human rights law principles has come before practice.[160] Indeed, general principles play an important role in the propagation of human rights protection, particularly among the rules of general international law. This is evident not least in the jurisprudence of the ICJ.[161]

Courts and tribunals have a wealth of norms to choose from given the proliferation of 'norm-generating bodies'[162] and have played a role in extending human rights as well as bringing greater protection and better

International Law 195; see also, Oscar Schachter, 'International Law in Theory and Practice: General Course in Public International Law' 178 (1982) *Collected Courses of the Hague Academy of International Law* 21, 333–342 and 334 (noting that human rights come into existence in a multitude of ways, including beyond the 'usual processes of customary law formation').

159 Simma and Alston, 'The Sources of Human Rights Law: Custom, Jus Cogens and General Principles', 105. Similarly, Judge Tanaka in the *South West Africa Cases* argued that general principles under Article 38(1)(c) of the ICJ Statute encompassed 'the concept of human rights and of their protection' and that Article 38(1)(c) 'does not require the consent of States as a condition of the recognition of the general principles'. As such, '[f]rom this kind of source international law could have the foundation of its validity extended beyond the will of States, that is to say, into the sphere of natural law and assume an aspect of its supra-national and supra-positive character'. *South West Africa Cases (Ethiopia* v. *South Africa; Liberia* v. *South Africa)*, Second Phase, Dissenting Opinion of Judge Tanaka (1966) ICJ Rep. 6, 298.

160 Simma and Alston, 'The Sources of Human Rights Law: Custom, Jus Cogens and General Principles', 107.

161 See, for example, *Corfu Channel Case*, Judgment (1949) ICJ Rep. 4, 22 ('obligations … based … on certain general and well-recognized principles' as including 'elementary considerations of humanity'); *Reservations of the Genocide Convention*, Advisory Opinion (1951) ICJ Rep. 15, 23 ('the principles underlying the Convention are principles which are recognized by civilized nations as binding on States, even without any convention obligation'); *Barcelona Traction, Light & Power Co. (Belgium* v. *Spain)*, Second Phase (1970) ICJ Rep 3, 32 (*erga omnes* obligations derive 'from the principles and rules concerning the basic rights of the human person'); *United States Diplomatic and Consular Staff in Tehran*, Judgment (1980) ICJ Rep. 3, 42 (to '[w]rongfully deprive human beings of their freedom and to subject them to physical constraint in conditions of hardship is in itself manifestly incompatible with the principles of the Charter of the United Nations, as well as with the fundamental principles enunciated in the Universal Declaration of Human Rights').

162 Hamilton and Buyse, 'Human Rights Courts as Norm-Brokers', who emphasise the need for courts and tribunals to take so-called norm-brokering seriously. On the proliferation of courts and tribunals, and potential problems thereto, see Benedict Kingsbury,

standards of living to more people. More broadly, courts and tribunals are amassing a greater portfolio of functions, beyond simply the settlement of disputes.[163]

2.3 Concluding Remarks

In sum, it is through the agents of international law that values may infiltrate the legal system.[164] Legal systems are open to reflecting developments in social realties, and so the forces of globalisation, interconnectivity and empathy for others can have a material influence on the value-content of the law. Legal norms develop over time through interpretative practices that also have the effect of internalising social developments. This chapter has shown that states, individuals, institutions and international courts have all played a significant role in the humanisation of international law. In certain cases, this has been under the influence of the rhetoric of human rights or recourse to principles as a means of extending human rights protection.

Overall, the chapter has sought to reveal the connection between ideology and the law. It has sought to serve as a reminder that law does not exist in a vacuum but, rather, it is a reflection of the prevailing social forces over time. International law emerges from a context of shared values, empathy and altruism, as much as it does from a context of individual interests and selfish behaviour. In the next chapters, we turn to examine specific manifestations of altruism in international law.

'Foreword: Is the Proliferation of International Courts and Tribunals a Systemic Problem?' (1999) 31 *New York University Journal of International Law and Politics* 679.

163 See, for example, Laurence Boisson de Chazournes, 'Review Essay: The International Judicial Function in Its (In)finite Variety' (2015) 109(2) *American Journal of International Law* 433; Armin von Bogdandy and Ingo Venzke, 'On Functions of International Courts: An Appraisal in Light of Their Burgeoning Public Authority' (2013) 26 *Leiden Journal of International Law* 49.

164 Martti Koskenniemi, *From Apology to Utopia* (Re-issue, Cambridge University Press, 2005), 5. However, Koskenniemi argues that the practices, institutions and conceptual frameworks of international law need to be re-imagined to rectify global injustices.

3

The Substance of Altruism in International Law: Cooperation for the Other

3.1 Introduction

The evolution in the nature of legal relationships at the international level has been illustrated in the previous chapters. The result of this evolution is that there now exist horizontal legal relationships in the form of commitments between states and vertical legal relationships (with international oversight) in the form of commitments between states and people within their territory, but there are also altruistic legal relationships in the form of commitments between a state and people in other states. The object of the following chapters is to study these legal relationships in international law more closely. In so doing, an extensive exploration of these relationships will ensue through a consideration of the commitments themselves, *travaux préparatoires* where relevant, subsequent interpretations, state practice and academic commentary. As will become evident, some of these relationships are more legally binding than others, some more abstract than others and some more contested than others.

At the outset, however, it is important to point out that the altruistic legal relationships presented in the following chapters are to be found in positive law, and as such they are not law as it should be. These legal relationships can either exist in their own right, such as the duty to prevent genocide in a third country, or they may be contingent on other concepts, such as the obligation to cooperate, which we turn to first in this chapter.

International cooperation finds application in a wide variety of domains, including peace and security, human rights, international economic relations and others. This chapter will consider the provision for international cooperation under specific treaty regimes as well as in the context of particular rights. Given the cross-cutting nature of international cooperation, an exhaustive consideration of all manifestations of international cooperation would be beyond the scope of this project.

Thus, the aim is to provide an insight into the way international cooperation can operate in practice to establish altruistic legal relationships.

3.2 International Cooperation under the UN Charter

A duty to cooperate to realise certain rights is evident in a number of international instruments as well as the jurisprudence of courts and tribunals, treaty bodies and various other international institutions. Chapter IX of the UN Charter is dedicated to 'International Economic and Social Cooperation'.[1] In this context, Article 55 is directed at the UN itself, which is committed to promoting 'higher standards of living, full employment, and conditions of economic and social progress and development' (Article 55(a)), 'solutions of international economic, social, health, and related problems; and international cultural and educational cooperation' (Article 55(b)) and 'universal respect for, and observance of, human rights and fundamental freedoms for all without discrimination as to race, sex, language, or religion' (Article 55(c)). Article 56 of the UN Charter contains a concrete obligation for member states of the United Nations to 'take joint and separate action in cooperation with the Organization' on the pledges set out in the previous provision.

The aims of the United Nations as provided for in Article 1 of the UN Charter are to ensure the maintenance of international peace and security, to pursue international development and to promote and encourage international respect for and enjoyment of human rights and fundamental freedoms. Reading Articles 1, 55 and 56 together has led some to conclude that the text of these provisions create a binding legal obligation to work together in furthering the objectives of the United Nations and, as the UN Charter may be considered customary international law, these same obligations are also binding on states that are not members of the United Nations.[2] As such, an argument can be made that states have

[1] Charter of the United Nations, 26 June 1945, 1 UNTS XVI.

[2] See, for example, Bruno Simma and Philip Alston, 'The Sources of Human Rights Law: Custom, Jus Cogens, and General Principles' (1988–1989) 12 *Australian Yearbook of International Law* 82, 90, describing the 'authoritative interpretation' approach 'used to arrive at human rights obligations under international law independently of specific treaties'. Simma and Alston also note:

> It consists of treating the Universal Declaration and the body of soft law built upon it as an authoritative interpretation of the obligation contained in Articles 55 and 56 of the UN Charter according to which 'all Members pledge themselves to take joint and separate action in cooperation with the Organization' in order to achieve 'universal respect for, and observance of,

undertaken a commitment to engage in cooperative action for the realisation of human rights, development and international peace and security, not simply in their own countries but in other countries too. On the basis of the text of these provisions, the precise nature of cooperation remained somewhat unclear.

The Declaration on Principles of International Law Concerning Friendly Relations and Co-operation among States in accordance with the Charter of the United Nations of 24 October 1970[3] was intended to provide further clarity on the nature of international cooperation.[4] The Declaration reiterates that states have a duty to cooperate with one another in accordance with the UN Charter, and it goes on to elaborate that such cooperation should occur even if there are political, economic or social differences between them and should be aimed at maintaining international peace and security, promoting economic development and the general welfare of states. More specifically, states are directed to cooperate in the ways listed here for the following ends:

(a) States shall cooperate with other States in the maintenance of international peace and security;
(b) States shall cooperate in the promotion of universal respect for, and observance of, human rights and fundamental freedoms for all, and in the elimination of all forms of racial discrimination and all forms of religious intolerance;
(c) States shall conduct their international relations in the economic, social, cultural, technical and trade fields in accordance with the principles of sovereign equality and non-intervention;
(d) States Members of the United Nations have the duty to take joint and separate action in cooperation with the United Nations in accordance with the relevant provisions of the Charter.

human rights and fundamental freedoms for all without distinction as to race, sex, language or religion' (100).

3 General Assembly Resolution 2625 (XXV), Declaration on Principles of International Law Concerning Friendly Relations and Co-operation among States in accordance with the Charter of the United Nations, 24 October 1970, UN Doc. A/RES/25/2625. For a detailed analysis, see Laurence Boisson de Chazournes and Jason Rudall, 'Co-Operation' in Jorge E. Viñuales (ed.), *The UN Friendly Relations Declaration at 50: An Assessment of the Fundamental Principles of International Law* (Cambridge University Press, 2020), 105–132.

4 Philip Alston and Gerard Quinn, 'The Nature and Scope of States Parties' Obligations under the International Covenant on Economic, Social and Cultural Rights' (1987) 9(2) *Human Rights Quarterly* 156, 188.

> States should cooperate in the economic, social and cultural fields as well as in the field of science and technology and for the promotion of international cultural and educational progress. States should cooperate in the promotion of economic growth throughout the world, especially that of the developing countries.

Lacunae filling is one of the major functions of general principles like international cooperation and this function was one of the main reasons they were inserted into the Statute of the International Court of Justice (ICJ).[5] Such principles also help in the interpretation of legal norms, just as equity or good faith may be used in the interpretation of specific rules. Furthermore, principles may be needed to complement the operation of a series of legal rules. In its Advisory Opinion on the *Legal Consequences of the Separation of the Chagos Archipelago from Mauritius in 1965*, the ICJ referred to the Friendly Relations Declaration in calling upon states to cooperate with the United Nations to help realise the right of self-determination in completing the decolonisation of Mauritius:

> Since respect for the right to self-determination is an obligation *erga omnes*, all States have a legal interest in protecting that right (*East Timor; Barcelona Traction*). The Court considers that, while it is for the General Assembly to pronounce on the modalities required to ensure the completion of the decolonization of Mauritius, all Member States must co-operate with the United Nations to put those modalities into effect.
>
> . . .
>
> In response to Question (b) of the General Assembly, relating to the consequences under international law that arise from the continued administration by the United Kingdom of the Chagos Archipelago, the Court concludes that the United Kingdom has an obligation to bring to an end its administration of the Chagos Archipelago as rapidly as possible, and that all Member States must co-operate with the United Nations to complete the decolonization of Mauritius.[6]

Another milestone instrument for the expression of cooperation in international law is General Assembly Resolution 59/204 of 20 December 2004,[7] which is concerned with 'Respect for the purposes

[5] Béla Vitanyi, 'Les Positions doctrinales concernant le sens de la notion de "principes généraux de droit reconnus par les nations civilisées"' (1982) 86 *Revue générale de droit international public* 259.

[6] *Legal Consequences of the Separation of the Chagos Archipelago from Mauritius in 1965*, Advisory Opinion (2019) ICJ Rep. 95, paras 180 and 182.

[7] General Assembly Resolution 59/204, Respect for the purposes and principles contained in the Charter of the United Nations to achieve international cooperation in promoting and encouraging respect for human rights and for fundamental freedoms and in solving

and principles contained in the Charter of the United Nations to achieve international cooperation in promoting and encouraging respect for human rights and for fundamental freedoms and in solving international problems of a humanitarian character'. In particular, it adds further clarity to the scope of international cooperation in the context of the UN Charter. For example, it reaffirms in the Preamble that human rights and fundamental freedoms are central objectives of the United Nations and must be promoted and protected through, inter alia, international cooperation. The Preamble goes on to note that

> the enhancement of international cooperation in the field of human rights is essential for the full achievement of the purposes of the United Nations and that human rights and fundamental freedoms are the birthright of all human beings, the promotion and protection of such rights and freedoms being the first responsibility of Governments.[8]

This preambular language adds interesting contours to the duty of international cooperation. First, the use of terms such as 'enhancement', 'full achievement' and 'first responsibility' in the Preamble lend themselves to the proposition that this General Assembly resolution is a call for more, better and deeper international cooperation. Second, the reference to 'human rights and fundamental freedoms [as] the birthright of all human beings' underlines the universality of human rights and, in this connection, the universal nature of the duty to cooperate so that all human beings, regardless of their nationality, may benefit from human rights protection. Similarly, the resolution

> [c]alls upon all States to cooperate fully, through constructive dialogue, to ensure the promotion and protection of all human rights for all and in promoting peaceful solutions to international problems of a humanitarian character.

As such, the depth and breadth of the obligation to cooperate to ensure human rights is emphasised.

The inclusion of the phrase 'through constructive dialogue' in the resolution language suggests the primary modality is via diplomatic efforts. However, as we will see later in this chapter, international cooperation may involve other means of action and the commitment of resources. Indeed, Ian Brownlie observed that there was likely

international problems of a humanitarian character, 20 December 2004, UN Doc. A/59/503/Add.2.

[8] *Ibid.*, Preamble.

a collective duty upon states to take action to ensure reasonable living standards for their own peoples as well as those in other states.[9] Brownlie went on to observe that such aid may include loans, construction assistance or the transfer of technology or knowledge, for example. There are certain expectations around the giving of aid, including that they must not breach the principles of sovereign equality, *jus cogens* or permanent sovereignty over natural resources, and the United Nations Conference on Trade and Development recommended the application of certain principles in giving aid.[10]

The *travaux préparatoires* to Article 56 of the UN Charter, and in particular the notions of 'international cooperation' and 'joint and separate action', reveal some notable features as to what the drafters had in mind when they included the reference to international cooperation. In particular, the *travaux* sheds light on the extent to which member states of the UN would be expected to act either within the context of the UN or externally to the organisation. They indicate that although some were concerned with the potential ramifications of including a reference to 'separate action', other delegates saw little cause for concern and still others thought there was sufficient protection elsewhere in the Charter to allay fears of interference with the domestic affairs of other states.[11] There is little evidence that any of the delegates were concerned with the positive nature of the obligation of international cooperation, as inclusion of the term 'action' suggests. Given that 'separate action' was left in the revised draft and that draft was so widely accepted, we can surmise that states envisaged a commitment, at the very least to make individual and collective efforts on the diplomatic plane, to further the causes of human rights and development, and ensure peace and security. The *travaux préparatoires* of this article also reveal that the revised draft was widely agreed upon, including by the United States, Australia and

[9] Ian Brownlie, *Principles of International Law* (7th ed., Oxford University Press, 2008), 250. See also, General Assembly Resolution 1316 (XIII), International Co-operation for Economic Development of Under-Developed Countries, 12 December 1958; General Assembly Resolution 2158 (XXI), Permanent Sovereignty over Natural Resources, 25 November 1966; General Assembly Resolution 3281 (XXIX), Charter of Economic Rights and Duties of States, 12 December 1974; General Assembly Resolution 41/128, Declaration on the Right to Development, 4 December 1986.

[10] United Nations, *UN Monthly Chronicle* (United Nations, 1964), 49.

[11] The United Nations Conference on International Organization, Committee II, General Assembly, Committee 3: Economic and Social Cooperation (1945) 10 *Documents of the United Nations Conference on International Organization* 139–141.

the Soviet Union, and was ultimately adopted with thirty-four votes to one.[12]

With this insight as to the drafters' intention about the scope of international cooperation under the UN Charter, we now turn to consider its manifestation and practical application in the context of specific treaties and other legal contexts. As will be seen, the scope of international cooperation has expanded over time and an exploration of international cooperation under these treaties helps to define the contours of the positive action states are expected to take to assist people beyond their borders who may be in need of international assistance.

3.3 International Cooperation and the International Covenant on Economic, Social and Cultural Rights 1966

Article 2(1) of the International Covenant on Economic, Social and Cultural Rights 1966[13] contains one of the strongest formulations of international cooperation under international law. It provides:

> Each State Party to the present Covenant undertakes to take steps, individually and through international assistance and co-operation, especially economic and technical, to the maximum of its available resources, with a view to achieving progressively the full realization of the rights recognized in the present Covenant by all appropriate means, including particularly the adoption of legislative measures.

This provision obliges states to cooperate and assist, particularly by offering economic and technical resources, for the realisation of rights provided for in the Covenant. Beyond diplomatic efforts at cooperation, it also envisages the commitment of resources and assistance. The distinction made in the text between taking steps 'individually' and 'through international assistance and cooperation' is an indication that the Covenant binds states as regards their own citizens but also creates a commitment in respect of citizens of other countries. This indication is strengthened by having reference to the *travaux préparatoires*, other provisions of the Covenant and the interpretations of the Committee on Economic, Social and Cultural Rights, as will become evident.

The *travaux préparatoires* of Article 2(1) of the Covenant show that the Chairman of the Drafting Commission made reference to Article 22 of

[12] *Ibid.*

[13] International Covenant on Economic, Social and Cultural Rights, 16 December 1966, 993 UNTS 3.

the Universal Declaration of Human Rights.[14] Article 22 of the Declaration provides that

> [e]veryone, as a member of society, has the right to social security and is entitled to realization, through national efforts and international co-operation and in accordance with the organization and resources of each State, of the economic, social and cultural rights indispensable for his dignity and the free development of his personality.

The reference to this provision underscores the dual obligation on states to ensure their own citizens enjoy economic, social and cultural rights, but also that individuals beyond their jurisdiction in other states benefit from the guarantee of such rights. Further, lending clarity to the commitment of resources envisaged under Article 2(1), the French delegate on the Drafting Commission stated that

> [t]he expression 'their resources' was intended to convey, not that States should, in implementing the rights in question, renounce all progress which was beyond their own resources, but that countries with substantial resources should lend their assistance internationally.[15]

Similarly, recognising the need for developed states to provide assistance to developing states, the Iraqi delegate said that because 'the under-developed countries would be taking on much heavier commitments than the advanced countries ... [t]hey would certainly need international co-operation in discharging their obligations'.[16] The delegate of the United States emphasised that the provision would need 'to indicate the necessity of international co-operation in the matter',[17] and the delegate of Chile was of the view that 'international assistance to under-developed countries had in a sense become mandatory as a result of commitments assumed by States in the United Nations'.[18] All of these

[14] Commission on Human Rights, 'Summary Record of the Two Hundred and Thirty-Second Meeting', 2 July 1951, UN Doc. E/CN.4/SR.232, 7 UN ESCOR C.4, 5.

[15] Commission on Human Rights, 'Summary Record of the Two Hundred and Thirty-Third Meeting', UN Doc. E/CN.4/SR.233, 7 UN ESCOR C.4, 8.

[16] Iraq, General Assembly Third Committee, 1203rd Meeting, 17 UN GAOR C.3, UN Doc. A/C.3SR.1203 (1962), para 21.

[17] Commission on Human Rights, 'Summary Record of the Two Hundred and Seventieth Meeting', 14 May 1952, UN Doc. E/CN.4/SR.270, 8 UN ESCOR C.4, 10.

[18] Chile, General Assembly Third Committee, 1203rd Meeting, 17 UN GAOR C.3, UN Doc. A/C.3/SR.1203 (1962), para 10. However, it should be noted that there were several states opposed to the idea that financial assistance to developing states would be rendered mandatory; see, for example, the statement of Mr Bouquin of France, General Assembly Third Committee, 1205th Meeting, 17 UN GAOR C.3, UN Doc. A/C.3/SR.1205 (1962), para 12, the statement of Mr Ostrovsky of the USSR, General Assembly Third Committee,

statements support the claim that developed countries should commit resources and assistance towards the realisation of rights in developing countries.

The Maastricht Principles on the Extraterritorial Obligations of States in the Area of Economic, Social and Cultural Rights[19] set out several notable principles on the obligations of states extraterritorially as regards this category of rights. They offer several insights on international cooperation and assistance under the Covenant. These principles were adopted by human rights experts in September 2011 at a meeting convened by Maastricht University and the International Commission of Jurists. While states are not signatories to these principles, the signatories do include (former) members of UN human rights treaty bodies, Special Rapporteurs of the Human Rights Council, legal advisers to NGOs and eminent scholars. As such, they represent international expert opinion on the extraterritorial obligations of states. Set up around these principles is a network of experts and NGOs known as the Extraterritorial Obligations Consortium.[20] The principles aim to clarify the extraterritorial human rights obligations of states. The Preamble notes that the principles derive from international law and spell out the substance of extraterritorial state obligations to realise economic, social and cultural rights. Moreover, the Preamble also provides that

> [s]tates have recognized that everyone is entitled to a social and international order in which human rights can be fully realized and have undertaken to pursue joint and separate action to achieve universal respect for, and observance of, human rights for all.

Adding further support to the proposition that states must take positive action to help in the universal realisation of socio-economic rights, the Maastricht Principles note under Principle 33 that states are under an obligation 'to provide assistance' to ensure the realisation of socio-economic rights. In this way, Principle 33 sets out the following obligation to provide international assistance:

1203rd Meeting, 17 UN GAOR C.3, UN Doc. A/C.3/SR.1203 (1962), para 14, or Mr Mantzoulinos of Greece, General Assembly Third Committee, 1204th Meeting 17 UN GAOR C.3, UN Doc. A/C.3/SR.1204, para 14.

19 Maastricht Principles on the Extraterritorial Obligations of States in the Area of Economic, Social and Cultural Rights 2011, www.etoconsortium.org/nc/en/main-navigation/library/maastricht-principles/?tx_drblob_pi1%5BdownloadUid%5D=23.

20 See Extraterritorial Obligations Consortium website, www.etoconsortium.org.

> As part of the broader obligation of international cooperation, States, acting separately and jointly, that are in a position to do so, must provide international assistance to contribute to the fulfilment of economic, social and cultural rights in other States, in a manner consistent with Principle 32.

The Commentary to these principles also helps us to understand the scope of international assistance and cooperation better. For example, the Commentary to Principle 33 recalls that 'international assistance is to be understood as a component of international cooperation'.[21] The Commentary goes on to note that international assistance and cooperation under the International Covenant on Economic, Social and Cultural Rights is not limited to the provision of economic and technical assistance. It may also include, for example, giving information, offering assistance with tracing stolen public funds or helping with the adoption of measures to circumscribe human trafficking.[22]

The Commentary to Principle 31 of the Maastricht Principles (which deals with the capacity and resources of states) provides further guidance still on the specific action demanded by international cooperation, namely the need to mobilise all available resources to facilitate the fulfilment of economic, social and cultural rights.[23] The Commentaries also highlight that a state is not relieved of its obligation to cooperate because it does not have the resources to help. In this case, it must also make efforts to mobilise resources at the international level.[24]

Turning to the work of the Committee on Economic, Social and Cultural Rights, which monitors implementation of the Covenant and issues General Comments with a view to aiding the interpretation of its provisions, further clarity is offered on the nature of the commitments states must undertake towards people in other countries. Interpreting

[21] Olivier de Schutter, Asbjørn Eide, Ashfaq Khalfan, Marcos Orellana, Margot Salomon and Ian Seiderman, 'Commentary to the Maastricht Principles on the Extraterritorial Obligations of States in the Area of Economic, Social and Cultural Rights' (2012) 34(4) *Human Rights Quarterly* 1084, 1157.

[22] *Ibid.*

[23] *Ibid.*, 1153.

[24] *Ibid.*, 1154. This is a point noted by the UN Committee on Economic, Social and Cultural Rights, *General Comment No. 21 on the Right of Everyone to Take Part in Cultural Life*, 21 December 2009, UN Doc. E/C.12/GC/21, para 23:

> even in times of severe resource constraints, the most disadvantaged and marginalized individuals and groups can and indeed must be protected by the adoption of relatively low-cost targeted programmes.

Article 2(1) of the Covenant in its General Comment No. 3 of 1990, the Committee has said of international cooperation and assistance that

> the phrase 'to the maximum of its available resources' was intended by the drafters of the Covenant to refer to both the resources existing within a State and those available from the international community through international cooperation and assistance. Moreover, the essential role of such cooperation in facilitating the full realization of the relevant rights is further underlined by the specific provisions contained in Articles 11, 15, 22 and 23.
>
> ...
>
> In accordance with Articles 55 and 56 of the Charter of the United Nations, and with the provisions of the Covenant itself, international cooperation for development and thus for the realization of economic, social and cultural rights is an obligation of all States. It is particularly incumbent upon those States which are in a position to assist others in this regard. ... It emphasizes that, in the absence of an active programme of international assistance and cooperation on the part of all those States that are in a position to undertake one, the full realization of economic, social and cultural rights will remain an unfulfilled aspiration in many countries.[25]

This interpretation again emphasises the universal nature of the obligation to cooperate for the realisation of rights for all individuals, but it also underscores the need for states with plentiful resources to bear a heavier commitment to 'the other'. Moreover, such states are concretely encouraged to develop an 'active programme of international assistance and cooperation', thereby urging positive individual action and the commitment of national resources for the benefit of peoples in less developed states. This conception of assistance and cooperation thus goes well beyond diplomatic efforts.

Moreover, the Committee on Economic, Social and Cultural Rights has indicated that states can partly discharge the obligation of international assistance by meeting the internationally agreed[26] commitment to set aside a minimum net amount of 0.7 per cent of its gross national product for development assistance.[27] This is yet further evidence that

[25] UN Committee on Economic, Social and Cultural Rights, *General Comment No. 3 on the Nature of States Parties' Obligations*, paras 13 and 14.

[26] See, for example, General Assembly Resolution 2626 (XXV), International Development Strategy for the Second United Nations Development Decade, 24 October 1970, UN Doc. A/RES/25/2626.

[27] See de Schutter, Eide, Khalfan, Orellana, Salomon and Seiderman, 'Commentary to the Maastricht Principles on the Extraterritorial Obligations of States in the Area of Economic, Social and Cultural Rights'.

a commitment of resources, particularly by developed countries to developing countries, is expected. We will return to appraise official development assistance (ODA) in more detail in Chapter 5.

The Committee has also provided states with guidance on how to approach their cooperation and assistance efforts. First, in its General Comment No. 3, the Committee set out that the rights of the disadvantaged, such as women and refugees, and those of marginalised or vulnerable groups, such as children, should be prioritised. Second, they must ensure that 'minimum essential levels' of economic, social and cultural rights are realised. Third, the pace of cooperation to realise these rights must be as expeditious as possible. Fourth, the modalities chosen should be as effective as possible. Finally, all regressive measures should be avoided.[28] Further still, in its General Comment No. 14, the Committee noted that

> [p]riority in the provision of international medical aid, distribution and management of resources, such as safe and potable water, food and medical supplies, and financial aid should be given to the most vulnerable or marginalized groups of the population.[29]

As for core rights under the Convention, the Committee has indicated that these should be prioritized with the aim, as said, of ensuring minimum essential levels of rights. As such, the Committee set out that 'core obligations give rise to national responsibilities for all States, and international responsibilities for developed States, as well as others that are in a "position to assist"'.[30] This statement of the Committee goes on to note that

> [w]hen grouped together, the core obligations establish an international minimum threshold that all developmental policies should be designed to

[28] See UN Committee on Economic, Social and Cultural Rights, *General Comment No. 3 on the Nature of States Parties' Obligations*, paras 9–12. See also UN Committee on Economic, Social and Cultural Rights, *General Comment No. 19 on the Right to Social Security (Article 9 of the Covenant)*, 4 February 2008, UN Doc. E/C.12/GC/19, para 31; UN Committee on Economic, Social and Cultural Rights, *General Comment No. 15 on the Right to Water (Articles 11 and 12 of the Covenant)*, 20 January 2003, UN Doc. E/C.12/2002/11, para 16; UN Committee on Economic, Social and Cultural Rights, *General Comment No. 14 on the Right to the Highest Attainable Standard of Health (Article 12 of the Covenant)*, 11 August 2000, UN Doc. E/C.12/2000/4, para 40.

[29] UN Committee on Economic, Social and Cultural Rights, *General Comment No. 14 on the Right to the Highest Attainable Standard of Health (Article 12 of the Covenant)*, para 40.

[30] Commission on Economic, Social and Cultural Rights, 'Substantive Issues Arising in the Implementation of the International Covenant on Economic, Social and Cultural Rights: Poverty and the International Covenant on Economic, Social and Cultural Rights', 4 May 2001, UN Doc. E/C.12/2001/10 (2001), para 16.

> respect. . . . [I]t is particularly incumbent on all those who can assist, to help developing countries respect this international minimum threshold. If a national or international anti-poverty strategy does not reflect this minimum threshold, it is inconsistent with the legally binding obligations of the State party.[31]

Further dimensions to the commitment of international assistance and cooperation are provided by the Committee's General Comments 15 and 19, which underline that international assistance must be consistent with the Covenant and other human rights, as well as being sustainable and culturally appropriate.[32] Moreover, in response to a request for assistance and cooperation, states must take stock of their own available resources and capacities.[33]

Emphasis on the universal nature of the rights in the Covenant, the need for cooperation and assistance for their universal realisation, may also be detected in other provisions of the Covenant. Moreover, several of these other provisions illustrate the action required of states in fulfilling their duties of international assistance and cooperation. For example, Article 11(1) of the Covenant specifically places an obligation on states to ensure the realisation of the right of *everyone* to an adequate standard of living for themselves and their family, including adequate food, clothing and housing, and to the continuous improvement of living conditions. In this context, cooperation based on free consent is recognised as a means for such realisation. Reiterating similar language to that found in Article 2(1), Article 11 places states under an obligation to 'take appropriate steps to ensure the realization of this right, recognizing to this effect the essential importance of international co-operation based on free consent'. Article 15(4) of the Covenant also reaffirms the need for international cooperation.

As regards the right to adequate food under Article 11 of the Covenant, the Committee on Economic, Social and Cultural Rights has referred to the role that international cooperation plays in respect of this right, in particular that states must take joint and separate action to achieve its full

31 *Ibid.*, para 16.

32 UN Committee on Economic, Social and Cultural Rights, *General Comment No. 15 on the Right to Water (Articles 11 and 12 of the Covenant)*, para 34; UN Committee on Economic, Social and Cultural Rights, *General Comment No. 19 on the Right to Social Security (Article 9 of the Covenant)*, para 55.

33 De Schutter, Eide, Khalfan, Orellana, Salomon and Seiderman, 'Commentary to the Maastricht Principles on the Extraterritorial Obligations of States in the Area of Economic, Social and Cultural Rights', 1159.

realisation.[34] States must also 'take steps to respect the enjoyment of the right to food in other countries, to protect that right, to facilitate access to food and to provide the necessary aid when required'.[35] Moreover, states are expected to ensure that the right to adequate food is provided for in international agreements, as well as to seek the development of this right in other international instruments.[36]

Beyond respect for the right to food, the Committee calls upon states to take steps to 'facilitate access to food' as well as to 'provide necessary aid when required'.[37] The Committee added further colour to the commitment to take joint and separate action in the context of the right to food, and again emphasises that cooperating jointly and separately requires positive action directed at individuals beyond a state's own jurisdiction.[38] We will return to consider food assistance in other contexts in Chapter 5.

The importance of positive international action to realise the rights under the Covenant is further reinforced in Article 23. As such, this provision of the Covenant then provides for a non-exhaustive list of ways in which international cooperation may be operationalised. This can include the conclusion of treaties, adopting recommendations, offering technical assistance or holding meetings to consult on and study ways in which rights in the Convention may be achieved. This indicates a mix of diplomatic efforts as well as the commitment of resources, such as furnishing technical assistance. It indicates the minimum positive action expected under the Covenant, and provisions on specific rights encourage states to go further in terms of committing resources, as is the case with Article 11 and the realisation of the right to an adequate standard of living for everyone.

Article 12 of the Covenant obliges states to 'recognize the right of everyone to the enjoyment of the highest attainable standard of physical and mental health'. Once again, the universal nature of this right is underlined in the provision itself. Interestingly, in a General Comment, the Committee on Economic, Social and Cultural Rights has added greater detail as regards the obligations that states are under in respect of people in other countries. The Committee set out that

[34] Committee on Economic, Social and Cultural Rights, *General Comment No. 12 on the Right to Adequate Food (Article 11)*, para 36.
[35] *Ibid.*
[36] *Ibid.*
[37] *Ibid.*
[38] *Ibid.*

> [s]tates parties have to respect the enjoyment of the right to health in other countries, and to prevent third parties from violating the right in other countries, if they are able to influence these third parties by way of legal or political means, in accordance with the Charter of the United Nations and applicable international law. Depending on the availability of resources, States should facilitate access to essential health facilities, goods and services in other countries, wherever possible and provide the necessary aid when required.[39]

The Committee also underlined that it is particularly incumbent on developed states to provide 'international assistance and cooperation, especially economic and technical' that might help developing states fulfil their obligations to their own people.[40] Moreover, as General Comment No. 14 sets out, States are under an obligation to ensure third parties do not violate the right in other countries.[41] This is qualified by the means through which they must ensure the right is not violated and the extent to which they are able to influence such third parties. Also in the context of the right to health, the UN Special Rapporteur on the Right to Health has assessed that

> [t]he right to health places an obligation on developed states to take measures that help developing countries realize the right to health and indicators are needed to measure the degree to which donor states are fulfilling this responsibility.[42]

Clearly, this is a right which requires international cooperation and assistance, particularly from developed to developing countries, for its realisation. Similarly, as regards the right to water under the Covenant (Articles 11 and 12), the Committee on Economic, Social and Cultural Rights has said in its General Comment No. 15 that

> [d]epending on the availability of resources, States should facilitate realization of the right to water in other countries, for example through provision of water resources, financial and technical assistance, and provide the necessary aid when required. . . . International assistance should be provided in a manner that is consistent with the Covenant and other human rights standards. . . . The economically developed States parties

[39] UN Committee on Economic, Social and Cultural Rights, *General Comment No. 14 on the Right to the Highest Attainable Standard of Health*, para 39.

[40] *Ibid.*, paras 39 and 45, respectively.

[41] *Ibid.*, para 33.

[42] UN Commission on Human Rights, 'Report of the Special Rapporteur on the Right of Everyone to the Enjoyment of the Highest Attainable Standard of Physical and Mental Health, Paul Hunt', 3 March 2006, UN Doc. E/CN.4/2006/48.

> have a special responsibility and interest to assist the poorer developing States in this regard.[43]

Committing states to assist with the realisation of the right to water in other states, this General Comment spells out that the obligation includes such positive action as providing water resources, as well as financial, technical and other assistance, when this is necessary for the realisation of the right to water. Moreover, the General Comment speaks of a 'special responsibility' incumbent upon developed states to assist developing states. Emphasising the universal nature of the right to water, the Committee has also noted that '[t]he human right to water entitles everyone to sufficient, safe, acceptable, physically accessible and affordable water for personal and domestic uses'.[44]

While there may be a special responsibility upon developed states, particularly in respect of the assistance they must offer developing states, it is also clear that developing states themselves must also take steps towards the realisation of rights under the Covenant. Where these steps may be inadequate as a result of limited resources, developing countries may request assistance. In this way, as regards the right to adequate housing provided for under Article 11(1) of the Covenant, the Committee on Economic, Social and Cultural Rights has said of international cooperation in its General Comment No. 4 that, irrespective of the level of development in a country, every state must promote the right to housing. This requires all states to refrain from any action that would hinder realising the right and to facilitate 'self-help' among certain groups. Where a state does not have the necessary resources to fulfil the obligation, it should request help through international cooperation as well as inform the Committee.[45] Of the obligation incumbent on states to recognise 'the essential importance of international cooperation based on free consent' in Article 11(1), the Committee has said that

> [t]raditionally, less than 5 per cent of all international assistance has been directed towards housing or human settlements, and often the manner by which such funding is provided does little to address the housing needs of disadvantaged groups. States parties, both recipients and providers, should ensure that a substantial proportion of financing is devoted to

[43] UN Committee on Economic, Social and Cultural Rights, *General Comment No. 15 on the Right to Water (Articles 11 and 12 of the Covenant)*, para 34.

[44] *Ibid.*, para 2.

[45] UN Committee on Economic, Social and Cultural Rights, *General Comment No. 4 on the Right to Adequate Housing (Article 11(1) of the Covenant)*, 13 December 1991, UN Doc. E/1992/23, para 10.

> creating conditions leading to a higher number of persons being adequately housed. . . . States parties should, when contemplating international financial cooperation, seek to indicate areas relevant to the right to adequate housing where external financing would have the most effect. Such requests should take full account of the needs and views of the affected groups.[46]

Turning to the right to education under Article 13 of the Covenant, General Comment No. 13 of the Committee on Economic, Social and Cultural Rights reiterates the importance of assistance and cooperation in the full realisation of the right to education.[47] As is evident from this General Comment (and General Comment 3), the Committee envisages that international assistance and cooperation would 'especially' take the form of economic and technical support, in terms not only of the right to education but also of other rights under the Covenant. Paragraph 57 of the General Comment goes on to elaborate a minimum standard for the right to education in each state:

> In its General Comment 3, the Committee confirmed that States parties have a 'minimum core obligation to ensure the satisfaction of, at the very least, minimum essential levels' of each of the rights enunciated in the Covenant, including 'the most basic forms of education'. In the context of article 13, this core obligation includes an obligation: to ensure the right of access to public educational institutions and programmes on a non-discriminatory basis; to ensure that education conforms to the objectives set out in article 13 (1); to provide primary education for all in accordance with article 13 (2) (a); to adopt and implement a national educational strategy which includes provision for secondary, higher and fundamental education; and to ensure free choice of education without interference from the State or third parties, subject to conformity with 'minimum educational standards'. (art. 13 (3) and (4))[48]

These General Comments all contribute to the *acquis* of the International Covenant on Economic, Social and Cultural Rights, and help to clarify the nature of rights under it. The text of the obligations discussed, and the *acquis* show that altruistic legal relationships are created by the treaty through the vehicle of international cooperation and assistance.[49] These

[46] *Ibid.*, para 19.

[47] UN Committee on Economic, Social and Cultural Rights, *General Comment No. 13 on the Right to Education (Article 13 of the Covenant)*, para 56.

[48] *Ibid.*, para 57.

[49] Michael Nyongesa Wabwile, *Legal Protection of Social and Economic Rights of Children in Developing Countries: Reassessing International Cooperation and Responsibility* (Intersentia, 2010), 108.

obligations involve both the promotion of rights through diplomatic means, but also the commitment of resources, including financial and technical assistance, or the provision of food and water, particularly from developed states to developing states.

3.4 International Cooperation and the Convention on the Rights of the Child 1989

International cooperation is also present as a foundational principle of other more specialised treaty regimes. In the Preamble to the Convention on the Rights of the Child (CRC),[50] 'the importance of international cooperation for improving the living conditions of children in every country, in particular in the developing countries' is recognised in the Preamble. Article 4 provides that 'with regard to economic, social and cultural rights, States parties shall undertake such measures to the maximum extent of their available resources and, where needed, within the framework of international cooperation'. Indeed, international cooperation is emphasised throughout the CRC as a tool for the universal realisation of the rights in it.[51] While there are a number of examples, two concrete positive obligations that require specific action are highlighted for the purposes of this inquiry. Under Article 23(4) it is stated that

> States parties shall promote, in the spirit of international cooperation, the exchange of information in the field of preventive health care and of medical, psychological and functional treatment of disabled children. . . . In this regard, particular account shall be taken of the needs of developing countries.

Here states are encouraged to share information in an effort to improve the physical and mental health of disabled children in other countries.

The Optional Protocols to the CRC also set out extraterritorial obligations for state parties in the form of a call for international cooperation to ensure the effective implementation of these protocols. Under Article 7(1) of the Optional Protocol on Armed Conflict,[52] state parties are

[50] United Nations Convention on the Rights of the Child, 20 November 1989, 1577 UNTS 3.

[51] For example, Article 17(b) (right of children to access information and material), Article 22 (right of children to access appropriate protection and humanitarian assistance when seeking asylum or tracing their parents and family), Article 24(4) (general right of children to the highest attainable standard of health), and Article 28 (right of children to education).

[52] Optional Protocol to the Convention on the Rights of the Child on the Involvement of Children in Armed Conflict, 12 February 2002, 2173 UNTS 222.

obliged to cooperate in the implementation of the Protocol, and this cooperation can include, it goes on to stipulate, assistance of a technical or financial kind. Article 7(2) then provides that 'States parties in a position to do so shall provide such assistance through existing multilateral, bilateral or other programmes, or, *inter alia*, through a voluntary fund'. Similarly, Article 10(3) of the Optional Protocol on the Sale of Children, Child Prostitution and Child Pornography to the CRC provides that

> States Parties shall promote the strengthening of international cooperation in order to address the root causes, such as poverty and underdevelopment, contributing to the vulnerability of children to the sale of children, child prostitution, child pornography and child sex tourism.[53]

A call for international cooperation aimed at addressing the underlying causes of the exploitation of children is made in this context. Moreover, providing examples of the positive international action states are expected to take on behalf of potential victims abroad, Article 10(4) of the same protocol requires that states should provide financial, technical or other assistance where they can through existing programmes.

In addition to the explicit provisions of the CRC and its Optional Protocols, state practice in the area of children's rights would appear to confirm the presence of altruistic legal relationships. For example, in the context of the promotion of children's rights, Sweden has stated to the Committee on the Rights of the Child that 'the Convention creates a responsibility towards all the children of the world'.[54] Moreover, Canada has asserted in a periodic report to the Committee that it has sought to effect 'change by creating and sustaining constructive bilateral relationships with other countries and through cooperative efforts with international agencies such as UNICEF'.[55] Further still, the United Kingdom has recognised that there are legal obligations under Article 4 of the CRC to ensure that rights under the Convention are realised. For example, in a UK periodic report to the Child Rights Committee, it stated:

> The objective of [the UK Department for International Development] in promoting children's rights is to support international efforts to enhance

[53] Optional Protocol to the Convention on the Rights of the Child on the Sale of Children, Child Prostitution and Child Pornography, 18 January 2002, 2171 UNTS 227.

[54] *Initial Report of the State Party: Sweden*, 7 September 1992, UN Doc. CRC/C/3/Add.1, para 8.

[55] *Second Periodic Report: Canada*, 12 March 2003, UN Doc. CRC/C/83/Add.6, para 25.

> children's well-being through implementation of the Convention on the Rights of the Child, promoting children's protection and participation, alongside the provision of effective and sustainable services for children's survival and development. In partnership with Governments and civil society organizations, [the UK] supports, and ... assists in meeting the rights set out in the Convention on the Rights of the Child. Provision of services such as health care, education, and welfare is an essential part of the United Kingdom's contribution to promoting children's rights in the countries where [it] works.[56]

That State Parties to the CRC have obligations beyond their own jurisdiction in respect of the rights under the Convention is evident also in General Comment No. 5 of the UN Committee on the Rights of the Child, which recognises that a lack of financial or other resources can hinder the implementation of economic, social and cultural rights and advocates for the progressive realisation of these rights.[57] In this way, such rights must be implemented to the extent possible by all states according to their available resources. Where they require international cooperation for full implementation of these rights, states in need must seek this. And for those that are able to provide assistance, General Comment No. 5 provides that '[w]hen States ratify the Convention, they take upon themselves obligations not only to implement it within their jurisdiction, but also to contribute, through international cooperation, to global implementation'.[58]

As is the case under the International Covenant on Economic, Social and Cultural Rights, international cooperation has two dimensions in the context of the CRC: those in need of further resources for the realisation of rights under the Convention must seek them, and those who have committed to the Convention must contribute to the implementation of the treaty beyond their borders. Moreover, in General Comment No. 5, the Committee also emphasises the centrality of international cooperation to the Convention and, more particularly, in the realisation of the rights of all children:

> Article 4 emphasizes that implementation of the Convention is a cooperative exercise for the States of the world. This article and others in the Convention highlight the need for international cooperation. The

[56] *Periodic Report: UK*, 14 September 1999, CRC/C/83/Add.3, Section 5.5.2.

[57] UN Committee on the Rights of the Child, *General Comment No. 5 on General Measures of Implementation of the Convention on the Rights of the Child (Articles 4, 42 and 44)*, November 2003, UN Doc. CRC/GC/2003/527, para 4.

[58] *Ibid.*

> Charter of the United Nations (Arts. 55 and 56) identifies the overall purposes of international economic and social cooperation, and members pledge themselves under the Charter 'to take joint and separate action in cooperation with the Organization' to achieve these purposes. In the United Nations Millennium Declaration and at other global meetings, including the United Nations General Assembly special session on children, States have pledged themselves, in particular, to international cooperation to eliminate poverty.[59]

Indeed, in this statement the Committee infers that cooperation is a lynchpin to the operation and implementation of the entire Convention.[60]

In this treaty context, international cooperation is once again envisaged as a conduit through which the rights in the CRC can be realised universally and the shape of such cooperation can include technical or financial assistance provided by, in particular, those countries that have the resources to implement the CRC and those that do not. It is evident that an altruistic legal relationship to ensure children in other countries can benefit from the protection of the CRC is created.

3.5 International Cooperation in Other Legal Contexts

There are many other contexts in which the principle of international cooperation finds application under international law. From state responsibility[61] to international environmental law, and in other areas of human rights law (as well as the specific human rights regimes mentioned earlier).[62]

[59] *Ibid.*, para 60.

[60] Also in the area of the rights of the child, a further manifestation of the concept of international cooperation is evident in Article 8 of the International Labour Organisation's Convention No. 182 on the Elimination of the Worst Forms of Child Labour, 1 June 1999:

> Members shall take appropriate steps to assist one another in giving effect to the provisions of this Convention through enhanced international cooperation and/or assistance including support for social and economic development, poverty eradication programmes and universal education.

[61] Article 41 of the Draft Articles requires that 'States shall cooperate to bring to an end through lawful means any serious breach within the meaning of article 40' and 'States are under a positive duty to co-operate in order to bring to an end serious breaches . . . '. See Draft Articles on Responsibility of States for Internationally Wrongful Acts, with commentaries, (2001) II(2) *YBILC* 31, 114. This will be explored further in the next chapter.

[62] See, for example, Articles 4(2) and 32(1) of the Convention on the Rights of Persons with Disabilities, 13 December 2006, 2515 UNTS 3, which call on states to engage in

A particularly interesting context for this inquiry in which international cooperation finds important application is in the various declarations and agreements aimed at furthering development. Other dimensions of the law of development will be explored in Chapter 5. However, it is pertinent to note in this chapter that a positive obligation on states to cooperate internationally is provided by the 1986 Declaration on the Right to Development,[63] which recognises that all states are responsible for the realisation of the right to development. Its Article 3.3 provides that 'States have the duty to cooperate with each other in ensuring development and eliminating obstacles to development' and its Article 4.1 notes that 'States have the duty to take steps, individually and collectively, to formulate international development policies with a view to facilitating the full realization of the right to development'. States are under an affirmative duty to pursue a legislative programme that facilitates realisation of the right to development. That there is a reference to individual and collective action would suggest that states must both take measures themselves through their own domestic policies and engage in cooperative efforts with other countries to this end. Similarly, in the earlier Charter of Economic Rights and Duties of States, its Article 17 underlines the importance of international cooperation in the realisation of development. Indeed, it emphasises that international cooperation for development is both a shared goal and a common duty for states:

> Every State should co-operate with the efforts of developing countries to accelerate their economic and social development by providing favourable external conditions and by extending active assistance to them, consistent with their development needs and objectives, with strict respect for the sovereign equality of States and free of any conditions derogating from their sovereignty.

international cooperation and specify that this should take the form of ensuring development programmes are accessible to persons with disabilities, capacity-building, information-sharing, collaborating on research, scientific and technical knowledge as well as providing financial and technical assistance to ensure the progressive realisation of rights under the Convention. See also, for example, Article 9(1) of the Convention against Torture and Other Cruel, Inhuman or Degrading Treatment or Punishment, 10 December 1984, 1465 UNTS 85 and Article 15 of the International Convention for the Protection of all Persons from Enforced Disappearance, 23 December 2010, UN Doc. A/RES/61/177, in which states have committed to giving 'one another the greatest measure of mutual assistance with a view to assisting victims of enforced disappearance, and in searching for, locating and releasing disappeared persons and, in the event of death, in exhuming and identifying them and returning their remains'.

63 UN General Assembly Resolution 41/128, Declaration on the Right to Development, 4 December 1986, UN Doc. A/RES/41/128.

In Commitment 9 of the UN World Summit for Social Development,[64] States pledged 'to increasingly and/or utilizing more efficiently the resources allocated to social development in order to achieve the goals of the Summit through national action and regional and international cooperation'.[65] Commitment 9 goes on to set out the more concrete ways in which this may be achieved.

The UN Millennium Declaration, which included the Millennium Development Goals and was adopted by the UN General Assembly, also makes an implicit reference to international cooperation:

> In addition to our separate responsibilities to our individual societies, we have a collective responsibility to uphold the principles of human dignity, equality and equity at the global level. As leaders we have a duty therefore to all the world's people, especially the most vulnerable and, in particular, the children of the world, to whom the future belongs.[66]

Furthermore, the Millennium Development Goals made a call to developed countries in a number of areas. Goal 8 stipulated a 'global partnership for development' as well as targets to develop 'an open, rule-based predictable, non-discriminatory trading system' (Target 12) and to meet the needs of the least developed countries (Target 13). In so doing, the Declaration adds yet further colour to our understanding of international cooperation, particularly in the context of development. International cooperation has played a role in forging approaches to international development, which is called by some the law of development cooperation.[67] This can involve the transfer of ODA from industrialised countries to developing countries.[68] It has also assisted in mediating the distinction between the formal equality of sovereign States under international law and the need to ensure material differences in the expected commitments of developing countries, taking into account their capacity.

International cooperation is also central to the Sustainable Development Goals (SDGs), which are seventeen goals at the heart of the 2030 Agenda for Sustainable Development endorsed by United Nations member states in General Assembly Resolution 70/1 in

[64] UN World Summit for Social Development, 6–12 March 1995, UN Doc. A/CONF.166/9.
[65] *Ibid.*, Commitment 9.
[66] United Nations Millennium Declaration, UNGA Res 55/2 (8 September 2000), UN Doc. 55/2, para 2.
[67] See Philip Dann, *The Law of Development Co-operation: A Comparative Analysis of the World Bank, EU and Germany* (Cambridge University Press, 2013).
[68] *Ibid.*, 13. See also Chapter 5 of this book.

2015.[69] Indeed, UN member states committed to address a wide variety of global challenges through cooperation, including but not limited to pursuing development,[70] giving safe haven to refugees,[71] reducing greenhouse gases[72] and tackling desertification.[73] Several of the SDGs explicitly mention international cooperation and oblige states to take action through international assistance to meet the various targets and indicators specified under each goal.[74] These references to international cooperation in the United Nation's foremost agenda for the immediate future demonstrate the importance of

69 United Nations General Assembly Resolution A/RES/70/1, 'Transforming Our World: The 2030 Agenda for Sustainable Development', 25 September 2015, UN Doc. A/RES/70/1.

70 *Ibid.*, para 18.

71 *Ibid.*, para 29.

72 *Ibid.*, para 31.

73 *Ibid.*, para 33.

74 *Ibid.*, Goal 1 ('1.a. Ensure significant mobilization of resources from a variety of sources, including through enhanced development cooperation, in order to provide adequate and predictable means for developing countries, in particular least developed countries, to implement programmes and policies to end poverty in all its dimensions'), Goal 2 ('2.a. Increase investment, including through enhanced international cooperation, in rural infrastructure, agricultural research and extension services, technology development and plant and livestock gene banks in order to enhance agricultural productive capacity in developing countries, in particular least developed countries'), Goal 4 ('4.c. By 2030, substantially increase the supply of qualified teachers, including through international cooperation for teacher training in developing countries, especially least developed countries and small island developing States'), Goal 6 ('6.5. By 2030, implement integrated water resources management at all levels, including through transboundary cooperation as appropriate', '6.a. By 2030, expand international cooperation and capacity-building support to developing countries in water- and sanitation-related activities and programmes, including water harvesting, desalination, water efficiency, wastewater treatment, recycling and reuse technologies'), Goal 7 ('7.a. By 2030, enhance international cooperation to facilitate access to clean energy research and technology, including renewable energy, energy efficiency and advanced and cleaner fossil-fuel technology, and promote investment in energy infrastructure and clean energy technology'), Goal 14 ('14.3. Minimize and address the impacts of ocean acidification, including through enhanced scientific cooperation at all levels'), Goal 16 ('16.a. Strengthen relevant national institutions, including through international cooperation, for building capacity at all levels, in particular in developing countries, to prevent violence and combat terrorism and crime'), Goal 17 ('17.6. Enhance North-South, South-South and triangular regional and international cooperation on and access to science, technology and innovation and enhance knowledge sharing on mutually agreed terms, including through improved coordination among existing mechanisms, in particular at the United Nations level, and through a global technology facilitation mechanism', '17.9. Enhance international support for implementing effective and targeted capacity-building in developing countries to support national plans to implement all the Sustainable Development Goals, including through North-South, South-South and triangular cooperation').

cooperation in realising the ambitions of the international community throughout the world and bring into sharp focus the need for a well-defined understanding of cooperation that is supported by the rule of law.[75]

3.6 International Cooperation in Its Infinite Variety

International cooperation is an 'entrenched precept' of the UN Charter system besides being central to the universal realisation of human rights.[76] For some legal scholars, international cooperation can extend to reducing poverty by reshaping the international economic system as well as investment and financial systems, participatory trading, improving access to markets for developing countries, cancelling debt incurred by developing countries and creating a system for the transfer of resources to developing countries.[77] For others, it implies that states have committed to ensuring they offer international cooperation and assistance in all aspects of their external action, including, for example, trade, security, military assistance, development and cultural exchange.[78] Indeed, several scholars argue that international cooperation should inform every element of the external action of states. In doing so, they point out that international cooperation is connected to the principle of solidarity.[79] The principle of solidarity derives from Article 55 of the UN Charter and applies particularly to those states that have an impact on other states through their economic policies and, as such, should take the interests of other states into account through such action as consultation and avoiding any measures that cause significant injury to other states and their peoples.

[75] See Laurence Boisson de Chazournes, 'The Sustainable Development Goals (SDGs) and the Rule of Law: *A Propos* SDG 6 on Access to Water and Sanitation', *114th ASIL Annual Meeting Proceedings* (2020).

[76] Margot Salomon, *Global Responsibility for Human Rights: World Poverty and the Development of International Law* (Oxford University Press, 2007).

[77] *Ibid.*, 102–103.

[78] Sigrun Skogly, *Beyond National Borders: States' Human Rights Obligations in International Cooperation* (Intersentia, 2006); see also Sigrun Skogly and Mark Gibney, 'Economic Rights and Extraterritorial Obligations' in Shareen Hertel and Lanse Minkler (eds.), *Economic Rights: Conceptual, Measurement and Policy Issues* (Cambridge University Press, 2007), 267.

[79] See Alston and Quinn, 'The Nature and Scope of States Parties' Obligations under the International Covenant on Economic, Social and Cultural Rights', 191. For more on solidarity, see Chapters 5 and 7 of this book.

This is a view that has been reflected in the Draft Declaration on the Progressive Development of Principles of Public International Law Relating to the New International Economic Order,[80] and suggests that the external action of states, particularly as regards economic policy, should take into account the interests of other states. While this is a Declaration of the International Law Association (ILA), and therefore not a legally binding principle, the ILA is a distinguished NGO and forum for the study, clarification and development of international law,[81] and may provide an authoritative indication of the development of solidarity and cooperation. This resonates with Eyal Benvenisti's idea – explored in Chapter 1 – that states as trustees of humanity should take into account the interests of foreign stakeholders in decision-making.[82]

As to the type of legal commitment, the aforementioned analysis illustrates that international cooperation serves as an altruistic legal relationship through which states have committed to fulfilling rights, particularly socio-economic rights (but also many others), and to take steps to alleviate poverty in other countries. The obligation is heaviest on developed states, who should take positive action that will incur a cost to themselves and assist the people of other states, such as ensuring the terms of trade and investment with them are amenable, sharing knowledge and transferring technology, as well as the delivery of financial assistance.[83]

Finally, there remains disagreement as to whether international cooperation leads to enforceable rights. The negotiating history of the International Covenant on Economic, Social and Cultural Rights reveals that there was a division among the negotiating states on this point and, ultimately, the issue was avoided in the final text.[84] However, it had to be considered again when the Optional Protocol to the Covenant was under

[80] Draft Declaration on the Progressive Development of Principles of Public International Law relating to the New International Economic Order, submitted by the Committee on the Legal Aspects of the New International Economic Order to the 62nd Conference of the International Law Association, Seoul, August 1986.

[81] See, International Law Association website, www.ila-hq.org/en/about_us/index.cfm.

[82] See Chapter 1 of this book; Eyal Benvenisti, 'Sovereigns as Trustees of Humanity: On the Accountability of States to Foreign Stakeholders' (2013) 107(2) *American Journal of International Law* 295.

[83] For a similar argument, see Arjun Sengupta, 'Poverty Eradication and Human Rights' in Thomas Pogge (ed.), *Freedom from Poverty as a Human Right: Who Owes What to the Very Poor?* (Oxford University Press / UNESCO, 2007), 344.

[84] Alston and Quinn, 'The Nature and Scope of States Parties' Obligations under the International Covenant on Economic, Social and Cultural Rights', 188–190.

negotiation. Developed countries in those negotiations accepted there was a moral responsibility to cooperate internationally but did not accept the Covenant provided for a legally binding obligation to cooperate for the realisation of socio-economic rights.[85] However, General Assembly resolutions and other international agreements have indicated that certain extraterritorial obligations do flow from international cooperation.[86]

International cooperation is particularly effective and can be manifested in more elaborate ways when it is found within an institutional context.[87] This is evident, for example, in the protection and management of water resources through basin organisations. These institutions have been successful at ensuring and promoting cooperative activity.[88] In a similar way, the climate-change regime is beginning to create institutional machinery around the appraisal of cooperative efforts made by developed countries in providing technological and financial assistance to developing countries so that they can mitigate and adapt to the effects of climate change.[89] As a result, cooperation is operationalised in this particular context through transparency, reporting and accountability mechanisms. Manifestations of altruism in international environmental law will be considered in Chapter 6. In the final analysis, stronger institutional mechanisms that take account of and evaluate cooperative efforts are necessary to properly operationalise cooperation for the realisation of human rights, development and environmental justice.

[85] Commission on Human Rights, 'Report of the Open-ended Working Group to Consider Options Regarding the Elaboration of an Optional Protocol to the International Covenant on Economic, Social and Cultural Rights on its Third Session', 14 March 2006, UN Doc. E/CN.4/2006/47.

[86] See, for example, UN General Assembly Resolution 59/202, The Right to Food, 31 March 2005, UN Doc. A/RES/59/202, paras 20 and 32.

[87] See, for example, Wolfgang Friedmann, *The Changing Structure of International Law* (Stevens, 1964); Georges Abi-Saab, 'Cours général de droit international public (Volume 207)' in *Collected Courses of the Hague Academy of International Law* (Brill, 1987), 93; Georges Abi-Saab, 'Whither the International Community?' (1998) 9 *European Journal of International Law* 248, 256; Pierre-Marie Dupuy, 'International Law: Torn between Coexistence, Co-operation and Globalization: General Conclusions' (1998) 9 *European Journal of International Law* 278.

[88] Laurence Boisson de Chazournes, *Fresh Water in International Law* (Oxford University Press, 2013), 30–31.

[89] Laurence Boisson de Chazournes and Jason Rudall, 'Cooperation in a Transboundary and Global Context' in Yann Aguila and Jorge E. Viñuales (eds.), *A Global Pact for the Environment – Legal Foundations* (Cambridge Centre for Environment, Energy and Natural Resource Governance (C-EENRG), 2019), 149–156.

3.7 Concluding Remarks

Through a consideration of different legal instruments that make provision for international cooperation, it has been possible to trace its dimensions and evolution. This has been by recourse to the text of the legal instruments themselves, their *travaux préparatoires*, the interpretations of relevant bodies and state practice. Moreover, academic commentary illuminates yet further dimensions to and a more comprehensive understanding of international cooperation. The inquiry has revealed that international cooperation is much broader than the pursuit of efforts at the diplomatic level. It can also include a duty to provide assistance, positive action and the commitment of resources to ensure the realisation of human rights and the pursuit of development. Further still, it can imply specific action such as the offering of technological assistance, the adoption of international measures or sharing information, for example. While the duty to cooperate is particularly aimed at developed countries to assist with the realisation of rights in developing countries, all countries are bound to take certain steps, even if this means helping to mobilise global resources. In discharging the obligations to cooperate and provide assistance, states must have the consent of the receiving state and respect human rights.

Starting from its explicit recognition in the UN Charter, the obligation of international cooperation has gradually been developed through conventional practice and its interpretation by expert groups and states. As a result, this principle has become broader and deeper over time. Today, it should be understood as an inherently other-oriented concept and as involving an altruistic commitment to the populations of other countries. Moreover, international cooperation represents a cross-cutting framework for altruistic action by states in order to help realise the rights of citizens beyond the jurisdiction of those states. In addition to being a framework and regulatory space for altruistic action, the development of the concept of international cooperation over time has revealed it also has various normative dimensions that help guide, promote and strengthen the altruistic behaviour of states in this context.

4

The Substance of Altruism in International Law: Protection for the Other

4.1 Introduction

This chapter will consider the obligations that states are under to protect individuals in third states from harm. In particular, this will involve a consideration of the duty to prevent or arrest a genocide in a third state, the emerging duty to prevent torture and the duty to ensure respect for international humanitarian law. These all have their legal basis in multilateral treaties. Given the focus on the prevention of serious human rights abuses in other countries, consideration will also be given to the responsibility to protect (R2P) doctrine, which has been endorsed by states in several multilateral instruments and represents a significant commitment by states towards citizens beyond their borders but appears to have lost traction in recent years. Finally, the chapter will consider the duty to give safe haven to those fleeing persecution in their home state.

4.2 The Duty to Prevent Genocide in a Third State

A positive obligation to prevent and punish genocide is present under the Convention on the Prevention and Punishment of the Crime of Genocide 1948.[1] Article 1 of the Genocide Convention provides as follows:

> The Contracting Parties confirm that genocide, whether committed in time of peace or in time of war, is a crime under international law which they undertake to prevent and to punish.

The extent of this obligation, particularly its extraterritorial dimension, has been the subject of jurisprudence under the Convention. In this connection, a significant development is apparent in the judgment of the International Court of Justice (ICJ) in *Application of the Convention*

[1] Convention on the Prevention and Punishment of the Crime of Genocide, 9 December 1948, 78 UNTS 277.

on the Prevention and Punishment of the Crime of Genocide (Bosnia and Herzegovina v. *Serbia and Montenegro)*.[2] In this case, the ICJ found that states have a duty to prevent genocide in third states, and in doing so referred to the origin of the Genocide Convention.[3] It also referred to its earlier advisory opinion in *Reservations to the Convention on the Prevention and Punishment of the Crime of Genocide* to underline the universality of the prevention and punishment of genocide and that cooperation is required to 'liberate mankind from such an odious scourge (Preamble to the Convention)'.[4]

Moreover, the Court illuminated the purposes that underlie the Convention and the shared nature of the interest in preventing and punishing genocide by referring again to its earlier advisory opinion:

> The Convention was manifestly adopted for a purely humanitarian and civilizing purpose. It is indeed difficult to imagine a Convention that might have this dual character to a greater degree, since its object on the one hand is to safeguard the very existence of certain human groups, and on the other to confirm and endorse the most elementary principles of morality. In such a Convention the contracting States do not have any interests of their own; they merely have, one and all, a common interest, namely the accomplishment of those high purposes which are the *raison d'etre* of the Convention. Consequently, in a convention of this type, one cannot speak of individual advantages or disadvantages to States, or of the maintenance of a perfect contractual balance between rights and duties. The high ideals which inspired the Convention, provide, by virtue of the common will of the parties, the foundation and measure of all its provisions.[5]

This reference to a common interest in the accomplishment of the high purposes of the Convention reveals that the prevention of genocide is an obligation that should not be characterised in terms of reciprocity but rather in terms of solidarity to ensure no peoples, irrespective of their nationality, are subject to genocide. In this context, the duty to prevent will involve the commitment of a state to make all reasonable efforts to

[2] *Application of the Convention on the Prevention and Punishment of the Crime of Genocide (Bosnia and Herzegovina* v. *Serbia and Montenegro)*, Judgment (2007) ICJ Rep. 43.

[3] See Andrea Gattini, 'Breach of the Obligation to Prevent and Reparation Thereof in the ICJ's Genocide Judgment' (2007) 18(4) *European Journal of International Law* 695, 713.

[4] *Reservation to the Convention on the Prevention and Punishment of the Crime of Genocide*, Advisory Opinion (1951) ICJ Rep. 15, 23; see also, *Application of the Convention on the Prevention and Punishment of the Crime of Genocide (Bosnia and Herzegovina* v. *Serbia and Montenegro)*, Judgment (2007) ICJ Rep. 43, para 161.

[5] *Reservation to the Convention on the Prevention and Punishment of the Crime of Genocide*, Advisory Opinion (1951) ICJ Rep. 15, 23.

prevent a genocide being inflicted on citizens of a third country. Aside from the ideal of ensuring that genocide does not have a place in our world, there is no immediate reciprocity – in the classical legal sense of that term – to the state(s) on which this obligation falls. Moreover, it undoubtedly involves a cost to the state(s) that must engage in surveillance and, where necessary, act to prevent genocide.

Importantly for the purposes of this inquiry, the ICJ has explicitly set out that there is an obligation incumbent on states to take certain steps to prevent a genocide occurring in other countries. Indeed, the Court confirmed that 'responsibility is . . . incurred if the State manifestly failed to take all measures which were within its power, and which might have contributed to preventing the genocide'.[6] A state may even violate the obligation if it could not be sure that genocide would in fact be committed.[7] The Court noted that the obligation to act is triggered as soon as the state is aware of the risk that genocide may be committed and, to this end, a constructive knowledge test is applied.[8] Accordingly, since it is awareness of a risk that serves as the threshold, the obligation may in fact be triggered before the act of genocide is actually committed.[9]

[6] *Application of the Convention on the Prevention and Punishment of the Crime of Genocide (Bosnia and Herzegovina v. Serbia and Montenegro)*, Judgment (2007) ICJ Rep. 43, para 430.

[7] Rosalyn Higgins, 'Ethics and International Law' (2010) 23 *Leiden Journal of International Law* 277, 287.

[8] See *ibid.*, 287: This indicates the obligation is new given that the existing crime of complicity in genocide 'requires proof both that the State was aware that genocide was about to be committed or was in progress and that the state took positive action to furnish aid or assistance to the perpetrators'.

[9] Andreas Zimmermann has highlighted the scope of this obligation:

> One wonders whether States will over time realise the potential of this legal obligation, as carved out by the Court, and, eventually, the Court might itself have a chance to elaborate on it further. One example should be mentioned which might underline the far-reaching consequences of the duty to prevent genocide. If one takes the example of the genocide in Srebrenica, one wonders whether the Netherlands, which at the time was present in the area as part of the UN-mandated UN Protection Force (UNPROFOR), had indeed fulfilled its duty arising under Article 1 of the Genocide Convention.

Andreas Zimmermann, 'The Obligation to Prevent Genocide: Towards a General Responsibility to Protect?' in Ulrich Fastenrath *et al.* (eds.), *From Bilateralism to Community Interest: Essays in Honour of Judge Bruno Simma* (Oxford University Press, 2011), 629–645. In July 2019, the Dutch Supreme Court ruled that the Netherlands was 10 per cent responsible for the deaths that occurred while its battalion Dutchbat III was stationed at a nearby UN peacekeeping base during the Bosnian War that took place between 1992–1995. The Court revised this liability down from the 30 per cent that had

This is a very bold statement and indicates that there is an obligation to take all measures that may help to prevent genocide. That said, mass murder is likely to require both time and resources, both of which should make it evident to third states that certain individuals may be in danger.[10] Thus, a constructive knowledge test is not an unreasonable obligation to place on third states. In elaborating the nature of the measures to be taken, the Court considered the following elements were relevant in establishing whether an obligation to prevent genocide in another country had been fulfilled:

> The first, which varies greatly from one State to another, is clearly the capacity to influence effectively the action of persons likely to commit, or already committing, genocide. This capacity itself depends, among other things, on the geographical distances of the State concerned from the scene of the events, and on the strength of the political links, as well as links of all other kinds, between authorities of that State and the main actors in the events. The State's capacity to influence must also be assessed by legal criteria, since it is clear that every State may only act within the limits permitted by international law; seen thus, a State's capacity to influence may vary depending on its particular legal position vis-à-vis the situations and persons facing the danger, or the reality, of genocide.[11]

For the Court, influence was an important determining factor. It went on to define that influence included the capacity to effectively change the behaviour of those committing or likely to commit genocide.[12] This capacity to influence would turn upon proximity, including geographical proximity, and association between the state and the perpetrators of genocide.[13] If influence is in the test, it has been argued that the Court

been found by the Court of Appeals, adding that it was possible the Dutch forces could have prevented 350 deaths if these Muslim men fleeing Serbian forces had not been refused entry into the Dutch compound. *Mothers of Srebrenica Association et al.* v. *The Netherlands*, Supreme Court of the Netherlands, Judgment of 19 July 2019, ECLI:NL:HR:2019:1223 (English translation: ECLI:NL:HR:2019:1284). For a comprehensive critique of this judgment from the perspective of international law, see Cedric Ryngaert and Otto Spijkers, 'The End of the Road: State Liability for Acts of UN Peacekeeping Contingents after the Dutch Supreme Court's Judgment in *Mothers of Srebrenica* (2019)' (2019) 66 *Netherlands International Law Review* 537.

10 W. Michael Reisman, 'Acting before Victims Become Victims: Preventing and Arresting Mass Murder' (2008) *Faculty Scholarship Series*, Paper 962.

11 *Application of the Convention on the Prevention and Punishment of the Crime of Genocide (Bosnia and Herzegovina* v. *Serbia and Montenegro)*, Judgment (2007) ICJ Rep. 43, para 430.

12 *Ibid.*

13 *Ibid.*

had no reason to introduce geographical proximity.[14] Indeed, what the Court gives with one hand to extraterritorial obligations, it does partly take away with the other in this respect. The relevance of geographical proximity in the modern world in preventing one of the most heinous crimes known to humankind is certainly controversial. Nevertheless, influence is a significant step forward.[15]

It is also important to point out that the Court suggests the obligation to prevent genocide is not linked to the exercise of jurisdiction over a territory.[16] Under most human rights treaties, positive obligations are only applicable in respect of the territory over which a State exercises jurisdiction.[17] In this way the Court's interpretation of the Genocide Convention as extending to situations where a state does not exert jurisdiction or effective control but rather has influence, gives this particular obligation a special character. In his Separate Opinion, Judge Ranjeva said of the duty to prevent:

> [i]n law, international responsibility for omission is recognized in order to safeguard the fundamental interests of the international community. Stipulating the obligation to prevent is part of an approach to international legal relations based on international or even global solidarity. This approach thus adds a new international legal relations dimension to the interpretation of legal relations.[18]

In *Bosnia and Herzegovina* v. *Serbia and Montenegro*, the ICJ held that the duty to prevent genocide was 'normative and compelling' in response to Serbia's submission that fulfilment of the obligation to punish relieved it of any further obligation to prevent.[19] In so holding, the Court stressed that the obligation to prevent was one of conduct and not one of result, concluding that 'if the State manifestly failed to take all measures which

[14] Malcolm Langford, Martin Scheinin, Wouter Vandenhole and Willem van Genugten, 'Introduction and Key Themes' in Malcolm Langford, Martin Scheinin, Wouter Vandenhole and Willem van Genugten (eds.), *Global Justice, State Duties: The Extra-Territorial Scope of Economic, Social and Cultural Rights in International Law* (Cambridge University Press, 2012), 35.

[15] *Ibid.*

[16] Luke Glanville, 'The Responsibility to Protect Beyond Borders' (2012) 12(1) *Human Rights Law Review* 1.

[17] Marco Milanovic, 'State Responsibility for Genocide: A Follow-Up' (2007) 18 *European Journal of International Law* 669, 670–671.

[18] *Application of the Convention on the Prevention and Punishment of the Crime of Genocide (Bosnia and Herzegovina* v. *Serbia and Montenegro)*, Separate Opinion of Judge Ranjeva (2007) ICJ Rep. 43, para 1.

[19] *Application of the Convention on the Prevention and Punishment of the Crime of Genocide (Bosnia and Herzegovina* v. *Serbia and Montenegro)*, Judgment (2007) ICJ Rep. 43.

were within its power, and which might have contributed to preventing the genocide',[20] its obligation to prevent would not be fulfilled. As such, a state cannot claim that its efforts would not have prevented the genocide. Such a claim has been characterised as irrelevant as regards the violation of the obligation as well as excluding the possibility that several states may have been able to prevent the genocide through their collective action.[21] Giving further dimensions to the obligation, the Court said 'the obligation of States parties is rather to employ all means reasonably available to them, so as to prevent genocide as far as possible'. The Court then referred to 'due diligence' as the relevant standard of assessment.[22]

Importantly, the Court took the occasion to emphasise that the obligation to prevent has a separate legal existence from the obligation to punish.[23] The Court went on to note that

> [the duty to prevent] is not merged in the duty to punish, nor can it be regarded as simply a component of that duty. It has its own scope, which extends beyond the particular case envisaged in Article VIII, namely reference to the competent organs of the United Nations, for them to take such action as they deem appropriate.[24]

An approach of prevention, as an alternative or even supplementary to justice mechanisms after the fact is surely to be welcomed. Indeed, since Nuremberg the approach has been to act after a genocide or mass atrocity has taken place to set up a criminal tribunal or other process.[25] This is illustrated by the Genocide Convention itself, which provides for numerous means of punishment after the fact,[26] but has only one provision dedicated to prevention under Article 8. This is despite the apparent

20 *Ibid.*

21 Higgins, 'Ethics and International Law', 286. Knut Dörmann and Jose Serralvo, 'Common Article 1 to the Geneva Conventions and the Obligation to Prevent International Humanitarian Law Violations' (2014) 96 *International Review of the Red Cross* 707, 729. *Application of the Convention on the Prevention and Punishment of the Crime of Genocide (Bosnia and Herzegovina* v. *Serbia and Montenegro)*, Judgment (2007) ICJ Rep. 43, para 430.

22 *Application of the Convention on the Prevention and Punishment of the Crime of Genocide (Bosnia and Herzegovina* v. *Serbia and Montenegro)*, Judgment (2007) ICJ Rep. 43, para 430.

23 *Ibid.*, para 427.

24 *Ibid.*

25 Reisman, 'Acting before Victims Become Victims: Preventing and Arresting Mass Murder'.

26 See, for example, Articles 4, 5, 6 and 7, Genocide Convention.

priority that is accorded to prevention in Article 1 of the Convention. Elaborating on prevention, Article 8 provides that

> [a]ny Contracting Party may call upon the competent organs of the United Nations to take such action under the Charter of the United Nations as they consider appropriate for the prevention and suppression of acts of genocide or any of the other acts enumerated in Article III.

The text of this provision in particular – but also other provisions under the Genocide Convention – brings the progressive nature of the ICJ's judgment in this case into sharp focus. No mention is made of a hard obligation on third states to prevent a genocide occurring in another country. While Article 8 of the Genocide Convention refers to the possibility states have to request assistance from the relevant organs of the United Nations, the ICJ was quick to point out that the obligation to prevent has a scope beyond that particular possibility. The Court said,

> [e]ven if and when these organs have been called upon, this does not mean that the States parties to the Convention are relieved of the obligation to take such action as they can to prevent genocide from occurring, while respecting the United Nations Charter and any decisions that may have been taken by its competent organs.[27]

Moreover, the use of the words 'may' and 'as they consider appropriate' in Article 8 suggest something of a discretionary nature to the commitment under that provision. The Court's interpretation of the obligation to prevent is, evidently, a much stronger commitment on the part of states. Indeed, the previously opaque obligation to prevent or arrest genocide has been clarified and is acquiring real legal substance.[28]

The Court's judgment, however, was issued in a quickly developing context. In particular, it was preceded by several other developments in the early 2000s, including the R2P doctrine, which we will return to later. As such, it is possible the Court understood it had a mandate to develop the discretionary character of Article 8 into a harder commitment.[29]

In this case, the ICJ ultimately found that Serbia had failed to prevent the occurrence of a genocide and it had the means to do

[27] *Application of the Convention on the Prevention and Punishment of the Crime of Genocide (Bosnia and Herzegovina* v. *Serbia and Montenegro)*, Judgment (2007) ICJ Rep. 43, para 427.

[28] Reisman, 'Acting before Victims Become Victims: Preventing and Arresting Mass Murder', 84.

[29] *Ibid.*, 70.

so.[30] It is important to point out that the Court nevertheless placed several limits on the reach of its reasoning. For example, the ICJ noted that an omission to act cannot lead to complicity in the genocide.[31] Moreover, the Court emphasised that the duty to prevent may only be breached if a wrongful act is committed.[32] In so doing, the Court relied on Article 14(3) of the International Law Commission's (ILC) Draft Articles on State Responsibility, which provides that '[t]he breach of an international obligation requiring a State to prevent a given event occurs when the event occurs'. Previously, in its Provisional Measures Order, the Court had indicated that the obligation to prevent would require a 'positive obligation' to endeavour to ensure the acts in question do not occur. The Court has said that states were under a 'clear obligation to do all in their power to prevent the commission of any such acts in the future'.[33] This may be contrasted with the Court's assertion that the actions of the preventing state would only be judged when the violation occurs.[34]

There is agreement among scholars that this case is significant for the development of bystander responsibility in international law. Indeed, some have highlighted that states have an obligation to prevent genocide in third states and, significantly, can be held legally responsible for a breach of that obligation.[35] However, it is prudent to flag some of the other limitations that the Court built into its judgment. To this end, it stated that its decision does not 'purport to establish a general jurisprudence applicable to all cases where a treaty

30 *Application of the Convention on the Prevention and Punishment of the Crime of Genocide (Bosnia and Herzegovina* v. *Serbia and Montenegro)*, Judgment (2007) ICJ Rep. 43, paras 428–438.

31 *Ibid.*, para 432.

32 *Ibid.*

33 *Application of the Convention on the Prevention and Punishment of the Crime of Genocide (Bosnia-Herzegovina* v. *Serbia and Montenegro*), Provisional Measures Order (1993) ICJ Rep. 22, para 45. See also Laurence Boisson de Chazournes, 'Les ordonnances en indica tion de mesures conservatoires dans l'affaire relative à l'application de la convention pour law prevention et la repression du crime de genocide' (1993) 39 *Annuaire français de droit international* 515, 533; Pierre-Marie Dupuy, 'Reviewing the Difficulties of Codification: On Ago's Classification of Obligations of Means and Obligations of Result in Relation to State Responsibility' (1999) 10 *European Journal of International Law* 366, 384; Gattini, 'Breach of the Obligation to Prevent and Reparation Thereof in the ICJ's Genocide Judgment', 702.

34 Gattini, 'Breach of the Obligation to Prevent and Reparation Thereof in the ICJ's Genocide Judgment', 701.

35 André Nollkaemper, '"Failures to Protect" in International Law' in Marc Weller (ed.), *Handbook on the Prohibition of the Use of Force* (Oxford University Press, 2014), 442.

instrument, or other binding legal norm, includes an obligation for States to prevent certain acts'.[36] Similarly, it ruled out that there might be 'a general obligation on States to prevent the commission by other persons or entities of acts contrary to certain norms of general international law'.[37] However, as will be explored later, the Court may have left the door ajar to read a duty to prevent with an extraterritorial orientation into other treaties.

Despite the limitations employed by the Court, it has been suggested that the judgment provides a useful toolbox that can be used to develop a general notion of responsibility for the failure to act in other atrocity crimes. Some have characterised the obligation that the Court set out as a 'protection duty'.[38] This protection duty is multifaceted, including as it does the tort based notion of the duty of care, the standard of constructive knowledge of genocide and the distinction made between the responsibility to prevent and complicity in genocide.[39] Moreover, the Court's judgment in the *Bosnia and Herzegovina* v. *Serbia and Montenegro* case suggests that there may indeed be other obligations to protect people in third countries from mass atrocity crimes given the peremptory and *erga omnes* nature of such international crimes. Indeed, the Court did emphasise the need to safeguard certain humanitarian values, in particular those of an *erga omnes* character.[40]

[36] *Application of the Convention on the Prevention and Punishment of the Crime of Genocide (Bosnia and Herzegovina* v. *Serbia and Montenegro),* Judgment (2007) ICJ Rep. 43, para 429.

[37] *Ibid.*

[38] Steven Ratner, *The Thin Justice of International Law: A Moral Reckoning of the Law of Nations* (Oxford University Press, 2015), 310, also noting that '[w]e might be witnessing such a trend in the Security Council's decision to authorize aid agencies to deliver supplies to rebel-controlled areas of Syria despite the opposition of the government. SC Res. 2165 (14 July 2014)'.

[39] Louise Arbour, 'The Responsibility to Protect as a Duty of Care in International Law' (2008) 34(3) *Review of International Studies* 445.

[40] Glanville, 'The Responsibility to Protect Beyond Borders', 26. See also, Andrew Clapham, 'Rights and Responsibilities: A Legal Perspective' in Oliver Jütersonke and Keith Krause (eds.), *From Rights to Responsibilities: Rethinking Interventions for Humanitarian Purposes* (Geneva: Programme for Strategic and International Security Studies, 2006), 61. It is arguable that this is supported by the ILC Draft Articles on State Responsibility, which at Article 41(1) provide that 'States shall cooperate to bring an end through lawful means any serious breaches'. As to the form of cooperation, the ILC Commentaries to the Draft Articles state that cooperation could be 'organized in the framework of a competent international organization, in particular the United Nations' or it could take place outside of an institutional context. See Glanville, 'Responsibility to Protect Beyond Borders', 27.

The Court established that the concept of 'due diligence' requires *in concreto* evaluation.[41] As such, there now exists a standard for prevention based on a duty to act when a State has objective knowledge of a 'grave risk', which in turn acts as a benchmark to assess whether an extraterritorial obligation may be triggered.[42] The standard of due diligence has been applied in many legal systems with success and future situations might draw upon this practice to assess the operation of the protection duty. Two notable cases at the regional level include the *Velasquez-Rodriguez* case[43] before the Inter-American Court of Human Rights and *Osman* v. *UK* before the European Court of Human Rights.[44] The due diligence standard – to take reasonable measures to prevent violations in so far as possible in international practice, especially as articulated in the *Bosnia and Herzegovina* v. *Serbia and Montenegro* judgment – shows that there could be a trend towards the emergence of a positive obligation to protect people in third states from mass atrocities.[45]

On 11 November 2019, the Gambia instituted proceedings at the ICJ, alleging that Myanmar has committed a genocide through its treatment of the Rohingya people.[46] An Independent International Fact-Finding Mission on Myanmar was established by the UN Human Rights Council in 2017 and subsequently reported that it had prima facie evidence that Myanmar had engaged in the crime of genocide.[47] Moreover, the UN Special Adviser on the Prevention of Genocide and the UN Special Rapporteur on the Situation of Human Rights in Myanmar both indicated that a genocide could have been committed.[48] On 23 January 2020,

41 Sheri P. Rosenberg, 'Responsibility to Protect: A Framework for Prevention' (2009) 1 *Global Responsibility to Protect* 442, 467.

42 *Ibid.*, 472.

43 *Velasquez Rodriguez* v. *Honduras*, Judgment, Inter-Am.Ct.H. R. (ser. C) No. 4.

44 Case No. 87/1997/871/1083, *Osman* v. *United Kingdom* (1998) EHRR 101; [2000] 29 EHRR 245.

45 Rosenberg, 'Responsibility to Protect: A Framework for Prevention', 477.

46 *Application of the Convention on the Prevention and Punishment of the Crime of Genocide (The Gambia* v. *Myanmar)*, ICJ, 11 November 2019, www.icj-cij.org/files/case-related/178/178-20191111-APP-01-00-EN.pdf.

47 See Human Rights Council, Situation of human rights in Myanmar, Resolution of 24 March 2017 (A/HRC/RES/34/22); Human Rights Council, Report of the detailed findings of the Independent Fact-Finding Mission on Myanmar, 17 September 2018 (A/HRC/39/CRP.2).

48 See UN Secretary-General/Office on Genocide Prevention and the Responsibility to Protect, Note to Correspondents: Statement by Adama Dieng, United Nations Special Adviser on the Prevention of Genocide, on his visit to Bangladesh to assess the situation of Rohingya refugees from Myanmar, 12 March 2018, www.un.org/sg/en/content/sg/

the ICJ indicated provisional measures, in particular that Myanmar take measures in accordance with its obligations under the Genocide Convention to prevent, inter alia, the killing, injury or destruction of the group, as well as preserve any evidence in relation to the allegations of the breaches of the Genocide Convention.[49] The case is particularly significant because, while the prevention of genocide is an *erga omnes* obligation as alluded to previously, as well as an *erga omnes partes* obligation under the Genocide Convention, such situations are rarely brought to the ICJ. The Court emphasised the common interest that all states have in preventing genocide and that there was no need for a state to be specially affected to have standing, basing the standing of the Gambia on obligations *erga omnes partes* under the Convention instead.[50] It reasoned:

> In view of their shared values, all the States parties to the Genocide Convention have a common interest to ensure that acts of genocide are prevented and that, if they occur, their authors do not enjoy impunity. That common interest implies that the obligations in question are owed by any State party to all the other States parties to the Convention. In its Judgment in the case concerning *Questions relating to the Obligation to Prosecute or Extradite (Belgium* v. *Senegal)*, the Court observed that the relevant provisions in the Convention against Torture were 'similar' to those in the Genocide Convention. The Court held that these provisions generated 'obligations [which] may be defined as "obligations *erga omnes partes*" in the sense that each State party has an interest in compliance with them in any given case' (Judgment, I.C.J. Reports 2012(II), p.449, para. 68). It follows that any State party to the Genocide Convention, and not only a specially affected State, may invoke the responsibility of another State party with a view to ascertaining the alleged failure to

note-correspondents/2018-03-12/note-correspondents-statement-adama-dieng-united-nations. Office of the United Nations High Commission for Human Rights, Myanmar, 'UN expert says "lost optimism but still hopes for promised democratic transition"', 23 January 2020, www.ohchr.org/en/NewsEvents/Pages/DisplayNews.aspx?NewsID=25494&LangID=E.

49 *Application of the Convention on the Prevention and Punishment of the Crime of Genocide (The Gambia* v. *Myanmar)*, ICJ, Order of Provisional Measures, 23 January 2020, para 86, www.icj-cij.org/files/case-related/178/178-20200123-ORD-01-00-EN.pdf. Interestingly, the indication of provisional measures was unanimous, and included Myanmar's Judge ad hoc Kress (see also Declaration of Judge ad hoc Kress, www.icj-cij.org/files/case-related/178/178-20200123-ORD-01-03-EN.pdf).

50 *Ibid.*, paras 41–42. In coming to this conclusion, the Court relied on its previous findings in its Advisory Opinion on the *Reservations to the Convention on the Prevention and Punishment of the Crime of Genocide* (1951) ICJ Rep. 15 and *Questions relating to the Obligation to Prosecute or Extradite (Belgium* v. *Senegal)* (2012) ICJ Rep. 422.

> comply with its obligations *erga omnes partes*, and to bring that failure to an end.[51]

Legal commentators have characterised the Gambia's decision to bring the case (which has been expressly supported by the 57 other states of the Organization of Islamic Cooperation as well as the Netherlands and Canada[52]) as an act of 'legal altruism' because '[i]t has nothing to materially gain from the proceedings, indeed it will incur significant costs in taking the case'.[53] The Gambia is neither geographically connected nor likely to be significantly affected by the actions of Myanmar and yet it has undertaken to pursue the legal proceedings on behalf of the Rohingya people. Moreover, it has also been observed that the ICJ has been liberal in its approach to standing in the case as well as in its provisional measures order.[54] While the case has a long way to run (at the time of writing), the order of provisional measures is a positive sign that the Rohingya may benefit from the altruistic actions of those states that have brought the case and they will get the justice they deserve for any wrongdoing suffered because of what the Gambia and other countries have done on their behalf.

Another source of support that the obligation to prevent may be developed further in the future is the fact that the ICJ in its *Bosnia and Herzegovina* v. *Serbia and Montenegro* case also listed other international instruments which contain a specific obligation to prevent. Those it referred to included the Convention against Torture and Other Cruel, Inhuman or Degrading Treatment or Punishment 1984 (Article 2),[55] the

[51] *Ibid.*, para 41.

[52] Joint Statement of Canada and the Kingdom of the Netherlands Regarding Intention to Intervene in *The Gambia* v. *Myanmar* Case at the International Court of Justice, *Diplomatic Statement of the Government of the Netherlands*, 2 September 2020, www.government.nl/documents/diplomatic-statements/2020/09/02/joint-statement-of-canada-and-the-kingdom-of-the-netherlands-regarding-intention-to-intervene-in-the-gambia-v.-myanmar-case-at-the-international-court-of-justice; Priya Pillai, 'Canada and The Netherlands: New Intervention in *The Gambia* v. *Myanmar* at the International Court of Justice' *Opinio Juris*, 3 September 2020, http://opiniojuris.org/2020/09/03/canada-and-the-netherlands-new-intervention-in-the-gambia-v-myanmar-at-the-international-court-of-justice/.

[53] Joseph Powderly, 'Does "The Lady Doth Protest" Mark the Beginning of Myanmar's Reckoning?' *Justiceinfo.net*, 10 December 2019, www.justiceinfo.net/en/justiceinfo-comment-and-debate/opinion/43190-the-lady-doth-protest-beginning-myanmar-reckoning.html.

[54] Priya Pillai, 'Expanding the Scope of Provisional Measures under the Genocide Convention' (2020) 79(2) *Cambridge Law Journal* 201.

[55] Convention against Torture and Other Cruel, Inhuman or Degrading Treatment or Punishment, 10 December 1984, 1465 UNTS 85.

Convention on the Prevention and Punishment of Crimes against Internationally Protected Persons, Including Diplomatic Agents 1973 (Article 4),[56] the Convention on the Safety of United Nations and Associated Personnel 1994 (Article 11),[57] the International Convention on the Suppression of Terrorist Bombings 1997 (Article 15).[58] However, inserting a caveat, the Court noted that '[t]he content of the duty to prevent varies from one instrument to another, according to the wording of the relevant provisions, and depending of the nature of the acts to be prevented'.[59] We will explore the potential ramifications of this for obligations to prevent in other conventions, in particular Article 2 of the Convention against Torture and Other Cruel, Inhuman or Degrading Treatment or Punishment 1984, in the next section.

4.3 The Emerging Duty to Prevent Torture

This section analyses the potential for other positive duties to prevent international crimes, especially in light of the ICJ's judgment in *Bosnia and Herzegovina* v. *Serbia and Montenegro*. A focus will be placed on the prohibition of torture for illustrative purposes. Under the Convention against Torture and Other Cruel, Inhuman or Degrading Treatment or Punishment of 1984 (Convention against Torture), torture is prohibited in an absolute and non-derogable sense under international law.[60] Indeed, the prohibition of torture is a peremptory norm of international law. Article 2(1) of the Convention against Torture provides that '[e]ach State Party shall take effective legislative, administrative, judicial or other measures to prevent acts of torture in any territory under its jurisdiction'.

In accordance with this provision, states are obliged to act in order to reinforce the prohibition against torture in territories under their

[56] Prevention and Punishment of Crimes against Internationally Protected Persons, Including Diplomatic Agents, 14 December 1973, 1035 UNTS 167.

[57] Convention on the Safety of United Nations and Associated Personnel, 9 December 1994, 2051 UNTS 363.

[58] International Convention on the Suppression of Terrorist Bombings, 15 December 1997, 2149 UNTS 256.

[59] *Application of the Convention on the Prevention and Punishment of the Crime of Genocide (Bosnia and Herzegovina* v. *Serbia and Montenegro),* Judgment (2007) ICJ Rep. 43, para 429.

[60] The same prohibition exists under customary international law. Torture is also prohibited under Article 5 of the Universal Declaration of Human Rights, 10 December 1948, 999 UNTS 302 and Article 7 of the International Covenant on Civil and Political Rights, 16 December 1966, 999 UNTS 171.

jurisdiction, and these measures must be effective in preventing torture. Should the measures fail in preventing torture, the Convention against Torture requires that states revise the measures or adopt more effective measures. First and foremost, the Convention demands that states make torture a punishable offence under their criminal law in accordance with the elements of torture as defined under Article 1 of the Convention. This required action is, however, explicitly linked to the territories over which the states parties have jurisdiction.

However, given that the prohibition is a *jus cogens* norm,[61] it is incumbent upon states not only to refrain from engaging in torture within their territories, but it is also arguable that they have an obligation to help to ensure other countries do not engage in torture.[62] It has been argued that the obligation to prevent violations of peremptory norms is an emerging principle of international law and, in this context, Andrew Clapham observes that there exists 'the legal germs of a responsibility to protect people from torture in far-away lands'.[63] The legal basis for such a claim is Articles 40 and 41 of the ILC Draft Articles on State Responsibility, which oblige states to cooperate to bring serious breaches of an obligation arising under a peremptory norm of international law to an end.[64] As the Commentaries to the Draft Articles indicate, a peremptory norm of international law is defined by Article 53 of the Vienna Convention on the Law of Treaties of 1969 as a norm, which is accepted and recognised by the international community of states as a whole as a norm from which no derogation is permitted and which can be modified only by a subsequent norm of general international law having the same character.

[61] Case No. 15318/89, *Prosecutor* v. *Furundžija*, International Tribunal for the Prosecution of Persons Responsible for Serious Violations of International Humanitarian Law Committed in the Territory of the former Yugoslavia since 1991, Judgment, 10 December 1998, para 153.

[62] Andrew Clapham, 'Responsibility to Protect: "Some Sort of Commitment"' in Vincent Chetail (ed.), *Conflits, sécurité et coopération: Liber amicorum Victor-Yves Ghebali* (Bruylant, 2007), 169–192.

[63] Clapham, 'Rights and Responsibilities: A Legal Perspective', 65.

[64] See, Draft Articles on Responsibility of States for Internationally Wrongful Acts, with Commentaries, (2001) II(2) *YBILC* 31, 112–116. See also *Legal Consequences of the Construction of a Wall in the Occupied Palestinian Territory*, Advisory Opinion (2004) ICJ Rep. 136, para 159; *A* v. *Secretary of State for the Home Department* [2005] UKHL 71. In the latter case, Lord Bingham stated that Article 41 of the ILC Draft Articles on State Responsibility required 'states to cooperate to bring to an end through lawful means any serious breach of an obligation under a peremptory norm of general international law' (para 34).

While the Commentaries to the Draft Articles refrain from providing a full list of peremptory norms, it is noted that such norms result 'from those substantive rules of conduct that prohibit what has come to be seen as intolerable because of the threat it presents to the survival of States and their peoples and the most basic human values'.[65] However, the Commentaries to the Draft Articles do refer to peremptory norms around which there is broad consensus. Among these are the international crimes of aggression, slavery, genocide, racial discrimination and apartheid.[66] Also explicitly mentioned is the peremptory character of the prohibition against torture. This was not explicitly listed in the Commission's Commentary to the Draft Articles on the Law of Treaties of 1966,[67] but the Commentaries to the Draft Articles observe that this character has been confirmed by a variety of different national and international courts.[68]

As for the positive action that must be taken in respect of breaches of peremptory norms, paragraph 1 of Article 41 of the Draft Articles on State Responsibility requires that 'States ... co-operate to bring to an end through lawful means any serious breach within the meaning of article 40'. This is described by the ILC as part of the 'special legal obligations of States faced with the commission of "serious breaches" in the sense of article 40' and that 'States are under a positive duty to co-operate in order to bring to an end serious breaches'.[69] A positive legal obligation to take cooperative action is thus envisaged. Moreover, the duty to cooperate is incumbent on all states, regardless of whether they are directly affected by the serious breach.[70] The ILC concluded that, while paragraph 1 of Article 41 may be a reflection of the progressive development of international law,

[65] Draft Articles on Responsibility of States for Internationally Wrongful Acts, with Commentaries, 112.

[66] *Ibid.*

[67] International Law Commission, Draft Articles on the Law of Treaties, with Commentaries II (1966) *YBILC* 187.

[68] See, US Court of Appeals, Ninth Circuit, *Siderman de Blake and Others* v. *The Republic of Argentina and Others* (1992) 103 *ILR* 455, 471; the United Kingdom Court of Appeal in *Al Adsani* v. *Government of Kuwait and Others* (1996) 107 *ILR* 536, 540–541; the United Kingdom House of Lords in *R.* v. *Bow Street Metropolitan Stipendiary Magistrate, ex parte Pinochet* (1998) UKHL 41, 841 and 881; the US Court of Appeals, Second Circuit, *Filartiga* v. *Pena-Irala* (1980) 77 *ILR* 169, 177–179.

[69] Draft Articles on Responsibility of States for Internationally Wrongful Acts, with Commentaries, 114.

[70] *Ibid.*

> in fact such cooperation, especially in the framework of international organizations, is carried out already in response to the gravest breaches of international law and it is often the only way of providing an effective remedy. Paragraph 1 seeks to strengthen existing mechanisms of cooperation, on the basis that all States are called upon to make an appropriate response to the serious breaches referred to in article 40.[71]

Thus, under Article 41 of the Draft Articles, there is a positive obligation on states where a breach of a peremptory norm has taken place to cooperate to bring the serious breach to an end through lawful means, not to recognise as lawful a situation created by the breach, and not to render aid in maintaining that situation.

This obligation was given an expanded meaning by the ICJ in the *Legal Consequences of the Construction of a Wall in the Occupied Palestinian Territory (Wall Opinion)* case.[72] The Court underlined that, in accordance with Article 41(2) of the ILC's Draft Articles on State Responsibility, third states not parties to a conflict were under an obligation not to render aid or assistance to a breach of international law and had an additional obligation to see that the illegal situation be brought to an end.[73]

Moreover, this opinion appears to extend further these obligations to a violation of international human rights. While there has long been a duty on states to respect, protect and fulfil human rights, the *Wall Opinion* goes further by bringing the human rights obligations of third states within the framework of state responsibility.[74] The scope of this obligation is nonetheless defined when read alongside the ICJ's decision in *Military and Paramilitary Activities In and Against Nicaragua (Nicaragua* v. *United States of America),* where it made it clear that obligations under human rights treaties should not be enforced by resort to military intervention.[75]

In the case of *Questions relating to the Obligation to Prosecute or Extradite (Belgium* v. *Senegal)*, the ICJ found for the first time in its

71 *Ibid.*

72 *Legal Consequences of the Construction of a Wall in the Occupied Palestinian Territory*, Advisory Opinion (2004) ICJ Rep. 136. The Court noted that the Hague Regulations had become part of customary international law and thus immaterial that Israel was not a party to them.

73 *Ibid.*, para 159.

74 See Carlo Focarelli, 'Common Article 1 of the 1949 Geneva Conventions: A Soap Bubble?' (2010) 21(1) *European Journal of International Law* 125, who notes a similar development with Common Article 1 of the Geneva Conventions.

75 *Military and Paramilitary Activities In and against Nicaragua (Nicaragua* v. *United States of America),* Merits (1986) ICJ Rep. 14.

history that a state could have standing on the basis of *erga omnes partes* obligations.[76] Belgium had instituted proceedings against Senegal concerning the former President of Chad, Mr Hissène Habré, who was residing in Senegal having been granted political asylum there. Belgium claimed that Senegal was in violation of Article 7 of the Convention against Torture by failing to prosecute or extradite him for alleged acts of torture and crimes against humanity.

The case is particularly interesting for the way the ICJ approached the issue of standing to invoke breaches of human rights treaties by other states. It appears to mark a significant development from the Court's reasoning in *Barcelona Traction* whereby the Court held that 'the instruments which embody human rights do not confer on States the capacity to protect the victims of infringements of such rights irrespective of their nationality'.[77] In *Belgium* v. *Senegal*, the ICJ was of the view that 'each State party has an interest in compliance with [the rights involved] in any given case'.[78] In addition to basing its claims on the fact it was a Party to the Convention against Torture, Belgium had also argued that it had a 'special interest' in the case that distinguished it from other parties to the Convention. However, once it was satisfied that Belgium was a party, the Court did not think it necessary to address Belgium's alleged 'special interest'. The Court explained:

> The common interest in compliance with the relevant obligations under the Convention against Torture implies the entitlement of each State party to the Convention to make a claim concerning the cessation of an alleged breach by another State party. If a special interest were required for that purpose, in many cases no State would be in the position to make such a claim.[79]

If states are under an obligation to expend resources to bring an end to torture (or certain other breaches of international norms for that matter) committed in other countries, this is an obligation having an altruistic character. It is the right of a person in a third state not to be subject to torture that a state must act to ensure. Thus, the obligation is owed to

[76] *Questions relating to the Obligation to Prosecute or Extradite (Belgium* v. *Senegal)* (2012) ICJ Rep. 422. This had previously been opined on by the PCIJ in the *Case of the S.S. 'Wimbledon', Britain et al.* v. *Germany*, PCIJ Series A No. 1 (1923), ICGJ 235 (PCIJ 1923), 17 August 1923.

[77] *Barcelona Traction, Light & Power Co.*, Judgment (1970) ICJ Rep. 3, para 91.

[78] *Questions relating to the Obligation to Prosecute or Extradite (Belgium* v. *Senegal)* (2012) ICJ Rep. 422, para 68.

[79] *Ibid.*, para 69.

citizens beyond a given state's own polity of interest and there will likely be no immediate reciprocal benefit to the state, other than the promotion of the community interest in preventing violations of peremptory norms and promoting the rule of law.

Given that the ILC pointed out in its Commentaries to the Draft Articles that the explicitly referred to examples of peremptory norms were not exhaustively listed in the Commentaries, and that Article 64 of the Vienna Convention on the Law of Treaties of 1969 envisaged the emergence of new peremptory norms, this category may evolve over time. As such, the duty to cooperate to bring an end to serious breaches of peremptory norms may broaden.

4.4 Inducing Compliance and the Duty to Ensure Respect

The ICJ made a distinction in the *Wall Opinion*[80] between obligations *erga omnes* and obligations imposed on states to ensure respect in the context of Common Article 1 of the Geneva Conventions.[81] While both types of obligation apply in the area of international humanitarian law, this is an important distinction to make for the purposes of the present inquiry as the obligations are different in character. In particular, they differ in terms of the positive action that is required and whom this action is directed at.

As for the former, *erga omnes* obligations – where an obligation is owed to the international community as a whole – Article 48 of the ILC's Draft Articles on State Responsibility makes provision for any state, even if it is not the injured state, to invoke the responsibility of the violating state. Relatedly, Article 54 of the Draft Articles refers to '[m]easures taken by States other than an injured State', and explains that

> [t]his chapter does not prejudice the right of any State, entitled under article 48, paragraph 1, to invoke the responsibility of another State, to

[80] *Legal Consequences of the Construction of a Wall in the Occupied Palestinian Territory*, Advisory Opinion (2004) ICJ Rep. 136.

[81] *Ibid.*, paras 155–159. Previously, the ICJ in *Barcelona Traction, Light and Power Company, Limited (Belgium* v. *Spain)*, Judgment (1970) ICJ Rep. 3, para 33, laid the foundations for the normative category of *erga omnes* obligations owed to the international community as a whole:

> An essential distinction should be drawn between the obligations of a State towards the international community as a whole, and those arising vis-à-vis another State in the field of diplomatic protection. By their very nature, the former are the concern of all States. In view of the importance of the rights involved, all States can be held to have a legal interest in their protection: they are obligations *erga omnes*.

> take lawful measures against that State to ensure cessation of the breach and reparation in the interest of the injured State or of the beneficiaries of the obligation breached.

This may leave open the possibility for non-injured states in some instances to take countermeasures as a response to breaches of *erga omnes* obligations.[82] However, the Commentary to the Draft Articles emphasises the mixed practice on this point[83] and academic literature on third party countermeasures similarly reflects the controversial nature of this provision.[84] That said, in a recent study on the topic of third party countermeasures, which includes a detailed assessment of state practice since the entry into force of the UN Charter in 1945, Martin Dawidowicz observes that states have often adopted such countermeasures in an attempt to force compliance with communitarian norms.[85] These have included trade, investment and financial embargoes, the suspension of air services, development aid, the sale of agricultural commodities, membership in international organisations, military assistance and fishing rights, all of which were a breach of the responding state's treaty obligations in the first instance. Moreover, certain assets of responsible states have also been frozen on a regular basis, which would ordinarily be in breach of general international law.[86]

For Dawidowicz, this practice is neither 'limited nor embryonic', is 'more subtle and complex than the debate in the Sixth Committee taken in isolation would otherwise suggest' and 'overall decidedly points to a virtually uniform conduct capable of forming the basis of a general rule of custom'.[87] As to the effectiveness of third party countermeasures, Dawidowicz admits that they have not always been the best way of

[82] See the Commentary to Article 22 of the Draft Articles on Responsibility of States for Internationally Wrongful Acts, which notes in part that 'Article 54 leaves open the question whether any State may take measures to ensure compliance with certain international obligations in the general interest as distinct from its own individual interest as an injured State'. See also, Denis Alland, 'Countermeasures of General Interest' (2002) 13(5) *European Journal of International Law* 1211.

[83] Draft Articles on Responsibility of States for Internationally Wrongful Acts, with Commentaries, 137–139.

[84] See, for example, Martin Dawidowicz, *Third-Party Countermeasures in International Law* (Cambridge University Press, 2017); Alland, 'Countermeasures of General Interest'; Jonathan I. Charney, 'Third State Remedies in International Law' (1989) 10(1) *Michigan Journal of International Law* 57.

[85] Dawidowicz, *Third-Party Countermeasures in International Law*.

[86] *Ibid.*, 112–113.

[87] *Ibid.*, 283.

inducing compliance with communitarian norms but he perceives that they have helped with enforcement where the circumstances are right.[88]

The debate around inducing compliance with international law comes into particularly sharp focus in the context of ensuring respect for the norms of international humanitarian law. The special character of certain obligations of international humanitarian law under the Geneva Conventions was articulated clearly by the International Criminal Tribunal for the former Yugoslavia (ICTY) in *The Prosecutor* v. *Zoran Kupreskic and Others* case:

> As a consequence of their absolute character, these norms of international humanitarian law do not pose synallagmatic obligations, i.e. obligations of a State vis-à-vis another State. Rather – as was stated by the International Court of Justice in the *Barcelona Traction* case (which specifically referred to obligations concerning fundamental human rights) – they lay down obligations towards the international community as a whole, with the consequence that each and every member of the international community has a 'legal interest' in their observance and consequently a legal entitlement to demand respect for such obligations.[89]

Under Common Article 1 of the Geneva Conventions, there is a duty to both avoid encouraging violations of international humanitarian law and to take measures to prevent and end violations of international humanitarian law: 'The High Contracting Parties agree to respect and to ensure respect for the present Convention in all circumstances'.[90] This is a specific positive obligation to ensure that others respect the Geneva Conventions. However, a debate exists as to whether there is an external, that is to ensure respect by other states, as well as an internal, that is to ensure actors within a state's jurisdiction, dimension to this obligation.[91]

88 *Ibid.*, 284.

89 Case No. IT-95-16, *Prosecutor* v. *Zoran Kupreskic and Others*, International Tribunal for the Prosecution of Persons Responsible for Serious Violations of International Humanitarian Law Committed in the Territory of the former Yugoslavia since 1991, Judgment, 14 January 2000, para 519.

90 Common Article 1, Geneva Convention Relative to the Protection of Civilian Persons in Time of War, 12 August 1949, 75 UNTS 287.

91 For a comprehensive assessment of this debate, see Robin Geiß, 'The Obligation to Respect and to Ensure Respect for the Conventions' in Andrew Clapham, Paola Gaeta and Marco Sassòlli (eds.), *The 1949 Geneva Conventions: A Commentary* (Oxford University Press, 2015), 109–134. See also, Laurence Boisson de Chazournes and Luigi Condorelli, 'Common Article 1 of the Geneva Conventions Revisited: Protecting Collective Interests' (2000) 82(837) *International Review of the Red Cross* 67. However, for a diverging approach, see Focarelli, 'Common Article 1 of the 1949 Geneva Conventions: A Soap Bubble?'.

I will argue that Common Article 1 implies both an internal and external dimension to the duty to ensure respect.

To 'ensure respect' implies an active duty and not merely an entitlement to act when a state chooses. It requires states to go beyond refraining from endorsing or recognising breaches of international humanitarian law, and to actively take measures aimed at bringing an end to breaches of the Geneva Conventions, as well as preventing their occurrence in the first place.[92] This is confirmed by the Commentaries to the Geneva Conventions of 1952 and 2020.[93]

Jean Pictet's Commentaries to the Geneva Conventions also support the proposition that all contracting states are under an obligation to ensure respect by other countries:

> [I]n the event of a Power failing to fulfil its obligations, the other Contracting Parties (neutral, allied or enemy) may, and should, endeavour to bring it back to an attitude of respect for the Convention. The proper working of the system of protection provided by the Conventions demands in fact that the Contracting Parties should not be content merely to apply its provisions themselves, but should do everything in their power to ensure that the humanitarian principles underlying the Conventions are applied universally.[94]

This is even clearer in Pictet's French version of the Commentaries, particularly because the distinction between the power to act (*pouvoir*) and the obligation to act (*devoir*) is spelt out: 'Ainsi encore, si une Puissance manque a ses obligations, les autres Parties contractantes ... peuvent-elles – et doivent-elles – chercher a la ramener au respect de la Convention'.[95] Moreover, as regards the Third Geneva Convention Relative to the Treatment of Prisoners of War, the French Commentary reveals a reference only to a duty: 'Ceci vaut pour le respect que chaque

[92] Dörmann and Serralvo, 'Common Article 1 to the Geneva Conventions and the Obligation to Prevent International Humanitarian Law Violations', 707; Marco Sassòli, 'State Responsibility for Violations of International Humanitarian Law' (2002) 84 *International Review of the Red Cross* 401, 413.

[93] Jean Pictet (ed.), *Commentaries to the Geneva Conventions* (International Committee of the Red Cross, 1952), 17; Commentary of 2020 to Article 1 of the Convention (III) Relative to the Treatment of Prisoners of War, Geneva, 12 August 1949; Updated Commentaries to the Convention (I) for the Amelioration of the Condition of the Wounded and Sick in Armed Forces in the Field, Geneva, 12 August 1949 (International Committee of the Red Cross, 2016).

[94] Jean Pictet (ed.), *Commentary: IV Geneva Convention Relative to the Protection of Civilian Persons in Time of War* (International Committee of the Red Cross, 1958), 16.

[95] *Ibid.*, 21. See Dörmann and Serralvo, 'Common Article 1 to the Geneva Conventions and the obligation to prevent international humanitarian law violations', 707–736.

Etat doit lui-meme a la Convention mais, en outre, si une autre Puissance manque à ses obligations, chaque Partie contractante (neutre, alliee ou ennemie) doit chercher à la ramener au respect de la Convention.'[96]

The Commentary of 2020 to Common Article 1 provides that the obligation implies states 'do everything reasonably in their power "to ensure respect" for the Conventions'.[97] While the commitment to '"respect and ensure respect" applies first and foremost to the High Contracting Parties themselves',[98] the Commentaries go on to emphasise that the High Contracting Parties have a distinct obligation to 'undertake, whether or not they are themselves a party to an armed conflict, to ensure respect for the Conventions by other High Contracting Parties and non-State Parties to an armed conflict'.[99]

The Commentary underlines the universal nature of the need to ensure respect for the Geneva Conventions. Indeed, it provides that

> [t]he interests protected by the Conventions are of such fundamental importance to the human person that every High Contracting Party has a legal interest in their observance, wherever a conflict may take place and whoever its victims may be.[100]

As such, the phrase 'whoever its victims may be' suggests that all states parties must ensure all human beings benefit from the protection afforded by the Geneva Conventions. In this context, the Commentary also traces the two schools of thought that exist around the extent of the obligation to ensure respect. As alluded to, one school of thought is that the obligation simply requires states 'to adopt all measures necessary to ensure respect for the Conventions only by their organs and private individuals within their own jurisdictions'.[101] An alternative school of thought is that states must go beyond this basic commitment and 'ensure respect for the Conventions by other States and non-State parties'.[102] The Commentaries observe that the latter school of thought is the 'prevailing view', it is the position of the International Committee of the Red Cross and reflects customary

[96] Jean Pictet (ed.), *Commentaire: IIIeme Convention de Geneve Relative au Traitment des Prisonniers de Guerre* (International Committee of the Red Cross, 1960), 21.

[97] Commentary of 2020 to Article 1 of the Convention (III) Relative to the Treatment of Prisoners of War, Geneva, 12 August 1949, para 151.

[98] *Ibid.*

[99] *Ibid.*, para 152.

[100] *Ibid.*

[101] *Ibid.*, para 153.

[102] *Ibid.*

international law.[103] Further still, the Commentary cautions that 'Common Article 1 is not a mere stylistic clause' but instead has 'imperative force' and is critical to ensuring the Geneva Conventions are complied with.[104] It has also been argued that the obligation 'to ensure respect' under Common Article 1 of the Geneva Conventions is an expression of the emerging principle of solidarity, which suggests an obligation to those in third states.[105]

The *travaux préparatoires* of the Geneva Conventions around the addition of 'to ensure respect' do not reveal very much. Only the representatives of Italy, Norway and the United States commented on this addition. Interestingly, however, Mr Maresca of Italy stated that this phrase was 'either redundant or introduced a new concept into international law'.[106] It has been argued that the latter is more likely since, if the former was the case, it would probably have been deleted.[107] This proposition is strengthened by reference to a statement made by the delegate of the International Committee of the Red Cross at the Diplomatic Conference in Geneva in 1949, a statement which was not opposed by any delegate present at the time:

> [I]n submitting its proposals to the Stockholm Conference, the International Committee of the Red Cross emphasized that the Contracting Parties should not confine themselves to applying the Conventions themselves, but should do all in their power to see that the basic humanitarian principles of the Conventions were universally applied.[108]

The introduction of the obligation to ensure respect is one of the fundamental ways in which the Geneva Conventions of 1949 went further than those of 1929.[109] Similarly, this obligation was positioned upfront in

[103] *Ibid.*; see also ICRC Study on Customary International Humanitarian Law (2005), Rule 144; *Military and Paramilitary Activities in and against Nicaragua*, Merits (1986) ICJ Rep. 14, para 220.

[104] Commentary of 2020 to Article 1 of the Convention (III) Relative to the Treatment of Prisoners of War, Geneva, 12 August 1949, para 154.

[105] See Karel Wellens, 'Revisiting Solidarity as a (Re-)Emerging Constitutional Principle: Some Further Reflections' in Rüdiger Wolfrum and Chie Kojima (eds.), *Solidarity: A Structural Principle of International Law* (Springer, 2010), 13.

[106] Final Record of the Diplomatic Conference of Geneva of 1949, vol. 2, section B, 53.

[107] Dörmann and Serralvo, 'Common Article 1 to the Geneva Conventions and the obligation to Prevent International Humanitarian Law violations', 714.

[108] Final Record of the Diplomatic Conference of Geneva of 1949, vol. 2, section B, 53.

[109] Dörmann and Serralvo, 'Common Article 1 to the Geneva Conventions and the Obligation to Prevent International Humanitarian Law Violations', 711.

Common Article 1 of the 1949 Conventions, unlike the 1929 Convention where the obligation to respect the Convention features at the very end and only in the section concerned with executions. Under the 1949 Conventions, the duty to ensure respect is not preambular or introductory, it is an 'active provision' and has an 'imperative nature'.[110] Moreover, it has been observed that the obligation that '[t]he High Contracting Parties undertake to respect and ensure respect' is written in the active voice and this is of significance. Moreover, it differs from the way it was phrased in the 1929 Convention.[111] These developments, subsequent practice, and the obligation to respect a treaty in good faith all add weight to the proposition that every state must ensure all other states respect the Geneva Conventions.

The obligation to ensure respect is similar to the obligation to prevent genocide insofar as third states are under a duty of due diligence to pursue suitable measures to ensure that other states comply with their international obligations. It is an obligation of means.[112] If we draw guidance from the ICJ's decision in *Bosnia and Herzegovina* v. *Serbia and Montenegro*, an obligation of due diligence such as this implies that a state must engage all means reasonably available to them. This obligation is violated if the state fails to take measures to prevent genocide which are within its power and could have helped to prevent the genocide.[113]

The obligation to ensure respect is different from the obligations not to recognise an illegal situation and to refrain from aiding and assisting in breaches of international humanitarian law under Article 41(2) of the Draft Articles on State Responsibility. The ILC has clarified that the latter obligations are only triggered when the assisting state knows of the circumstances which render the conduct illegal and proceeds to assist despite that a violation of international humanitarian law would occur.[114] However, the standard of review attached to the ensure respect

[110] See Fateh Azzam, 'The Duty of Third States to Implement and Enforce International Humanitarian Law' (1997) 66 *Nordic Journal of International Law* 55, 60.

[111] Dörmann and Serralvo, 'Common Article 1 to the Geneva Conventions and the Obligation to Prevent International Humanitarian Law Violations', 711.

[112] *Application of the Convention on the Prevention and Punishment of the Crime of Genocide (Bosnia and Herzegovina* v. *Serbia and Montenegro)*, Judgment (2007) ICJ Rep. 43, para 430; Dörmann and Serralvo, 'Common Article 1 to the Geneva Conventions and the Obligation to Prevent International Humanitarian Law Violations', 724–725.

[113] *Application of the Convention on the Prevention and Punishment of the Crime of Genocide (Bosnia and Herzegovina* v. *Serbia and Montenegro)*, Judgment (2007) ICJ Rep. 43.

[114] Draft Articles on Responsibility of States for Internationally Wrongful Acts, with Commentaries, 114–116.

obligation is different in nature given that it is one of due diligence and is triggered when the third state fails to act.

As for the specific measures that states should take in the context of this obligation to ensure respect, they may include monitoring or fact-finding, diplomatic efforts, referral to the International Criminal Court, measures of retorsion, or action taken in cooperation with an international organisation. All of these measures must be intended to stop violations of the Geneva Conventions and to provide assistance to victims of such violations.[115] Turning to the consequences that may flow from a breach of the obligation to ensure respect for the Geneva Conventions, failure to act could trigger international responsibility where the conduct of the state falls short of the relevant due diligence standard.[116]

The International Committee of the Red Cross Study on Customary International Humanitarian Law 2005 has interpreted the standard set by this obligation as requiring states to 'exert their influence, to the extent possible'.[117] The obligation applies to all states and relevant international organisations and, given that the phrase 'in all circumstances' is included, it applies unconditionally.[118] The ICJ recognised this in the *Wall Opinion* and elaborated further on the type of action that is required under the duty to ensure respect for the Geneva Conventions in other countries. The Court said that it follows from Common Article 1 'that every State party to that Convention, whether or not it is a party to a specific conflict, is under an obligation to ensure that the requirements of the instruments in question are complied with'.[119] In the *Nicaragua* case referred to above, the ICJ also noted

[115] Dieter Fleck, 'International Accountability for Violations of the *Ius in Bello*: The Impact of the ICRC Study on Customary International Humanitarian Law' (2006) 10 *Journal of Conflict and Security Law* 179, 182. Dörmann and Serralvo, 'Common Article 1 to the Geneva Conventions and the Obligation to Prevent International Humanitarian Law Violations', 725–726.

[116] *Ibid.*, 726.

[117] Fleck, 'International Accountability for Violations of the *Ius in Bello*: The Impact of the ICRC Study on Customary International Humanitarian Law', 182.

[118] Pictet (ed.), *The Geneva Conventions of 12 August 1949: Commentary*, 1952, 15 *et seq*; Laurence Boisson de Chazournes, 'Responsibility to Protect: Reflecting Solidarity?' in Wolfrum and Kojima (eds.), *Solidarity: A Structural Principle of International Law*, 105. See also, Luigi Condorelli and Laurence Boisson De Chazournes, 'Quelques remarques à propos de l'obligation des États de "respecter et faire respecter" le droit international humanitaire "en toutes circonstances"' in Christophe Swinarski (ed.), *Studies and Essays on International Humanitarian Law and Red Cross Principles in Honour of Jean Pictet* (ICRC/Martinus Nijhoff, 1984), 17–35.

[119] *Legal Consequences of the Construction of a Wall in the Occupied Palestinian Territory*, Advisory Opinion (2004) ICJ Rep. 136, para 158.

that the United States had an obligation to 'respect' and 'even to ensure respect for' the Geneva Conventions, despite that it was not a party to the non-international armed conflict.[120]

The Security Council and General Assembly have also confirmed that states are under a legal obligation to ensure respect for the Geneva Conventions in conflicts they are not party to[121] and the Secretary-General of the United Nations has previously stated in respect of alleged violations of international humanitarian law committed by Israel:

> Under [the Fourth Geneva Convention], each Contracting State undertakes a series of unilateral engagements, vis-à-vis itself and at the same time vis-à-vis the others, of legal obligations to protect those civilians who are found in occupied territories following the outbreak of hostilities ... the Security Council should consider making a solemn appeal to all the High Contracting Parties to the Fourth Geneva Convention that have diplomatic relations with Israel, drawing their attention to their obligation under article 1 of the Convention to '... ensure respect for the present Convention in all circumstances' and urging them to use all the means at their disposal to persuade the Government of Israel to change its position as regards the applicability of the Convention.[122]

Further still, other provisions of the Geneva Conventions also reinforce the notion that all parties must ensure respect for the Conventions. Article 25 of the Geneva Convention on the Amelioration of the Condition of the Wounded and Sick in Armies in the Field 1929 and Article 82 of the Geneva Convention on the Treatment of Prisoners of War 1929 stated that the conventional obligations 'shall be respected by the High Contracting Parties in all circumstances'. It has been observed

[120] *Military and Paramilitary Activities in and against Nicaragua (Nicaragua* v. *United States of America)*, Merits (1986) ICJ Rep. 14, para 220, noting that

> [t]he Court considers that there is an obligation on the United States Government, in terms of Article 1 of the Geneva Conventions, to 'respect' the Conventions and even 'to ensure respect' for them 'in all circumstances', since such an obligation does not only derive from the Conventions themselves, but from the general principles of humanitarian law to which the Conventions merely give specific expression.

[121] See, for example, Security Council Resolution 681 (1990), Israel/Palestine, 20 December 1990; Security Council Resolution 764 (1992), Bosnia and Herzegovina, 13 July 1992, UN Doc. S/RES/764; Security Council Resolution (1994), Rwanda, 6 November 1994, UN Doc. S/RES/955.

[122] Report Submitted to the Security Council by the Secretary-General in Accordance with Resolution 605 (1987), 21 January 1988, UN Doc. A/19443, paras 24–27.

that these were the first provisions to oblige states to abide by a convention regardless of the behaviour of other states.[123]

In conclusion, the duty to ensure respect for international humanitarian law is a positive other-directed obligation. It is an obligation of means and a due diligence standard applies. In this respect, it is similar in nature to the duty to prevent or arrest genocide. The *travaux préparatoires*, the text itself, and subsequent interpretations all lend support to the proposition that it requires action on the part of states to ensure all other states obey the Geneva Conventions. We now turn to consider the R2P doctrine, which similarly promotes an obligation to prevent grave violations of international law.

4.5 The Responsibility to Protect

The cosmopolitan and altruistic nature of certain international commitments is also evident in developments around the regulation of the use of force and non-intervention in international law.[124] In this context, the role that solidarity has played in shaping obligations and processes in recent years will become clearer.[125] That said, humanitarian intervention predates the contemporary law on the use of force. Ideas of the just war have been explored by philosophers and lawyers from Thomas Aquinas onwards.[126] Indeed, it was long accepted that where there was right authority, just cause, right intention, last resort, proportionality and a reasonable prospect of success, resort to war was justified. While there may have been a moral obligation to intervene (or to use the now archaic formulation: a right to intervene), there has never been a legal obligation to intervene. R2P began to play a role in shifting the narrative of intervention for humanitarian purposes from rights to responsibility,

[123] See Condorelli and Boisson De Chazournes, 'Quelques remarques à propos de l'obligation des États 'de respecter et faire respecter le droit international humanitaire en toutes circonstances'; Frits Kalshoven, 'The Undertaking to Respect and Ensure Respect in All Circumstances: From Tiny Seed to Ripening Fruit' (1999) 2 *Yearbook of International Humanitarian Law* 7; Alexandre Devillard, 'L'obligation de faire respecter le droit international humanitaire: l'article 1 commun aux Conventions de Genève et leur Première Protocol Additionnel, fondement d'une droit international humanitaire de coopération?' (2007) 75 *Revue Québécoise de droit international* 77.

[124] Robert Fine, *Cosmopolitanism* (Routledge, 2007), 79.

[125] Boisson de Chazournes, 'Responsibility to Protect: Reflecting Solidarity?'.

[126] See Ratner, *The Thin Justice of International Law: A Moral Reckoning of the Law of Nations*, 296.

as well as the focus from the intervening state to the victims of atrocity.[127] As will be seen in the following section, it is unlikely that this doctrine has created new legal obligations as such, but it has sought to provide some clarity around the collective security mechanism of the UN system and the situations when states are under a moral obligation to act on behalf of people in other countries who are subject to the most serious human rights abuses. Moreover, R2P places an emphasis on preventing such abuses in the first place, as well as the availability of a range of measures to arrest them.

The background to the emergence of the R2P doctrine was the humanitarian interventions that took place in the 1990s. One prominent example in this context is the NATO intervention in Kosovo in 1999. Despite the absolute nature of the principle of non-intervention under the UN Charter, save for the explicit exceptions of self-defence and collective security, states intervened in Kosovo for what they claimed were humanitarian purposes. Some have suggested that this intervention was formally illegal but morally necessary.[128] The reason for this judgment was that more good would be done by breaching the law than would be done by conforming to it. As such, international law did not permit an ethical outcome in this situation and ethics demanded intervention. In order for international law to respond to the charge that it allowed for such fundamental human rights abuses, a systemic and fundamental rethink was required.

This began with a reconceptualisation of sovereignty. That a state's legitimacy could determine its sovereignty gave sovereignty new meaning. This paradigm shift is reflected in the work of the International Commission on Intervention and State Sovereignty

[127] Interestingly, José Alvarez advocates for a return to humanitarian intervention as the latter is more focused on human rights. José Alvarez, 'The Schizophrenias of R2P' in Euan MacDonald and Philip Alston (eds.), *Human Rights, Intervention, and the Right to Force* (Oxford University Press, 2008), 275; see also Ratner, *The Thin Justice of International Law: A Moral Reckoning of the Law of Nations*, 308. For a scholarly exploration of the legal bases for R2P, see Jutta Brunneé and Stephen Toope, 'The Responsibility to Protect and the Use of Force: Building Legality?' (2010) 2 *Global Responsibility to Protect* 191; Gareth Evans, 'The Responsibility to Protect: An Idea Whose Time Has Come … And Gone?' (2008) 22 *International Relations* 283; Rosenberg, 'Responsibility to Protect: A Framework for Prevention'.

[128] Antonio Cassese, '*Ex iniuria ius oritur*: Are We Moving towards International Legitimation of Forcible Humanitarian Countermeasures in the World Community?' (1999) 10 *European Journal of International Law* 23, 25 (noting that 'from an *ethical* viewpoint resort to armed force was justified' (emphasis in original)).

(ICISS),[129] which is published in its report of 2001 and represents one of the first major milestones in the story of the R2P doctrine. In this context, a real innovation of the ICISS Report was that it recharacterised sovereignty as responsibility rather than control. As such, sovereignty implied a dual responsibility: externally to respect the sovereignty of other states and internally to respect the dignity and basic rights of all people within the state.

This also served to humanise the principle of sovereignty[130] and the *raison d'être* of sovereignty was intended to be the needs of human beings. The state commits itself to protect its population in exchange for respect of its sovereignty by the international community. As the ICISS Report made clear, sovereignty as responsibility has become the minimum content of good international citizenship.[131] Further still, sovereignty became intertwined with solidarity and former UN Secretary-General Kofi Annan saw the evolution of sovereignty as 'testimony to a humanity that cares more, not less, for the suffering in its midst, and a humanity that will do more, not less, to end it'.[132]

This evolution in the understanding of sovereignty allowed R2P to emerge. In their report, ICISS elaborated a three-phase framework whereby states were obligated with a responsibility to prevent, react and rebuild. They emphasised that the prevention phase was the most important of these but there was also a broad consensus that military intervention should be a last resort and that the idea of a right to intervention should be rearticulated as a responsibility to protect.[133] In this way, the terminology used by ICISS oriented towards the rights of victims rather than the rights of those proposing intervention helped to change the way in which intervention was conceived by states.[134]

129 Hereinafter 'ICISS'. International Commission on Intervention and State Sovereignty, 'The Responsibility to Protect', December 2001, http://responsibilitytoprotect.org/ICISS%20Report.pdf.

130 Anne Peters, 'Humanity as the A and Ω of Sovereignty' (2009) 20(3) *European Journal of International Law* 513.

131 International Commission on Intervention and State Sovereignty, 'The Responsibility to Protect', para 1.35.

132 Kofi Annan, 'Two Concepts of Sovereignty 1999', *The Economist*, 16 September 1999, www.economist.com/node/324795.

133 International Commission on Intervention and State Sovereignty, 'The Responsibility to Protect', XI. See also, Francis Deng, Sadikiel Kimaro, Terrence Lyons, Rothchild Donald and I. William Zartman, *Sovereignty as Responsibility: Conflict Management in Africa* (Brookings Institution Press, 1996).

134 Alex J. Bellamy, *Responsibility to Protect: The Global Effort to End Mass Atrocities* (Wiley, 2009), 65.

The major innovation of the ICISS report was its suggestion that, while the state whose people are affected has the primary responsibility to protect, a residual responsibility also lies with the broader community of states for the rights of those affected people. As such, it made a distinction between a state's internal and external responsibility. It also suggests that if the Security Council fails to act, unilateral action becomes a possibility. Such a situation would require a balancing assessment and must meet the stipulated criteria of just cause, right intention, last resort, proportionality of means and reasonable prospects of success.[135]

Following the ICISS report, in 2004, the High-level Panel on Threats, Challenges and Change (HLPTCC) produced its report entitled *A More Secure World: Our Shared Responsibility.*[136] This text endorsed a broader reading of the concept of 'responsibility' under which the responsibility of the state at issue shifts to every other state where the former is unwilling to act. The HLPTCC associated the concept of collective responsibility, in particular, with action by the Security Council. It also urged responsible use of the veto that permanent members of the Security Council have to block the adoption of measures. Significantly, the HLPTCC did not necessarily envisage action outside of the Security Council in situations of R2P and stressed collective R2P was only exercisable by the Security Council. Furthermore, it set out five criteria of legitimacy, similar to those suggested in the ICISS report, but this time aimed at the Security Council in its calculus of R2P situations. They include the seriousness of the threat, proper purpose, last resort, proportionality of means and balance of consequences.[137]

A year later, the then Secretary-General Kofi Annan published his report entitled *In Larger Freedom: Toward Development, Security and Human Rights for All*, in which he made the case that the pillars of the United Nations were the rule of law, democracy and human rights. In doing so, he strongly endorsed R2P.[138] In a reference to the ICISS and HLPTCC reports, he agreed that there was an emerging norm while also

[135] Incidentally, these are identical to those that constituted the *jus ad bello* regime of just war.

[136] UN General Assembly Resolution 59/565, 'A More Secure World: Our Shared Responsibility: Report of the High-Level Panel on Threats, Challenges and Change', 2 December 2004, UN Doc. A/59/565.

[137] *Ibid.*, para 56.

[138] UN Secretary-General, 'In Larger Freedom: Towards Security, Development and Human Rights for All', 21 March 2005, UN Doc. A/59/2005, 35.

recognising that there remained sensitivities around it. This embracing of the concept and characterisation as an emerging norm was significant, not least because it was by a Secretary-General of the UN who had witnessed and criticised the international community's inaction in situations like Rwanda.[139]

At the United Nations World Summit in 2005, the principle of R2P was affirmed. This is expressed in the World Summit Outcome Document's paragraphs 138 and 139,[140] which elaborate the three pillars on which R2P is based. First, the primary responsibility of states is to protect their own populations from the four crimes of genocide, war crimes, ethnic cleansing and crimes against humanity, as well as their incitement. Second, the international community has a responsibility to assist a state to fulfil its R2P. Third, the international community also has a responsibility to take timely and decisive action, in accordance with the UN Charter, in cases where the state has manifestly failed to protect its own population from one or more of the four crimes.

After six months of debating the subject, the Security Council unanimously adopted Resolution 1674 in a move that was meant to reaffirm R2P as conceived by the World Summit Outcome.[141] However, this was not an easy consensus to achieve as the negotiations surrounding the resolution indicate.[142] Despite this, the Security Council affirmed R2P again in 2009[143] and had referred to the concept in its consideration of the situation in Darfur in 2006.[144]

A new Secretary-General of the United Nations signalled a new direction for R2P. Upon taking office, Ban Ki-Moon appointed a special advisor on R2P. The person to assume the role would be UN expert Edward Luck. Subsequently, Ban Ki-Moon published a report entitled *Implementing the Responsibility to Protect*, which was an attempt to

139 'If humanitarian intervention is, indeed, an unacceptable assault on sovereignty, how should we respond to a Rwanda, to a Srebrenica – to gross and systematic violations of human rights that offend every precept of our common humanity?', UN Secretary-General, '"We the Peoples" The Role of the United Nations in the 21st Century' (United Nations, 2000), 48, www.un.org/en/events/pastevents/pdfs/We_The_Peoples.pdf.

140 UN General Assembly Resolution 60/1, 'World Summit Outcome', 24 October 2005, UN Doc. A/RES/60/1, paras 138 and 139.

141 UN Security Council Resolution 1674, 28 April 2006, UN Doc. S/RES/1674.

142 Alex Bellamy, 'The Responsibility to Protect – Five Years On' (2010) 24(2) *Ethics and International Affairs* 143, 145.

143 UN Security Council Resolution 1894, 11 November 2009, UN Doc. S/RES/1894.

144 UN Security Council Resolution 1706, 31 August 2006, UN Doc. S/RES/1706, although several Security Council members expressed concern and China abstained.

effectively realise R2P and included the establishment of a joint office for R2P and the prevention of genocide.[145]

Despite this rapid development of R2P, intervention for humanitarian purposes remains controversial for many different reasons. The concerns around the application of R2P are reflected in the inconsistent reference to R2P in practice. For example, R2P has not been engaged in respect of the civil war in Syria, where there had been a case for its application. It is likely that it is today something of a poisoned chalice after it was used ultimately for regime change in Libya, despite that the explicit mandate was a no-fly zone in that conflict.[146]

One of the implications of the R2P doctrine is that it is an endorsement by the international community that the role of the UN Security Council is evolving. In particular, the UN Security Council is evolving from a mechanism for the prevention of inter-state conflict to a mechanism that regulates situations within particular states. In this context, it has been said that R2P signals an enlargement of the Security Council's 'circle of empathy' and has helped to institutionalise altruistic responses to certain situations where people require external assistance by placing the responsibility for action squarely on the Security Council.[147]

One particular value-added aspect of the R2P concept is that it places a renewed emphasis on de facto rather than *de jure* grounds for authority. It has been observed that R2P rests on the idea that authority should ensure protection in order for it to be legitimate, and a failure to protect should invite a response from the international community.[148] This resonates with the claim by Marlier and Crawford that R2P represents an institutionalisation of empathy and altruism, as mentioned in Chapter 1.[149] In particular, the institutional mechanisms that gather facts (or in other words serve as the eyes and ears of the Security Council) are also mechanisms of empathy, insofar as they take into account the plight of others, and mechanisms of altruism, insofar as they are an

[145] See, UN Office on Genocide Prevention and the Responsibility to Protect, www.un.org/en/genocideprevention/.

[146] UN Security Council Resolution 1970, 26 February 2011, UN Doc. S/RES/1970 and UN Security Council Resolution 1973, 17 March 2011, UN Doc. S/RES/1973.

[147] Grant Marlier and Neta C. Crawford, 'Incomplete and Imperfect Institutionalisation of Empathy and Altruism in the "Responsibility to Protect" Doctrine' (2013) 5 *Global Responsibility to Protect* 397, 398.

[148] Anne Orford, *International Authority and the Responsibility to Protect* (Cambridge University Press, 2011).

[149] Marlier and Crawford, 'Incomplete and Imperfect Institutionalisation of Empathy and Altruism in the "Responsibility to Protect" Doctrine'.

impetus for positive action. It should also be borne in mind in this context that the very roots of the word 'responsibility' are in the Latin word '*respondeo*', meaning 'I answer'.[150] This provides further support that responsibility requires some form of positive response or action from the responsible.

While Marlier and Crawford have argued that R2P represents the institutionalisation of empathy and altruism through the mechanism of the UN Security Council and the processes of international law, they also admit, however, that this institutionalisation of empathy and altruism has been 'incomplete and imperfect' because the mechanisms have the potential to allow abusive and improper use of the R2P doctrine.[151] They suggest that this risk of abuse or improper use can be remedied by a more acute institutionalisation of empathy and that this is a process that is ongoing.[152]

A further fundamental question is whether, if there is a failure to respond, does liability follow? While there may be an ethical obligation to act, it would seem that this has not yet translated into an enforceable legal obligation.[153] In this context, the legal nature of the obligations as expressed in paragraphs 138 and 139 of the World Summit Outcome have been questioned.[154] Others argue that, aside from the lack of legal obligations, the constructional ambiguity in the doctrine, whereby there exists a distinction between the primary responsibility of the state and the fall back responsibility of the international community, could allow states to argue that their primary responsibility should constrain rather than enable Security Council involvement.[155]

[150] Hannes Peltonen, 'Modelling International Collective Responsibility: The Case of Grave Humanitarian Crises' (2010) 36(2) *Review of International Studies* 235, 239.

[151] Marlier and Crawford, 'Incomplete and Imperfect Institutionalisation of Empathy and Altruism in the "Responsibility to Protect" Doctrine', 399.

[152] *Ibid.*

[153] The intervention in Libya seemed to represent the high water mark for the R2P doctrine and evidence for any legal obligation to intervene, while Syria and the (weak) language of the World Summit Outcome indicate that no such obligation exists.

[154] See, for example, Ekkehard Strauss, 'A Bird in the Hand is Worth Two in the Bush: On the Assumed Legal Nature of the Responsibility to Protect' (2009) 1(3) *Global Journal on the Responsibility to Protect* 291; Stephen Marks and Nicolas Cooper, 'The Responsibility to Protect: Watershed or Old Wine in New Bottles?' (2010) 2(1) *Jindal Global Law Review* 86. The better school of thought is that there is not a legal obligation to intervene on the basis of the text ultimately adopted in Paragraph 139 of the World Summit Outcome, which reflects the version of R2P that states have consented to; UN General Assembly Resolution 60/1, 'World Summit Outcome', 24 October 2005, UN Doc. A/RES/60/1, para 139.

[155] Carsten Stahn, 'Responsibility to Protect: Emerging Norm or Political Rhetoric?' (2007) 101(1) *American Journal of International Law* 99.

Despite the debate over whether any new legal obligations have been added by R2P, its influence has certainly been useful in a number of ways. Indeed, some have argued that R2P's contribution lies in the way it structures and conceptualises responses to certain issues.[156] In this way, R2P provides a useful continuum from the responsibility to prevent, to the responsibility to react and to rebuild.[157] In turn, this ensures that elements vital to adequate humanitarian protection, such as in the prevention and rebuilding phase, are not overlooked by states.[158] Furthermore, real institutional advances have been made with additions like a Peacebuilding Commission, early warning systems and advocating a norm of international solidarity.[159]

It is fair to conclude, therefore, that R2P has added some value[160] and also demonstrates 'a developing cosmopolitan sentiment within the field, leading in turn to a more compassionate jurisprudence with a greater concern for responsibility towards others and an increased willingness to accept at least limited forms of external obligations'.[161] While in the heat of humanitarian crises characterised by political fallout the practice of R2P has proved to be inconsistent, its lasting contribution may well lie in the role it has played in recharacterising sovereignty and establishing pathways, though imperfect, for empathy and altruism within the UN system.[162]

We turn next to a pathway for altruism intended to protect those fleeing their home states that are unable or unwilling to protect them. It is the long-standing duty to provide safe haven for refugees and others who benefit from the obligation of *non-refoulement* under international law.

[156] Anne Peters, 'The Responsibility to Protect: Spelling out the Hard Legal Consequences for the UN Security Council and Its Members' in Fastenrath *et al.* (eds.), *From Bilateralism to Community Interest: Essays in Honour of Judge Bruno Simma*, 297–325.

[157] Strauss, 'A Bird in the Hand is Worth Two in the Bush: On the Assumed Legal Nature of the Responsibility to Protect'.

[158] Rosenberg, 'Responsibility to Protect: A Framework for Prevention'.

[159] Boisson de Chazournes, 'Responsibility to Protect: Reflecting Solidarity?'.

[160] Clapham, 'Responsibility to Protect: "Some Sort of Commitment"', 169–192.

[161] Trevor Redmond, *People, States and Hope: Cosmopolitanism and the Future of International Law* (Wolf Legal Publishers, 2012), 306.

[162] Marlier and Crawford, 'Incomplete and Imperfect Institutionalisation of Empathy and Altruism in the "Responsibility to Protect" Doctrine'; see also Wabwile, *Legal Protection of Social and Economic Rights of Children in Developing Countries: Reassessing International Cooperation and Responsibility*, 116.

4.6 The Duty to Protect Those Fleeing Their Home State

International refugee law protects the rights of refugees and stipulates the obligations of host states that have committed to safeguarding the welfare of refugees in the absence of protection from their home state.[163] The duty of *non-refoulement*, which is a cornerstone of international refugee law, implies the provision of safe haven to individuals facing a particular threat in another country. The obligation applies to refugees and asylum seekers,[164] and Article 3 of the Convention against Torture applies *non-refoulement* to those who are facing a risk of torture in a third state.[165] These obligations are concerned with the relationship between a state and the citizens of another state, and in this sense they differ conceptually from traditional human rights law that is concerned with the way a state treats its own citizens.[166]

While Article 14(1) of the Universal Declaration of Human Rights of 1948 provided that '[e]veryone has the right to seek and to enjoy in other countries asylum from persecution', the centrepiece of the regime concerning the protection of refugees came with the 1951 United Nations Convention relating to the Status of Refugees (Refugee Convention). Under the Refugee Convention a refugee is anyone who is in fear of persecution because of their race, religion, nationality, membership in a particular social group or political opinions, who is outside of their country of origin and whose country of origin is unable or unwilling to protect them, or who is unwilling to return to it owing to a fear of persecution.[167] The principle of non-discrimination, which is expressed

[163] Alice Edwards, 'International Refugee Law' in Daniel Moeckli, Sangeeta Shah and Sandesh Sivakumaran (eds.), *International Human Rights Law* (Oxford University Press, 2017), 539.

[164] Article 33, Convention Relating to the Status of Refugees, 28 July 1951, 189 UNTS 137.

[165] Article 3, Convention against Torture and Other Cruel, Inhuman or Degrading Treatment or Punishment, 4 February 1984, UN Doc A/39/51.

[166] See Karen Costa, 'Meeting the Challenges of a Globalized World: Extraterritorial Obligations in the Field of Human Rights' (October 2010) *H-Human Rights* 1–2; Thomas Gammeltoft-Hansen, 'Growing Barriers: International Refugee Law' in Mark Gibney and Sigrun Skogly (eds.), *Universal Human Rights and Extraterritorial Obligations* (University of Pennsylvania Press, 2010), Chapter 3.

[167] The Protocol Relating to the Status of Refugees, 31 January 1967, 606 UNTS 267 confirms this definition. The Organization of African Unity Convention Governing the Specific Aspects of Refugee Problems in Africa adds to this definition of a refugee in its Article 1(2) by providing that: 'The term "refugee" shall also apply to every person who, owing to external aggression, occupation, foreign domination or events seriously disturbing public order in either part or the whole of his country of origin or nationality, is compelled to leave his place of habitual residence in order to seek refuge in another

in Article 3 of the Refugee Convention, extends protection to all refugees irrespective of their country of origin, race or religion.

Given that all states must abide by the Refugee Convention in good faith, they are obliged to offer protection to individuals fitting the definition of a refugee within their territory. The principle of *non-refoulement* is provided for in Article 33(1) of the Convention.[168] The Commentaries to the Refugee Convention elaborate that the principle of *non-refoulement* applies to any person fitting the definition of a refugee within the territory of the Contracting State, regardless of whether they have entered the country legally or illegally.[169] Moreover, Article 33(1) must be applied on a prima facie basis to those who may fit the definition of a refugee before a final determination on that status is made.[170] While Article 33(2) goes on to set out the circumstances under which a refugee may be considered a danger to the national security of the country giving refuge, the Commentaries clarify that states are under an obligation to act in good faith when making such a determination. If a state expels the refugees under the guise of Article 33(2) when 'reasonable grounds' for believing that the refugee is a threat to national security do not exist, the concerned state may be held responsible for a breach of their treaty obligations.[171]

The drafters of the 1951 Convention intended for the *non-refoulement* principle to be broad in scope, so as to offer meaningful protection for refugees.[172] Further, the broad scope is reflected in the language of the

place outside his country of origin or nationality'. Similarly, in 1984, the Cartagena Declaration on Refugees (adopted by the Colloquium on the International Protection of Refugees in Central America, Mexico and Panama, held at Cartagena, Colombia from 19–22 November 1984) added to the definition under the 1951 Refugee Convention such that refuges also include 'persons who have fled their country because their lives, safety or freedom have been threatened by generalized violence, foreign aggression, internal conflicts, massive violation of human rights or other circumstances which have seriously disturbed public order'.

168 On the principle, see Elihu Lauterpacht and Daniel Bethlehem, 'The Scope and Content of the Principle of *Non-Refoulement*: Opinion' in Erika Feller, Volker Türk and Frances Nicholson (eds.), *Refugee Protection in International Law* (Cambridge University Press, 2003), 107; Erika Feller, 'Asylum, Migration and Refugee Protection: Realities, Myths and the Promise of Things to Come' (2006) 18 *International Journal of Refugee Law* 509, 523.

169 Commentary on the Refugee Convention 1951, Articles 2–11, 13–37 (Division of International Protection of the United Nations High Commissioner for Refugees, 1997), www.unhcr.org/publ/PUBL/3d4ab5fb9.pdf.

170 *Ibid.*

171 *Ibid.*

172 David Weissbrodt and Isabel Hortreiter, 'The Principle of Non-Refoulement: Article 3 of the Convention against Torture and Other Cruel, Inhuman or Degrading

provision. In particular, the obligation not to 'expel or return ("refouler") a refugee in any manner whatsoever' covers any act of removing an individual that puts them at risk.[173] It has also been interpreted that this means there should be no exceptions on the basis of any other treaty obligations that the state may be under, including extradition for example.[174] Moreover, it has been suggested the condition that 'his life or freedom . . . be threatened' should be construed broadly, and the fact that the scope of the provision includes a wide range of individuals (e.g. asylum seekers and those already granted asylum, those that have entered the country legally and those that have not) adds to this argument for broad application.[175]

The principle of *non-refoulement* is also part of customary international law, and as such it is an obligation that all states are under.[176] Further still, it is considered a general principle of international law,[177] and some contend that it is an emerging norm of *jus cogens*.[178] The principle of *non-refoulement* may also be found explicitly or has been read into other international conventions. For example, Article 3 of the Convention against Torture, which prevents sending an individual to a country where they are at risk of being tortured,[179] the Convention on the Rights of the Child,[180] Article 3 of the European Convention for the

Treatment or Punishment in Comparison with the Non-Refoulement Provisions of Other International Human Rights Treaties' (1999) 5 *Buffalo Human Rights Law Review* 1, 18.

173 Lauterpacht and Bethlehem, 'The Scope and Content of the Principle of *Non-Refoulement*: Opinion', 112.

174 *Ibid.*

175 *Ibid.*, 115–116.

176 See, for example, Declaration of States Parties to the 1951 Convention and or Its 1967 Protocol relating to the Status of Refugees, HCR/MMSP/2001.09 (16 January 2002), para 4; see also, Jean Allain, 'The Jus Cogens Nature of Non-Refoulement' (2001) 13(4) *International Journal of Refugee Law* 533, 538.

177 See, for example, Guy Gooodwin-Gill, *The Refugee in International Law* (Oxford University Press, 1996).

178 Allain, 'The Jus Cogens Nature of Non-Refoulement'.

179 The principle of *non-refoulement* is also part of Article 7 of the International Covenant on Civil and Political Rights 1966 (prevention of torture), as confirmed by Human Rights Committee, *General Comment No. 20: Article 7 (Prohibition of Torture, or Other Cruel, Inhuman or Degrading Treatment or Punishment)*, 10 March 1992, UN Doc. HRI/HEN/1/Rev.1 of 28 July 1994, para 9.

180 See, for example, the interpretation of the Committee on the Rights of the Child, *General Comment No. 6 (2005) on the Treatment of Unaccompanied and Separated Children Outside their Country of Origin*, 1 September 2005, UN Doc. CRC/GC/2005/6, para 27, noting that States Parties to the Convention on the Rights of the Child shall not return a child to a country where there are substantial grounds for believing that there is a real

Protection of Human Rights and Fundamental Freedoms (ECHR),[181] Article 22(8) of the American Convention on Human Rights[182] and Article 5 of the African Charter on the Protection of Human and Peoples' Rights.[183] Similarly, the Geneva Conventions make provision for the protection of refugees and displaced persons. In particular, Article 45 of the Fourth Geneva Convention Relative to the Protection of Civilian Persons in Time of War provides that '[i]n no circumstances shall a protected person be transferred to a country where he or she may have reason to fear persecution for his or her political opinions or religious beliefs'.

Interestingly, there would appear to be growing support for the proposition that the principle of *non-refoulement* may be applied extraterritorially.[184] In the case of *Hirsi Jamaa and Others* v. *Italy*, the European Court of Human Rights found that the principle of *non-refoulement* (in this case captured by Article 3 of the ECHR) can apply extraterritorially.[185] Here, the interception of Libyan migrants at sea by Italian ships meant that the former came under the jurisdiction of the latter. In addition to finding that the principle of *non-refoulement* under the ECHR was engaged, the Court also found that Italy had violated Article 4 of Protocol 4 of the ECHR, namely the prohibition on the collective expulsion of aliens. Noting that neither the text nor the *travaux préparatoires* of Article 4 of Protocol 4 preclude the extraterritorial application of the obligation, the Court found 'that a Contracting State has, exceptionally, exercised its jurisdiction outside its national territory, [and] it does not see any obstacle to accepting that the exercise of extraterritorial jurisdiction by that State took the form of collective expulsion'.[186]

risk of irreparable harm to the child, such as, but by no means limited to, those contemplated under articles 6 [right to life] and 37 [right to be free from torture or other cruel, inhuman or degrading treatment or punishment and right not to be arbitrarily deprived of liberty] of the Convention.

181 European Convention for the Protection of Human Rights and Fundamental Freedoms, 4 November 1950, 213 UNTS 221.

182 American Convention on Human Rights, 22 November 1969, 1144 UNTS 123.

183 African [Banjul] Charter on Human and Peoples' Rights, 27 June 1981, 21 ILM 58.

184 Ralph Wilde, '"Let Them Drown": Rescuing Migrants at Sea and the Non-refoulement Obligation as a Case Study of International Law's Relationship to "Crisis"', *EJIL: Talk!* (25 February 2017).

185 Case No. 27765/09, *Hirsi Jamaa and Others* v. *Italy*, Grand Chamber of the ECtHR, 23 February 2012.

186 *Ibid.*, para 178.

The Court also addressed the issue of potential legal vacuums where individuals may not be afforded their human rights:

> [A]s regards the exercise by a State of its jurisdiction on the high seas, the Court has already stated that the special nature of the maritime environment cannot justify an area outside the law where individuals are covered by no legal system capable of affording them enjoyment of the rights and guarantees protected by the Convention which the States have undertaken to secure to everyone within their jurisdiction.[187]

This finding has been reinforced in a number of other cases. In a subsequent case before the European Court of Human Rights, namely *Sharifi and Others* v. *Italy and Greece*, Italy had intercepted asylum seekers and pushed them back to Greece, where they were in danger of being refouled to their country of origin, Afghanistan.[188] The Court found that there had been a breach of Article 4 of Protocol 4 of the ECHR, which provides for the prohibition of collective expulsion. In particular, the Court was concerned that the asylum seekers had not been given an opportunity to contest their transfer back to Greece.[189] Outside of the European context, the Inter-American Commission on Human Rights has also opined that the United States violated various human rights under the American Declaration on Human Rights by pushing back boats with Haitian asylum seekers on board to their country of origin.[190] That said, the Commission found it did not have jurisdiction to consider Article 33 of the Refugee Convention.[191]

These cases also serve to illustrate a potentially broader application for the prohibition on return under human rights law in certain circumstances compared to the principle of *non-refoulement* under Article 33 of the Refugee Convention.[192] In the former case, human rights law protects all individuals from being returned to face various human rights violations, including at a minimum return to torture and other inhuman or degrading treatment, and the scope of potential human rights violations this includes is evolving. Moreover, certain *non-refoulement* under

[187] *Ibid.* See also Case No. 3394/03, *Case of Medvedyev and Others* v. *France*, Grand Chamber of the ECtHR, 29 March 2010, para 81.

[188] *Sharif and Others* v. *Italy and Greece*, ECHR Second Section, Application No. 16643/09, Judgment of 21 October 2014.

[189] *Ibid.*

[190] Case No. 10.675, *The Haitian Centre for Human Rights et al* v. *United States*, IACommHR Report No 51/96, 13 March 1999.

[191] *Ibid.*, para 76.

[192] Edwards, 'International Refugee Law', 549.

human rights law is absolute, such as where there is a risk of torture. In contrast, Article 33 of the Refugee Convention protects refugees or asylum seekers from return to threats against their life or freedom, other serious human rights violations or persecution, but there are also certain exceptions under Article 33(2) of the Refugee Convention. That said, human rights law has rendered these somewhat irrelevant.[193]

In this developing context, the extraterritorial application of the *non-refoulement* principle (or related human rights that could apply) may represent a double-edged sword. On the one hand, it means that states intercepting migrants at sea must not bring these migrants to places where they may be subject to harm, and therefore the intercepting state has a responsibility for their safety. On the other hand, this extraterritorial application of the *non-refoulement* principle could deter states from rescuing migrants who find themselves in trouble at sea.[194] Perhaps a stronger link between the obligation of *non-refoulement* and the duty to rescue could provide a solution to this problem.[195]

This section has provided an insight into those commitments made by states under international law to give safe haven to persons from third countries fleeing harm. In practice, receiving refugees is an act for others that invariably involves a cost to the host country and, as such, it has an altruistic character.

4.7 Concluding Remarks

This chapter has focused on those obligations that are directed at protecting people in other countries from mass atrocities and serious human rights violations. One of the most significant of these obligations is the duty to prevent genocide. The judgment of the ICJ in the *Bosnia and*

[193] *Ibid.*

[194] For a more elaborate discussion, see Wilde, '"Let Them Drown": Rescuing Migrants at Sea and the Non refoulement Obligation as a Case Study of International Law's Relationship to "Crisis"' and Itamar Mann, *Humanity at Sea: Maritime Migration and the Foundations of International Law* (Cambridge University Press, 2016).

[195] See, for example, Article 98 of the United Nations Convention on the Law of the Sea, 10 December 1982, 1822 UNTS 3; Chapter V, Regulation 33 of the International Convention on Maritime Search and Rescue, 27 April 1979, 1405 UNTS 98; see, also, International Law Commission, Draft Articles on the Protection of Persons in the Event of Disasters II(2) *YBILC* (2016); Giulio Bartolini, 'The Draft Articles on "The Protection of Persons in the Event of Disasters": Towards a Flagship Treaty?', *EJIL: Talk* (2 December 2016); Erik Røsæg, 'The Duty to Rescue Refugees and Migrants at Sea', *Oxford Border Criminologies Blog* (25 March 2020), www.law.ox.ac.uk/research-subject-groups/centre-criminology/centreborder-criminologies/blog/2020/03/duty-rescue.

Herzegovina v. *Serbia and Montenegro* case has had a significant influence on the interpretation of this obligation. The Court confirmed that states have an obligation to prevent or arrest genocide in a third state. Beyond the crime of genocide, the texts of other treaties when read in the context of this case, and bearing in mind the ILC's Draft Articles on State Responsibility, imply that the duty to prevent serious breaches of international law could be much wider, and it will be interesting to see how this evolves over time.

There is also an obligation under the Geneva Conventions to ensure respect for international humanitarian law. There are several important commonalities among the duties to prevent and to ensure respect. First, they are obligations of conduct and involve due diligence on the part of the state.[196] They are imperative duties that require states to take positive action aimed at preventing or bringing to an end the relevant breach of international law. Second, both the obligation to prevent genocide and to ensure respect with the Geneva Conventions envisage a best efforts test and require states to take measures that may contribute to preventing or ending the illegal situation. It is therefore no defense for a state to claim that their best efforts alone would not have prevented the illegal act of a third state. Third, and importantly for this study, the beneficiaries of the positive action taken by states in fulfilling these obligations are the potential or actual victims of genocide, torture or grave breaches of the Geneva Conventions located in a foreign state.

The emergence of R2P represents an institutionalisation of empathy and altruism. The various mechanisms that constitute the framework of R2P allow for the international community to empathise with the victims of mass atrocity and grave human rights abuses through fact-finding, reporting and rhetorical tools. Similarly, the framework also facilitates altruistic action in order to protect these victims. As can be seen from the

[196] Although there is some disagreement amongst scholars as to whether the obligation to prevent genocide is really an obligation of due diligence per se. Marco Milanović argues that the ICJ 'made it clear that the obligation to prevent genocide is by nature a due diligence obligation', while James Crawford has contended that 'although the Court acknowledged that due diligence is an important factor in discharging the obligation of prevention, the latter cannot be categorised as an obligation of due diligence per se, because such an obligation would be breached by a state party's failure to take action, regardless of whether the prohibited event in fact took place'. See, respectively, Milanović, 'State Responsibility for Genocide: A Follow-Up', 669, 685 and James Crawford, *State Responsibility: The General Part* (Cambridge University Press, 2014), 231–232.

practice of the doctrine, however, the institutionalisation of empathy and altruism in this context has been imperfect and is incomplete.

Finally, the protection of those fleeing harm is a long-standing commitment made by states to help those people in other countries who fear for their life and well-being. The duty involves a positive action at the cost of the receiving state that will have to spend resources on behalf of the beneficiaries and, as such, it may be considered a manifestation of altruism.

5

The Substance of Altruism in International Law: Development for the Other

5.1 Introduction

This chapter will explore altruistic commitments that are specifically between developed countries and developing countries. In particular, an emphasis will be placed on the right to development, official development assistance (ODA), the right to food and particular aspects of the international economic order, as well as the special role played by the principle of solidarity in this context. The international law of development has been characterised as 'the ferment introduced into the dough of classic international law to contribute to its evolution'.[1] Indeed, the aims of the United Nations as provided for in Article 1 of its Charter include a commitment to pursue international development. Development is also mentioned in the UN Charter's Article 55, which provides for the promotion of development by the United Nations. Further still, the United Nations Economic and Social Council was created to further the aims of the UN in this area. In a similar way, the Declaration on Principles of International Law Concerning Friendly Relations and Cooperation among States[2] provides for the promotion of development through international cooperation in particular.[3] As such, this chapter will explore the various instruments, institutions and processes that are directed at furthering the cause of development by facilitating the transfer of resources from developed to developing countries.

[1] J Touscoz, 'Le régime juridique international des hydrocarbures et le droit international du développement' (1973) 2 *Clunet* 296, 303. Translation in Ahmed Mahiou, 'International Law of Development' (2013) *Max Planck Encyclopedia of Public International Law*, https://opil.ouplaw.com/view/10.1093/law:epil/9780199231690/law-9780199231690-e1428.

[2] Declaration on Principles of International Law Concerning Friendly Relations and Co-operation among States in accordance with the Charter of the United Nations, UNGA Res 2625 (XXV), 24 October 1970, UN Doc A/RES/25/2625.

[3] See also Chapter 3 of this book.

5.2 Development Assistance

The creation of the post-war international institutions and decolonisation led to a new focus on development in the 1960s. This, the United Nations proclaimed, was the 'development decade'.[4] The 1969 UN General Assembly Declaration on Social Progress and Development provides that all Member States of the United Nations 'have a responsibility to pursue internal and external policies designed to promote social development throughout the world, and in particular to assist developing countries to accelerate their economic growth'.[5] It recognises that social progress and development are the concerns of the international community at large and calls upon all members of the international community to raise living standards. Further, Article 23 of the Declaration calls specifically on developed countries to provide financial support to developing countries. It stated that this financial support should be of a magnitude of at least 1 per cent[6] of the gross national domestic product (GNP) of the developed country. Further still, Article 23 requires developed states to provide technical, financial and material assistance to developing countries through various means and on the most favourable terms possible. In addition, the Declaration calls for better co-ordination of international assistance to allow for the most effective implementation of national development plans.[7]

It should be noted that the aid volume target of 1 per cent was subsequently lowered to 0.7 per cent of GNP in Resolution 2626 (XXV) of the General Assembly on the International Development Strategy for the Second United Nations Development Decade in 1970.[8] In that resolution, the general spirit of development assistance was expressed as being 'a major part of financial resource transfers to the developing countries' and developed countries should progressively increase their ODA to developing countries such that they do their best to reach a minimum of 0.7 per cent of GNP.[9]

[4] Report of the Secretary-General, The United Nations Development Decade: Proposals for Action, UN Doc. E/3613 of 1962, www.un.org/ga/search/view_doc.asp?symbol=E/3613.

[5] Preamble, UN General Assembly Resolution 2542 (XXIV), 11 December 1969, UN Doc. A/RES/24/2542.

[6] Although this has subsequently been revised down to 0.7 per cent of gross national product.

[7] Article 23(b) and (c), *ibid.*

[8] UN General Assembly Resolution 2626 (XXV) on the International Development Strategy for the Second United Nations Development Decade 1970, 24 October 1970, UN Doc. A/RES/25/2626.

[9] *Ibid.*, para 43.

A right to development began to emerge in the 1970s and 1980s. It was affirmed in a number of resolutions of the UN Commission on Human Rights, such as Resolution 5 (XXXV) of 2 March 1979, which expressly stated that development was a human right.[10] A positive obligation on States to cooperate internationally is provided by the 1986 Declaration on the Right to Development,[11] which recognises that all states are responsible for the realisation of the right to development. Its Article 1 provides that

> [t]he right to development is an inalienable human right by virtue of which every human person and all peoples are entitled to participate in, contribute to, and enjoy economic, social, cultural and political development, in which all human rights and fundamental freedoms can be fully realized.[12]

This Declaration goes on to specify the duty bearers of the right to development in its Article 3 and makes explicit that states should create the conditions that facilitate the realisation of the right to development. Article 4(1) notes that 'States have the duty to take steps, individually and collectively, to formulate international development policies with a view to facilitating the full realization of the right to development'. It has been argued that these provisions, combined with the duty to cooperate, offer a basis for the proposition that States are under an affirmative duty to pursue a legislative programme that facilitates realisation of the right to development.[13] In the specific case of indigenous peoples, the guarantee of the right to development is more explicit, as is evident in Articles 20(1) and 23 of the Declaration on the Rights of Indigenous Peoples, which provide that 'indigenous peoples have the right to maintain and develop their political, economic and social systems or institutions, to be secure in the enjoyment of their own means of subsistence and development, and to engage freely in all their traditional and other economic activities' and the right to determine and develop priorities and strategies for exercising their right to development, respectively.[14]

[10] UN Commission on Human Rights, Resolution 5 (XXXV) of 2 March 1979.

[11] UN General Assembly Resolution 41/128, Declaration on the Right to Development, 4 December 1986, UN Doc. A/RES/41/128.

[12] *Ibid.*, Article 1.1.

[13] Laurence Boisson de Chazournes and Jason Rudall, 'Co-Operation' in Jorge E. Viñuales (ed.), *The UN Friendly Relations Declaration at 50: An Assessment of the Fundamental Principles of International Law* (Cambridge University Press, 2020), 105–132.

[14] Article 20(1), UN General Assembly Resolution 61/295, Declaration on the Rights of Indigenous Peoples, UN Doc. A/RES/61/295, Annex, UN Doc A/HRC/RES/1/2, Annex, UN Doc A/HRC/RES/2006/2, Annex, GAOR 61st Session Supp. 49, Vol III, 15.

In a similar way to Resolution 2542 (XXIV) and 2626 (XXV) described earlier, under Article 23(b) of the Declaration on the Right to Development, states have committed to improving the assistance they provide to other states as well as to implementing the target level of assistance. Moreover, states should ease lending terms via lower interest rates and longer repayment periods, as well as make the provision of loans based purely on socio-economic criteria rather than any political considerations.

Other references to the right to development can also be found, though not all of its expressions are in binding legal instruments. Article 10 of the Vienna Declaration and Programme of Action[15] and Article 26(j) of the Copenhagen Declaration on Social Development of the United Nations World Summit for Social Development in 1995[16] expresses the commitment states made to '[p]romote universal respect for, and observance and protection of, all human rights and fundamental freedoms for all, including the right to development', thereby apparently confirming its universal nature and that all states have a responsibility to ensure it is realised everywhere. The right is similarly contained in regional treaties such as Article 37 of the Arab Charter on Human Rights 2004[17] and Article 22 of the African Charter on Human and Peoples' Rights 1981,[18] which provides that

> 1. All peoples shall have the right to their economic, social and cultural development with due regard to their freedom and identity and in the equal enjoyment of the common heritage of mankind.
> 2. States shall have the duty, individually or collectively, to ensure the exercise of the right to development.

This particular provision has also been the subject of jurisprudence before the African Commission on Human and Peoples' Rights and the African Court on Human and Peoples' Rights. With respect to the former, the Commission found that the Endorois community had their general right to development breached by the Kenyan government's

[15] Vienna Declaration and Programme of Action, UN Doc. A/CONF.157/23, para 10.

[16] Copenhagen Declaration on Social Development, UN Doc. A/CONF.166/9, Annex I, Part B Principles and Goals.

[17] Arab Charter on Human Rights, 22 May 2004, (2005) 12 International Human Rights Reports 893.

[18] African Charter on Human and Peoples' Rights, 27 June 1981, OAU Doc. CAB/LEG/67/3 rev.5.

construction of a game reserve.[19] In so deciding, the Commission based its reasoning on both Article 22 of the African Convention and Article 2(3) of the UN Declaration on Development. This approach was affirmed in a case before the African Court, which found that Kenya had violated the Ogiek community's right to development by failing to take measures that would secure their other rights under the African Convention.[20]

These attempts to consolidate the emergence of a right to development have been accompanied by efforts to define the right. Indeed, the High-Level Task Force on the Implementation of the Right to Development helped to draw the contours of the right to development by elaborating on the nature and type of action states should take to ensure its realisation:

> [T]he responsibility for the creation of this enabling environment encompasses three main levels: (a) States acting collectively in global and regional partnerships ... ; (b) States acting individually as they adopt and implement policies that affect persons not strictly within their jurisdiction ... ; and (c) States acting individually as they formulate national development policies and programmes affecting persons within their jurisdiction.[21]

The Office of the United Nations High Commissioner for Human Rights has clarified that the obligation to facilitate the right to development calls for states to, among other elements, take the responsibility of crafting a national and international enabling environment to ensure all human rights are realised, construct a development policy that is both comprehensive and human-centred and includes participatory development processes, social justice and equity, as well as cultivate friendly relations with other states, international solidarity, cooperation and assistance for developing countries in particular areas where they need it, including technology transfer, access to essential medicines, debt sustainability, development aid, international trade and policy space in

[19] Communication 276/2003, *Centre for Minority Rights Development (Kenya) & Minority Rights Group International on behalf of the Endorois Welfare Council* v. *The Republic of Kenya*, 25 November 2009.

[20] Ogiek Community of the Mau Forest Case, *African Commission on Human and Peoples' Rights* v. *Kenya*, Judgment, App No 006/2012, 26 May 2017, African Court on Human and Peoples' Rights.

[21] Report of the high-level task force on the implementation of the right to development on its sixth session, 8 March 2010, UN Doc. A/HRC/15/WG.2/TF/2/Add.2, 8 (original footnotes omitted).

decision-making.[22] As such, it is clear that positive action and a commitment of resources that would benefit others are expected from developed countries in this context.

The law of development cooperation has also been referred to as the law of official development transfers.[23] This legal system co-ordinates the processes, mechanisms and criteria according to which such assistance is offered. These include the budgetary decision to set aside an amount for official development assistance, the country or sector-specific planning, negotiating and agreeing on how the assistance should be spent through projects, initiatives or programmes, and implementing the delivery of the assistance.[24] The Organisation for Economic Co-operation and Development's (OECD) Development Assistance Committee has defined ODA as 'government aid that promotes and specifically targets the economic development and welfare of developing countries'.[25] It does not include military aid nor any aid that promotes the donor's security interests.[26] Moreover, transactions having a primarily commercial objective, such as export credits, are also not characterised as ODA.[27] That said, ODA can include project or programme assistance, technical and financial cooperation, humanitarian or disaster relief or debt relief.[28]

Commitments to give financial and technical assistance have been affirmed in many other significant multilateral instruments since the turn of the millennium and illustrate that they are at the top of the international agenda. In the Millennium Declaration, adopted unanimously by the UN General Assembly in 2000,[29] states recognised the existence of an obligation owed to the most vulnerable people in the world:

> We recognize that, in addition to our separate responsibilities to our individual societies, we have a collective responsibility to uphold the

[22] Office of the United Nations High Commissioner for Human Rights, 'The Right to Development at a glance', www.un.org/en/events/righttodevelopment/pdf/rtd_at_a_glance.pdf.

[23] Philipp Dann, *The Law of Development Cooperation: A Comparative Analysis of the World Bank, the EU and Germany* (Cambridge University Press, 2013), 13.

[24] *Ibid.*

[25] OECD, 'Official Development Assistance', April 2020, www.oecd.org/dac/financing-sustainable-development/development-finance-standards/What-is-ODA.pdf.

[26] *Ibid.*

[27] *Ibid.*

[28] Dann, *The Law of Development Cooperation: A Comparative Analysis of the World Bank, the EU and Germany*, 16.

[29] UN General Assembly Resolution 55/2, 8 September 2000, UN Doc. A/RES/2.

> principles of human dignity, equality and equity at the global level. As leaders we have a duty therefore to all the world's people, especially the most vulnerable and, in particular, the children of the world, to whom the future belongs.[30]

Its paragraphs 15 and 28 call upon developed countries to give more generous financial assistance to developing countries. Moreover, it reaffirms the right to development. The Roadmap towards the Implementation of the Millennium Development Goals (MDGs) of 2001 aimed at the creation of a partnership between developed and developing states for the realisation of various goals.[31] The Roadmap reaffirmed that developed states allocate at least 0.7 per cent of their GNP to assist development in developing countries.[32] Both the Millennium Declaration and the Roadmap set out a framework through which their goals are financed by developed countries for developing countries. Goal 8 of the Roadmap was specifically concerned with concrete targets for development in respect of ODA, market access or debt sustainability.

The 2030 Agenda for Sustainable Development aims to build on the MDGs, and states have committed to making up for what was not achieved by the MDGs.[33] Indeed, through the United Nations, states have expressed that this Agenda should eradicate poverty and place the world on a sustainable path to the future. As alluded to previously, the centrepiece of Agenda 2030 is the 17 Sustainable Development Goals (SDGs) and their 169 targets. In particular, the Preamble of the General Assembly resolution in which Agenda 2030 is expressed provides that the 'Goals and targets will stimulate action over the next fifteen years in areas of critical importance for humanity and the planet.'[34] These goals are universal in their application, both in terms of their beneficiaries and of the states required to take action or commit resources to ensure they are realised, though they do take into account the varying capacity of developed and developing countries.[35]

The first SDG is particularly worthy of note, the substance of which is to 'end poverty in all its forms everywhere'.[36] In particular, Target 1.a of SDG 1 is to

[30] *Ibid.*, para 2.

[31] Report of the Secretary General, 'Road Map Towards the Implementation of the United Nations Millennium Declaration', 6 September 2001, UN Doc. A/56/326.

[32] *Ibid.*, Goal 8.

[33] United Nations General Assembly Resolution A/RES/70/1, 'Transforming Our World: The 2030 Agenda for Sustainable Development' (25 September 2015).

[34] *Ibid.*, Preamble.

[35] *Ibid.*, para 5.

[36] *Ibid.*, para 59.

> [e]nsure significant mobilization of resources from a variety of sources, including through enhanced development cooperation, in order to provide adequate and predictable means for developing countries, in particular least developed countries, to implement programmes and policies to end poverty in all its dimensions.[37]

Progress on this target would be evidenced by the '[p]roportion of resources allocated by the government directly to poverty reduction programmes' and the '[p]roportion of total government spending on essential services (education, health and social protection)'.[38] Target 1.b of SDG 1 is to '[c]reate sound policy frameworks at the national, regional and international levels, based on pro-poor and gender-sensitive development strategies, to support accelerated investment in poverty eradication actions',[39] with the indicator of progress on this target being the '[p]roportion of government recurrent and capital spending to sectors that disproportionately benefit women, the poor and vulnerable groups'.[40]

In 2015, the Addis Ababa Action Agenda for financing development was also launched.[41] In it, states committed to 'address the challenge of financing and creating an enabling environment at all levels for sustainable development in the spirit of global partnership and solidarity'.[42] Its expressed goals include bringing an end to poverty and hunger, as well as promoting sustainable development in the form of economic growth, environmental protection and social inclusion.[43] The Action Agenda was agreed upon by all 193 UN Member States that attended the Third International Conference on Financing for Development and includes more than 100 measures as well as detailing the sources of finance and calling for cooperation in the areas of technology, science, innovation, capacity building and trade.[44] The Action Agenda was also intended to support the 2030 Agenda for Sustainable Development, which includes the SDGs as mentioned earlier.[45]

[37] *Ibid.*, Target 1.a.
[38] *Ibid.*, Indicator 1.a.1 and 1.a.2, respectively.
[39] *Ibid.*, Target 1.b.
[40] *Ibid.*, Indicator 1.b.1.
[41] United Nations, *Addis Ababa Action Agenda of the Third International Conference on Financing for Development* (United Nations, 2015) endorsed by UN General Assembly Resolution 69/313, 27 July 2015, UN Doc. A/RES/69/313.
[42] *Ibid.*, para 1.
[43] *Ibid.*
[44] *Ibid.*
[45] *Ibid.*, para 2.

Prior to this, two International Conferences on Financing for Development had been held in 2002 and 2008 respectively. The first in 2002 was held in Monterrey, Mexico and resulted in the so-called Monterrey Consensus.[46] This included six main areas of action, including the mobilisation of domestic financial resources for development, international resources for development, as well as a commitment to using international trade as an engine for development, increasing international financial and technical cooperation for development, harnessing sustainable debt for development and seeking opportunities for debt relief for developing countries, as well as addressing systemic issues such as enhancing the coherence and consistency of international monetary, financial and trading systems for development.[47] This was followed by a second conference in 2008, which led to the Doha Declaration reaffirming the Monterrey Consensus and which sought new ways to strengthen financing for development, primarily within the six issue-areas identified earlier.[48] These instruments also reaffirm the level of ODA – 0.7 per cent GNP – that developed countries should provide to developing countries.

Over time, specific programmes and institutions dedicated to development and the provision of aid have also been created and elaborated. Examples include the United Nations Fund for Economic Development and the Expanded Programme of Technical Assistance, which were merged in 1965 to create the United Nations Development Programme (UNDP).[49] Similarly, the United Nations Conference on Trade and Development (UNCTAD), the United Nations Capital Development Fund and the United Nations Industrial Development Organization (UNIDO) are United Nations institutions dedicated to economic development. In the story of development within the United Nations context, the Agenda for Development, which began in 1994 and was followed up in 1997, also played an important role in re-cementing development at the top of the international agenda.[50] It should also be noted that this

[46] United Nations, *Monterrey Consensus on Financing for Development* (United Nations, 2002), www.un.org/esa/ffd/wp-content/uploads/2014/09/MonterreyConsensus.pdf.

[47] *Ibid.*

[48] United Nations, *Doha Declaration on Financing for Development* (United Nations, 2008), www.un.org/esa/ffd/wp-content/uploads/2014/09/Doha_Declaration_FFD.pdf.

[49] See *Yearbook of the United Nations* (1965), 283–300, www.unmultimedia.org/searchers/yearbook/page.jsp?volume=1965&page=1.

[50] Report of the UN Secretary General, An Agenda for Development, 6 May 1994, UN Doc. A/48/935; Report of the Ad Hoc Open-ended Working Group of the General Assembly on an Agenda for Development, 19 September 1997, UN Doc A/51/45.

Agenda called for the mobilisation of domestic resources as well as external aid, including technical and financial assistance.[51] Moreover, the Economic Commissions for Europe, Asia and the Far East, Latin America and Africa all assist in co-ordinating state policies on development and the provision of aid. The International Bank for Reconstruction and Development, the International Development Association and the International Finance Corporation at the international level, as well as the Inter-American, Asian and African Development Banks at the regional level, all provide finance for development efforts. In addition to multilateral efforts, there are of course many bilateral agreements which facilitate the provision of aid to developing countries.

As explored earlier, the obligation of international cooperation, such as that found under Article 11(2) of the International Covenant on Economic, Social and Cultural Rights committing states to take measures 'individually and through international cooperation' to realise the right to be free from hunger, provides a further basis for the broader right to development with a correlative obligation on developed states to ensure realisation of such rights.[52] Indeed, the Inter-American Commission on Human Rights concluded in respect of economic, social and cultural rights that 'the more developed countries have an obligation vis-à-vis the less developed countries. Without solid support from the wealthy countries within the area, development of the poorer countries is almost impossible.'[53] Similarly, the General Assembly of the Organization of American States has emphasised the 'responsibility of the economically more developed member states to make every possible effort to participate fully in cooperation for hemispheric development'.[54] This also illustrates the significant role played by international cooperation as

[51] Report of the UN Secretary General, An Agenda for Development, 6 May 1994, UN Doc. A/48/935, para 142; Report of the Ad Hoc Open-ended Working Group of the General Assembly on an Agenda for Development, 19 September 1997, UN Doc A/51/45, para 203.

[52] See, for example, statement of M'Baye (Senegal), 33rd Session of the UN Commission on Human Rights, 33 UN ESCOR C.4, UN Doc. E/CN.4/SR.1391, para 18, (1978); Philip Alston and Gerard Quinn, 'The Nature and Scope of States Parties' Obligations under the International Covenant on Economic, Social and Cultural Rights' (1987) 9(2) *Human Rights Quarterly* 156, 187.

[53] Annual Report of the Inter-American Commission on Human Rights 1979–1980, OAS Doc. OEA/Ser. G/CP/doc. 110/80, 152–153.

[54] OAS General Assembly Resolution AG/RES.510 (X-O/80), 27 November 1980.

a vehicle for the implementation of the right to development in all its manifestations.

Efforts to provide development assistance and the emergence of the right to development largely took place in parallel to the creation of the New International Economic Order, elements of which remain today and other elements that seek to further development have been added to the international economic order as we know it now. We turn to consider these in the next section.

5.3 The International Economic Order and Development

Since World War II, various efforts that, at least in part, aim at promoting international economic justice have been pursued.[55] The Bretton Woods institutions are particularly prominent in this respect. The records of the oral debates at the 1974 Sixth Special Session of the General Assembly on the New International Economic Order evidence an effort to develop economic relations based on the principle of solidarity.[56] That the foundation of the Order would be the principles of equity, interdependence and cooperation is stipulated in the Preamble to the Declaration of 1 May 1974 Concerning the Establishment of a New International Economic Order.[57] It has been observed that these initiatives 'reinforc[ed] the moral commitment of industrial States'.[58] Moreover, as mentioned earlier, an institutional structure in the form of UNCTAD was created in 1964 by the UN General Assembly with the aim of integrating development with international trade, investment and finance: 'convinced of the benefits of international co-operation with a view to helping the developing

[55] See, for example, UN General Assembly Resolution 3201, New International Economic Order, 1 May 1974, UN Doc. A/RES/3201; UN General Assembly Resolution 3202, Programme of Action on the Establishment of a New International Economic Order, 1 May 1974, UN Doc. A/RES/3201(S/VI); UN General Assembly Resolution 3281 (XXIX), Charter of Economic Rights and Duties of States, 12 December 1974, UN Doc. A/RES/3281 (XXIX).

[56] Mohammed Bedjaoui, 'Droit du développement et jus cogens' (1984–1986) 54–56 *Annuaire de l'A.A.A.* 275; Ronald St. J. Macdonald, 'Solidarity in the Practice and Discourse of Public International Law' (1996) 8 *Pace International Law Review* 259, 263.

[57] Preamble, UN General Assembly Resolution 3201 (S-VI), Declaration on the Establishment of a New International Economic Order, 1 May 1974, UN Doc. A/RES/ 3201 (S-VI).

[58] Domenico da Empoli, 'Financial Assistance' (2011) *Max Planck Encyclopedia of International Law*, https://opil-ouplaw-com.ezproxy.leidenuniv.nl:2443/view/10.1093/law:epil/9780199231690/law-9780199231690-e1523?rskey=y5SODi&result=1&prd=MPIL.

countries to reach a higher standard of life, the States ... are resolved, in a sense of human solidarity, "to employ international machinery for the promotion of economic and social advancement of all people"'.[59] As such, it sought to address some of the structural issues in the international economic order, not least in terms of commodity prices, trade terms and the issue of foreign debt. UNCTAD became a permanent organ of the UN General Assembly in December 1964.[60] This resonated with the stated objectives of the New International Economic Order, which was also intended to 'correct inequalities and redress existing injustices, ... eliminate the widening gap between the developed and developing countries and ensure steadily accelerating economic and social development ... for present and future generations'.[61]

It has been pointed out that the Declaration on the Establishment of a New International Economic Order of 1974 was the first occasion on which the UN General Assembly had called for action on inequality and injustice.[62] In it an obligation was placed on states to do no harm and also provided that development was a common goal and duty for all.[63] Indeed, '[t]he purpose of cooperation is declared to be elimination of disparities among states and preferential treatment of and active assistance to the [Least Developed Countries]'.[64] Further, under the Declaration of 1974, duties regarding the transfer of assistance, financial resources, scientific know-how and technology were included.[65]

A somewhat stronger obligation is evident in the Charter of Economic Rights and Duties of States, adopted by General Assembly resolution on 12 December 1974, and which provides in its Article 24 that

[59] Preamble, Final Act, Proceedings of the United Nations Conference on Trade and Development 1964, Volume 1, UN Doc. E/CONF.46/141, para 2.

[60] United Nations General Assembly Resolution 1995 (XIX), The establishment of the United Nations Conference on Trade and Development as an organ of the General Assembly (United Nations General Assembly [UNGA]), 21 September 1979, UN Doc. A/RES/1995(XIX).

[61] United Nations General Assembly Resolution 3201 (S-VI), Declaration on the Establishment of a New International Economic Order, 1 May 1974, UN Doc. A/RES/3201(S-VI).

[62] Macdonald, 'Solidarity in the Practice and Discourse of Public International Law', 263.

[63] United Nations General Assembly Resolution 3201 (S-VI), Declaration on the Establishment of a New International Economic Order, 1 May 1974, UN Doc. A/RES/3201(S-VI).

[64] *Ibid.*

[65] *Ibid.*; Holger Hestermeyer, *'Reality or Aspiration? Solidarity in International Environmental and World Trade Law' Diversity and Homogeneity, Outcome Paper 2/2012* (Max Planck Institute, 2012).

> [a]ll States have the duty to conduct their mutual economic relations in a manner which takes into account the interests of other countries. In particular, all States should avoid prejudicing the interests of developing countries.[66]

Similarly, Article 6 notes the duty on states to take into consideration the interests of producers and consumers, and to contribute to the development of international trade.[67] Stronger again are those obligations under the Charter of Economic Rights and Duties of States that speak to the duty on states to cooperate to promote social, economic and cultural development (Article 7), to cooperate in achieving more equitable economic relations (Article 8), to encourage structural changes for a more 'balanced world economy' that serves the 'needs and interests of all countries, especially developing countries', and to cooperate in promoting 'economic and social progress throughout the world, especially that of the developing countries'.[68] Moreover, Article 18 provides that developed countries should take into account the interests and needs of developing countries by endeavouring to 'avoid measures having a negative effect on the development of the national economies of the developing counties' and should promote development through the use of generalised tariff preferences as well as adopting other measures that favour developing countries.[69]

That developed countries are under an obligation to respect the needs and interests of developing countries is also underlined in Article 22. As such, it provides that the needs and objectives of developing countries must be promoted through 'increased net flows of real resources to the developing countries from all sources' not least 'to reinforce the efforts of developing countries to accelerate their economic and social development'.[70] In particular, developed countries are expected, over time, 'to increase the net amount of financial flows from official sources to developing countries' as well as ensure the conditions of such financial flows are as favourable as possible.[71] Finally, development assistance should also include technical assistance as well as economic assistance.[72]

66 Charter of Economic Rights and Duties of States, 12 December 1974, UN Doc. A/RES/3281 (XXIX).
67 *Ibid.*
68 *Ibid.*
69 *Ibid.*
70 Article 22(1), *ibid.*
71 Article 22(2), *ibid.*
72 Article 22(3), *ibid.*

The 1986 Declaration on the Right to Development, mentioned earlier, underlined that New International Economic Order should play a role in the realisation of the right to development.[73] In particular, the Declaration recognises that the promotion and protection of human rights should be linked to the efforts to establish the New International Economic Order. Moreover, the Declaration envisages that the New International Economic Order should be based on sovereign equality, interdependence, mutual interest and cooperation between states.

The principles of solidarity and cooperation also influenced the mechanisms of the New International Economic Order in a very real way. In fact, it has been said that, while the Declaration on the Establishment of a New International Economic Order and the Charter of Economic Rights and Duties of States do not explicitly refer to the principle of solidarity, they do reflect it.[74] In 1986, the International Law Association issued a Draft Declaration on the Progressive Development of Principles of Public International Law relating to the New International Economic Order, which would commit states,

> whose economic, monetary and financial policies have a substantial impact on other States, [to] conduct their economic policies in a manner which takes into account the interests of other countries by appropriate procedures of consultation; in the legitimate exercise of their economic sovereignty, they should seek to avoid any measure which causes substantial injury to other States, in particular to those interests of developing States and their peoples.[75]

This suggests states should take into account the interests of others in setting national policies and particularly when conducting their economic affairs, and especially resonates with the idea that states should be accountable to foreign stakeholders and serve as trustees of humanity, as argued by Eyal Benvenisti.[76]

[73] Preamble and Article 3, UN General Assembly Resolution 41/128, Declaration on the Right to Development, 4 December 1986, UN Doc. A/41/128.

[74] Philipp Dann, 'Solidarity and the Law of Development Cooperation' in Rüdiger Wolfrum and Chie Kojima (eds.), *Solidarity: A Structural Principle of International Law* (Springer, 2010), 55.

[75] UN General Assembly Resolution 58/251, Draft Declaration on the Progressive Development of Principles of Public International Law Relating to the New International Economic Order, 5 November 2003, UN Doc. A/58/251.

[76] See Chapter 1 of this book for a full account of the argument; Eyal Benvenisti, 'Sovereigns as Trustees of Humanity: On the Accountability of States to Foreign Stakeholders' (2013) 107(2) *American Journal of International Law* 295.

Turning now to the area of international trade, it has been said that the purpose of international trade law is 'to limit the negative international externalities that countries create when they set their trade and industrial policies'.[77] The goal of economic development was in fact inserted into the Preamble to the Agreement Establishing the World Trade Organization (WTO Agreement).[78] This had not been a feature of its predecessor agreement: the General Agreement on Tariffs and Trade of 1947 (GATT 1947). That said, a particularly notable development under the GATT regime, which continues to exist today, was the 'Enabling Clause' in 1979.[79] The Enabling Clause permits Member States (including of the WTO today) to afford differential and more favourable treatment to developing countries. This of course is a broad exception to one of the foundational principles of the world trading system, namely the most favoured nation (MFN) principle provided for under Article I of the General Agreement on Tariffs and Trade of 1994 (GATT 1994), which is part of the WTO Agreement. Under the Enabling Clause, the Generalized System of Preferences (GSP) allows developed Member States to accord more favourable tariff rates (lower than their MFN rate) to developing Member States. This has been described as resulting 'from an altruistic concern for the less fortunate'.[80]

Prior to the Enabling Clause, a system of preferences for developing countries was established under the 1971 Waiver Decision, which sought to facilitate the 'promotion of the trade and export earnings of developing countries for the furtherance of their economic development'.[81] This scheme had been intended, like the Enabling Clause, to 'eliminate the fragmented system of special preferences that were, in general, based on historical and political ties between developed countries and their former

[77] Gene Grossman and Alan Sykes, 'A Preference for Development: The Law and Economics of GSP' in George Bermann and Petros Mavroidis (eds.), *WTO Law and Developing Countries* (Cambridge University Press, 2007), 277.

[78] Preamble, Agreement Establishing the World Trade Organization, 15 April 1994, 1867 UNTS 154.

[79] World Trade Organisation, Decision on Differential and Most Favourable Treatment, Reciprocity and Fuller Participation of Developing Countries, 28 November 1979, GATT Doc. L/4903. Hestermeyer, 'Reality or Aspiration? Solidarity in International Environmental and World Trade Law'.

[80] Gene Grossman and Alan Sykes, 'A Preference for Development: The Law and Economics of GSP' (2005) 4 *World Trade Review* 41, 67.

[81] Preamble, Decision on Generalized System of Preferences (the '1971 Waiver Decision'), 25 June 1971, WT/L/3545.

colonies'.[82] These are, as such, interesting developments as they seek to apply trade preferences more fairly on the basis of need rather than vested interests. While such schemes are not mandatory for Member States of the WTO, many countries have in fact provided favourable treatment. According to the WTO, in the first decade of this millennium, twenty-three Member States pursued thirty-six initiatives that had as a goal the improvement of market access for Least Developed Countries.[83]

The Enabling Clause has also been interpreted by the WTO's Dispute Settlement Body, and the dimensions of the Clause have become more apparent. The *EC – Tariff Preferences* case[84] between India and the European Communities concerned the European Community according tariff preferences under its generalised system of preferences. In the case, India argued that the way in which tariff preferences were accorded by the European Community created obstacles for Indian exports to the European Community and mitigated any benefits it could accrue under the MFN provisions of the GATT 1994. More particularly, India considered that the Enabling Clause did not require developing countries to waive their MFN rights as regards other developing countries.[85] India was of the view that, were this to be the case, it would be inconsistent with certain provisions of the Enabling Clause, which was overall intended to benefit developing countries. The Panel in this case accepted that tariff preferences accorded by developed countries must be extended to all developing countries.[86] On appeal, the Appellate Body upheld the Panel's finding that the Enabling Clause operates as an exception to the MFN provision in Article I:1 of the GATT 1994. However, the Appellate Body also found that preference-granting countries did not have to accord the same treatment to all GSP beneficiaries, reversing the finding of the Panel.[87] In this respect, the Appellate Body was of the view that:

> [h]aving examined the text and content of footnote 3 to paragraph 2(a) of the Enabling Clause, and the object and purpose of the WTO Agreement

[82] DS246, *European Communities – Conditions for the Granting of Tariff Preferences to Developing Countries*, WT/DS246/AB/R.

[83] WTO, Market Access for Products and Services of Export Interest to Least Developed Countries, WT/COMTD/LDC/W/46/Rev.1 (Geneva, 2010).

[84] DS246, *European Communities – Conditions for the Granting of Tariff Preferences to Developing Countries*, WT/DS246/AB/R.

[85] DS246, *European Communities – Conditions for the Granting of Tariff Preferences to Developing Countries*, WT/DS246/AB/R (Panel Report), para 7.162.

[86] *Ibid.*, para 7.174.

[87] DS246, *European Communities – Conditions for the Granting of Tariff Preferences to Developing Countries*, WT/DS246/AB/R (Appellate Body Report), paras 173–174.

> and the Enabling Clause, we conclude that the term 'non-discriminatory' in footnote 3 does not prohibit developed-country Members from granting different tariffs to products originating in different GSP beneficiaries, provided that such differential tariff treatment meets the remaining conditions in the Enabling Clause.[88]

As far as the extent of this right to differentiate is concerned, differentiation may only be made where there is a need that a developed country is responding to, and this need must be defined by an objective standard. Moreover, the differentiation must only be on the basis of ameliorating the development, financial or trade circumstances of the developing state in view of the identified need.[89] Further still, any differentiation on the basis of a particular need must be equally accorded to similarly situated beneficiaries.[90] The WTO's Appellate Body noted that making it easier to justify preferences given to developing countries would facilitate greater returns from the increasing exports of developing countries. It also pointed out that these returns are central to the economic development of these countries.[91]

More generally, special and differential treatment for developing countries has gradually been extended under the WTO regime.[92] In fact, it has been observed that a significant number of provisions in the WTO Agreements, as well as related decisions, provide for special and differential treatment that benefits developing countries. These provisions include those that increase trade opportunities and safeguard the interests of developing countries, those that offer flexibility in commitments, action, transitional time periods and policies that apply to developing countries as well as those that offer technical assistance.[93]

It should also be highlighted that, in the contemporary WTO system, the obligations of developed countries in respect of developing countries

[88] *Ibid.*, para 173.

[89] Lorand Bartels, 'Internet Roundtable: The Appellate Body's GSP Decision' (2004) 3(2) *World Trade Review* 239, 244 (footnotes omitted).

[90] *Ibid.*

[91] DS246, *European Communities – Conditions for the Granting of Tariff Preferences to Developing Countries*, WT/DS246/AB/R (Appellate Body), para 106.

[92] For example, General Council, Preferential Tariff Treatment for Least Developed Countries, Decision on Waiver, 17 June 1999, WT/L/3014; prolonged by General Council, Preferential Tariff Treatment for Least-Developed Countries, Decision on Extension of Waiver, 29 May 2009, WT/L/759.

[93] Hestermeyer, 'Reality or Aspiration? Solidarity in International Environmental and World Trade Law', drawing information from WTO Secretariat, Special and Differential Treatment Provisions in WTO Agreements and Decisions, 8 June 2010, TN/CTD/W/33, paras 2–5.

under the WTO Agreements are considered as non-reciprocal. This is made explicit in Article XXXVI:8 of the GATT 1994, which provides that:

> [t]he developed contracting parties do not expect reciprocity for commitments made by them in trade negotiations to reduce or remove tariffs and other barriers to the trade of less-developed contracting parties.

Other trade agreements in the WTO system encourage states to give consideration to the interests and effects of trade measures on third states. For example, Article 12(1) of the Agreement on Agriculture provides that '[w]here any Member institutes any new export restrictions on foodstuffs . . . the Member instituting the export restriction shall give due consideration to the effects of such prohibition or restriction on importing Members' food security'. This once again demonstrates the expectation that states act as agents of humanity and be accountable to all foreign stakeholders when crafting their policies.[94]

In a different way, the 2001 Doha Declaration, which resulted from the fourth WTO Ministerial Meeting in Doha, represented an occasion for developed states to reaffirm their commitments to developed states, and in particular to commit to providing 'incentives to their enterprises and institutions to promote and encourage technology transfer to least-developed country Members'.[95] And Article 6 of the Declaration recognised that

> WTO Members with insufficient or no manufacturing capacities in the pharmaceutical sector could face difficulties in making effective use of compulsory licensing under the [Agreement on Trade-Related Aspects of Intellectual Property Rights (TRIPS)]. We instruct the Council for TRIPS to find an expeditious solution to this problem.[96]

As a consequence, in 2003, WTO Member States agreed to make it easier for poor countries to import generic drugs they are unable to manufacture themselves.[97] In particular, it waived the application of Article 31(f)

[94] See Benvenisti, 'Sovereigns as Trustees of Humanity: On the Accountability of States to Foreign Stakeholders'.

[95] Article 7, WTO Ministerial Conference, Declaration on the TRIPS Agreement and Public Health, 14 November 2001, WT/MIN(01)/DEC/2.

[96] *Ibid.*

[97] Implementation of paragraph 6 of the Doha Declaration on the TRIPS Agreement and public health, Decision of the General Council, 30 August 2003, WT/L/540. For a more detailed analysis, see Isabel Feichtner, 'The Waiver Power of the WTO: Opening the WTO for Political Debate on the Reconciliation of Competing Interests' (2009) 20(3) *European Journal of International Law* 615. See also Benvenisti, 'Sovereigns as Trustees of Humanity: On the Accountability of States to Foreign Stakeholders', 324.

of the TRIPS Agreement, which requires that such drugs made under compulsory licencing be primarily reserved for consumption in the domestic market. This had the effect of preventing poor countries' access to these drugs as patented versions of the drugs were often too expensive. The Director-General of the WTO at the time, Supachai Panitchpakdi, said of the decision:

> This is a historic agreement for the WTO .... The final piece of the jigsaw has fallen into place, allowing poorer countries to make full use of the flexibilities in the WTO's intellectual property rules in order to deal with the diseases that ravage their people. It proves once and for all that the organization can handle humanitarian as well as trade concerns .... The fact that WTO members have managed to find a compromise in such a complex issue bears testimony to their goodwill.[98]

It has been observed that this decision fulfils the 'criteria for an action to be considered altruistic'.[99] This is because, first of all, any self-interest for developed countries in the decision is coincidental. The decision in fact disadvantages their own corporations so that those in developing countries can have affordable drugs. Secondly, any self-interest that there may be in the desire to prevent the spread of disease was not the primary motivating factor. In the final analysis of this decision, it has been argued that it 'proves the potential for purely altruistic actions at the international level'.[100]

In a similar vein, in 2006, the European Union adopted a regulation on Compulsory Licensing of Patents Relating to the Manufacture of Pharmaceutical Products for Export to Countries with Public Health Problems, which permitted the compulsory licensing authorities of EU Member States to address public health issues in developing countries, particularly by improving access to safe, effective and affordable medicines.[101] Moreover, the regulation promoted technology transfer to and capacity-building in developing countries with inadequate pharmaceutical manufacturing capabilities.[102] In this context, there

[98] 'Decision removes final patent obstacle to cheap drug imports', 30 August 2003, www.wto.org/english/news_e/pres03_e/pr350_e.htm.

[99] Jeffrey Ding, 'An Altruistic Approach to Human Rights Policy', *Iowa Center for Human Rights* 2013, 4, www.drake.edu/media/departmentsoffices/international/nelson/ding.pdf.

[100] *Ibid.*

[101] Regulation (EC) 816/2006 of the European Parliament and of the Council of 17 May 2006 on Compulsory Licensing of Patents Relating to the Manufacture of Pharmaceutical Products for Export to Countries with Public Health Problems, 2006 OJ (L 157) 1.

[102] *Ibid.*

have also been more informal commitments made to complement the formal legal commitments.[103] For example, the Global Fund to Fight AIDS, Tuberculosis and Malaria and UNITAID are both organisations established by states with the objective of ameliorating the health of those in developing countries.

In respect of a different commodity, WTO Member States have also been known to exercise altruism – again arguably in spite of their own short-term economic interests – with respect to conflict diamonds.[104] As such, in 2003, the WTO allowed Member States to adopt trade restrictions on countries that were not members of the Kimberley Process Certification Scheme for Rough Diamonds. The Kimberley Process is an international certification scheme that aims to prevent conflict diamonds from entering the international market.[105] In the WTO context, a waiver was proposed by Australia, Brazil, Canada, Israel, Japan, Korea, the Philippines, Sierra Leone, Thailand, the United Arab Emirates and the United States in an effort to fight the trade in conflict diamonds.[106] The WTO's General Council subsequently issued the waiver.[107] The Decision recognised

> the extraordinary humanitarian nature of this issue and the devastating impact of conflicts fuelled by trade in conflict diamonds on the peace, safety and security of people in affected countries and the systematic and gross human rights violations that have been perpetrated in such conflicts.[108]

[103] Benvenisti, 'Sovereigns as Trustees of Humanity: On the Accountability of States to Foreign Stakeholders', 324.

[104] See, for example, Joost Pauwelyn, 'WTO Compassion or Superiority Complex?: What to Make of the WTO Waiver for "Conflict Diamonds"' (2003) 24(4) *Michigan Journal of International Law* 1177; Feichtner, 'The Waiver Power of the WTO: Opening the WTO for Political Debate on the Reconciliation of Competing Interests', 615; Krista Nadakavukaren Schefer, 'Stopping Trade in Conflict Diamonds: Exploring the Trade and Human Rights Interface with the WTO Waiver for the Kimberley Process' in Thomas Cottier, Joost Pauwelyn and Elisabeth Bürgi Bonanomi (eds.), *Human Rights and International Trade* (Oxford University Press, 2005), 420–440; Kevin Gray, 'Conflict Diamonds and the WTO: Not the Best Opportunity to be Missed for the Trade-Human Rights Interface' in Cottier, Pauwelyn and Bonanomi (eds.), *Human Rights and International Trade*.

[105] The Kimberley Process [website], www.kimberleyprocess.com/.

[106] See WTO, 'Agreement reached on WTO waiver for "Conflict Diamonds"', 26 February 2003, www.wto.org/english/news_e/news03_e/goods_council_26fev03_e.htm.

[107] WTO General Council, Waiver Concerning Kimberley Process Certification Scheme for Rough Diamonds, Decision of 15 May 2003, WTO Doc. WT/L/518.

[108] Council for Trade in Goods, Waiver Concerning Kimberley Process Certification Scheme for Rough Diamonds, 24 February 2003, G/C/W/432. The Waiver was extended by General Council Decision of 15 December 2006, WT/L/676.

Some have said that WTO Members adopted this decision for noble reasons. In particular, the nexus between the trade in such diamonds and the proliferation of war, humanitarian crises and terrorism, in Africa and beyond, is well known. Indeed, legal scholars have noted that efforts at ceasing this trade must be characterised as humanitarian acts of 'compassion'.[109] Furthermore, it has been noted that this development has helped to 'guarantee the basic human rights not only of [states'] own citizens, but also of those *abroad*. For the states involved in Kimberley that do not themselves export diamonds are all using trade as a foreign policy measure – seeking to protect *another state's* residents by requiring the certificates as a condition of importation'.[110]

The Kimberley Process Certification Scheme for Rough Diamonds is itself an effort to prevent gross human rights abuses by suppressing the valuable trade in conflict diamonds.[111] The Preamble to the Kimberley Process Certification Scheme provides in part that trade in conflict diamonds can fuel conflicts and cause 'systematic and gross human rights violations'.[112] Moreover, the UN General Assembly has unanimously adopted a resolution which recognises the role that trade in conflict diamonds plays in catalysing conflict and leading to human rights violations.[113] The Scheme has also been endorsed by the Security Council.[114]

While the Kimberley Process Certification Scheme is not a binding treaty, its link to the WTO waiver provided a new legal dimension to

[109] Pauwelyn, 'WTO Compassion or Superiority Complex?: What to Make of the WTO Waiver for "Conflict Diamonds"', 1198.

[110] Steven Ratner, *The Thin Justice of International Law: A Moral Reckoning of the Law of Nations* (Oxford University Press, 2015), 330(emphasis in original).

[111] See Interlaken Declaration of 5 November 2002 on the Kimberley Process Certification Scheme for Rough Diamonds, www.kimberleyprocess.com/documents/basic_core_documents_en.html; see also its endorsement in General Assembly and Security Council Resolutions, e.g. UN General Assembly Resolution 57/302, The role of diamonds in fuelling conflict: Breaking the link between the illicit transaction of rough diamonds and armed conflict as a contribution to prevention and settlement of conflicts, 20 April 2003, UN Doc. A/RES57/302; UN Security Council Resolution 1459, 28 January 2003, UN Doc. S/RES/1459.

[112] *Ibid.*

[113] UN General Assembly Resolution 55/56, The role of diamonds in fuelling conflict: Breaking the link between the illicit transaction of rough diamonds and armed conflict as a contribution to prevention and settlement of conflicts, 29 January 2001, UN Doc. A/RES/55/56; UN General Assembly Resolution 56/263, The role of diamonds in fuelling conflict: Breaking the link between the illicit transaction of rough diamonds and armed conflict as a contribution to prevention and settlement of conflicts, 9 April 2002, UN Doc. A/RES/56/263.

[114] UN Security Council Resolution 1459, 28 January 2003.

measures aimed at preventing the trade in conflict diamonds. For some, the Kimberley Process Certification Scheme and the WTO waiver both show that WTO rules could be interpreted as attempts to stem conflict and propagate peace, particularly in Africa.[115] More generally, they are an expression of solidarity, which has played a significant role in shaping commitments to developing countries in the area of development and the international economic order, as has been alluded to earlier and as will be explored in more detail in the following section.

5.4 The Role of Solidarity in Development

The right to development has been characterised as a 'solidarity right'.[116] Such solidarity rights also include the rights to peace, to a healthy environment, to share in the common heritage of humankind and to communication and are sometimes referred to as third-generation human rights.[117] While certain scholars have noted that such rights are generally aspirational in nature, others have pointed to the fact that individual third-generation rights have been referred to in international and regional treaties, as well as by treaty bodies, experts and courts.[118] For example, most recently the Addis Ababa Action Agenda in creating a framework to finance the post-2015 sustainable development agenda and the SDGs, emphasises 'global partnership and solidarity'.[119]

[115] Ratner, *The Thin Justice of International Law: A Moral Reckoning of the Law of Nations*, 329.

[116] Petra Minnerop, Naomi Roht-Arriaza and Sara Aminzadeh, 'Solidarity Rights (Development, Peace, Environment and Humanitarian Assistance)' (2018) *Max Planck Encyclopedia of Public International Law*, https://opil-ouplaw-com.ezproxy.leidenuniv.nl:2443/view/10.1093/law:epil/9780199231690/law-9780199231690-e1470?rskey=jN1sV1&result=1&prd=MPIL; see also Karel Vasak, 'For the Third Generation of Human Rights: The Right of Solidarity' (Inaugural Lecture Tenth Study Session International Institute of Human Rights, July 1979); Karel Vasak, 'Pour une troisième génération des droits de l'homme' in Christophe Swinarski (ed.), *Studies and Essays on International Humanitarian Law and Red Cross Principles in Honour of Jean Pictet* (Martinus Nijhoff, 1984), 837–850.

[117] *Ibid.*

[118] *Ibid.* See, for example, Articles 19–24, African Charter on Human and Peoples' Rights 1981; Article 11, Additional Protocol to the American Convention on Human Rights in the Area of Economic, Social and Cultural Rights; Article 37, Arab Charter of Human Rights 2004; Chapter IV, Charter of Fundamental Rights of the European Union 2000.

[119] United Nations, *Addis Ababa Action Agenda of the Third International Conference on Financing for Development* (United Nations, 2015) endorsed by UN General Assembly Resolution 69/313, 27 July 2015, UN Doc. A/RES/69/313, para 1.

The principle of solidarity has a long history in the context of international law.[120] Indeed, Emer de Vattel saw this principle as both essential to the international legal order and also voluntary and unenforceable.[121] Today, the principle of solidarity has been described as a 'multifunctional principle'.[122] It is visible across various fragments of international law, from international economic law and international human rights law to international environmental law, and it has a differing role across these different disciplines.[123] Solidarity involves the pursuit of common objectives. While there are varying definitions of the notion of solidarity, UN Resolution 56/151 of 19 December 2001,[124] 57/213 of 18 December 2002[125] and 59/193 of 18 March 2005[126] provide a helpful articulation of the principle:

> [s]olidarity as a fundamental value, by virtue of which global challenges must be managed in a way that distributes costs and burdens fairly, in accordance with basic principles of equity and social justice, and ensures that those who suffer or benefit the least receive help from those who benefit the most.

The latter part of this provision in particular expresses a responsibility that is incumbent on those individuals who are privileged and which is owed to those who are least privileged, and makes no mention of any

[120] Emer de Vattel, *Le Droit des Gens ou Principes de la Souveraineté* (1758, reprinted, 1958), Préliminaires ss. 13.

[121] Macdonald, 'Solidarity in the Practice and Discourse of Public International Law', 261.

[122] Rüdiger Wolfrum, 'Solidarity amongst States: An Emerging Structural Principle of International Law', in Pierre-Marie Dupuy (ed.), *Völkerrecht als Weltordnung. Festschrift für Christian Tomuschat* (NP Engel, Kehl, 2006), 1087. For other scholarly explorations of solidarity, see generally Rüdiger Wolfrum and Chie Kojima (eds.), *Solidarity: A Structural Principle of International Law* (Springer, 2010).

[123] Karel Wellens, 'Revisiting Solidarity as a (Re-)Emerging Constitutional Principle: Some Further Reflections' in Wolfrum and Kojima (eds.), *Solidarity: A Structural Principle of International Law*, 13; Holger Hestermeyer, *'Reality or Aspiration? Solidarity in International Environmental and World Trade Law' Diversity and Homogeneity, Outcome Paper 2/2012* (Max Planck Institute, 2012), 18–19, www.mpil.de/ww/de/pub/forschung/forschung_im_detail/projekte/otto_hah. Hestermeyer provides a presentation of the various nuances of solidarity we see in the different fragments of international law as well as pointing to some of the less obvious shortcomings of solidarity, particularly in the area of international trade. He concludes that the distinction between self-centred solidarity and altruistic solidarity reveals that obligations of the latter type, while they may be as widespread as those of the former type, are in practice implemented to a lesser degree than obligations of the former, self-centred type.

[124] UN General Assembly Resolution 56/151, 19 December 2001, UN Doc. A/RES/56/151.

[125] UN General Assembly Resolution 57/213, 18 December 2002, UN Doc. A/RES/57/213.

[126] UN General Assembly Resolution 59/193, 18 March 2005, UN Doc. A/RES/59/193.

barrier to such an obligation in the form of nationality or otherwise. Subsequently, the General Assembly has reiterated the importance of solidarity and attempted to refine it over time.[127] Article 29(1) of the Universal Declaration of Human Rights provides that '[e]veryone has duties to the community', and evidences an expanded conception of legal obligation that reaches across state borders. In this and other areas of international law, authors have noted that there exists a principle of solidarity,[128] which redefines obligations in respect of humanitarian intervention and assistance.

The Commission on Human Rights and the Human Rights Council have each played a role in developing the principle. Often, these institutions have linked the principle of solidarity to a call for assisting developing countries.[129] The Human Rights Council also appointed Mr Rudi Muhammad Rizki as the Independent Expert on Human Rights and International Solidarity, who subsequently published a 'Report on Human Rights and International Solidarity' in 2010.[130] Mr Rizki noted that solidarity represented

> the union of interests or purposes among countries, and social cohesion between them, based upon the dependence of States and other international actors on each other, in order to preserve the order and very survival of international society, and in order to achieve collective goals, which require international cooperation and joint action.[131]

The principle has evolved over time from its first existence as a concept, then as a political principle and finally as a principle of international law. In fulfilling its function as a constitutional principle of international law, it plays various roles in the area of development assistance.[132] As the

127 UN General Assembly Resolution 55/2, 18 September 2000, UN Doc. A/RES/52/2, para 6; UN General Assembly Resolution 64/157, 8 March 2010, UN Doc. A/RES/64/157, para 4, lits e, f (referring to both solidarity among states and as a right of peoples and individuals); UN General Assembly Resolution 63/189, 18 March 2009, UN Doc. A/RES/63/189; UN General Assembly Resolution 61/160, 21 February 2007, UN Doc. A/RES/61/160; See also, Hestermeyer, 'Reality or Aspiration? Solidarity in International Environmental and World Trade Law'.

128 See, for example, Wolfrum and Kojima (eds.), *Solidarity: A Structural Principle of International Law* (Springer, 2010), 12.

129 Commission on Human Rights, Resolution 2005/55, 20 April 2005; Human Rights Council Resolution A/HRC/RES/15/13, 6 October 2010, para. 2; Human Rights Council Resolution A/HRC/RES/12/9, 12 October 2009.

130 Human Rights Council Resolution A/HRC/15/32, 5 July 2010.

131 *Ibid.*, 13.

132 Wolfrum and Kojima (eds.), *Solidarity: A Structural Principle of International Law.*

Independent Expert on International Solidarity has pointed out, the Vienna Declaration and Programme of Action,[133] the Monterrey Consensus,[134] the Paris Declaration on Aid Effectiveness[135] and the Accra Agenda for Action 2008[136] all spell out state obligations in respect of international solidarity.[137]

In the context of international development, aid provided by international financial institutions can be compelled by solidarity.[138] While there are certain conditions that have to be fulfilled under the Articles of Agreement and Operational Policies of the World Bank[139] (e.g. an eligible country, an eligible project and no other sources of funding available, contribution to the eradication of poverty, absence of political motives), the Articles also provide that if these conditions are met, the 'Association shall provide financing' under Article V(1)(a) of the Articles. There is in this respect a requirement to commit resources evidenced by the use of the word 'shall' rather than 'may' (as is also the case in the Articles of Agreement of the International Bank for Reconstruction and Development).[140]

The breadth of its application in international law can also reveal an elusive conceptual nature to solidarity,[141] which in turn would appear to have led to differences in the understanding of solidarity among international legal scholars. Hanspeter Neuhold has adopted a simple definition of international solidarity 'understood as the readiness of a State to

[133] The World Conference on Human Rights, 'Vienna Declaration and Programme of Action', 25 June 1993, www.ohchr.org/Documents/ProfessionalInterest/vienna.pdf.

[134] Monterrey Consensus on Financing for Development (United Nations, 2003), www.un.org/esa/ffd/monterrey/MonterreyConsensus.pdf.

[135] Paris Declaration on Aid Effectiveness (2005), www.oecd.org/dac/effectiveness/34428351.pdf.

[136] Accra Agenda for Action (2008), www.oecd.org/dac/effectiveness/34428351.pdf.

[137] Report of the independent expert on human rights and international solidarity, Rudi Muhammad Rizki, 5 July 2010, UN Doc. A/HRC/15/32, 11.

[138] Dann, 'Solidarity and the Law of Development Cooperation' in Wolfrum and Kojima (eds.), *Solidarity: A Structural Principle of International Law.*

[139] See International Bank for Reconstruction and Development, Articles of Agreement, as amended effective 27 June 2012, http://pubdocs.worldbank.org/en/722361541184234501/IBRDArticlesOfAgreement-English.pdf; see also, World Bank Environmental and Social Policies, www.worldbank.org/en/projects-operations/environmental-and-social-policies.

[140] Dann, 'Solidarity and the Law of Development Cooperation', in Wolfrum and Kojima (eds.), *Solidarity: A Structural Principle of International Law,* 69; Article III.4, AoA/IBRD.

[141] Hanspeter Neuhold, 'Common Security: The Litmus Test of International Solidarity' in Wolfrum and Kojima (eds.), *Solidarity: A Structural Principle of International Law*, 193.

provide assistance to another State and to accept the resulting costs'[142] while Philipp Dann has suggested that solidarity should be conceived as having three main elements: 'helping each other to achieve a common objective, equality of the partners and mutuality of obligations'.[143] The latter suggests an aspect of reciprocity while the former would suggest no reciprocity. In fact, Neuhold confirms that his understanding does not involve any reciprocity, as is exemplified by unilateral security guarantees or development aid.[144]

Laurence Boisson de Chazournes also sets out in detail the core elements of solidarity, and suggests that reciprocity is not a required element.[145] Boisson de Chazournes perceives that solidarity can be a form of help offered by one set of actors to benefit another set of actors, with the benefit being the attainment of a certain objective or recovery from crisis. Boisson de Chazournes notes that forms of international assistance do not have to be understood in the context of state-to-state relations, but rather as 'help provided by a State, or a group of States, to the population of another State'.[146]

This suggests an altruistic character to the nature of the legal relationship that solidarity creates. Solidarity implies taking the interests of others into account and acting on their interests where they require assistance. It is owed by certain members of a community to other members of that community, and the specific direction of the obligation depends on the situation. The solidaristic actor does not act with the aim of deriving a direct and concrete benefit.[147]

Thus, solidarity can be understood in two ways: horizontally, between States as a way of mitigating inequalities, and diagonally, as a part of rescuing peoples from danger who cannot be rescued by their own state. As Boisson de Chazournes has described, '[t]his is a form of solidarity where the relationship is between States and populations of other States (and between international organisations and populations)'.[148]

The practice and scholarship around the principle of solidarity would suggest that it has a wide application and can be understood differently in

[142] *Ibid.*, 193–194.
[143] Dann, 'Solidarity and the Law of Development Cooperation' in Wolfrum and Kojima (eds.), *Solidarity: A Structural Principle of International Law*, 77.
[144] Neuhold, 'Common Security: The Litmus Test of International Solidarity', 195.
[145] Laurence Boisson de Chazournes, 'Responsibility to Protect: Reflecting Solidarity?' in Wolfrum and Kojima (eds.), *Solidarity: A Structural Principle of International Law*.
[146] *Ibid*, 94–95 (original footnotes omitted).
[147] *Ibid.*
[148] *Ibid.*, 102.

different contexts. As such, a distinction can be drawn between what might be termed 'self-centred solidarity' and 'altruistic solidarity'.[149] 'Self-centred solidarity' is used to describe situations when states pursue goals that are also directly in their self-interest. An example of this is the action that has been taken on climate change. It is a problem upon which collective action will benefit all states directly. This conception may be contrasted with 'altruistic solidarity', which is used to describe the pursuit of goals that are not directly or immediately in the self-interest of states. An example that is given in the latter case is action on development.[150] Here, the developing state is the direct and immediate beneficiary of the action pursued.[151] In this respect, the principle is other-oriented. These dimensions give an insight into the various types of behaviour the principle of solidarity can serve to motivate, as well as its capacity to embrace both community interests and the needs of those in developing countries.

In response to his questionnaire on human rights and international solidarity sent to a wide range of states, UN departments and bodies, specialised agencies, other international organisations, NGOs and special mandate holders of the Human Rights Council, the Independent Expert on Human Rights and International Solidarity Mr Rudi Muhammad Rizki, observed that '[i]nternational solidarity is perceived by virtually all respondents as a principle, and by several as a right in international law'.[152] In his report, the Independent Expert points out that Article 1 of the Universal Declaration of Human Rights states that 'all human beings are born free and equal in dignity and rights. They are endowed with reason and conscience and should act towards one another in a spirit of brotherhood'.[153] He concludes that '[i]nternational solidarity is a precondition to human dignity, the basis of all human rights, and a human-centred approach to development, and has a bridge building function across all divides and distinctions'.[154] This also points to the principle of solidarity having a constitutional character insofar as it provides the foundations for so many other aspects of international law.

149 Hestermeyer, 'Reality or Aspiration? Solidarity in International Environmental and World Trade Law'.

150 *Ibid.*

151 *Ibid.* Although it may be argued that in the long term all states benefit from development.

152 *Report of the independent expert on human rights and international solidarity, Rudi Muhammad Rizki*, 3.

153 *Ibid.*, 4.

154 *Ibid.*, 18.

5.5 Food Assistance

Closely connected to commitments to provide development assistance is the commitment to end hunger and the emergence of the right to food. Several instruments and the jurisprudence of treaty bodies and special rapporteurs indicate the importance of this issue on the international agenda.

This is illustrated not least by the most recent 2030 Agenda for Sustainable Development. Ending hunger is a shared aim of the Addis Ababa Action Agenda on Financing for Development of 2015,[155] and SDG 2 has as its purpose to '[e]nd hunger, achieve food security and improved nutrition and promote sustainable agriculture'.[156] Target 2.a of this goal is to '[i]ncrease investment, including through enhanced international cooperation in rural infrastructure, agricultural research and extension services, technology development and plant and livestock gene banks in order to enhance agricultural productive capacity in developing countries, in particular least developed countries'.[157] The progress on this target will in part be measured by reference to official development assistance and other official flows of investment to the agricultural sector of developing countries.[158] Prior to the SDGs, a similar objective was evident in the MDGs, of which Goal 1 was 'to eradicate extreme poverty and hunger'.[159] Such commitments have been elaborated in various treaties, which in turn have been given further meaning by special rapporteurs and treaty bodies.

The Food Assistance Convention of 25 April 2012 contains what might be characterised as other-regarding obligations.[160] Its overarching objective is 'to improve the effectiveness, efficiency, and quality of food assistance in preserving the lives and alleviating the suffering of the most vulnerable populations'.[161] Article 5 of the Convention provides for the commitments made by states to ensure the objectives of the Convention are met. As such, parties are expected to make an annual commitment of

155 United Nations, Addis Ababa Action Agenda of the Third International Conference on Financing for Development (United Nations, 2015) endorsed by UN General Assembly Resolution 69/313, 27 July 2015, UN Doc. A/RES/69/313, para 1.

156 United Nations General Assembly Resolution 70/1, Transforming Our World: The 2030 Agenda for Sustainable Development, 25 September 2015, UN Doc. A/RES/70/1.

157 *Ibid.*, Target 2.a.

158 *Ibid.*, Target 2.a.2.

159 Report of the Secretary General, 'Road Map Towards the Implementation of the United Nations Millennium Declaration', 6 September 2001, UN Doc. A/56/326, Goal 1.

160 Food Assistance Convention, 25 April 2012, 2884 UNTS 3.

161 Preamble, *ibid.*

food assistance, which is called its 'minimum annual commitment'. This is expressed as a value or quantity of food assistance that the country must provide to eligible recipient countries. Not less than 80 per cent of this commitment should be in grant form, and parties must seek to progressively exceed this amount. This commitment is notified to the Secretariat when the Party accedes to the Convention and in advance of each year that it intends to change its minimum annual commitment. The Secretariat communicates the minimum annual commitments to all other parties of the Convention. Where a party is unable to meet its minimum annual commitment, it is obliged to provide an explanation in its annual report and the shortfall is added to the state's minimum annual commitment for the following year, unless there are exceptional circumstances that justify a different course of action. Not more than 5 per cent of any excess to annual minimum commitment may be counted towards the next year.

As alluded to earlier, there are also obligations in respect of access to food under the International Covenant on Economic, Social and Cultural Rights, which provides for an obligation on states to '[take] into account the problems of both food-importing and food-exporting countries, to ensure an equitable distribution of world food supplies in relation to need',[162] and has been interpreted by the Committee on Economic, Social and Cultural Rights as requiring states to 'take steps to respect the enjoyment of the right to food in other countries . . . [and] refrain at all times from food embargoes or similar measures which endanger conditions for food production and access to food in other countries'.[163]

The former Special Rapporteur on the Right to Food assessed that there was a 'complementary obligation' on external states to act where the 'principal obligation' to guarantee the right to food incumbent on the territorial state was not met.[164] Indeed, Mr Jean Zigler said that while '[t]he principal obligation to guarantee the right to food is incumbent on the national government', if other states have the resources they 'have a complementary obligation to help the national State when it does not have the resources to realize the right to food of

[162] Article 11(b), International Covenant on Economic, Social and Cultural Rights, 16 December 1966, 999 UNTS 171.

[163] Committee on Economic, Social and Cultural Rights, 'Substantive Issues Arising in the Implementation of the International Covenant on Economic, Social and Cultural Rights', 12 May 1999, UN Doc. E/c.12/1999/5.

[164] Report of the Special Rapporteur on the Right to Food, *Economic, Social and Cultural Rights: The Right to Food*, UN Doc. E/CN.4/2005/47 (2005), para 47.

its population'.[165] This implies there is an altruistic legal relationship between states and individuals in other countries such that the former must ensure they support fulfilment of the right to food by the latter where necessary.[166]

The Committee on Economic, Social and Cultural Rights has emphasised that the respect, protect and fulfil framework applies to the right to food and outlined the specific duties on third states in this respect. For the Committee, the obligation to fulfil

> means the State must pro-actively engage in activities intended to strengthen people's access to and utilization of resources and means to ensure their livelihood, including food security. Finally, whenever an individual or group is unable, for reasons beyond their control, to enjoy the right to adequate food by the means at their disposal, States have the obligation to fulfil (provide) that right directly. This obligation also applies for persons who are victims of natural or other disasters.[167]

In a similar way, and further underlining the positive character of the obligation to fulfil (as well as noting a duty to promote), the African Commission on Human and Peoples' Rights in the case of *The Social and Economic Rights Action Center and the Center for Economic and Social Rights* v. *Nigeria*[168] observed that

> [t]he last layer of obligation requires the State to fulfil the rights and freedoms it freely undertook under the various human rights regimes. It is more of a positive expectation on the part of the State to move its machinery towards the actual realisation of the rights. This is also very much intertwined with the duty to promote .... It could consist in the direct provision of basic needs such as food or resources that can be used for food (direct food aid or social security).

This brings into sharp focus the role that the respect, protect and fulfil framework can have in providing states with guidance on their human rights obligations. In this context, an argument can be made that the

165 *Ibid.*

166 Michael Nyongesa Wabwile, *Legal Protection of Social and Economic Rights of Children in Developing Countries: Reassessing International Cooperation and Responsibility* (Intersentia, 2010), 109.

167 UN Committee on Economic, Social and Cultural Rights, *General Comment No. 12 on The Right to Adequate Food*, para 15.

168 *The Social and Economic Rights Action Center and the Center for Economic and Social Rights* v. *Nigeria*, African Commission on Human and Peoples' Rights, Comm. No. 155/96 (2001) AHRLR 60 (ACHPR 2001) (15th Annual Activity Report), para 47.

fulfil-bound obligation demands positive action to promote or even ensure the realisation of human rights in a third state.

Other regimes also have a role in furthering the right to food. Indeed, the former Director-General of the WTO has remarked that international trade law can help to open trade that creates efficiency that in turn raises standards and living conditions in such a way as to help with the implementation of human rights like the right to food.[169]

5.6 Concluding Remarks

This chapter has sought to consider those legal relationships in which developed countries have committed to providing assistance to developing countries. In particular, the focus of consideration has been on the right to development, specific manifestations of altruism that have emerged through the international economic order and the right to food, as well as the principle of solidarity.

As for the right to development, developed countries have committed to giving at least 0.7 per cent of their GNP to development assistance. As for the right to food, states are under a negative obligation to ensure their actions do not hinder access to food in third countries (i.e. through trade embargoes, etc.). Moreover, the work of the Special Rapporteur on the Right to Food also indicated there is a complementary obligation on those states with the resources to help those that do not. As for the international economic order, several initiatives intended to benefit developing countries that represented a real cost to developed countries and show an intention to help developing countries were explored.

Elements of the New International Economic Order, contemporary international economic governance, international trade, fair access to the commodity markets for developing countries, along with ensuring the right to development and the provision of development aid, can be oriented at helping to further development and fulfil international economic and social rights.[170] Moreover, it has become apparent that international cooperation and solidarity play an important role in development efforts through the mechanisms outlined. In fact, economic

[169] Pascal Lamy, 'Globalization and trade opening can promote human rights', World Trade Organization, 5 June 2009, www.wto.org/english/news_e/sppl_e/sppl128_e.htm.

[170] Glenn Mower, *International Cooperation for Social Justice: Global and Regional Protection of Economic and Social Rights* (Greenwood Press, 1985).

development effected through the international trade regime has been characterised as representing a form of 'altruistic solidarity'.[171]

More recent efforts at furthering development have been connected to the notion of sustainable development and the pursuit of environmental justice, to which we turn in the next chapter.

[171] Hestermeyer, 'Reality or Aspiration? Solidarity in International Environmental and World Trade Law'.

6

The Substance of Altruism in International Law: Environmental Justice for the Other

6.1 Introduction

This chapter will consider the major features of international environmental governance that are manifestations of altruism. It begins from the observation that the very premise of international environmental law is the no-harm principle according to which states must not cause significant transboundary harm to their neighbouring countries or their populations. While not altruistic, this illustrates the structurally inherent concern for the other that exists at the heart of international environmental law. There is as such a recognition that the actions of those in one state affect those of another state.[1]

The chapter continues by appraising the emergence of concern for the individual in international environmental law, and in particular procedures through which those in other countries can participate in environmental decision-making or have recourse to justice where they are subject to environmental harm caused by a state other than their own. Moreover, international human rights law is interacting with international environmental law to extend the environmental obligations that states have to people in third countries. It will also become apparent that the universality of international environmental law obligations is manifested in principles such as intergenerational equity, which is an altruistic consideration for people of the future.

Finally, the chapter will consider the increasing prevalence of common but differentiated responsibilities and commitments made to developing countries in the area of environmental protection. A particular focus will

[1] Center on Law and Globalization, 'International Law to Cosmopolitan Law', https://clg.portalxm.com/library/keytext.cfm?keytext_id=39; Andrew Linklater, 'Cosmopolitan Harm Conventions' in Steven Vertovec and Robin Cohen (eds.), *Conceiving Cosmopolitanism: Theory, Context and Practice* (Oxford University Press, 2002), 255.

be placed on the importance of financial and technical assistance for those countries in need of it.

6.2 The Other in International Environmental Law

6.2.1 The Duty to Prevent Transboundary Harm

The actions of states often affect the environment of people living in another state. International environmental law has evolved from the premise that activities in one state can have consequences for the environment and people beyond that state's borders. Today, the degradation of the international environment is a threat to all humanity, whether in terms of climate change, the degradation of natural resources or biodiversity. The early origins of international environmental law are in the no-harm principle itself. The basic principle of international environmental law was set out by an arbitral tribunal long ago in the middle of the twentieth century. Indeed, the *Trail Smelter* case[2] was one of the first international cases in which environmental damage was addressed and in it the Tribunal asserted that a State was 'not to use or permit the use of its territory in such a manner as to cause injury by fumes in or to the territory of another or the properties or persons therein, when the case is of serious consequences and the injury is established by clear and convincing evidence'.[3] As such, this case stands for the so-called no-harm principle according to which States must not cause significant transboundary harm to their neighbouring countries or peoples.

The International Court of Justice (ICJ) reaffirmed this principle in its *Corfu Channel (United Kingdom of Great Britain and Northern Ireland* v. *Albania)* case in 1949.[4] Notably, in the *Legality of the Threat or Use of Nuclear Weapons* and the *Pulp Mills on the River Uruguay (Argentina* v. *Uruguay)* cases, the ICJ confirmed that customary international law obliged states to take all possible measures to avoid activities taking place

2 *Trail Smelter Case (United States/Canada)* III (1938 and 1941) Reports of International Arbitral Awards 1905.

3 *Ibid.* Similarly in the more recent *Iron Rhine* case, the Tribunal observed that '[m]uch of international environmental law has been formulated by reference to the impact that activities in one territory may have on the territory of another', *Award in the Arbitration regarding the Iron Rhine Railway between the Kingdom of Belgium and the Netherlands*, Final Award, 24 May 2005, XXVII (2008) Reports of International Arbitral Awards 35, para 59.

4 *Corfu Channel case (United Kingdom of Great Britain and Northern Ireland* v. *Albania)*, Judgment (1949) ICJ Rep. 4.

in their jurisdiction which might cause significant damage to another state's environment.[5]

Beyond international courts and tribunals, the no-harm principle has also been affirmed by states in the 1972 United Nations Stockholm Declaration on the Human Environment.[6] Principle 21 of the Stockholm Declaration provides explicitly that states have 'the responsibility to ensure that activities within their jurisdiction or control do not cause damage to the environment of other States or of areas beyond the limits of national jurisdiction'. Similarly, Principle 2 of the 1992 Rio Declaration on Environment and Development[7] indicates that the main obligation on states in respect of the environment has long concerned the duty not to cause environmental damage to neighbouring states. This principle confirms that sovereignty does not give states the right to cause environmental harm to their neighbours. While this is not a manifestation of altruism, it nevertheless illustrates the other-directed commitments made in the context of international environmental law. This is further supported by the emergence of mechanisms that allow individuals to participate in environmental decision-making or that compel states to consider the interests of individuals in third states when conducting environmentally hazardous activities.

6.2.2 The Rise of the Individual in International Environmental Law

The individual has gradually found a place in the regulatory framework of international environmental protection.[8] Ellen Hey has observed that substantive international environmental law 'reflects ideals associated with moral cosmopolitanism'[9] and that '[s]ubstantive elements in global

[5] *Legality of the Threat or Use of Nuclear Weapons*, Advisory Opinion (1996) ICJ Rep. 226, para 29; *Case Concerning Pulp Mills on the River Uruguay (Argentina* v. *Uruguay)*, Judgment (2010) ICJ Rep. 14, 56.

[6] United Nations Stockholm Declaration on the Human Environment, 15 December 1972, UN Doc. A/RES/2994.

[7] Rio Declaration on Environment and Development, 12 August 1992, UN Doc. A/CONF.151/26.

[8] Roger Crisp, 'Ethics and International Environmental Law' in Samantha Besson and John Tasioulas (eds.), *The Philosophy of International Law* (Oxford University Press, 2010), 473.

[9] Ellen Hey, 'Global Environmental Law and Global Institutions: A System Lacking 'Good Process'' in Roland Pierik and Wouter Werner (eds.), *Cosmopolitanism in Context: Perspectives from International Law and Political Theory* (Cambridge University Press, 2010), 45.

environmental law reflect concerns associated with the well-being of individuals and groups and seek to further distributive justice'.[10] Indeed, public participation has also become a cornerstone principle of international environmental law. And there is increasingly wide recognition of the importance of including all individuals in environmental decision-making. For example, Principle 10 of the Rio Declaration provides that '[e]nvironmental issues are best handled with the participation of all concerned citizens', while an emphasis on public participation features very strongly in instruments related to the United Nations Economic Commission for Europe (UNECE).[11] The public participation principle is in fact evident in a number of treaties, such as the UN Convention on the Non-navigational Uses of International Watercourses.[12] Other instruments such as UN Environment's Guidelines on Developing National Legislation on Access to Information, Public Participation in Decision-Making and Access to Justice in Environmental Matters are intended to help countries to develop effective participation mechanisms in their domestic legal systems.[13]

Practically speaking, environmental impact assessments are a way in which the interests of individuals can be taken into account in the evaluation of projects prior to their implementation. The idea that such interests should be taken into account in environmental decision-making can be detected as early as 1957 in the *Lake Lanoux* case, in which an arbitral tribunal underlined that 'consideration must be given to all interests, whatever their nature, which may be affected by the works undertaken, even if they do not amount to a right'.[14] The Rio

[10] *Ibid.*, 50.

[11] See for example, Article 16, Convention on the Protection and Use of Transboundary Watercourses and International Lakes, 17 March 1992, 1936 UNTS 269; Articles 5(1), 6(2), 8(1)(a)(iii), 9 and 10, Protocol on Water and Health to the 1992 Convention on the Protection and Use of Transboundary Watercourses and International Lakes, 17 June 1999, 2331 UNTS 202; Article 2(6), Convention on Environmental Impact Assessment in a Transboundary Context, 25 February 1991, 1989 UNTS 309.

[12] UN Convention on the Law of the Non-Navigational Uses of International Watercourses, 21 May 1997, 2999 UNTS 12; See Roberta Greco, 'Access to Procedures and the Principle of Non-Discrimination' in Laurence Boisson de Chazournes, Mara Tignino, Makane Mbengue, Komlan Sangbana and Jason Rudall (eds.), *The UN Convention on the Law of the Non-Navigational Uses of International Watercourses: A Commentary* (Oxford University Press, 2018), 325–345.

[13] Decision SS.XI/5, Part A, 'Guidelines on Developing National Legislation on Access to Information, Participation in Decision-Making and Access to Justice in Environmental Matters', 26 February 2012, Doc GCSS.XI/11.

[14] *Lake Lanoux Arbitration (France* v. *Spain)*, Award 12 (1957) Reports of International Arbitration Awards 281, 16 November 1957, para 22.

Declaration of 1992 also provides for environmental impact assessments in its Principle 17, while various international treaties and much national legislation now make provision for such assessments.[15] Under certain treaties, like the Convention on Environmental Impact Assessment in a Transboundary Context (Espoo Convention),[16] states must consult with potentially affected local communities. In the *Pulp Mills* case,[17] the ICJ confirmed that there is a customary international law obligation to conduct an environmental impact assessment prior to the execution of projects or activities that may have transboundary effects.

A related principle of international environmental law is that of prior informed consent. In this context, there is a requirement to consult with affected populations, particularly indigenous communities, to ensure that their interests are taken into account in projects that they may be affected by. This is provided for in a very wide range of international instruments.[18]

Transboundary environmental impact assessments and prior informed consent are connected to the principle of non-discrimination insofar as they require the interests of all stakeholders to be taken into account in the planning of measures likely to have transboundary consequences, including the impact on those beyond the territorial jurisdiction of the

[15] See, for example, Convention on Environmental Impact Assessment in a Transboundary Context, 25 February 1991, 1989 UNTS 309; Article 206, UN Convention on the Law of the Sea, 10 December 1982, 1833 UNTS 3; Article 8 and Annex 1 of the Protocol to the Antarctic Treaty, 4 October 1991, 30 ILM 1455 (Madrid Protocol); Article 12, UN Convention on the Law of the Non-Navigational Uses of International Watercourses, 21 May 1997, 2999 UNTS 12; Neil Craik, *The International Law of Impact Assessment* (Cambridge University Press, 2008).

[16] Articles 2(6) and 3(8), Convention on Environmental Impact Assessment in a Transboundary Context, 25 February 1991, 1989 UNTS 309.

[17] *Case Concerning Pulp Mills on the River Uruguay (Argentina* v. *Uruguay)*, Judgment (2010) ICJ Rep. 14. See also, *Certain Activities Carried Out by Nicaragua in the Border Areas (Costa Rica* v. *Nicaragua)* and *Construction of a Road in Costa Rica Along the San Juan River (Nicaragua* v. *Costa Rica)*, Judgment (2015) ICJ Rep. 665, para 104; *Responsibilities in the Area*, Advisory Opinion, 1 February 2011, ITLOS Seabed Chamber, para 145; *Case 2013–19, South China Sea Arbitration (The Republic of Philippines* v. *The People's Republic of China)*, PCA Award of 12 July 2016, paras 947–8.

[18] See, for example, Articles 16(2) and 6, Convention (No. 169) concerning Indigenous and Tribal Peoples in Independent Countries, 27 June 1989, 28 ILM 1382; Annex, Articles 10 and 19, United Nations Declaration on the Rights of Indigenous Peoples, 2 October 2007, UN Doc. A/RES/61/295; Article 8(j), Convention on Biological Diversity, 5 June 1992, 1760 UNTS 79; Articles 6(2) and 7, Nagoya Protocol on Access to Genetic Resources and the Fair and Equitable Sharing of the Benefits Arising from their Utilization to the Convention on Biological Diversity, 29 October 2010, Doc. UNEP/CBD/COP/DEC/X/1.

state.[19] The principle has several dimensions. First, it accords the same substantive rights that residents of a particular state have to non-residents.[20] Second, on a procedural level, the principle of non-discrimination requires states to afford both residents and non-residents equal access to judicial remedies and administrative decision-making mechanisms.[21] Third, the principle of non-discrimination in international environmental law requires states to take into account the environmental consequences of measures within and beyond their territory.

The growing importance of the principle of non-discrimination is evidenced by its presence in many multilateral environmental agreements. For example, the Arhus and Espoo Conventions,[22] as will be explored later, employ the principle of non-discrimination in a way that extends the scope of its environmental protection. Similarly, the 1909 Boundary Waters Treaty between Canada and the United States,[23] the 1974 Nordic Convention on the Protection of the Environment,[24] the 1974 Organization for Economic Co-operation and Development (OECD) Recommendations of the Council on the Principles concerning Transfrontier Pollution,[25] the 1982 Montreal Rules on Water Pollution in an International Drainage Basin[26] and the 1992 Convention on the

[19] John Knox, 'The Myth and Reality of Transboundary Environmental Impact Assessment' (2002) 96 *American Journal of International Law* 291, 293.

[20] *Legality of the Threat or Use of Nuclear Weapons*, Advisory Opinion (1996) ICJ Rep 226, para 29; *Case Concerning Pulp Mills on the River Uruguay (Argentina* v. *Uruguay)*, Judgment (2010) ICJ Rep. 14, para 101.

[21] See Greco, 'Access to Procedures and the Principle of Non-Discrimination (Article 32)'; see also, Jonas Ebbesson, 'Access to Justice in Environmental Matters' (2009) *Max Planck Encyclopedia of Public International Law*, www.mpepil.com, para 3.

[22] Aarhus Convention on Access to Information, Public Participation in Decision-Making, and Access to Justice in Environmental Matters, 25 June 1998, 2161 UNTS 447; Convention on Environmental Impact Assessment in a Transboundary Context, 25 February 1991, 1989 UNTS 309.

[23] Article 2, Treaty between the United States and Great Britain Relating to Boundary Water, and Questions arising between the United States and Canada, 11 January 1909, 36 Stat. 2448, T.S. 548.

[24] Article 3, Convention on the Protection of the Environment between Denmark, Finland, Norway and Sweden, 19 February 1974, http://www2.ecolex.org/server2neu.php/libcat/docs/TRE/Full/En/TRE-000491.txt.

[25] Organization for Economic Co-operation and Development (OECD), Recommendation C(74)224 (1974), see Annex C(4)(*d*), D(5)(*a*)(*b*). See also OECD, Recommendation of the Council for Implementation of a Regime of Equal Right of Access and Non-Discrimination in Relation to Transfrontier Pollution, 17 May 1977, Doc. C(77)28/FINAL.

[26] International Law Association, Report of the 60th Conference, Montreal, 60 ILA 531, 535 (1982) (1982 Montreal Rules), Article 8.

Transboundary Effects of Industrial Accidents, all provide for non-discrimination and suggest a broad application of treaty provisions under those conventions.[27] The OECD has set out that the non-discrimination principle requires 'each Country should ensure that its regime of environmental protection does not discriminate between pollution originating from it which affects or is likely to affect the area under its national jurisdiction and pollution originating from it which affects or is likely to affect an exposed Country'.[28] It has also highlighted the procedural dimensions of the principle and recommended that those affected by transboundary pollution should have the same rights as those in the country of origin, particularly as regards access to information, participation in decision-making and recourse to a remedy to stop or be compensated for environmental damage.[29]

The Aarhus Convention on Access to Information, Public Participation in Decision-Making and Access to Justice in Environmental Matters of 1998[30] provide an important example of the way in which the non-discrimination principle can be best used to accord rights to non-residents. It obliges states to release environmental information where this is requested by individuals, as well as setting requirements on environmental information dissemination more generally, and for public participation in particular projects, policies or law-making in the area of the environment. The intention is 'to contribute to the protection of the right of every person of present and future generations to live in an environment adequate to his or her health and well-being'.[31]

Article 2(5) of the Arhus Convention provides that those 'affected or likely to be affected by, or having an interest in, the environmental decision making' have a right to have their interests in environmental

[27] Preamble and Article 9, Convention on the Transboundary Effects of Industrial Accidents, 17 March 1992, 2105 UNTS 457, as amended on 15 December 2015.

[28] Organisation for Economic Co-operation and Development, Recommendation of the Council for the Implementation of a Regime of Equal Right of Access and Non-Discrimination in Relation to Transfrontier Pollution 1977, Doc. OECD/LEGAL/0152, para 3.

[29] *Ibid.*, Annex, para 4

[30] Aarhus Convention on Access to Information, Public Participation in Decision-Making, and Access to Justice in Environmental Matters, 25 June 1998, 2161 UNTS 447.

[31] *Ibid.* The Rio+20 Conference on Sustainable Development in 2012 gave states an opportunity to underline the importance they ascribe to public participation in realising sustainable development (see Outcome of the United Nations Conference on Sustainable Development (Rio+20), The Future We Want, 11 September 2012, UN Doc. A/RES/66/288, para 13).

decision-making taken into account. In this context, the UN Economic and Social Council recommended that states identify, notify and involve 'the public concerned in decision-making on projects in border areas affecting the public in other countries'.[32] Moreover, Article 3(9) of the Aarhus Convention embraces the non-discrimination principle, and spells out that

> [w]ithin the scope of the relevant provisions of this Convention, the public shall have access to information, have the possibility to participate in decision-making and have access to justice in environmental matters *without discrimination as to citizenship, nationality or domicile* and, in the case of a legal person, without discrimination as to where it has its registered seat or an effective centre of its activities.[33]

Further still, Article 4(1)(a) of the Aarhus Convention provides for the release of environmental information from public authorities without an interest having to be demonstrated. This would suggest that a broad formulation has been adopted in respect of access and participation in environmental matters under the Aarhus Convention, which is further supported by the wide definitions of 'environmental information' and 'public authority' under the Convention (wider in fact than many definitions under national law).[34]

The Aarhus Convention also provides for a compliance mechanism.[35] As such, states parties, the Convention Secretariat, individuals and NGOs may make submissions to a committee comprising eight independent experts.[36] As alluded to, the party making the submission need not be a national of the state being complained about. According to a decision taken at the Meeting of the Parties in 2002, the Compliance Committee 'shall consider any such communication unless it determines that the communication is: (a) Anonymous; (b) An abuse of the right to make such

[32] UN Economic and Social Council, Findings and Recommendations with Regard to Compliance by Ukraine with the Obligations Under the Aarhus Convention in the Case of Bystre Deep-Water Navigation Canal Construction, 14 March 2005, UN Doc. ECE/MP.PP/C.1/2005/2/Add.3.

[33] Emphasis added.

[34] Laurence Boisson de Chazournes, *Fresh Water in International Law* (Oxford University Press, 2013), 162.

[35] On the other-regarding nature of this mechanism, see also Eyal Benvenisti, 'Sovereigns as Trustees of Humanity: On the Accountability of States to Foreign Stakeholders' (2013) 107(2) *American Journal of International Law* 295, 319–320.

[36] See UNECE, Communications from the Public, www.unece.org/env/pp/cc/com.html.

communications; (c) Manifestly unreasonable; (d) Incompatible with the provisions of this decision or with the Convention'.[37]

A submission made by the Moldovan-based Biotica Ecological Society in respect of Turkmenistan, which had passed legislation restricting environmental NGOs, is a case in point.[38] The Committee found that

> [t]he exclusion of foreign citizens and persons without citizenship from the possibility to found and participate in an NGO might constitute a disadvantageous discrimination against them. The Committee is, therefore, of the opinion that article 5 of the [Turkmenistani] Act is not in compliance with article 3, paragraph 9, of the Convention.[39]

The Committee recommended that Turkmenistan bring its legislation into compliance with the Aarhus Convention, as well as to take interim measures to ensure obligations under the Convention were complied with.[40]

A further example is the Convention on Environmental Impact Assessment in a Transboundary Context (Espoo Convention),[41] which employs the principle of non-discrimination in a way that facilitates the realisation of the rights of those in third countries. In respect of individuals in other countries, Article 2(6) establishes a legal relationship such that

> [t]he Party of origin shall provide, in accordance with the provisions of this Convention, an opportunity to the public in the areas likely to be affected to participate in relevant environmental impact assessment procedures regarding proposed activities and shall ensure that the opportunity provided to the public of the affected Party is equivalent to that provided to the public of the Party of origin.

The impact on all those affected must be taken into account in decision-making, as noted in Article 6(1):

[37] Economic Commission for Europe, Compliance Committee, Decision I/7 of the Meeting of the Parties, 2002, ECE/MP.PP/2/Add.8, 2004, para 20.

[38] See Economic Commission for Europe, Compliance Committee, Report on the Seventh Meeting – Findings and Recommendations with regard to compliance by Turkmenistan with the obligations under the Aarhus Convention in the case of Act on Public Associations (Communication ACCC/C/2004/05 by Biotica (Republic of Moldova) (14 March 2005) (ECE/MP.PP/C.1/2005/2/Add.5), www.unece.org/fileadmin/DAM/env/documents/2005/pp/c.1/ece.mp.pp.c1.2005.2.Add.5.e.pdf.

[39] *Ibid.*, para 16.

[40] *Ibid.*, paras 25–28.

[41] Convention on Environmental Impact Assessment in a Transboundary Context, 25 February 1991, 1989 UNTS 309 (Espoo Convention).

> The Parties shall ensure that, in the final decision on the proposed activity, due account is taken of the outcome of the environmental impact assessment, including the environmental impact assessment documentation, as well as the comments thereon received pursuant to Article 3, paragraph 8 and Article 4, paragraph 2, and the outcome of the consultations as referred to in Article 5.

The principle of non-discrimination can therefore serve as a basis for establishing what have been referred to as diagonal environmental legal relationships.[42] This principle accords the same rights that residents of a particular country have to non-residents.

Reference should also be made to the Permanent Court of Arbitration's 2001 Optional Rules for Arbitration of Disputes relating to Natural Resources and/or the Environment, which allow states, international organisations and non-state actors to settle disputes pursuant to mixed arbitration.[43] Under its Article 1.1, the Optional Rules allow for broad application since 'the characterisation of the dispute as relating to the environment or natural resources is not necessary for jurisdiction, where all the parties have agreed to settle a specific dispute under these rules'. Moreover, although it is not yet in force as it has only been ratified by one country so far, the 2003 Protocol on Civil Liability and Compensation for Damage caused by the Transboundary Effects of Industrial Accidents on Transboundary Waters to the 1992 Convention on the Protection and Use of Transboundary Watercourses and International Lakes provides for recourse to the PCA's Optional Rules for Arbitration of Disputes relating to Natural Resources and/or the Environment.[44] Under the 2003 Protocol, victims would be able to seek compensation in accordance with Article 13 in the courts of a Party to the Protocol either where the damage was suffered or where the industrial accident occurred, and Article 13(2) goes on to oblige Parties that their 'courts possess the necessary competence to entertain such claims for

[42] See, for example, John Knox, 'Diagonal Environmental Rights' in Mark Gibney and Sigrun Skogly (eds.), *Universal Human Rights and Extraterritorial Obligations* (University of Pennsylvania Press, 2010), 82–103.

[43] Permanent Court of Arbitration, Optional Rules for Arbitration of Disputes relating to Natural Resources and/or the Environment 2001.

[44] Protocol on Civil Liability and Compensation for Damage Caused by the Transboundary Effects of Industrial Accidents on Transboundary Waters to the 1992 Convention on the Protection and Use of Transboundary Watercourses and International Lakes and to the 1992 Convention on the Transboundary Effects of Industrial Accidents, 21 May 2003, Doc. ECE/MP.WAT/11-ECE/CP.TEIA/9 (not yet in force). Presently it has only been ratified by Hungary. The Protocol will enter into force when sixteen states have ratified it.

compensation'. Article 14 makes provision for the pursuance of claims for compensation via arbitration under the PCA's Optional Rules.

These developments in procedural mechanisms in international environmental law have been accompanied by an increasing tendency for environmental matters to be considered in the field of human rights, and by human rights courts. We turn next to the emergence of the human right to a healthy environment, particularly in its extraterritorial dimension.

6.2.3 *Human Rights, Extraterritoriality and the Environment*

This section will explore the emergence of a human right to a healthy environment and how this has begun to acquire an extraterritorial dimension. In addition to the fact that environmental degradation may interfere with the realisation of well-established human rights like the right to life or health, for example, it has also been suggested that there exists a human right to a healthy environment.[45] This right has been characterised as a solidarity right because it is an expression of solidarity between states as well as a 'programmatic mandate for States to act upon'.[46] The emergence of the right can be detected as early as the 1970s. Indeed, Principle 1 of the 1972 Stockholm Declaration of the UN Conference on the Human Environment set out that

> [m]an has the fundamental right to freedom, equality and adequate conditions of life, in an environment of a quality that permits a life of dignity and well-being, and he bears a solemn responsibility to protect and improve the environment for present and future generations.

Subsequently, Principle 1 of the 1992 Rio Declaration on Environment and Development stipulated that

> [h]uman beings are at the centre of concerns for sustainable development. They are entitled to a healthy and productive life in harmony with nature.

Since then, many resolutions of the UN Human Rights Council have recognised the relationship between a healthy environment and the full

[45] Simon Caney, 'Human Rights and Global Climate Change' in Pierik and Werner (eds), *Cosmopolitanism in Context: Perspectives from International Law and Political Theory*, 20.
[46] Petra Minnerop, Naomi Roht-Arriaza and Sara Aminzadeh, 'Solidarity Rights (Development, Peace, Environment and Humanitarian Assistance)' (2018) *Max Planck Encyclopedia of Public International Law*, www.mpepil.com.

realisation of human rights.[47] Moreover, in 2012 an Independent Expert on Human Rights and the environment was appointed by the Council,[48] in 2015 this mandate became the Special Rapporteur on Human Rights and the Environment,[49] and in 2017 the Special Rapporteur warned in his annual report that pollution is one of the main causes of biodiversity degradation which, in turn, hinders the full realisation of human rights.[50] The Special Rapporteur concluded that

> [b]iodiversity is necessary for ecosystem services that support the full enjoyment of a wide range of human rights, including the rights to life, health, food, water and culture. In order to protect human rights, States have a general obligation to protect ecosystems and biodiversity.[51]

In 2018, the Special Rapporteur also set out the Framework Principles on Human Rights and the Environment, which reflect many obligations that already exist under treaty law and the jurisprudence of human rights bodies.[52] Principles 1 and 2 emphasise the link between human rights and the environment, as well as the duty on states both to ensure a safe, clean, healthy and sustainable environment, and to respect, protect and fulfil human rights. Principle 3 goes on to highlight the importance of prohibiting discrimination in the enjoyment of a healthy environment.

General Comment No. 36 of the Human Rights Committee on the right to life also addresses the environment in the context of the International Covenant on Civil and Political Rights 1966.[53] The General Comment provides in part that '[t]he duty to protect life also

[47] See, for example, Human Rights Council (HRC) Resolution 16/11 of 24 March 2011 on human rights and the environment; HRC Resolutions 7/23 of 28 March 2008, 10/4 of 25 March 2009 and 18/22 of 30 September 2011 on human rights and climate change; HRC Resolutions 9/1 of 24 September 2008 and 12/18 of 2 October 2009 on the adverse effects of the movement and dumping of toxic and dangerous products and wastes on the enjoyment of human rights; and HRC Resolution 18/11 of 29 September 2011 on the mandate of the Special Rapporteur on the implications for human rights of the environmentally sound management and disposal of hazardous substances and wastes.

[48] HRC Resolution 19/10.

[49] HRC Resolution 28/11.

[50] Report of the Special Rapporteur on the issue of human rights obligations relating to the enjoyment of a safe, clean, healthy and sustainable environment, UN Doc. A/HRC/34/49, 3.

[51] *Ibid.*, 21.

[52] Framework Principles to the UN Human Rights Council, March 2018, UN Doc. A/HRC/37/59.

[53] Human Rights Committee, General comment No. 36 (2018) on article 6 of the International Covenant on Civil and Political Rights, on the right to life, 30 October 2018, UN Doc. CCPR/C/GC/36.

implies that States parties should take appropriate measures to address the general conditions in society that may give rise to direct threats to life or prevent individuals from enjoying their right to life with dignity [. . . including] degradation of the environment'.[54] The Comment goes on to underline the risk that environmental degradation presents to current and future generations and, in particular, their right to life.[55] Moreover, it highlights that international environmental law obligations should inform the content of the right to life, and vice versa, as well as that states are expected to take measures to preserve and protect the environment to ensure the implementation of the right to life.[56]

The latter reference to the need for states to take measures that 'preserve the environment and protect it against harm' suggests there may be extraterritorial reach of the right to life in the context of environmental degradation, not least because it resonates with other obligations to protect and preserve the environment that can be observed in other regimes where such extraterritorial effect has been clarified.[57] As a consequence, states are likely under an obligation to prevent transboundary harm that would result in the violation of the right to life of people in other countries.

The Human Rights Committee has since decided several cases finding that a state's failure to prevent environmental damage can amount to a violation of Article 6 of the International Covenant on Civil and Political Rights, which provides for the right to life.[58] Indeed, it has confirmed that 'environmental degradation, climate change and unsustainable development constitute some of the most pressing and serious threats to the ability of present and future generations to enjoy the right to life'.[59] It has also said that the effects of climate change may 'propel

[54] *Ibid.*, para 26.
[55] *Ibid.*, para 62.
[56] *Ibid.*
[57] *Ibid.* Ginevra Le Moli, 'The Human Rights Committee, Environmental Protection and the Right to Life' (2020) *International and Comparative Law Quarterly* 735, who highlights Articles 192 to 237 of the United Nations Convention on the Law of the Sea of 1982, the South China Sea Arbitration before and Arbitral Tribunal constituted under Annex VII of the United Nations Convention on the Law of the Sea, PCA Case No. 2013–19, Award (12 July 2016), paras 927 and 941, and the Inter-American Court of Human Rights' Advisory Opinion OC/23/17 on The Environment and Human Rights, 15 November 2017, paras 101–102.
[58] *Portillo Cáceres* v. *Paraguay*, HRC, 9 August 2019, Comm No. 2751/2016, CCPR/C/126/D/2751/2016; *Teitiota* v. *New Zealand*, HRC, 24 October 2019, Comm No. 2728/2016, CCPR/C/127/D/2728/2016.
[59] *Teitiota* v. *New Zealand*, HRC, 24 October 2019, Comm No. 2728/2016, CCPR/C/127/D/2728/2016, para 9.4.

cross-border movement of individuals seeking protection from climate change-related harm' and that national and international efforts would be required to prevent individuals being deprived of the right to life.[60] Significantly, the Committee has observed that life does not need to be lost and entire states do not need to be submerged under water for there to be a violation of the right to life.[61] This suggests a more acute realisation that requiring evidence of significant harm to prove environmental damage may be too high a threshold.

The connection between environmental damage and human rights violations is evident in other contexts as well. For example, in the area of toxic dumping, the Human Rights Commission appointed a Special Rapporteur in 1995 with a mandate to investigate toxic dumping and its effects on human rights. The Special Rapporteur identified a number of human rights whose enjoyment is interfered with by toxic dumping.[62] These include, but are not limited to, the rights to life, health, self-determination, permanent sovereignty over natural resources, development, adequate food and safe and healthy working conditions, freedom of expression, to form and join trade unions, to strike and to collective bargaining, social security and the right to enjoy the benefits of scientific progress.[63] It is evident, therefore, that dumping waste can have profound consequences, not just for the natural environment, but also for human beings and the realisation of their fundamental rights.

Where private entities are responsible for toxic dumping, the Special Rapporteur has indicated that there may be an obligation on the home state of that entity to prevent or punish the toxic dumping by the private entity.[64] This further implies that a state may owe a diagonal obligation to those at risk of harm from toxic dumping in a third state.[65] Indeed, the Special Rapporteur urged states to allow non-residents access to mechanisms of judicial recourse for the redress of harm they have experienced

[60] *Ibid.*, para 9.11.

[61] *Ibid.*, para 9.11; *Portillo Cáceres* v. *Paraguay*, HRC, 9 August 2019, Comm No. 2751/2016, CCPR/C/126/D/2751/2016, para 7.3; Amnesty International, 'UN Landmark Case for People Displaced by Climate Change', 20 January 2020, www.amnesty.org/en/latest/news/2020/01/un-landmark-case-for-people-displaced-by-climate-change/.

[62] See also, Commission on Human Rights, Special Rapporteur to the UN Commission on Human Rights, 'Adverse effects of the illicit movement and dumping of toxic and dangerous products and wastes on the enjoyment of human rights', 21 December 2000, UN Doc. E/CN.4/2001/55/Add.1, para 58.

[63] *Ibid.*, para 58.

[64] *Ibid.*

[65] Knox, 'Diagonal Environmental Rights', 92.

and human rights breached as a result of toxic substances being dumped in their countries. Moreover, the Special Rapporteur has had the occasion to investigate and report on US entities with subsidiaries in Mexico who deal in toxic substances. In this respect, the Special Rapporteur recommended that the US government should cooperate with Mexico and enforce Mexican judgments, but also encouraged the government to

> facilitate the prosecution of United States corporations whose subsidiary entities in Mexico are responsible for failing to deal with imports of toxic and dangerous products and wastes in accordance with United States, Mexican or international law.[66]

This link between the environment and human rights is reflected in certain regional treaty practice as well. Article 24 of the African Charter on Human and Peoples' Rights provides that '[a]ll peoples shall have the right to a general satisfactory environment favourable to their development'. Interpreting the scope of this provision and indicating the specific measures that should be taken by states, the African Commission on Human and Peoples' Rights has noted that

> [g]overnment compliance with the spirit of Articles 16 and 24 of the African Charter must also include ordering or at least permitting independent scientific monitoring of threatened environments, requiring and publicising environmental and social impact studies prior to any major industrial development, undertaking appropriate monitoring and providing information to those communities exposed to hazardous materials and activities and providing meaningful opportunities for individuals to be heard and to participate in the development decisions affecting their communities.[67]

Ultimately, the African Commission concluded that Nigeria had violated the right to a satisfactory environment and the right to health. In coming to this finding, the Commission underlined that the right to environment 'imposes clear obligations upon a government' and will require the positive action of a state in the form of measures to prevent environmental damage and pollution.[68] The Commission went on to assess that the

[66] Commission on Human Rights, Special Rapporteur to the UN Commission on Human Rights, 'Adverse effects of the illicit movement and dumping of toxic and dangerous products and wastes on the enjoyment of human rights', 10 January 2003, UN Doc. E/CN.4/2003/56/Add.1, para 72(c).

[67] *Social and Economic Rights Action Center (SERAC) and Center for Economic and Social Rights (CESR)* v. *Nigeria*, African Commission on Human Rights, 27 October 2001, 155/96, para 55.

[68] *Ibid.*, para 52.

violated rights in this case in fact oblige states at three levels. First, not to interfere with the rights as such. Second, to ensure third parties do not affect the enjoyment of the rights by the beneficiaries. And third, to actively ameliorate enjoyment of the rights.[69]

In another treaty context, the Additional Protocol to the American Convention on Human Rights in the Area of Economic, Social and Cultural Rights (San Salvador Protocol)[70] guarantees that '[e]veryone shall have the right to live in a healthy environment' in its Article 11, which also places an obligation on states Parties to 'promote the protection, preservation, and improvement of the environment'. Though this particular provision may not be the subject of an individual petition.

The Inter-American Commission on Human Rights has also noted that the rights to life, personal safety and integrity and to property may be interfered with by environmental degradation in the context of the American Convention on Human Rights.[71] In *Saldano* v. *Argentina*, the Inter-American Commission noted that 'a party to the American Convention may be responsible under certain circumstances for the acts and omissions of its agents which produce effects or are undertaken outside that state's own territory'.[72] That said, the Inter-American Court

[69] *Ibid.*, paras 45–47. See also, Minnerop, Roht-Arriaza and Aminzadeh, 'Solidarity Rights (Development, Peace, Environment, Humanitarian Assistance)' (2018) *Max Planck Encyclopedia of International Law.*

[70] Additional Protocol to the American Convention on Human Rights in the Area of Economic, Social and Cultural Rights (San Salvador Protocol), 16 November 1999, Organization of American States A-52.

[71] See, for example, Case No. 12.053, *Maya Indigenous Community of the Toledo District* v. *Belize (2004)* Inter-Am. C.H.R. OEA/Ser.L/V/II.122, where the Commission held:

> 193. The State violated the right to property enshrined in Article XXIII of the American Declaration to the detriment of the Maya people, by failing to take effective measures to recognize their communal property right to the lands that they have traditionally occupied and used, without detriment to other indigenous communities, and to delimit, demarcate and title or otherwise established the legal mechanisms necessary to clarify and protect the territory on which their right exists.
>
> 194. The State further violated the right to property enshrined in Article XXIII of the American Declaration to the detriment of the Maya people, by granting logging and oil concessions to third parties to utilize the property and resources that could fall within the lands which must be delimited, demarcated and titled or otherwise clarified and protected, in the absence of effective consultations with and the informed consent of the Maya people.

[72] Report No. 38/99, *Saldano* v. *Argentina* (1998) Inter-Am. C.H.R. OEA/Ser.L/V/II.95, para 17.

of Human Rights has recently gone further in its landmark Advisory Opinion on *The Environment and Human Rights (State Obligations in Relation to the Environment in the Context of the Protection and Guarantee of the Rights to Life and to Personal Integrity – Interpretation and Scope of Articles 4(1) and 5(1) of the American Convention on Human Rights).*[73] Confirming the link between the realisation of human rights and the existence of a healthy environment, the Court found that states should take measures to ensure significant environmental harm is not caused to individuals within and beyond their territory.[74] In establishing a right to a healthy environment under the American Convention on Human Rights, which is justiciable under Article 26 of the Convention, this Opinion may well open the door for individual litigants to bring a case where this right has been interfered with.

Suggesting extraterritorial reach, the Court asserted in this Advisory Opinion that the jurisdiction of a state can extend beyond its territory where activities conducted within its territory have cross-border effects.[75] Moreover, the Court noted that states have a duty to ensure the rights of persons outside their territory are not impaired.[76] The Court observed that

> the obligation to prevent environmental transboundary damage is an obligation recognised by international environmental law, by virtue of which States can be held responsible for significant damage caused to persons located outside their territory as a result of activities originating in their territory or under their authority or effective control.[77]

This has led some commentators to suggest that the principal significance of the Advisory Opinion 'is that it signals the possibility of "diagonal" human rights claims in circumstances far broader than those which have been held admissible under the Inter-American system, or indeed any other system, to date'.[78] In this respect, a stronger argument can now be

[73] *The Environment and Human Rights (State Obligations in Relation to the Environment in the Context of the Protection and Guarantee of the Rights to Life and to Personal Integrity – Interpretation and Scope of Articles 4(1) and 5(1) of the American Convention on Human Rights)*, Advisory Opinion OC-23/17, Inter-Am. Ct. H.R. (ser. A) No. 23.

[74] *Ibid.*

[75] *Ibid.*, para 81.

[76] *Ibid.*, paras 81, 95 and 101.

[77] *Ibid.*, para 103.

[78] Monica Feria-Tinta and Simon Milnes, 'The Rise of Environmental Law in International Dispute Resolution: Inter-American Court of Human Rights Issues Advisory Opinion on Environment and Human Rights' *EJIL: Talk!* (26 February 2018), www.ejiltalk.org/the-rise-of-environmental-law-in-international-dispute-resolution-inter-american-court-of-

made that greenhouse gases emitted by a state could lead to the attribution of responsibility for damage caused to people in other states. It has also been said that this case contributes to the evolving case law on 'cross border human rights claims arising from transboundary environmental impacts',[79] and it will be interesting to see if this innovative interpretation of jurisdiction, a common limitation in the applicability of human rights treaties, may be followed in other contexts.

Another case of the Inter-American Court, *Kaliña and Lokono Peoples* v. *Suriname*, concerned environmental damage caused to the land of an indigenous community.[80] Of interest in this case is that the Court ordered, among other reparation, compensation for damage caused to 'the environment and the lands of the Kaliña and Lokono peoples owing to the bauxite mining operations in the Wane Kreek Nature Reserve'.[81] It thus offers an example of a human rights court ordering compensation for environmental damage and contributes to the recent trend among international courts and tribunals, which appear to be developing better tools to value damage caused to the environment so that just reparation can be awarded.[82]

Other regional human rights systems have recognised that environmental degradation can violate human rights as well. In the context of the European Court of Human Rights (ECtHR), it has held that environmental pollution may violate Article 8 of the European Convention on Human Rights (ECHR), which includes the right to respect for private

human-rights-issues-landmark-advisory-opinion-on-environment-and-human-rights3/.

[79] Monica Feria-Tinta and Simon Milnes, 'The Rise of Environmental Law in International Dispute Resolution: Inter-American Court of Human Rights Issues Advisory Opinion on Environment and Human Rights' (2016) 27 *Yearbook of International Environmental Law* 64.

[80] *Kaliña and Lokono Peoples* v. *Suriname* (2015) Inter-Am. Ct. H.R. (ser C) No. 309.

[81] *Ibid.*, para 290.

[82] See, for example, *Certain Activities Carried Out by Nicaragua in the Border Area (Costa Rica* v. *Nicaragua)*, Compensation, Judgment (2018) ICJ Rep. 15; *Burlington Resources* v. *Ecuador*, Decision on Ecuador's Counterclaim, ICSID Case No. ARB/08/5, 7 February 2017; *Perenco* v. *Ecuador and Empresa Estatal Petróleos del Ecuador (Petroecuador)*, Interim Decision on the Environmental Counterclaim, ICSID Case No. ARB/08/6, 11 August 2015; *Perenco Ecuador Ltd.* v. *The Republic of Ecuador and Empresa Estatal Petróleos del Eduador (Petroecuador)*, Final Award, ICSID Case No. ARB/08/6, 27 September 2019. For a comprehensive analysis of this topic, see Jason Rudall, *Compensation for Environmental Damage Under International Law* (Routledge, 2020); Jason Rudall, 'Certain Activities Carried out by Nicaragua in the Border Area (*Costa Rica* v. *Nicaragua*) – Compensation Owed by the Republic of Nicaragua to the Republic of Costa Rica' (2018) 112(2) *American Journal of International Law* 288.

and family life, home and correspondence.[83] The ECtHR has also said that 'in exceptional circumstances the acts of Contracting States performed outside their territory, or which produce effects there, may amount to exercise by them of their jurisdiction within the meaning of Article 1 of the Convention',[84] which could allow those in another country to make a claim for a breach of human rights caused by environmental pollution. In several cases, it is also notable that the ECHR has said that environmental harm may cause a denial of the right to life.[85]

The reach of human rights treaties and the extent to which states must ensure that actions within their territory do not impinge upon the rights of those outside it is likely to come into even sharper focus as the present wave of litigation concerning climate change grows stronger.[86] Indeed, there has been a steady increase in litigation on the climate in domestic and regional jurisdictions.[87] These cases have been brought on various bases. For example, in the United States the Clean Air Act,[88] the public nuisance doctrine[89] and the public trust doctrine[90] have all been bases for

[83] See, for example, *Guerra and Others* v. *Italy*, ECtHR, 19 February 1998, Application No. 14967/89, para 60; *López Ostra* v. *Spain*, ECtHR, 9 December 1994, Application No. 16798/90, para 51; *Tătar* v. *Romania*, ECtHR, 27 January 2009, Application No. 67021/01; *Dubetska and Others* v. *Ukraine*, ECtHR, 10 February 2011, Application No. 30499/03; *Dzemyuk* v. *Ukraine*, ECtHR, 4 September 2014, Application, 42488/02.

[84] *Ilaşcu and others* v. *Moldova and Russia*, ECtHR, 8 July 2004, Application No. 48787, para 314. Although note that the ECtHR has at times been reluctant to extend the jurisdictional reach of the ECHR (see *Banković and others* v. *Belgium and 16 Other Contracting States*, ECtHR, 12 December 2001, Application No. 52207/99).

[85] *M. Özel and others* v. *Turkey*, ECtHR, 17 November 2015, Application No. 46221/99, paras 170, 171 and 200; *Budayeva and others* v. *Russia*, 20 March 2008, Application No. 15339/02, 21166/02,20058/02, 11673/02 and 15343/02, paras 128–130, 133 and 159; *Öneryildiz* v. *Turkey*, ECtHR, 30 November 2004, Application No. 48939/99, paras 71, 89, 90 and 118.

[86] See, for example, *The Netherlands* v. *Urgenda*, No. 19/00135, 13 January 2020; *Juliana* v. *United States*, No. 6:15-cv-1517-TC (2016); *Air Transport of America and others* v. *Secretary of State for Energy and Climate Change* [2001] ECR II-864; *People's Climate Case (Armando Ferrão Carvalho and others* v. *The European Parliament and the Council*, No. T-330/18.

[87] For a good overview, see United Nations Environment Programme, 'The Status of Climate Litigation: A Global Review' (UN Environment and Columbia Law School, 2017); Margaretha Wewerinke-Singh, *State Responsibility, Climate Change and Human Rights under International Law* (Hart, 2019).

[88] See, for example, *Massachusetts* v. *EPA* 549 US 497 (2007).

[89] See, for example, *Am. Elec. Power Co.* v. *Connecticut* 564 US 410 (2011); *Native Vill. of Kivalina* v. *ExxonMobil Corp.* 696 F.3d 849 (9th Cir. 2012).

[90] See, for example, *Juliana* v. *United States*, No. 6:15-cv-1517-TC, 2016 WL 183903 (D. Or. 14 January 2016). The federal appeals courts ruled in favour of twenty-one teenagers suing the US government for its energy and climate change policies.

litigation. In Canada, the United Nations Framework Convention on Climate Change of 1992 (UNFCCC)[91] and its Kyoto Protocol of 1997[92] have been the subject of certain cases.[93] In Pakistan, principles of sustainable development, precaution and intergenerational equity have been invoked in climate litigation.[94] In Nigeria, human rights law has been the foundation of certain cases[95] while in New Zealand domestic environmental legislation has been the source of claims related to climate change.[96] In the Netherlands, Dutch courts have ordered the government to reduce emissions so that its citizens may be protected from climate change.[97] In particular, it stipulated the Dutch government must be more ambitious in its emission reduction targets. This case, *The Netherlands* v. *Urgenda*, was brought under human rights and tort law as a climate liability suit. The Dutch courts have warned that the threat posed by global warming is acute, and that the Dutch government had committed to act through international treaties. In particular, one judge noted specifically that the state should not hide behind the argument that the solution to the global climate problem does not depend solely on Dutch efforts.[98]

These cases once again illustrate the growing importance of the individual in propagating environmental protection through courts and tribunals. Combined with the expanding notions of jurisdiction and the connection between human rights and environmental degradation, courts and tribunals may reinforce the emerging norm that states must take the interests of those beyond their borders into account when formulating their environmental policies as well as in other decisions that may lead to environmental harm for those living in third countries. Once again, this resonates with

[91] United Nations Framework Convention on Climate Change, 9 May 1992, 1771 UNTS 107.

[92] Kyoto Protocol to the United Nations Framework Convention on Climate Change, 11 December 1997, 2303 UNTS 162.

[93] See, for example, *Friends of the Earth* v. *Canada* (2008) F.C. 1183 (Can. Fed. Ct.).

[94] See, for example, *Leghari* v. *Fedn. of Pakistan*, W.P. No. 25501/2015 (Lahore High Court) (4 September 2015).

[95] See, for example, *Gbemre* v. *Shell Petroleum Dev. Co. Nigeria* (2005) Afr. Hum. Rts. L. Rep. 151

[96] See, for example, *Greenpeace New Zealand* v. *Northland Reg'l Council* (2006) NZHC CIV 2006-404-004617; *Genesis Power Ltd.* v. *Franklin Dist. Council* (2005) NZRMA 541.

[97] *The Netherlands* v. *Urgenda*, No. 200.178.245/01 (2018). The case has been upheld by the Hague Court of Appeal on 9 October 2018 and the Dutch Supreme Court on 13 January 2020 (*The Netherlands* v. *Urgenda*, No. 19/00135, 13 January 2020). For a commentary on this decision, see, Oksana Lutak, 'The Urgenda Decision: The Landmark Dutch Climate Change Case' (2020) *Leiden Law Blog*, https://leidenlawblog.nl/contributors/oksana-lutak.

[98] *The Netherlands* v. *Urgenda*, No. 200.178.245/01 (2018).

Eyal Benvenisti's idea that sovereigns should act as agents of humanity and have consideration for 'the other'.[99] Such consideration for the other in international environmental protection is also evident in a different direction, namely those who will live in the future, through the principle of intergenerational equity, to which we turn next.

6.2.4 *Intergenerational Equity*

Intergenerational equity is an embodiment of cosmopolitan altruism since it extends the universal application of rights to, and demands consideration for the needs of, individuals not yet born. Its overall function is to strike a balance between the needs of different generations. The principle appears in a broad cross-section of environmental agreements. For example, Principle 1 of the 1972 Stockholm Declaration on the Human Environment provides that human beings bear 'a solemn responsibility to protect and improve the environment for present and future generations' and Principle 2 that '[t]he natural resources of the earth ... must be safeguarded for the benefit of present and future generations' while Principle 5 expresses the objective that '[t]he non-renewable resources of the earth must be employed in such a way as to guard against the danger of their future exhaustion'. The spirit of the principle was expressed by the Brundtland Commission, who defined the notion of sustainable development to which intergenerational equity is closely connected, as 'development that meets the needs of the present without compromising the ability of future generations to meet their own needs'.[100] Principle 3 of the Rio Declaration similarly affirmed that the 'right to development must be fulfilled so as to equitably meet developmental and environmental needs of present and future generations'. The principle of intergenerational equity is evident in treaty practice too, as shown by the 1992 Convention on Biological Diversity,[101] which has been ratified by most of the world's countries and whose Article 10 requires that states '[i]ntegrate consideration of the conservation and sustainable use of biological resources into national decision-making'.

While the principle has featured in the reasoning of courts and tribunals, this has often been in a rather oblique way at the international level.

[99] Benvenisti, 'Sovereigns as Trustees of Humanity: On the Accountability of States to Foreign Stakeholders'.

[100] The World Commission on Environment and Development, *Our Common Future* (Oxford University Press, 1987), 43.

[101] Convention on Biological Diversity, 5 June 1992, 1760 UNTS 79.

It has been hinted at in two cases of the ICJ, namely its Advisory Opinion in the *Legality of the Threat or Use of Nuclear Weapons*[102] and in the *Gabčikovo-Nagymaros Project (Hungary/Slovakia)* dispute.[103] In both cases, the Court observed that '[t]he environment is not an abstraction but represents the living space, the quality of life and the very health of human beings, including generations unborn'.[104]

Aside from the ICJ, regional and domestic courts have applied the principle in a more concrete way. For example, the Inter-American Court of Human Rights referred to future generations in *Mayagna (Sumo) Awas Tingni Commission* v. *Nicaragua.*[105] It noted the importance of protecting land and the indigenous community's relationship with it to 'preserve their cultural legacy and transmit it to future generations'.[106] In a Joint Separate Opinion in this case, Judges Cançado-Trindade, Pacheco-Gómez and Abreu-Burelli were of the view that 'we relate ourselves . . . in time, with other generations (past and future), in respect of which we have obligations'.[107] At the domestic level, the principle has also provided the basis for a case in which the Supreme Court of the Philippines reasoned that the principle of intergenerational equity rendered admissible a collective action suit that had been brought by several Philippine children.[108] Finally, the High Court of Kenya has applied the principle in its *Waweru* v. *Kenya* case, which concerned water pollution that resulted from disposing of waste water and sewage, and in which the Court stated that 'intergenerational equity obligates the present generation to ensure that health, diversity and productivity of natural resources are maintained or enhanced for the benefit of future generations'.[109]

[102] *Legality of the Threat or Use of Nuclear Weapons*, Advisory Opinion (1996) ICJ Rep. 226.

[103] *Case Concerning the Gabčikovo-Nagymaros Project (Hungary/Slovakia)*, Judgment (1997) ICJ Rep. 7.

[104] *Legality of the Threat or Use of Nuclear Weapons*, Advisory Opinion (1996) ICJ Rep. 226, para 29; *Case Concerning the Gabčikovo Nagymaros Project (Hungary/Slovakia)*, Judgment (1997) ICJ Rep. 7, para 112.

[105] *Mayagna (Sumo) Awas Tingni Community* v. *Nicaragua*, Judgment (2001) IACtHR (ser C) No. 79 .

[106] *Ibid.*, para 149.

[107] *Ibid.*, Separate Opinion of Judge Cançado-Trindade, Pacheco-Gómez and Abreu-Burelli, para. 10.

[108] *Juan Antonio Oposa and others* v. *Fulgenico S. Factoran Jr. and others*, Supreme Court of the Philippines, 30 June 1993, para 22.

[109] *Waweru, Mwangi (joining) and others (joining)* v. *Kenya*, Misc Civil App No 118 of 2004, (2006) 1 KLR (E & L) 677, ILDC 880 (KE 2006), (2007) AHRLR 149, 2nd March 2006, Nairobi High Court, 13.

The principle of intergenerational equity is closely connected to the principle of the common heritage of humankind. The latter is also concerned with consideration for the interests of future generations. It advocates for the sustainable use of common resources to ensure people in the future may benefit from them.[110] This principle is in fact most commonly associated with the law of the sea regime. It can be found in UN General Assembly Resolution 2749 (XXV) of 17 December 1970, which provides that the 'sea-bed and ocean floor, and the subsoil thereof, beyond the limits of national jurisdiction . . . as well as the resources of the area, are the common heritage of mankind'[111] and Article 136 of the 1982 United Nations Convention on the Law of the Sea,[112] which sets out that the seabed and its resources are the common heritage of humankind, while Article 311(6) enshrines this latter provision with a special status by noting that 'there shall be no amendments to the basic principle relating to the common heritage of mankind set forth in article 136 and [there shall be] no derogation thereof'. That said, it has also found application in relation to other common heritage, such as outer space,[113] Antarctica,[114] the environment[115] or cultural heritage[116] as well as having been incorporated into the domestic law of many states.[117]

110 Rüdiger Wolfrum, 'Common Heritage of Humankind' (2009) *Max Planck Encyclopedia of International Law*, www.mpepil.com.

111 UN General Assembly Resolution 2749 (XXV), Declaration of Principles Governing the Sea-Bed and the Ocean Floor, and the Subsoil Thereof, beyond the Limits of National Jurisdiction, 17 December 1970, UN Doc. A/RES/2749 (XXV), para 1.

112 United Nations Convention on the Law of the Sea, 10 December 1982, 1833 UNTS 3.

113 Article 1, UN General Assembly Resolution 1962 (XVIII), Declaration of Legal Principles Governing the Activities of States in the Exploration and Use of Outer Space, 13 December 1963, UN Doc. A/RES/1962 (XVIII); Article 1, Treaty on Principles Governing the Activities of States in the Exploration and Use of Outer Space, Including the Moon and Other Celestial Bodies, 27 January 1967, 610 UNTS 205; Articles 4(1), 5 and 11, Agreement Governing the Activities of States on the Moon and Other Celestial Bodies ('Moon Treaty'), 5 December 1979, 1363 UNTS 3.

114 Recommendation ATCM XI-1: Regime on Antarctic Mineral Resources (Antarctic Treaty Consultative Meeting [ATCM]), para 5(d); Preamble, Protocol on Environmental Protection to the Antarctic Treaty, 4 October 1991, 2941 UNTS 3.

115 United Nations Stockholm Declaration on the Human Environment, 15 December 1972, UN Doc. A/RES/2994; the notion of common concern of mankind is also used: see, for example, UN General Assembly Resolution 43/53, Protection of global climate for present and future generations of mankind, 6 December 1988, UN Doc. A/RES/43/53.

116 See, for example, the endeavour to protect cultural heritage for future generations: Convention for the Protection of Cultural Property in the Event of Armed Conflict (United Nations Educational, Scientific and Cultural Organization [UNESCO]), 14 May 1954, 249 UNTS 240.

117 Wolfrum, 'Common Heritage of Humankind' (2009) *Max Planck Encyclopedia of International Law*.

Several efforts at the international level have been made to operationalise the principle of intergenerational equity further, as can be seen by the UN Secretary-General's 2013 report on *Intergenerational Solidarity and the Needs of Future Generations*, which was requested in the Outcome Document of the Rio+20 conference of 2012 and appraises how intergenerational solidarity could be addressed through the UN system.[118] The proposals put forward included the creation of a 'High-Commissioner for Future Generations', a 'Special Envoy of the Secretary-General on Future Generations', an 'Agenda item in a high-level political forum' or an 'Inter-agency coordination mechanism on the needs of future generations'.[119] These would all help advocate for the interests of future generations to be taken into account, within the UN system or in individual member states, to ensure the best practices and policies are developed in contexts that concern intergenerational equity.

In theory, a strong moral argument can be made for intergenerational equity since, as Simon Caney argues, '[i]f persons, by virtue of their humanity, have interests then this should apply to those who are alive and those who will be born'.[120] That said, this principle is difficult to apply in practice, and particularly as a basis for deciding legal disputes, given the indeterminacy that surrounds its implications.[121] Questions such as what would be unfair to future generations, what will their needs be, and what resources or technology will they have, make the objective calculus of this principle almost impossible.

While this principle may be difficult to apply in respect of certain issues, such as the use of non-renewable energy sources, it may be easier in relation to others, like action on climate change. Its utility can be to encourage more effective action to prevent or slow climate change now to ensure that future generations do not suffer from its effects. In this context, intergenerational equity in fact serves as a reminder of our duty to future generations as regards the environment they inherit, which should at least be as favourable as that which our generation inherited.[122] The application of this principle, and other tools for guarding against global climate change, has a further

[118] UN Secretary-General, *Intergenerational Solidarity and the Needs of Future Generations*, 15 August 2013, UN Doc. A/68/322.
[119] *Ibid.*, para 63–67.
[120] Caney, 'Human Rights and Global Climate Change', 31.
[121] See Edith Brown Weiss, *In Fairness to Future Generations: International Law, Common Patrimony and Intergenerational Equity* (Transnational Publishers, 1989).
[122] Caney, 'Human Rights and Global Climate Change', 23.

important dimension. That is, since climate change is most likely to affect those in foreign states who are the poorest in global society, but who have contributed least to environmental degradation, the obligation should be shouldered mostly by wealthy industrialised countries today.[123] In a similar way, though without the temporal aspect, intragenerational equity is directed at achieving equity within a generation and is concerned primarily with the South–North divide between developing and developed countries. We turn to specific duties to people in developing countries in the context of environmental governance in the next section.

6.3 Special Commitments to Developing Countries

Equity in environmental governance is one of the most significant sources of contestation in the field today. Recent efforts have been focused on seeking to balance the need for universal action on environmental degradation with the different financial and technical capacities of states (as well as their historical and present responsibility for the damage caused).[124] The vehicle that has been engineered to resolve this tension in international environmental law is the principle of common but differentiated responsibilities.

6.3.1 Common but Differentiated Responsibilities

The principle of common but differentiated responsibilities applies to environmental obligations. It is a principle that is intended to guide global environmental governance on the basis of responsibility for environmental damage and the capacity to shoulder the burden of managing environmental problems.[125] In other words, the principle helps to bridge the gap between the formal legal equality of states recognised under the UN Charter (Article 2(1)) and the reality that developing countries do not have the means to undertake the same obligations as developed countries, nor are historically responsible for

123 *Ibid.*, 24.

124 Pierre-Marie Dupuy and Jorge E. Viñuales, *International Environmental Law* (2nd ed., Cambridge University Press, 2018), 83.

125 *Ibid.*; Philippe Cullet, 'Principle 7: Common but Differentiated Responsibilities', in Jorge E. Viñuales (ed.), *The Rio Declaration on Environment and Development: A Commentary* (Oxford University Press, 2015), 229–244; Lavanya Rajamani, *Differential Treatment in International Environmental Law* (Oxford University Press, 2006).

the same amount of damage to the environment.[126] Principle 7 of the 1992 Rio Declaration encapsulates the core idea of common but differentiated responsibilities:

> States shall cooperate in a spirit of global partnership to conserve, protect and restore the health and integrity of the Earth's ecosystem. In view of the different contributions to global environmental degradation, States have common but differentiated responsibilities.
>
> The developed countries acknowledge the responsibility that they bear in the international pursuit of sustainable development in view of the pressures their societies place on the global environment and of the technologies and financial resources they command.

The principle of common but differentiated responsibilities is also evident in a number of treaties. For example, the 1985 Vienna Convention for the Protection of the Ozone Layer attempts to take account of 'the circumstances and particular requirements of developing countries', 'the means at their disposal and their capabilities' and commits developed countries to cooperation and technology transfer.[127] In the same context, the Montreal Protocol to the Vienna Convention provides specifically for differentiated obligations for developing countries in its Article 5. Turning to the climate change regime, the UNFCCC provides the following in Article 3:

> 1. The Parties should protect the climate system for the benefit of present and future generations of humankind, on the basis of equity and in accordance with their common but differentiated responsibilities and respective capabilities. Accordingly, the developed country Parties should take the lead in combating climate change and the adverse effects thereof.
> 2. The specific needs and special circumstances of developing country Parties, especially those that are particularly vulnerable to the adverse effects of climate change, and of those Parties, especially developing country Parties, that would have to bear a disproportionate or abnormal burden under the Convention, should be given full consideration.

Under the Kyoto Protocol to the UNFCCC developed countries were required to meet new emissions targets while developing countries were

[126] Christopher Stone, 'Common but Differentiated Responsibilities in International Law' (2004) 98 *American Journal of International Law* 276.

[127] Preamble, para 3, Article 2(2) and Article 4, Vienna Convention for the Protection of the Ozone Layer, 22 March 1985, 1513 UNTS 293.

not.[128] With the Paris Agreement of 2015, all states set their own nationally determined contributions to the common effort of mitigating and adapting to climate change.[129] Moreover, as will be explored further below, developing countries should receive financial, technical and capacity-building assistance to help them reduce their emissions.[130] Further still, the Paris Agreement relies on transparency to encourage states to meet the commitments they have made, but this mechanism also emphasises the importance of taking into account the differing capabilities of states.[131]

The principle of common but differentiated responsibilities is similar in a certain respect to the differential treatment accorded to developing countries in the context of the international trade regime, considered in Chapter 5, or the law of the sea and the legal framework that applies to Antarctica.[132] These areas of law also attempt to resolve the tension between common challenges and differential capacities in tackling those challenges. Like the equivalent doctrines in those regimes, the principle of common but differentiated responsibilities is an expression of solidarity with other countries.[133] Indeed, it has been argued that common but differentiated responsibilities are an expression of the principle of solidarity.[134] It has also been observed that the principle of common but differentiated obligations exhibits aspects of so-called self-centred solidarity, because action on goals that ultimately benefit all states is pursued, as well as so-called altruistic solidarity because the structure of action often benefits certain states more directly and

[128] Articles 3(1) and 10, Kyoto Protocol to the United Nations Framework Convention on Climate Change, 11 December 1997, 2303 UNTS 148.

[129] Articles 3 and 4, Paris Agreement, adopted on 12 December 2015 at the twenty-first session of the Conference of the Parties to the United Nations Framework Convention on Climate Change held in Paris from 30 November to 13 December 2015.

[130] Articles 9–11, *ibid.*

[131] Article 13(1)–(3), *ibid.*

[132] Dupuy and Viñuales, *International Environmental Law*, 84. See also Chapter 5 of this book; United Nations General Assembly Resolution 3201 (S-VI), Declaration on the Establishment of a New International Economic Order, 1 May 1974, UN Doc. A/RES/3201(S-VI), para 4(n)–(p); Articles 69 and 254, United Nations Convention on the Law of the Sea, 10 December 1982, 1833 UNTS 3; Preamble, para 2, The Antarctic Treaty, 1 December 1959, 402 UNTS 71.

[133] Holger Hestermeyer, 'Reality or Aspiration? Solidarity in International Environmental and World Trade Law' *Diversity and Homogeneity, Outcome Paper 2/2012* (Max Planck Institute, 2012).

[134] See Karel Wellens, 'Revisiting Solidarity as a (Re-)Emerging Constitutional Principle: Some Further Reflections' in Rüdiger Wolfrum and Chie Kojima (eds.), *Solidarity: A Structural Principle of International Law* (Springer, 2010), 13.

immediately.[135] The principle tempers the obligations that developing states may be under and, even beyond international environmental law, could prove to be an important principle in constructing altruistically oriented commitments that are fair for all states.[136]

In the context of environmental governance, the emergence of common but differentiated responsibilities serves to highlight that the altruism such principles encourage can play a critical role in shaping certain norms, targets and assistance in a more equitable way. Indeed, the principle of common but differentiated responsibilities is also an important justification for technical and financial assistance for those states that lack the capability to meet environmental targets. We turn next to this topic of technical and financial assistance.

6.3.2 *Financial and Technical Assistance*

As alluded to earlier, financial assistance is becoming increasingly critical to international environmental governance in order to help developing countries meet the costs of environmental protection. This can include the costs of mitigating environmental damage as well as of adapting to environmental change, and can extend to capacity-building, pollution control, compliance assistance or disaster-relief, among other areas. Moreover, technology transfer that can assist in environmental monitoring, and management frequently accompanies the call for financial assistance. Such assistance is provided for in a variety of multilateral environmental agreements as well as through the activities of financial institutions. Evidence of this commitment to assist others in meeting environmental and development challenges is also apparent in the Sustainable Development Goals (SDGs), not least SDG 17, which provides a reiteration of the need to 'strengthen the means of implementation and revitalize the global partnership for sustainable development'.[137]

Official development assistance (ODA) is an important channel through which financial assistance for sustainable development

135 Hestermeyer, 'Reality or Aspiration? Solidarity in International Environmental and World Trade Law'.

136 Michael Nyongesa Wabwile, *Legal Protection of Social and Economic Rights of Children in Developing Countries: Reassessing International Cooperation and Responsibility* (Intersentia, 2010), 159; Benvenisti, 'Sovereigns as Trustees of Humanity: On the Accountability of States to Foreign Stakeholders', 328.

137 United Nations General Assembly Resolution A/RES/70/1, 'Transforming Our World: The 2030 Agenda for Sustainable Development', 25 September 2015, UN Doc. A/RES/70/1, Sustainable Development Goals.

initiatives may flow.[138] ODA may also be accompanied by such financial instruments as green bonds, local currency financing, blended finance, guarantee mechanisms and public–private partnerships.[139] In fact, the private sector is playing an increasing role in the provision of financial assistance for developing countries so that they can achieve environmental objectives. This role was affirmed, in particular at the 1992 Rio Conference as well as the Monterrey Conference and Johannesburg Summit.[140]

Financial and technical assistance for environmental purposes is provided for in a variety of multilateral instruments or funds. It is notable that such mechanisms have assisted with avoiding bias in funding decisions that can occur in bilateral aid channels.[141] They are evident in various initiatives that have been designed to address environmental pollution or disasters. For example, financial and technical assistance can be offered in response to oil spills, as can be seen in Article 198 of the UN Convention on the Law of the Sea 1982[142] or Article 9 of the International Maritime Organization (IMO) Convention on Oil Pollution Preparedness, Response and Cooperation 1990.[143] It can also take the form of assistance in monitoring pollution through technical equipment as well as sharing the resources needed to ensure that those responsible for such monitoring are trained to do so, as is the case with the General Trust Fund established by the 1984 Geneva Protocol on Long-term Financing of the Cooperative Programme for Monitoring and Evaluation of the Long-range Transmission of Air Pollutants in Europe (EMEP

[138] Report of the International Conference on Financing for Development (UN, 2002) 9, para 42; see also Report of World Summit on Sustainable Development (UN, 2002), para 85(a).

[139] UNDP and French Development Agency, 'Financing the SDGs in the Least Developed Countries (LDCs): Diversifying the Financing Tool-box and Managing Vulnerability' (2016); Pedro Conceição and Philippe Orliange, 'To leave no one behind, Least Developed Countries need new financing tools' *UNDP* (14 December 2016).

[140] See United Nations Conference on Environment and Development, Agenda 21, 3 to 14 June 1992, para 33.16; World Summit on Sustainable Development, Johannesburg, 26 August–4 September 2002, UN Doc. A/C.2/57/L.83, paras 86(d)-(e), 87 and 88.

[141] Antonella Angelini, 'A Trouble Shared is a Trouble Halved: How the Structure of Cooperation Matters for the Engagement of Responsibility in the World Bank Partnership Programmes' (2016) 13(1) *International Organizations Law Review* 171.

[142] United Nations Convention on the Law of the Sea, 10 December 1982, 1833 UNTS 3.

[143] Convention on Oil Pollution Preparedness, Response and Cooperation, 30 November 1990, 1891 UNTS 51.

Protocol) to the 1979 Convention on Long-Range Transboundary Air Pollution (LRTAP Convention).[144]

Assistance may also be targeted at developing domestic capacity and national legislation to meet environmental objectives, such as the Convention on International Trade in Endangered Species of Wild Fauna and Flora (CITES) Trust Fund of 1973[145] or Article 20(2) of the Convention on Biodiversity, which provides that developed states should assist developing countries by delivering sufficient financial resources so that they can meet the costs of implementing measures set out under the Convention and, in turn, benefit from the biodiversity promotion that the Convention offers.[146] It also emphasises 'the need for adequacy, predictability and timely flow of funds'.[147] Significantly, Article 20(4) of the same convention stipulates that the formal compliance of developing countries is conditional upon the financial and technical support provided by developed countries.

Certain assistance takes the form of specific support to help with the implementation of multilateral environmental agreements (MEAs). This is the case, for example, with the Basel Technical Cooperation Trust Fund in the context of the 1989 Basel Transboundary Wastes Convention, which provides financial and technical assistance for capacity-building, specific projects and the response to accidents involving the transboundary movement of hazardous wastes.[148]

There has also been an increase in the number of financial mechanisms that seek to provide assistance to states dealing with broader environmental challenges.[149] In this context, it is also important to underline that environmental degradation, including climate change, is likely to affect developing countries most severely. These mechanisms come in various forms and can be targeted at specific environmental challenges.

[144] Convention on Long-Range Transboundary Air Pollution, 13 November 1979, 1302 UNTS 217.

[145] CITES, Decisions 13.74–13.75, 'National wildlife trade policy reviews' (2004); Decisions 14.21–14.24, 'National wildlife trade policy reviews' (2007).

[146] Convention on Biodiversity, 5 June 1992, 1760 UNTS 79.

[147] Article 20(2), *ibid.*

[148] Decision V/32, 'Enlargement of the scope of the Technical Cooperation Trust Fund' (10 December 1999) UN Doc UNEP/CHW.5/29, elaborated/amended by Decisions VI/14, XI/14, and XII/11.

[149] Laurence Boisson de Chazournes, 'Financial Assistance' in Lavanya Rajamani and Jacqueline Peel (eds.), *Oxford Handbook on International Environmental Law* (2nd ed., Oxford University Press, 2021).

The Montreal Multilateral Fund under the 1987 Montreal Protocol on Substances that Deplete the Ozone Layer is aimed at financing the costs incurred by developing countries as they transition away from technologies and substances that have a significantly negative effect on the ozone layer to those that do not.[150] In a different way, the Global Environment Facility (GEF) provides finance for projects that concern biodiversity, land degradation, pollution, international water resources, forest management and climate change.[151] In particular, GEF projects help support the implementation of sustainable development initiatives at the domestic level and also facilitate public participation. Contributions to the GEF are increased every four years and in the latest GEF Replenishment, states have committed to providing $4.1 billion to the Fund.[152] In the context of the GEF, there is also a Small Grants Programme, administered by the UN Development Programme (UNDP), in which NGOs or local community organisations may benefit directly from funding of up to $50,000 where their activities promote sustainable development.[153] Moreover, the GEF has a Medium-sized Grants Programme within which local NGOs can apply for grants up to the value of $2 million.[154] A particular emphasis has been placed on facilitating access to funding from the GEF by least developed countries, small island developing states and African states.[155]

In the context of the climate change regime, a number of funds have been created.[156] The Least Developed Countries Fund was adopted in 2001 under the Marrakesh Accords, adopted at the Seventh Conference of Parties of the UNFCCC, and is aimed at supporting such countries as

150 Montreal Protocol on Substances that Deplete the Ozone Layer, 16 September 1987, 1522 UNTS 3.

151 See GEF, www.thegef.org/.

152 See 'Fourth Meeting of the Seventh Replenishment of the GEF Trust Fund – Working Documents', GEF/R.7/18–22, www.thegef.org/council-meetings/gef-7-replenishment-fourth-meeting.

153 See GEF Small Grants Programme, https://sgp.undp.org/about-us-157.html.

154 See GEF Types of Projects, www.thegef.org/about/funding/project-types.

155 Decision 4/CP.14, 'Additional Guidance to the Global Environment Facility', 18 March 2009, UN Doc. FCCC/CP/2008/7/Add.1, 6; Decision 5/CP.16, 'Further guidance for the operation of the Least Developed Countries Fund', 15 March 2011, UN Doc. FCCC/CP/2010/7/Add.2, 9.

156 For a comprehensive survey of this topic, see Laurence Boisson de Chazournes, 'Climate Change and Financial Assistance: A Fragmented Unified or Coordinated Approach?' in Sharif Bhuiyan, Philippe Sands, and Nico Schrijver (eds.), *International Law and Developing Countries: Essays in Honour of Kamal Hossain* (Martinus Nijhoff, 2014), 126–152.

they adapt to the changes resulting from climate change.[157] Following the 2009 Copenhagen Accord, adopted at the Fifteenth Conference of Parties of the UNFCCC, collective commitments to provide annual funding incrementally up to $100 billion by 2020 were made and the Green Climate Fund (GCF) was also created.[158] The latter was established by 194 governments in order to mitigate greenhouse gas emissions in developing states as well as to assist those most affected by climate change to mitigate and adapt to its consequences.[159]

Climate finance also played a major role in negotiations around the 2015 Paris Agreement.[160] Moreover, the Paris Agreement aims to promote sustainable development through incentive schemes that are addressed to public and private actors.[161] Specific legal structures have been developed within the Paris Agreement to encourage the flow of financial and technical assistance.[162] This is evident, for example, in its aim to ensure $100 billion is available in additional resources and for specific legal structures to avoid double-counting. Article 9(9) stipulates that there should be 'efficient access to financial resources through simplified approval procedures and enhanced readiness support for developing country Parties'. Progressively increasing contributions by developed countries are expected and financial assistance will play a role in the review of progress that takes place every five years (known as the Global Stocktake).[163]

Transparency also plays a role in this context as developed countries must report on the assistance that they provide to developing countries. The Paris Agreement envisages, for example, an 'enhanced transparency framework for action and support'.[164] This includes an augmented reporting mechanism that is concerned with the action

157 Decision 5/CP.7, 'Implementation of Article 4, paragraphs 8 and 9, of the Convention (Decision 3/CP.3 and Article 2, paragraph 3, and Article 3, paragraph 14, of the Kyoto Protocol)', 21 January 2002, UN Doc. FCCC/CP/2001/13/Add.1, 32.

158 Decision 2/CP.15, 'Copenhagen Accord', 30 March 2010, UN Doc. FCCC/CP/2009/11/Add.1, 4–9, Articles 8 and 10.

159 See Green Climate Fund, www.greenclimate.fund/.

160 Decision 5/CP.20, 'Long-Term Climate Finance', 2 February 2015, UN Doc. FCCC/CP/2014/10/Add.2, 9, paras 9–10.

161 See, for example, Article 6(4), Paris Agreement.

162 See Laurence Boisson de Chazournes, 'The Paris Climate Change instruments as a blueprint for new legal approaches?', *Thomas Franck Lecture – KFG The International Rule of Law – Rise or Decline?*, 4 February 2019, www.kfg-intlaw.de/News%20and%20Events/Events/videos/Lectures_video.php?ID=86.

163 See, for example, Article 9(3), Paris Agreement.

164 Article 13, *ibid.*

and support of States. Developed countries must report on financial, technology transfer and capacity-building support provided to developing country parties under Articles 9, 10 and 11 of the Paris Agreement. This information provided by developed countries will also be subject to a technical expert review. In addition, interestingly, developing countries should report on financial, technology transfer and capacity-building support needed and received under Articles 9, 10 and 11. In fact, more generally, the propagation of transparency through reporting requirements and other compliance mechanisms under international environmental regulation is to be welcomed. It has been shown that information about harm caused by behaviour tends to prompt pro-social behaviour and self-sacrifice, rather than defection and selfishness.[165] In the context of environmental governance, this has been described as environmental norm activation.[166] The finding correlates with the evidence that people are more likely to act altruistically if they perceive their contribution is going to make a more significant social impact than less.[167] Moreover, pro-social behaviour is more likely to occur when people observe others acting in a pro-social way and, as a result, a virtuous circle results.[168]

In addition to financial assistance, technology development and transfer between developed and developing countries are also provided for under the Paris Agreement.[169] Article 10(5) encourages 'collaborative approaches to research and development, and facilitating access to technology . . . to developing country Parties,' while Article 10(2) recommends cooperation on technology development and transfer to assist with climate change mitigation and adaptation.

Aside from the climate change regime, funds aimed at addressing other particular issues are also a feature of international environmental governance. The Rainforest Trust helps to preserve threatened tropical rainforests, protect wildlife and conserve ecosystems through funding local initiatives via a range of sources, creating partnerships and

[165] Michael Vandenbergh, 'Order without Social Norms: How Personal Norm Activation Can Protect the Environment' (2005) 99 *Northwestern University Law Review* 1101.

[166] *Ibid.*

[167] Lynn Stout, 'Law and Prosocial Behaviour', in Eyal Zamir and Doron Teichman (eds.), *The Oxford Handbook of Behavioural Economics and the Law* (Oxford University Press, 2014), 204.

[168] *Ibid.*

[169] Article 10(4), Paris Agreement.

interacting with local communities.[170] Alternatively, the Prototype Carbon Fund (PCF)[171] and the Clean Development Mechanism (CDM)[172] are aimed at providing public–private finance for climate-related projects in developing countries and countries with economies in transition. Public sector participants in the PCF are required to contribute $10 million while private sector participants must pay $5 million to the Fund.[173] Similarly addressing the issues of carbon reduction in developing countries is the Forest Carbon Partnership Facility (FCPF), which includes the Readiness Fund and the Carbon Fund.[174]

These financial and technical assistance mechanisms demonstrate a recognition not only of the shared challenge presented by environmental degradation but also of the particularly severe consequences that developing and least developed countries will face as well as their reduced capacity in responding to the challenge. They are an expression of solidarity in facing a common threat, but they also prompt altruism among states because they require positive action in the form of contributions from developed countries in order to assist developing countries.

6.4 Concluding Remarks

This chapter has revealed two major features in the evolving architecture of international environmental law. First, an increasing anthropocentrism in substantive international environmental law, which includes a growing number of avenues for individuals to seek recourse for environmental damage against third states. Second, while international environmental law has always included duties to 'the other', particularly as regards the foundational obligation to avoid transboundary harm, it is also possible to see the emergence of different manifestations of duties to 'the other', such as more meaningful commitments to individuals in

[170] See Rainforest Trust, www.rainforesttrust.org/about/what-we-do/; Rainforest Trust, '2017 Annual Report', available at https://online.anyflip.com/zzrd/ekhf/mobile/index.html, 37.

[171] See Prototype Carbon Fund, www.eea.europa.eu/themes/climate/links/carbon-markets/Link1033460005.

[172] See Clean Development Mechanism, available at https://cdm.unfccc.int/.

[173] International Bank for Reconstruction and Development (IBRD), Resolution 99–1, Article IV, 'Authorising Establishment of the Prototype Carbon Fund'.

[174] See IBRD, 'Charter establishing the Forest Carbon Partnership Facility', August 2010; see also Forest Carbon Partnership Facility, www.forestcarbonpartnership.org/about; FCPF, 'Information Memorandum', 13 June 2008, 2.

other countries through their participation in environmental decision-making and opportunities for redress. The emergence of a human right to a healthy environment, particularly with extraterritorial effect, is assisting in this respect.

Other principles in international environmental law also underline the importance of action for 'the other'. This is evident in the principle of intergenerational equity and the common heritage of humankind, which both encourage states to consider people who will live in the future. The principle of common but differentiated responsibilities reflects the expectation that developed countries should make the most significant contributions to efforts designed to combat environmental challenges. The principle is also connected to another growing cornerstone of international environmental law, namely financial and technical assistance. The elaboration of funds and emphasis on technology transfer have become increasingly prominent features of recent MEAs, as well as other instruments and institutions designed to tackle environmental concerns in developing countries or global environmental problems that have a particularly devastating effect in developing countries.

Overall, this increased consideration for 'the other' in international environmental governance further highlights that states should not be oblivious to any interest but their own. Instead, international environmental law gives states a reason to take into account the interests of others and to alter their behaviour accordingly. The polluting state that causes transboundary harm through its heavy industry and consumption is a paragon of self-interest. To paraphrase Duncan Kennedy, 'the law provides [it] a conscience'.[175]

[175] Duncan Kennedy, 'Form and Substance in Private Law Adjudication' (1976) 89 *Harvard Law Review* 1685, 1719, making an analogous point about the legal prohibition on theft:

> The thief is a very paragon of self-reliance, and the property owning victim has failed to act effectively in his own defense. The point for the altruist is not that the thief is a slacker, but that he is oblivious to any interest but his own. The law, as the expression goes, 'provides him a conscience'.

7

The Form of Altruism in International Law

7.1 Introduction

This chapter explores the legal mechanisms that facilitate altruism in the international legal system. It starts from Duncan Kennedy's proposition that legal substance may be inherently connected to legal form.[1] In particular, consideration is given to his claim that altruistic norms lend themselves to expression as standards in the legal system. An examination of specific standards in the international legal order that provide a regulatory space for altruism will ensue in this chapter. In doing so, the chapter builds on the insights offered in the previous chapters on substantive international law and will reveal that there are certain common legal vehicles through which altruism is compelled or promoted by the law. The chapter also brings into sharper focus my overall claim that, while altruism is evident in the fabric of international law, it is rarely expressed in prescriptive highly administrable rules. In a context where the altruistic behaviour of individual states waxes and wanes, I conclude this chapter by making a call for greater institutionalisation of altruism.

7.2 Jurisprudence of Form

The jurisprudence of rules is concerned with the form that law takes. There are two poles of the spectrum: rules and standards. In other words, there is ultimately a distinction in legal form between 'mechanically applicable rules' and 'situation-sensitive, ad hoc standards'.[2] The distinguishing characteristic between rules and standards is formal

1 This is an insight provided in particular by the Critical Legal Studies and Law and Literature movements. See, for example, Duncan Kennedy, 'Form and Substance in Private Law Adjudication' (1976) 89 *Harvard Law Review* 1685; Jerry Frug, 'Argument as Character' (1988) 40 *Stanford Law Review* 869, 872–875; J. Paul Oetken, 'Form and Substance in Critical Legal Studies' (1991) 100(7) *The Yale Law Journal* 2209, 2210.

2 Nikolaos Tsagourias, *Jurisprudence of International Law: The Humanitarian Dimension* (Juris Publishing, 2000), 57; Kennedy, 'Form and Substance in Private

realisability.[3] This is the extent to which a legal norm has the character of 'ruleness', namely the automaticity of its application to a particular set of facts because of its specificity. Where a rule specifies a factual scenario for its application, it must be applied.[4] The official who is tasked with application of the legal norm has little to no discretion in applying the norm. A good example of a formally realizable rule is the setting of a specific age of legal capacity for liability or the fixing of a fine amount for given crimes.

Rules have a high degree of formal realisability. In contrast, standards or principles have a low degree of formal realisability. A standard instantiates an overriding objective of the legal order. Under the common law, an example of a standard is the legal norm to act in the best interests of the child. Other examples of standards in domestic contexts are due diligence, good faith, reasonableness or fairness, among others. Standards leave a broad margin of discretion to the official tasked with their application. However, the application of standards to particular fact scenarios can generate more particular rules by virtue of the precedential value that application in certain circumstances will have for application in similar circumstances in the future. There is also the possibility that no sufficiently general formally realizable rule will emerge from case law that applies to very particular factual scenarios.

Standards are more equitable and lend themselves to tailored justice in individual cases. Decisions are made on an ad hoc basis, and those officials tasked with applying standards have a broad margin of discretion. In this way, standards have an informal character. The critique of standards is that they lead to uncertainty as they may be applied differently in different situations. On the other hand, rules tend to be more clearly defined and are highly administrable. They favour giving little discretion to the judge that will apply them and they have a formal character. The critique of rules is that they tend to be either over or under-inclusive and may lead to injustices in the individual case.

Law Adjudication', 1687; Mark Kelman, *A Guide to Critical Legal Studies* (Harvard University Press, 1987), 3.

[3] Kennedy, 'Form and Substance in Private Law Adjudication', 1687–1688.

[4] *Ibid.*, Kennedy notes:

> The extent to which particular words or categories are regarded as sufficiently 'factual' to serve as the basis of formally realisable rules changes through time, is subject to dispute at any particular time, and is a matter of degree (at 1688, fn 6).

Duncan Kennedy observes that altruism favours equitable standards and ad hoc decision-making.[5] Standards allow for the application of moral norms and this is in contradistinction to the rigid application of rules divorced from any moral consideration, which is favoured in the individualist approach. In an altruistic system, the judge who engages with these standards must offer communitarian, paternalistic and regulatory solutions. Thus, while individualist rules tend to reinforce the goals of individualism (such as individual freedom), altruistic standards introduce and reinforce values in a given community.[6] An altruistic critique of the individualist perspective is the negative sense in which freedom is guaranteed in such a system, namely through a lack of constraint on individual choice. Moreover, individualism implies an indifference to the plight of the other.

The form of the law is shaped by values in the same way that the substance of the law is shaped by these values.[7] Indeed, Kennedy has observed in the context of private law that '[t]he substantive and formal dimensions are related because the same moral and economic political arguments appear in each'.[8] The ideal-type legal system for the individualist is constituted by (1) property rules, which demarcate individual ownership and define individual rights, and (2) contract rules, which regulate how individual actors interact with each other.[9] The individualist legal order is concerned with creating individual autonomy through rules designed to create separation, as well as ensuring smooth interactions between autonomous individuals through rules that govern how individuals deal with each other. Rules are intended to limit the discretion that officials who are tasked with applying them have. Moreover, individuals may act in whichever way they wish to pursue their self-interest as long as they do not breach these rules. Finally, non-intervention plays a central role in the individualist approach. Kennedy notes that 'non-intervention is consistent with the liberal premises [of individualism] because it means the refusal of the group to use the state to enforce its vision of altruistic duty against the conflicting visions of individuals pursuing their self-interest'.[10]

5 *Ibid.*, 1776.
6 Tsagourias, *Jurisprudence of International Law*, 57.
7 Kennedy, 'Form and Substance in Private Law Adjudication', 1776.
8 *Ibid.*
9 *Ibid.*, 1768.
10 *Ibid.*, 1771.

It is in this way that individualism is analogous to statism in the context of international law. Statism is an individualist approach that relies on (1) the centrality of sovereignty and the rule on non-intervention (like property rules), and (2) rules that govern how states interact (like contract rules).[11] In the case of an individualist statist order, spheres of autonomy are created through separation rules (property/sovereignty/non-intervention rules) and are linked by rules which regulate how states should deal with each other (treaties or contracts between states that ensure harmonious coexistence). In Kennedy's words, 'each member declares her indifference to her neighbor's salvation – washes her hands of him the better to "deal" with him'.[12]

As for the ideal-type of altruism, it is rooted in the premise of collectivism.[13] Altruism favours the application of standards and the pursuit of shared ends. Where this is not the case, the altruist argues that moral agnosticism and injustice prevail. While the individualist legal order embraces rules to secure the interests of the individual, the altruistic legal order embraces standards to direct the individual to pursue those collectivist ends.[14] In contrast to the individualist approach of emphasising the independence of individualistic actors, the altruistic approach is to emphasise the interdependence of moral agents because '[m]y neighbor's experience is anything but a closed book to me'.[15] Thus, sacrifice and sharing are demanded.

With these characteristics of individualist and altruistic legal form in mind, we now turn to consider whether the form of those international legal norms with an altruistic nature identified in the previous chapters conform to Kennedy's observation about standards in private law.

11 This was, for example, the approach symbolised by the *The Case of the S.S. Lotus (France v. Turkey)*, PCIJ Series A, no. 10 (1927), 18.

12 Kennedy, 'Form and Substance in Private Law Adjudication', 1774.

13 On coexistence and collectivism, see Holger Hestermeyer, *et al.* (eds.), *Co-existence, Cooperation and Solidarity: Liber Amicorum Rüdiger Wolfrum* (Martinus Nijhoff Publishers, 2012).

14 Tom Campbell, *The Left and Rights: A Conceptual Analysis of the Idea of Socialist Rights* (Routledge, 1983), 42–55; Christine Sypnowich, 'Law as a Vehicle of Altruism' (1985) 5(2) *Oxford Journal of Legal Studies* 276, 280.

15 Kennedy, 'Form and Substance in Private Law Adjudication', 1772. For a similar claim that a legal order must recognise relationally organised society through a new conception of feudalism, see Roscoe Pound, 'The New Feudalism' (1930) 16(9) *American Bar Association Journal* 553, 558, arguing that we do seem to be developing a relationally organised society. Our picture can no longer be one of free competitive activity of economically self-sufficing units. It must be redrawn as one of adjusted relations of economically interdependent units.

7.3 The Form of Altruism in International Law

As will become evident, the form of the legal norms in the chapters on the substance of altruism in international law more often have the character of flexible standards rather than of strict rules. These standards have served as regulatory spaces for altruism in many different contexts. Moreover, it is apparent that there are certain altruistic standards that operate across different areas of international law and have been an impetus for the creation of more specific altruistic standards. The following sections will offer several examples of altruistic standards with a view to revealing their inherent flexibility and lack of formal realisability.

7.3.1 Standards for International Cooperation

In 1964, Wolfgang Friedmann noted that the development of international cooperation was part of a changing structure in international law 'from an essentially negative code of rule abstention to positive rules of cooperation'.[16] As can be seen from the previous chapters on the substance of altruism in international law, cooperation is a cross-cutting principle and appears in many different areas of international legal regulation, from human rights to development and state responsibility. International cooperation can be employed to prompt specific behaviour in certain contexts, such as the exchange of information to protect children or the adoption of national or international measures aimed at promoting development and reducing poverty.

One notable expression of the positive duty to cooperate is in the International Covenant on Economic, Social and Cultural Rights of 1966, where it has a special role to play in the realisation of rights.[17] The altruistic character of the duty to cooperate and assist in the realisation of economic, social and cultural rights, as well as the special responsibility placed on developed countries in this context is evident in the statement of the Committee on Economic, Social and Cultural Rights in its General Comment No. 3 on the 'Nature of States Parties' Obligations (Art. 2, Para. 1, of the Covenant)' that

> international cooperation for development and thus for the realization of economic, social and cultural rights is an obligation of all States. It is

[16] Wolfgang Friedmann, *The Changing Structure of International Law* (Stevens, 1964), 62.

[17] International Covenant on Economic, Social and Cultural Rights, 16 December 1966, 993 UNTS 3.

> particularly incumbent upon those States which are in a position to assist others in this regard.[18]

This statement appeals to the moral sensitivities of states and underlines that, without international cooperation and assistance, the full realisation of socio-economic rights will be hindered. Rather than attaching liability to a failure to pursue a programme of international assistance and cooperation, the prospect of non-fulfilment of rights in third countries is offered as a consequence. International cooperation, in this legal form, can be used as a vehicle for encouraging altruistic behaviour. It provides a framework for states to transcend the *de minimis* duties imposed by the legal order.[19]

It has been suggested that the repeated reference to the concept of international cooperation in international law is an expression of the desire to create a cosmopolitan community of states.[20] General international law has sketched a basic formulation of the duty to cooperate, as is evident not least under the UN Charter. However, over time, it has been adopted in specific contexts, and it is in specialised regimes of international law that real meaning has been given to the general obligation.[21] For example, cooperation for the realisation of human rights has provided more specific content, expected action and scope to the duty. In the area of development cooperation, a special responsibility has been placed on developed countries to provide financial and technical assistance to developing countries through, for example, the mechanism of official development assistance (ODA). In the area of environmental governance, there have been new attempts to compel cooperation through transparency and accountability mechanisms.

Overall, while international cooperation is undoubtedly a flexible standard, it has been hardened in its application as a tool to respond to specific global challenges, even if cooperative efforts have not always met expectations.

[18] UN Committee on Economic, Social and Cultural Rights, *General Comment No. 3 on the Nature of States Parties' Obligations*, para 14.

[19] Kennedy, 'Form and Substance in Private Law Adjudication', 1722.

[20] Michael Nyongesa Wabwile, *Legal Protection of Social and Economic Rights of Children in Developing Countries: Reassessing International Cooperation and Responsibility* (Intersentia, 2010), 89.

[21] Laurence Boisson de Chazournes and Jason Rudall, 'Co-Operation' in Jorge E. Viñuales (ed.), *The UN Friendly Relations Declaration at 50: An Assessment of the Fundamental Principles of International Law* (Cambridge University Press, 2020), 105–132.

7.3.2 Standards for Protection

In another major area of international law that calls for altruistic action, namely the protection of the other where they are subject to harm, a closer examination of the architecture reveals that flexible standards rather than highly administrable rules are predominant as well.

Turning first to the duty to prevent a genocide in a third country, it will be recalled that the International Court of Justice (ICJ) in the *Application of the Convention on the Prevention and Punishment of the Crime of Genocide (Bosnia and Herzegovina* v. *Serbia and Montenegro)* case confirmed that 'responsibility is . . . incurred if the State manifestly failed to take all measures which were within its power, and which might have contributed to preventing the genocide'.[22] The due diligence standard is the legal test as to whether this obligation is discharged. A test of due diligence indicates that the duty to prevent is a duty of conduct rather than an obligation of result, and the former is inordinately less formally realisable than the latter. It will also be recalled that due diligence in the duty to prevent is contingent on the capacity to influence. As such, the '"capacity to influence" effectively now emerges as an applicable standard for the obligation to prevent'.[23] The capacity to influence is a standard that requires an assessment of many variables such that it accords a wide margin of discretion to the official tasked with making this appraisal. Those variables include geographical proximity and the associations with the genocide perpetrating state.[24] Moreover, the Court in *Bosnia and Herzegovina* v. *Serbia and Montenegro* indicated that the capacity to influence should be appraised against legal criteria as states must only act within the bounds of international law and, as such 'a State's capacity to influence may vary depending on its particular legal position vis-à-vis the situations and persons facing the danger, or the reality, of genocide'.[25]

[22] *Application of the Convention on the Prevention and Punishment of the Crime of Genocide Bosnia and Herzegovina* v. *Serbia and Montenegro*, Judgment (2007) ICJ Rep. 43, para 430.

[23] Vladyslav Lanovoy, 'Complicity in an Internationally Wrongful Act' in André Nollkaemper and Illias Plakokefalos (eds.), *Principles of Shared Responsibility in International Law* (Cambridge University Press, 2014), 146, citing *Application of the Convention on the Prevention and Punishment of the Crime of Genocide (Bosnia and Herzegovina* v. *Serbia and Montenegro)*, Judgment (2007) ICJ Rep. 43, para 432.

[24] *Ibid.*

[25] *Application of the Convention on the Prevention and Punishment of the Crime of Genocide (Bosnia and Herzegovina* v. *Serbia and Montenegro)*, Judgment (2007) ICJ Rep. 43, para 430.

This flexibility in the capacity to influence test comes into even sharper focus when the capacity to influence is contrasted with the criteria for complicity in genocide, which requires a 'full knowledge of the facts'.[26] While the latter standard still demands a level of assessment as to whether the state knew it was contributing to a genocide, the capacity to influence standard is much less determinate. Similarly, complicity turns on actual knowledge while due diligence is subject to a constructive knowledge appraisal.

Aside from the lack of formal realisability in altruistic standards, the latter are also characterised by their propensity to allow for the infiltration of community values. In the context of the duty to prevent genocide, the Court made it clear that under the Genocide Convention, states do not have their own interests but rather one common interest. The common interest is in achieving 'the high ideals which inspired the Convention' and these ideals 'provide, by virtue of the common will of the parties, the foundation and measure of all its provisions'.[27] Thus, the Court makes explicit that a community interest underpins the Convention and the duty to prevent genocide. The peremptory character of genocide further confirms the community interest in its prevention.

As noted in Chapter 4, it is arguable that the duty to protect is also emerging in respect of other *erga omnes* norms, such as the prohibition on torture. This too illustrates the influence of community interests. As is well known, the category of obligations *erga omnes* emerged following the ICJ's judgment in *Barcelona Traction, Light and Power Company (Belgium* v. *Spain)*, in which the Court confirmed that there were certain obligations owed to the international community as a whole.[28] According to the Court, these obligations were derived 'from the principles and rules concerning the basic rights of the human person'.[29] It has been observed that this moment 'seemed to purport a restructuring of the

[26] *Ibid.*, para 432.

[27] *Ibid.*, para 430.

[28] *Barcelona Traction, Light and Power Company (Belgium* v. *Spain)*, Second Phase, Judgment (1970) ICJ Rep. 3, para 34: an essential distinction should be drawn between the obligations of a State towards the international community as a whole, and those arising vis-à-vis another State in the field of diplomatic protection. By their very nature the former are the concern of all States. In view of the importance of the rights involved, all States can be held to have a legal interest in their protection: they are obligations *erga omnes*.

[29] Bruno Simma and Philip Alston, 'The Sources of Human Rights Law: Custom, Jus Cogens, and General Principles' (1988–1989) 12 *Australian Yearbook of International Law* 82, 106.

international community on a set of common values and interests'.[30] Moreover, the UN Human Rights Committee has stated that internationally recognised human rights must be accorded the status of *erga omnes* obligations. In its General Comment 31 on the Nature of the General Legal Obligation on States Parties to the Covenant, the Committee said:

> [E]very State Party has a legal interest in the performance by every other State Party of its obligations. This follows from the fact that the 'rules concerning the basic rights of the human person' are *erga omnes* obligations and that, as indicated in the fourth preambular paragraph of the Covenant, there is a United Nations Charter obligation to promote universal respect for, and observance of, human rights and fundamental freedoms.[31]

As for *jus cogens* norms, while their origin lies in Article 53 of the Vienna Convention on the Law of Treaties of 1969,[32] it was not until the ICJ's judgment in its *Case Concerning Armed Activities in the Territory of the Congo between the Democratic Republic of the Congo (Democratic Republic of the Congo* v. *Rwanda)* that the notion materialised more fully.[33] Almost in passing, the Court noted that there existed 'peremptory norms of general international law', which it referred to as *jus cogens.*[34] In his separate opinion in that case, Judge Ad Hoc Dugard agreed with the judgment of the Court but elaborated further on the category of *jus cogens.*[35] Interestingly, Judge Dugard observed that

[30] Andrea Bianchi, 'Human Rights and the Magic of Jus Cogens' (2008) 19(3) *European Journal of International Law* 491, 194.

[31] Human Rights Committee, *General Comment No. 31 on the Nature of the General Legal Obligation on States Parties to the Covenant*, para 2.

[32] Vienna Convention on the Law of Treaties, 23 May 1969, 1155 UNTS 331.

[33] *Case Concerning Armed Activities on the Territory of the Congo (Democratic Republic of the Congo* v. *Rwanda)* (New application: 2002), Jurisdiction and Admissibility (2006) ICJ Rep. 1. Although they had been referred to in scholarship: see, for example, Simma and Alston, 'Sources of Human Rights Law', 103; Theodor Meron, 'On a Hierarchy of International Human Rights' (1986) 80 *American Journal of International Law* 1. The ILC had also noted in 1966 that '[i]t is not the form of a general rule of international law but the particular nature of the subject matter with which it deals that may . . . give it the character of *jus cogens*', ILC, (1966) 2 *YBILC* 248.

[34] *Case Concerning Armed Activities on the Territory of the Congo (Democratic Republic of the Congo* v. *Rwanda)* (New application: 2002), Jurisdiction and Admissibility (2006) ICJ Rep. 1, para 64. Indeed, it also affirmed that the norm preventing genocide had the character of *jus cogens*. Although the fact that a *jus cogens* norm was at stake in this case was not enough to establish the jurisdiction of the Court.

[35] *Case Concerning Armed Activities on the Territory of the Congo (Democratic Republic of the Congo* v. *Rwanda)* (New application: 2002), Jurisdiction and Admissibility, Separate Opinion of Judge Ad Hoc Dugard (2006) ICJ Rep. 1.

> [n]orms of *jus cogens* are a blend of principle and policy. On the one hand, they affirm the high principles of international law, which recognize the most important rights of the international order – such as the right to be free from aggression, genocide, torture and slavery and the right to self-determination; while, on the other hand, they give legal form to the most fundamental policies or goals of the international community – the prohibitions on aggression, genocide, torture and slavery and the advancement of self-determination.[36]

This provides support for the proposition that such legal norms in the international legal order should be considered as principles, standards or policies. Moreover, it has been said that '[t]he inner moral aspiration of the law thus materialized in international law with the advent of *jus cogens*',[37] which resonates with Duncan Kennedy's claim that standards express goals of the legal system.[38] Further still, both the International Law Commission (ILC) and international courts have shown a preference for purposeful interpretation rather than the mechanical application of hierarchically superior rules in this context.[39]

Turning now to the duty to ensure respect for international humanitarian law, violations of the 1949 Geneva Conventions similarly have a peremptory character and thus their prevention is a fundamental community interest. The duty to ensure respect has many other dimensions that are similar to the duty to prevent. Indeed, it is an obligation of means rather than of result, and a due diligence approach is expected.[40] Moreover, a state can pursue a variety of measures in order to discharge its duty to ensure respect, including monitoring or fact finding, diplomatic efforts, referral to an international court, measures of retortion or action in cooperation with an international organisation. The array of

36 *Ibid.*, para 10.

37 Bianchi, 'Human Rights and the Magic of *Jus Cogens*', 495.

38 Kennedy, 'Form and Substance in Private Law Adjudication', 1754.

39 See, for example, Bianchi, 'Human Rights and the Magic of Jus Cogens', 504, citing Article 41, Draft Articles on State Responsibility; Case No. IT-95-17/1-T, *Prosecutor* v. *Anto Furundzija*, International Tribunal for the Prosecution of Persons Responsible for Serious Violations of International Humanitarian Law Committed in the Territory of the former Yugoslavia since 1991, Judgment, 10 December 1998, paras 155–156; the principle of systemic integration elaborated in Report of the Study Group of the International Law Commission, 'Fragmentation of International Law: Difficulties Arising from the Diversification and Expansion of International Law', Appendix, UN Doc. A/CN.4/L.682/Add.1, 15.

40 Knut Dörmann and Jose Serralvo, 'Common Article 1 to the Geneva Conventions and the Obligation to Prevent International Humanitarian Law Violations' (2014) 96 *International Review of the Red Cross* 707, 724–725.

options open to states leave the standard with a low degree of formal realisability and afford a wide margin of discretion in assessing whether the standard has been complied with. Further still, the flexibility in the standard is evident by the interpretation of the International Committee of the Red Cross Study Group on Customary International Humanitarian Law that an influence test should apply to the duty to ensure respect. As such, the Study Group was of the view that states should 'exert their influence, to the extent possible'.[41]

In the context of the *non-refoulement* of a refugee, the standard employed in Article 31(1) of the Convention Relating to the Status of Refugees 1951 is that refuge must be given where the individual's 'life or freedom was threatened'.[42] Assessing the *travaux préparatoires* and the opinion of experts, it has been observed that this standard requires an assessment as to whether the individual has a 'well-founded fear of persecution'.[43] It has also been suggested that this is a standard that should be construed broadly for a number of reasons, including that there has been an evolution in the scope of who may be a refugee, that the humanitarian character of the Convention favours greater protection not less, that broad formulations have been adopted by subsequent treaties dealing with *non-refoulement*, and that there have been developments in human rights law such as the absolute prohibition on *refoulement* where a person is at risk of torture or cruel, inhuman or degrading treatment.[44] As to whether a refugee does indeed possess a well-founded fear of persecution, this 'will be something to be established "to a reasonable degree" taking account of all the relevant facts' and '[t]he threshold will require more than mere conjecture concerning a threat but less than proof to a level of probability or certainty', which is likely to demand that a "real risk' of persecution is present.[45] The nature of these elements to be assessed reveals the inherent flexibility of the standard of *non-refoulement* in the context of protecting those fleeing their country of origin for fear of harm.

[41] Dieter Fleck, 'International Accountability for Violations of the *Ius in Bello*: The Impact of the ICRC Study on Customary International Humanitarian Law' (2006) 10 *Journal of Conflict and Security Law* 179, 182.

[42] Convention Relating to the Status of Refugees, 28 July 1951, 189 UNTS 137.

[43] Elihu Lauterpacht and Daniel Bethlehem, 'The Scope and Content of the Principle of Non-refoulement: Opinion' in Erika Feller, Volker Türk and Frances Nicholson (eds.), *Refugee Protection in International Law* (Cambridge University Press, 2003), 123.

[44] *Ibid.*, 125.

[45] *Ibid.*, 125–126.

This exploration has revealed both the inherent flexibility in legal standards around the protection of others under international law and also the centrality of community values in shaping those standards. This is also evident in the context of development standards, to which we turn next.

7.3.3 Standards for Development

International solidarity has played a role in shaping development efforts, and not least initiatives to establish a right to development.[46] In practice, it serves to create an enabling national and international environment by recognising the needs and interests of others. That said, the objective of development is very often stipulated as a goal to be achieved rather than a prescription to be judged by. Even where targets or indicators are set, these rarely offer a degree of highly administrable specificity. This is evident, for example, in the recent Sustainable Development Goals (SDGs) that form part of the United Nation's current flagship Agenda 2030 for Sustainable Development.[47] Indeed, SDG 1 aims to 'end poverty in all its forms everywhere'.[48] While a target is set, such as significant mobilisation of resources to implement programmes and policies that help to end poverty,[49] this will be measured against rather broad parameters, such as the '[p]roportion of resources allocated by the government directly to poverty reduction programmes' and the '[p]roportion of total government spending on essential services'.[50] No concrete rule is as such established.

This is similarly the case in the area of ODA. As for the obligations on developed countries in this context, the stipulated amount of ODA as 0.7 per cent of gross national product suggests at face value a high degree of formal realisability. However, upon closer inspection, it is clear that the best efforts approach is expected. Indeed, General Assembly Resolution 2626 (XXV), which provides for this figure, sets out that economically advanced countries should 'exert best efforts to reach'

46 See, for example, Article 3(g), Draft Convention on the Right to Development, Advance Edited Version, 17 January 2020, UN Doc. A/HRC/WG.2/21/2.

47 United Nations General Assembly Resolution A/RES/70/1, 'Transforming Our World: The 2030 Agenda for Sustainable Development', 25 September 2015, UN Doc. A/RES/70/1, Sustainable Development Goals.

48 *Ibid.*, para 59.

49 *Ibid.*, Target 1.a.

50 *Ibid.*, Indicator 1.a.1 and Indicator 1.a.2, respectively.

this minimum amount.[51] This evidently gives developed states the flexibility to choose the policies they deem most appropriate. Moreover, according to the Declaration on Social Progress and Development of 1969, developed states are under a 'responsibility to pursue internal and external policies' to promote development and to assist developing countries in growing their economies.[52] Affording equivalent levels of discretion, Article 3 of the 1986 Declaration on the Right to Development imposes on states an obligation to create 'international conditions favourable to the realization of development'.[53] Furthermore, akin to the best efforts standard set by the UN General Assembly, the General Assembly of the Organisation of American States has imposed a best efforts obligation on economically advanced countries to cooperate for development.[54] Similarly again, the Charter of Economic Rights and Duties of States of 1974 requires in Article 24 that developed countries 'conduct their mutual economic relations in a manner which takes into account the interests of other countries'.[55] This undoubtedly demands other-regarding behaviour, but the language used suggests an obligation of means or the best efforts standard is that which states will be judged by.

In the context of international economic governance, the Declaration on the Establishment of a New International Economic Order of 1974 provided for 'the necessity to ensure the accelerated development of all developing countries' and the 'extension of active assistance to developing countries by the whole international community',[56] and the goal of economic development was inserted into the Preamble of the WTO Agreement.[57] These too express broad objectives and show a recognition that the international economic order should serve to benefit all states as well as further the cause of development in developing countries. That said, these overarching ideals have taken the form of

[51] General Assembly Resolution 2626 (XXV) on the International Development Strategy for the Second United Nations Development Decade 1970, para 43.

[52] UN General Assembly Resolution 2542 (XXIV), Declaration on Social Progress and Development, 11 December 1969, UN Doc. A/RES/2542 (XXIV).

[53] UN General Assembly Resolution 41/128, Declaration on the Right to Development, 4 December 1986, UN Doc. A/RES/41/128.

[54] OAS General Assembly Resolution AG/RES.510 (X-O/80), 27 November 1980.

[55] UN General Assembly Resolution 3281 (XXIX), Charter of Economic Rights and Duties of States, 12 December 1974, UN Doc. A/RES/3281 (XXIX).

[56] UN General Assembly Resolution 3201 (S-VI), Declaration on the Establishment of a New International Economic Order, 1 May 1974, UN Doc. A/RES/3201 (S-VI).

[57] Preamble, Agreement Establishing the World Trade Organization (WTO), 15 April 1994, 1867 UNTS 154.

more specific institutions, programmes and initiatives that have also played an important role in prompting altruistic behaviour among states. Indeed, the experience of the international trading system reveals that in specific contexts, often supported by an institution, development as an objective can inspire more realisable initiatives, as can be seen by the creation of the Enabling Clause to help cultivate trade from developing countries, waiving certain intellectual property rules to ensure access to medicines or efforts to end the trade in conflict diamonds.[58]

As has become evident, the international law of development also contains flexible standards such as best efforts tests to realise the goals set by the legal regime.

7.3.4 *Standards for Environmental Justice*

While it is not a standard, the growing means through which individuals, particularly those residing in other countries, can participate in environmental decision-making or have recourse to redress for environmental harm evidences an increasing anthropocentrism and concern for 'the other' in international environmental governance. Moreover, the growing recognition of the connection between environmental degradation and human rights, the emergence of a human right to the environment, and the consideration of environmental matters by human rights courts are helping to reinforce this trend. This has led to a notable development in the jurisprudence of certain international courts and tribunals. In particular, several recent cases suggest an extraterritorial duty to ensure the human rights of those in third countries are not violated by environmental degradation such as climate change. As is the case with the longstanding duty to avoid transboundary harm, this is not altruism per se but it does demonstrate a consideration for 'the other' in the fabric of international law.

Other developments in international environmental law provide good examples of altruistic standards. Intergenerational equity is a principle of international environmental law that is closely related to the concept of sustainable development. In its altruistic dimension, it is an expression

[58] See WTO, Decision on Differential and Most Favourable Treatment, Reciprocity and Fuller Participation of Developing Countries, 28 November 1979, GATT Doc. L/4903; Implementation of Paragraph 6 of the Doha Declaration on the TRIPS Agreement and Public Health, Decision of the General Council, 30 August 2003, WT/L/540; WTO General Council, Waiver Concerning Kimberley Process Certification Scheme for Rough Diamonds, Decision of 15 May 2003, WTO Doc. WT/L/518.

of the importance of protecting the environment and preserving resources for future generations. It requires that present generations pass on the resources of the Earth to future generations in no worse condition than they inherited them.[59] It has similarly been conceived as a form of trust in which present generations serve as trustees, stewards or custodians to ensure a healthy environment and sufficient resources for future generations.[60]

The difficulties of administering this principle are linked to its indeterminacy, and it has only been referred to a handful of times in dispute settlement as illustrated in Chapter 6. That said, the principle touches almost all aspects of environmental governance and has helped to set commitments that future generations will benefit from. Indeed, it is a critical reason for regulating toxic waste disposal, biodiversity, forests, the ozone layer and climate change, among other issues. To see its influence in shaping commitments in practice, we need only think of the nationally determined contributions made by states under the 2015 Paris Agreement in the collective effort to ensure global temperatures stay well below 2 °C above pre-industrial levels, and ideally no more than 1.5 °C.[61] As the objectives of the Paris Agreement are largely to be realised in the second half of this century, it has been pointed out that most of us will not be around then to benefit from the Paris Agreement, and that it is an example of action for future generations.[62]

Related to the principle of intergenerational equity is the principle of intra-generational equity, which serves to redress environmental injustice between peoples, particularly rich and poor, today. The notion of common but differentiated responsibilities has become an increasingly important principle of international environmental law, though other expressions of the idea can be found in earlier instruments of international law outside the area of environmental governance.[63] It

[59] Edith Brown Weiss, 'Intergenerational Equity' (2013) *Max Planck Encyclopedia of International Law*, para 6.

[60] *Ibid.*, para 7.

[61] Article 2(1)(a), Paris Agreement on Climate Change, UN Doc. FCCC/CP/2015/L.9/Rev.1, 12 December 2015.

[62] Laurence Boisson de Chazournes, 'One Swallow Does Not a Summer Make, but Might the Paris Agreement on Climate Change a Better Future Create?' (2016) 27(2) *European Journal of International Law* 253.

[63] See, for example, Article 405(3), Versailles Peace Treaty, 28 June 1919; Article 19(3), Instrument for the Amendment of the Constitution of the International Labour Organization, 22 June 1962, 15 UNTS 40; Article XVIII, General Agreement on Tariffs and Trade, 1947 and 1994, Agreement Establishing the WTO, 15 April 1994, 1867 UNTS

recognises the special situation of developing countries and can serve to structure obligations such that all states contribute to remedying damage relative to their historical responsibility and present capacity. It has been observed that, while the concept of common but differentiated responsibilities has 'normative dimensions', it is 'unlikely to qualify as a rule, given that it cannot apply in an all or nothing fashion' and is 'more likely to qualify as a principle'.[64] An insight into its operation, as shown in Chapter 6, supports this view. That said, it does serve to guide decision-making, shape rules and establish institutions in the area of international environmental governance.

Among the institutions that have emerged in the area of environmental governance are mechanisms for the provision of financial and technical assistance. Financial mechanisms have been developed to facilitate assistance from developed to developing countries for the purpose of mitigating or adapting to environmental change. A significant number of such mechanisms have now come into existence.[65] These represent manifestations of altruism and have been shown to function in an effective way providing significant resources to countries that need them to deal with specific environmental challenges they face. Such institutions, like in the context of the responsibility to protect (R2P) doctrine,[66] illustrate how altruistic commitments may be hardened.

7.4 Concluding Remarks

This chapter provides support for Duncan Kennedy's claim that there is a connection between form and substance, and this connection is apparent in the international legal system. Indeed, it is apparent that the altruistic commitments analysed generally conform to the mould of standards that Kennedy claims populate altruistic legal orders. Altruistic norms tend to find their expression in ad hoc and flexible standards. Such standards are characterised by a lack of formal

154; Articles 61(3) and 62, United Nations Convention on the Law of the Sea, 10 December 1982, 1833 UNTS 3.

64 Ellen Hey, 'Common but Differentiated Responsibilities' (2011) *Max Planck Encyclopedia of International Law*, para 18.

65 See Laurence Boisson de Chazournes, 'Is There Room for Coherence in Climate Financial Assistance?' (2015) 4 *Laws* 541.

66 Grant Marlier and Neta C. Crawford, 'Incomplete and Imperfect Institutionalisation of Empathy and Altruism in the "Responsibility to Protect" Doctrine' (2013) 5 *Global Responsibility to Protect* 397.

realisability, allow a broad margin of discretion in application and are sensitive to community interests.

It is also apparent from an examination of the nature of the altruistic standards identified in the previous chapters that some are particularly transversal and cross-cut many different areas of international law. They serve the same purpose of prompting action on a wide variety of community objectives and create regulatory spaces for altruism in specific issue areas. As is evident from the discussion earlier, this is the case with international cooperation. It is also increasingly the case for the concept of solidarity. While its status as a principle of international law has been more contested, it is clear that solidarity has played a similar cross-cutting role as a standard in a wide range of areas.[67] Indeed, it has been used as a mechanism for furthering common objectives by imposing common obligations in international humanitarian law, as an instrument to achieve common objectives via differentiated obligations in international environmental law and international trade law, and as an instrument for benefiting particular states in the context of Articles 49 and 50 of the UN Charter.[68] The standard undoubtedly propagates community values and some go as far as to argue that 'the principle of solidarity reflects the transformation of international law into a value based international legal order'[69] and characterise it as a structural or constitutional principle of international law.[70]

An appraisal of the form of altruism in international law also reveals, however, that altruistic standards are vulnerable to abuse because of the discretion and flexibility they afford. Such hijacking of altruistic

[67] Hestermeyer, 'Reality or Aspiration? Solidarity in International Environmental and World Trade Law'.

[68] See Karel Wellens, 'Revisiting Solidarity as a (Re-)Emerging Constitutional Principle: Some Further Reflections' in Rüdiger Wolfrum and Chie Kojima (eds.), *Solidarity: A Structural Principle of International Law* (Springer, 2010), 13, who also points out that in its role as a means of achieving differentiated obligations and for benefiting particular states, 'the principle of solidarity becomes operational in case of a State's failure to meet a particular challenge, thus working in tandem with the principle of subsidiarity' (at fn 50).

[69] Rüdiger Wolfrum, 'Solidarity amongst States: An Emerging Structural Principle of International Law' in Pierre-Marie Dupuy, Bardo Fassbender and Malcolm N. Shaw (eds.), *Völkerrecht als Wertordnung: Festschrift für Christian Tomuschat* (N. P. Engel, 2006), 1087.

[70] See, for example, *ibid* (as a structural principle); Wolfrum and Kojima (eds.), *Solidarity: A Structural Principle of International Law* (authors of the edited volume characterising it as either a structural or constitutional principle); Wellens, 'Revisiting Solidarity as a (Re-) Emerging Constitutional Principle: Some Further Reflections' (as a constitutional principle).

standards by a self-interested minority seems inevitable in the light of nationalist tendencies that come and go in world politics. To ensure that the promise of altruism in the fabric of international law is kept, I submit that institutions should have a more significant role to play. Institutions can help to widen the circle of empathy, appeal to reason by sharing information and harden altruistic responses.[71] Various international mechanisms for monitoring the domestic implementation of international human rights norms, such as expert committees and special rapporteurs, have been developed.[72] Bodies like the Human Rights Council, the Human Rights Committee and the Committee on Economic, Social and Cultural Rights, all help to bring human rights abuses and suffering to the attention of the rest of the world and doctrines like R2P have attempted to establish an institutional response, albeit imperfect. Similarly, reporting mechanisms under international environmental law represent attempts to institutionalise altruism. In this context, developing countries should report on financial, technology transfer and capacity-building support needed and received from developed countries, while developed countries must also report on financial, technology transfer and capacity-building support provided to developing countries.[73] Moreover, the institutionalisation of the provision of financial assistance, for environmental or development purposes, has also helped to address the problem of bias in the provision of such aid.[74] Overall, altruism in international law is often more effective when it is found within an institutional context.

[71] Marlier and Crawford, 'Incomplete and Imperfect Institutionalisation of Empathy and Altruism in the "Responsibility to Protect" Doctrine', 399.

[72] Jack Donnelly, *Universal Human Rights in Theory and Practice* (3rd ed., Cornell University Press, 2013), 34.

[73] Articles 9, 10, and 11, Paris Agreement, adopted on 12 December 2015 at the twenty-first session of the Conference of the Parties to the United Nations Framework Convention on Climate Change held in Paris from 30 November to 13 December 2015.

[74] Antonella Angelini, 'A Trouble Shared is a Trouble Halved: How the Structure of Cooperation Matters for the Engagement of Responsibility in the World Bank Partnership Programmes' (2016) 13(1) *International Organizations Law Review* 171.

Conclusion

Overview

This book has inquired into the existence of altruism in international law. It has challenged the perception that international law can be reduced to the maximisation of individual states' interests. Instead, alongside the policies of states adopted out of self-interest, international law can also reflect and encourage altruistic behaviour among states. Indeed, the point of the book's departure was this observation about the fundamental contradiction in international law. The book engaged with definitions, concepts and studies of altruism from a wide range of disciplines and sought to identify common themes in altruistic theory. A deeper understanding of altruism revealed an inherent symbiosis between altruism and cosmopolitanism in our global society. The catalytic role that cosmopolitan ideology plays in expanding circles of empathy and altruism was revealed, and the centrality of the common humanity perspective was highlighted. In this context, it was also argued that the underlying impetus for the common humanity perspective lies in globalisation, the increasing interconnectedness and communication between peoples across borders, and the emotive force of major world events.

Consideration was then given to literature on altruism and other-regarding concepts in legal scholarship, concerning both national and international legal systems. This exposed a gap in the literature on altruism in respect of the international legal system. That said, there is growing support in international legal scholarship that there exist other-regarding commitments in international law. This was reviewed and the key elements were identified.

The focus of the book then turned to the formation, substance and form of international law. First, the ways in which cosmopolitan and altruistic values become imbued as legal norms were assessed. Drawing on systems theory, the specific mechanisms and actors involved in this process were presented. Second, the substantive elements of positive international law that are altruistic in character were given detailed consideration. Similarly, the book considered several legal developments that showed various trends towards a more altruistic approach in different international law disciplines. Third, the book turned to appraise the relationship between substance and form. In particular, it analysed the proposition that there exists a connection between individualism and a preference for rules and altruism and a preference for standards in the international legal order.[1] This inquiry has revealed several fundamental insights to which this concluding chapter now turns.

A Growing Concern for the Other

The last century has witnessed a remarkable evolution in the nature of legal obligations at the international level. Traditionally, international law regulated the horizontal relationships between states. Following World War II, international legal regulation became concerned with the vertical relationship between a state and its own citizens. In this context, human rights have gained increasing prominence in the overall architecture of international law and the individual, rather than the state, has been recognised more acutely as the ultimate unit of moral concern in the international legal order. With the focus on the individual and the universalist rhetoric of human rights law, a normative turn in the orientation of legal regulation is presently underway. While horizontal and vertical legal relationships continue to be formed and remain dominant in the corpus of international law, there is increasing evidence for the existence of altruistic legal relationships between states and people in third countries. Such altruistic legal relationships involve taking into account their needs and interests in policy-making, positive action and a commitment of resources to ensure their well-being and welfare are respected and realised.

Moral cosmopolitanism, focused as it is on human relationships, can explain the phenomena that result from globalisation and the increasing interconnection between people across borders. It is 'the belief that our duty to ameliorate the suffering of individuals is more important than any artificial political barrier that may stand in our way'.[2] As such, it is an

[1] Duncan Kennedy, 'Form and Substance in Private Law Adjudication' (1976) 89 *Harvard Law Review* 1685.

[2] Daniel Levy and Natan Sznaider, 'The Institutionalization of Cosmopolitan Morality' (2004) 3(2) *Journal of Human Rights* 143, 155. It is a close cousin of the Grotian tradition, but it may be distinguished, in particular, by the emphasis placed on the human being as

ideology that broadens the horizon of our moral concern. This is motivated by the belief that we belong to a common humanity, that state borders should not inhibit our concern for the welfare of all human beings. In this context, moral cosmopolitanism can be a driver for a widening circle of altruistic behaviour.

The Common Humanity Perspective and Cosmopolitan Altruism

A study of altruistic theory has illuminated various fundamental characteristics of altruism. In particular, it has revealed that altruism involves acting in the interests of others at a cost to the actor. Moreover, the presence of reasons for acting other than the intention to help a beneficiary and of a self-regarding pay-off for the actor do not necessarily mitigate the altruistic nature of a given act. Further still, contrary to rational actor theories, behavioural science provides evidence that human beings do not always act as a homo economicus. In fact, human beings regularly act in altruistic ways. As such, studying altruism can help us to understand the natural human urge to help the other. Where that urge comes from has also been the subject of investigation.

Central to altruism is the presence of a common humanity perspective. This is, in essence, identification with the plight of the other. As has become apparent, the common humanity perspective is also implied by the ideology of moral cosmopolitanism. This ideology can serve to drive attitudes and behaviour towards cosmopolitan altruism, which is 'the motivationally effective desire to assist needy or endangered strangers'.[3] Globalisation has led to increasing interconnectedness and interaction between peoples and this has facilitated identification with strangers in faraway countries. In this context, global markets, technological advancement, institutional connections and significant world events all bring people of different nationalities together and help them to understand and identify with one another as being part of a common human group. These influences and an abiding ideology of cosmopolitan altruism among international law actors have been the normative forces that have helped to broaden commitments by states to people in other countries.[4]

the ultimate unit of moral concern, in keeping with cosmopolitan theory more generally. See Hedley Bull, *The Anarchical Society: A Study of Order in World Politics* (2nd ed., Columbia University Press, 1977), Chapter 2.

3 William A. Galston, 'Cosmopolitan Altruism' (1993) 10(1) *Social Philosophy & Policy* 118.

4 Arguing that modern human rights are a result of a moral cosmopolitan response to particular events, which is driven by globalisation and interdependency, see Levy and

The Making of Altruism in International Law

Examining the link between ideology and law is a powerful reminder that law does not exist in a vacuum but rather reflects the prevailing social forces at a given time. Agents and institutional processes within the international legal order play a role in imbuing the law with altruistic values and help to motivate altruistic action. In this context, the rhetoric of universal human rights has had an especially powerful influence on the propagation of more human- and other-oriented law. Indeed, states, individuals, international institutions and courts have all in different ways contributed to the creation of altruistic international law.

As for the processes in the international legal order that motivate altruistic action, certain mechanisms, institutions or practices help the international community empathise with the plight of those suffering in the world and in this way can motivate altruistic behaviour among states or other international actors. Human rights agencies, special rapporteurs, the Human Rights Council, and treaty bodies all serve, to greater or lesser degrees, as the eyes and ears of the international community[5] and help identification with the suffering or needs of people in other countries. A similar phenomenon is apparent in the realms of development cooperation and environmental protection with the propagation of institutions that facilitate more effective altruism in those fields. Indeed, bringing to light the suffering and needs of others, such processes should invoke empathy and prompt altruism, as well as improve transparency around altruistic action.

The Substance of Altruism in International Law

Just as altruism has been shown to manifest itself in domestic legal systems,[6] this book has argued that altruism is similarly manifested in the substance of international law. Indeed, altruism has touched many different areas of international law. It is evident, for example, in the guarantee of fundamental human rights, the realisation of socio-economic rights, the

Sznaider, 'The Institutionalization of Cosmopolitan Morality: The Holocaust and Human Rights'.

5 Grant Marlier and Neta C. Crawford, 'Incomplete and Imperfect Institutionalisation of Empathy and Altruism in the 'Responsibility to Protect' Doctrine' (2013) 5 *Global Responsibility to Protect* 397, 419.

6 See, for example, Kennedy, 'Form and Substance in Private Law Adjudication'; Jeroen Kortmann, *Altruism in Private Law: Liability for Nonfeasance and Negotiorum Gestio* (Oxford University Press, 2005).

protection of refugees, commitments regarding development and in the extension of environmental rights, obligations and financial assistance. Altruism may be characterised as a concept to describe certain kinds of legal relationship that exist in the strata of international law, and we should not underestimate its influence in law-making, interpretation and application. Even if it is not a principle of international law, it should be recalled that '[n]ormative concepts and prescriptions of a varied nature may exercise significant influence on international legal processes regardless of their formal status'.[7]

Obligations such as international cooperation imply a positive duty to act in the interests of other people. As the evolution of cooperation has shown, it can involve a commitment of resources at a cost to the actor. International cooperation is, as such, a regulatory space for altruism. The interpretations of relevant bodies and state practice, as well as *travaux préparatoires* of various international instruments, all provide normative guidance for the way in which states are expected to cooperate. In certain contexts, especially as regards social, economic and cultural rights, states are expected to take positive action to provide assistance to ensure the universal realisation of human rights. Obligations to provide assistance are particularly incumbent on developed countries, but there are also obligations on all countries relative to their capacity, such as the obligation to mobilise global resources.

The duty to prevent is a similar standard that has been given more precision in respect of certain mass atrocity crimes. The judgment of the International Court of Justice (ICJ) in *Application of the Convention on the Prevention and Punishment of the Crime of Genocide (Bosnia and Herzegovina* v. *Serbia and Montenegro)* has had a significant influence on the interpretation of this obligation.[8] Moreover, some have suggested that this judgment is having a ripple effect on other duties to prevent, such as that regarding torture.[9] This also shows the role that actors like the international judiciary can have in developing regulatory spaces for altruism, and even attaching liability for failures to act as expected.

[7] Andrea Bianchi, 'On Power and Illusion: The Concept of Transparency in International Law' in Andrea Bianchi and Anne Peters (eds.), *Transparency in International Law* (Cambridge University Press, 2013), 6.

[8] *Application of the Convention on the Prevention and Punishment of the Crime of Genocide (Bosnia and Herzegovina* v. *Serbia and Montenegro)*, Judgment (2007) ICJ Rep. 43.

[9] See, for example, Andrew Clapham, 'Responsibility to Protect: "Some Sort of Commitment"' in Vincent Chetail (ed.), *Conflits, sécurité et coopération: Liber amicorum Victor-Yves Ghebali* (Bruylant, 2007), 169–192.

Moreover, the Court furnished the duty to prevent with various analytical tools, such as the due diligence standard and constructive knowledge test, which may be helpful for a wider application of the duty to prevent in the future.

The responsibility to protect (R2P) doctrine provides an example of the institutionalisation of altruism. Through its institutional structure, R2P is a mechanism that enables the international community to empathise with the victims of mass atrocity and grave human rights violations, and to act upon that empathy through altruistic behaviour. It thus provides a framework for action and normative guidance. However, its practice reveals that the institutionalisation has been imperfect and incomplete, and there remain systemic obstacles that have hindered its effective functioning.

Certain commitments under international law require all states to give safe haven to foreign persons who may have had their fundamental rights violated or are in danger of having those rights violated. This is particularly the case with the obligation of *non-refoulement*, which has its basis in several sources of international law. The principle of non-discrimination demands that this commitment applies to any individual, irrespective of their origin, race or religion, who is outside of their country of origin. It is, as such, an obligation that differs in a conceptual way from traditional human rights law in the sense that is exclusively concerned with the way a host state treats foreigners. It is, in this way, other-directed, cosmopolitan and, because it inevitably involves some commitment of resources, altruistic in nature.

As with international cooperation, the principle of solidarity also finds application across a range of areas of international law. One such application is in motivating specific commitments to developing countries. Indeed, both solidarity and international cooperation have served as impulses for enhancing the right to development, and the commitment to give at least 0.7 per cent of gross national product to developing countries in official development assistance (ODA), the right to food, which encompasses both negative and positive obligations, and initiatives pursued in the context of the international economic order. These all have an altruistic dimension. The cost to developed countries and the intention to help the people of developing countries are relatively self-evident, even though there may be other self-interested reasons to act as well. In this context, altruistic theory helps us to understand that the existence of such additional reasons to act or the presence of a self-regarding payoff does not necessarily mitigate the altruistic character.

The rhetoric of universal human rights has begun to have a transformative effect on the scope of environmental protection. Indeed, the transformation has involved an increasing anthropocentrism, the emergence of a human right to a healthy environment and the proliferation of mechanisms for the individual to participate in decision-making and seek redress for environmental harm. Further, there are growing opportunities for those of third countries in this context as well. Similarly, the principles of inter and intra-generational equity encourage states to take the needs and interests of the other into account, whether they are the interests of people in third countries or of future generations. Finally, there is a wider recognition of the importance of funding mechanisms to help other countries deal with their specific environmental challenges as well as meet broader environmental objectives.

An aspect ripe for clarification in the area of altruistic legal relationships is how burdens to assist the other are shared. In other words, what are the precise obligations incumbent on developed countries and on developing countries? Certain mechanisms may be helpful in achieving a fair balance of responsibility. For example, the Committee on Economic, Social and Cultural Rights has indicated that developed countries have a special responsibility in certain contexts. Moreover, in the Commentary to the Maastricht Principles it is noted that '[c]apacity offers both a specific and a general requirement: specific in that it is one of the bases that points to the requisite duty-bearers, e.g. "those in a position to assist", and general in that it is a prerequisite to discharging any obligation'.[10] Capacity has also found application in other contexts. Indeed, the capacity to influence is an important factor in determining whether the duty to prevent genocide has been violated.[11] In a different approach to burden sharing, and as alluded to above, the principle of common but differentiated responsibilities has become an increasingly important cornerstone of international environmental governance. Extending this principle and expanding upon the other notions mentioned in the realm of altruistic legal relationships may help to clarify the obligations each state is under to people in other countries as well as

[10] Olivier de Schutter, Asbjørn Eide, Ashfaq Khalfan, Marcos Orellana, Margot Salomon and Ian Seiderman, 'Commentary to the Maastricht Principles on the Extraterritorial Obligations of States in the Area of Economic, Social and Cultural Rights' (2012) 34(4) *Human Rights Quarterly* 1084, 1153, fn 179.

[11] *Application of the Convention on the Prevention and Punishment of the Crime of Genocide (Bosnia and Herzegovina* v. *Serbia and Montenegro),* Judgment (2007) ICJ Rep. 43.

ensuring fairness in the allocation of legal burdens.[12] Future research should be dedicated to the role that common but differentiated responsibilities and the assessment of capacity can play in shaping international legal obligations.

Overall, it is argued that altruistic legal relationships serve an important function in the universal realisation of peace, human rights, development and environmental justice. States have a wide margin of discretion as to how altruistic legal relationships may be executed. As such, it has been observed that these types of obligations can be performed

> through bilateral collaboration with the domestic state, multilateral engagement using intergovernmental organizations, unilateral mechanisms and even contracting non-state actors such as specialist local and global non-governmental organizations.[13]

This means, for example, that if horizontal relations between two concerned states break down, the obligations owed to citizens are not affected.[14] This provides yet another argument for institutionalising altruistic commitments in the international legal order. In light of a rapidly changing geopolitical landscape, it must be emphasised that the legal framework for altruism should be robust enough that altruistic behaviour continues despite any political, economic or social differences states may have.

The Form of Altruism in International Law

A consideration of the substance of altruism in international law also reveals that altruistically oriented legal norms possess certain common characteristics. This resonates with the observation made by Duncan Kennedy in the context of private law adjudication.[15] Kennedy asserted that there is a preference for standards in altruistic legal orders while there is a preference for rules in individualist legal orders. In an individualist legal order, the rules have a high degree of formal realisability and are strictly applied while in an altruistic legal order, the standards are

[12] For an argument along these lines, see Eyal Benvenisti, 'Sovereigns as Trustees of Humanity: On the Accountability of States to Foreign Stakeholders' (2013) 107(2) *American Journal of International Law* 295, 328.

[13] Michael Wabwile, *Legal Protection of Social and Economic Rights of Children in Developing Countries: Reassessing International Cooperation and Responsibility* (Intersentia, 2010), 87.

[14] *Ibid.*

[15] Kennedy, 'Form and Substance in Private Law Adjudication'.

flexible and leave a large measure of discretion in their application, as well as allowing for the infiltration of community values. The reason for this distinction lies in the ultimate goals each system pursues. One seeks increased individual autonomy while the other recognises the interconnected nature of humanity.

The common characteristic in the altruistically oriented legal norms examined in the chapters of this book on the substance of altruism in international law is that they tend to leave a sizeable margin of appreciation for states as to how they fulfil the altruistic legal relationships that they have with people in other countries. While such relationships represent a regulatory space in which normative encouragement towards certain behaviour may be present, a standard lacks the characteristic of being a highly administrable, formally realisable, strict legal rule. Even the stronger altruistic commitments in international law are subject to flexible legal standards. For example, the duty to prevent genocide in a third country relies on such standards as due diligence and influence.

This reveals that there is a connection between substance and form in international law. As such, the pursuit of either individualist or altruistic approaches in international law can affect the form that the law takes. Individualist rules divide up the international legal order (akin to property rights in domestic law) and regulate the manner in which individual entities, like states, interact with each other (akin to contract rules in domestic law). This resonates with the statist and realist approaches to international relations. In contrast, altruistic standards rely on the assumption that people will instinctively aspire towards human brotherhood, which resonates with cosmopolitan notions. This is the reason why standards leave a wide measure of discretion to those tasked with applying them. The cynic would of course argue that there are other reasons why there might be a preference for standards around positive duties at the international level. Indeed, states may be reluctant to commit in a highly administrable and formally realisable way to far reaching obligations that they may be unable to deliver on in the future. But that there are multiple reasons for the emergence of such standards may illustrate the constant tension among and within human beings, which is in turn reflected in international law, between individualism and altruism. It is all the more reason to encourage the institutionalisation of altruistic commitments.

A further insight about the form of altruism in international law is that there are certain standards that cross-cut different areas of international law, and serve to shape legal norms and state behaviour. They have a transformative effect on the creation and interpretation of other standards as well as the way in which certain rights are realised or assistance to other countries is provided. As became evident in this book, standards like international cooperation or solidarity have found application in many of the more specific areas examined, and their normative influence has been to catalyse certain commitments to the other in those areas.

The Promise of Altruism in International Law

The present study has illuminated several apparent contradictions in the architecture of international law. These are, not least, between statism and cosmopolitanism, between individualism and altruism, and between rules and standards. As alluded to previously, these may reflect 'the contradictory character of moral existence . . . that every one of us exists in a situation of doubleness and ambivalence in our ethical orientation'.[16] Given the simplicity with which these competing positions have traditionally been treated, they have tended to be presented as irreconcilable: one approach must be chosen to the exclusion of the other. However, by developing more nuanced understandings, this book has sought to show that they may not be as mutually exclusive as they appear at face value. Indeed, the experience of the international legal order has been that spaces for altruistic behaviour can be created within an essentially individualist legal order which is organised primarily around the sovereignty of states.

International law is formed in a global society of (some) shared values and expectations. While altruism may not always take precedence in this society, it often coexists with other, sometimes opposite, value-systems. This is not, however, to suggest that different legal orders exist in the same space and time, as legal pluralists may argue. Instead, this study has highlighted the inevitability of the contradictions in any legal system, which are – incidentally – not necessarily flaws to be remedied. The system functions as a unified whole, and its capacity to reflect societal norms and behaviour ensures that it does not harbour a level of rigidity that would ultimately be unsustainable.

As explained, altruistic standards lend themselves to flexibility because the altruistic approach to legal regulation 'asserts that we understand our own goals and purposes and those of others to be at all times in a state of

[16] Tor Krever, Carl Lisberger and Max Utzscneider, 'Law on the Left: a Conversation with Duncan Kennedy' (2015) 10(1) *Unbound* 1.

evolution, progress or retrogression, in terms of a universal ideal of human brotherhood'.[17] As such, the very structure of an altruistic system allows oscillations towards or away from the altruistic ideal. And so the system relies on the behaviour of its actors. If the international system is to become more altruistic, this will largely depend on the extent to which its actors are influenced by an ideology of cosmopolitanism, perceive that all peoples of the world are part of the same common humanity and, as a result, are inclined to act altruistically.

If cosmopolitan altruism continues to have an influence on the content of international legal relations, we have reason to believe that the system will become more altruistic over time. In this context, institutions have a role to play in consolidating, reinforcing and propagating altruism in international law. And in order to perfect the institutionalisation of altruism in the international legal order it will be necessary to improve the mechanisms aimed at perspective-taking. Where actors can better identify with the suffering or needs of others, this will facilitate empathy and, ultimately, altruistic action. As explained earlier in this book, perspective-taking mechanisms allow for a process of rationalisation such that the altruistically inclined actor is able to understand the plight of 'the other' and is motivated to act in their interests.[18] The law and its institutions can give such actors a reason and the impetus to act altruistically. If international mechanisms do not effectively allow for perspective-taking, then identification with the other's suffering is less likely to occur.

Recent geopolitical events do suggest that cosmopolitan altruism may be under threat. This has the potential to result in what Theodor Adorno and Max Horkheimer once referred to as the collapse or regression of reason,[19] a phenomenon which has had devastating consequences at various points in the history of the world. Such regressions in reason are driven by myth, superstition and rhetoric, rather than fact, and result in a reversion to smaller communities. Similarly, Hannah Arendt viewed the rise of Nazism as a breakdown in Enlightenment thinking, democracy, critical judgment and reason.[20] In an environment of 'fake news' and isolationist rhetoric, the role of reason is diminished and this may contribute to a fear or suspicion of the other. Such a development is likely

[17] Kennedy, 'Form and Substance in Private Law Adjudication', 1772.
[18] Galston, 'Cosmopolitan Altruism', 124.
[19] Max Horkheimer and Theodor W. Adorno, *Dialectic of Enlightenment: Philosophical Fragments* (Gunzelin Scmid Noerr ed., Edmund Jephcott trans., Stanford University Press, 2002).
[20] Hannah Arendt, *The Origins of Totalitarianism* (Allen and Unwin, 1958).

to lead to less rather than more cosmopolitan altruism in international society.

Aside from avoiding prejudicial attitudes toward the other, there are further reasons to embrace an ideology of cosmopolitan altruism. Indeed, altruism in society has been shown to have various benefits for the overall welfare of society. Indeed, several studies have found that 'societies characterized by a high degree of trust and cooperation have higher levels of investment and show greater economic growth than societies in which people in fact behave more consistently like *homo economicus*'.[21] This supports the enlightened conclusion that altruism is, in fact, in our self-interest.

We must also, however, be cognizant of the threat posed by acts that may be carried out under the cloak of altruism but which in reality have ulterior motives. This might be termed 'the dark side of altruism'.[22] Indeed, imperialism and Western universalism present a risk that inherently flexible and morally charged altruistic standards may be abused. In certain areas of scholarship, international law has long been critiqued for making empty utopian promises.[23] Instead, in reality, it is vulnerable to being used as a tool to serve the interests of the wealthy and powerful. In particular, Third World Approaches to International Law (TWAIL) and other critical scholars have sought to expose the imperial and oppressive reality of international law.[24] The purpose of this book has not been to deny such claims but rather to highlight some of the altruistic

21 Lynn Stout, 'Law and Prosocial Behaviour', in Eyal Zamir and Doron Teichman (eds.), *The Oxford Handbook of Behavioural Economics and the Law* (Oxford University Press, 2014), 210; Paul Zak and Stephen Knack, 'Trust and Growth' (2001) 111 *Economic Journal* 295; Stephen Knack and Phillip Keefer, 'Does Social Capital Have an Economic Payoff? A Cross-Country Investigation.' (1997) 112 *Quarterly Journal of Economics* 1251.

22 The risks and critique may be similar to those made of international human rights and international humanitarianism: see, for example Frédéric Mégret, 'Where Does the Critique of International Human Rights Stand? An Exploration in 18 Vignettes' in José Maria Beneyto and David Kennedy (eds.), *New Approaches to International Law: The European and the American Experiences* (Springer, 2012), 3–40; David Kennedy, *The Dark Sides of Virtue: Reassessing International Humanitarianism* (Princeton University Press, 2005); Ben Golder, 'Beyond Redemption? Problematising the Critique of Human Rights in Contemporary International Legal Thought' (2014) 2(1) *London Review of International Law* 77.

23 See, for example, Martti Koskenniemi, *From Apology to Utopia: The Structure of International Legal Argument* (Cambridge University Press, 2006).

24 See, for example, on Third World Approaches to International Law: B.S. Chimni, 'Third World Approaches to International Law: A Manifesto' (2006) 8(1) *International Community Law Review* 27; James T. Gathii, 'TWAIL: A Brief History of its Origins, its Decentralized Network and a Tentative Bibliography' (2011) 3(1) *Trade, Law and*

commitments made and emphasise that states and other guardians of the international legal order should ensure those promises are kept, as well as to suggest the best means for doing so. Moreover, an emphasis has been placed on the importance of ensuring equity in the distribution of legal burdens and the principle of common but differentiated responsibilities should have a greater role to play in the wider framework of international law.

Finally, this book has illuminated that legal systems can accommodate and oscillate between distinct ideological approaches. The domination of individualist or statist approaches does not preclude the emergence of regulatory spaces for altruism in international law. Indeed, the architecture of international law is constituted by both individualist rules and altruistic standards. Given that altruistic standards are by nature malleable, in a context of changing state behaviour, it is hoped that states will fulfil rather than retrench from the commitments made to the other. There is much hope for altruism in international law and the role it can play in ensuring the universal realisation of human rights, peace among nations, development and environmental protection. While altruism is undoubtedly present in the fabric of international law, the form that brings altruism to life can mean that in practice it waxes and wanes over time. If the promise of altruism in international law is to be kept, states must – to paraphrase Martin Luther King on the promise of domestic civil rights – 'be true to what [they] said on paper'.[25]

Development 26; Antony Anghie, *Imperialism, Sovereignty and the Making of International Law* (Cambridge University Press, 2012).

25 Martin Luther King, 'I've been to the Mountaintop', 3 April 1968, www.americanrhetoric.com/speeches/mlkivebeentothemountaintop.htm.

SELECT BIBLIOGRAPHY

Books

Allott, Philip, *Eunomia: New Order for a New World* (2nd ed., Oxford University Press, 2001).

Alvarez, José, 'State Sovereignty Is Not Withering Away: A Few Lessons for the Future' in Antonio Cassese (ed.), *Realizing Utopia: The Future of International Law* (Oxford University Press, 2012).

Alvarez, José, 'The Schizophrenias of R2P' in Euan MacDonald and Philip Alston (eds.), *Human Rights, Intervention, and the Right to Force* (Oxford University Press, 2008).

Anghie, Antony, *Imperialism, Sovereignty and the Making of International Law* (Cambridge University Press, 2012).

Appiah, Kwame Antony, *Cosmopolitanism: Ethics in a World of Strangers* (Allen Lane, 2006).

Arendt, Hannah, *The Origins of Totalitarianism* (Allen and Unwin, 1958).

Attfield, Robin, *Environmental Ethics: An Overview for the 21st Century* (Polity Press, 2003).

Bagnoli, Carla, 'Humanitarian Intervention as Perfect Duty: A Kantian Argument' in Terry Nardin and Melissa Williams (eds.), *Humanitarian Intervention* (New York University Press, 2006).

Barnett, Michael and Weiss, Thomas G., 'Humanitarianism: A Brief History of the Present' in Michael Barnett and Thomas G. Weiss (eds.), *Humanitarianism in Question: Politics, Power, Ethics* (Cornell University Press, 2008).

Batson, Daniel C., *The Altruism Question: Toward a Social-Psychological Answer* (Lawrence Erlbaum Associates, 1991).

Beitz, Charles R., 'Cosmopolitan Liberalism and the States System' in Chris Brown (ed.), *Political Restructuring in Europe: Ethical Perspectives* (Routledge, 1994).

Beitz, Charles R., *Political Theory and International Relations* (Princeton University Press, 1999).

Berman, Franklin, 'The International Court of Justice as an Agent of Development?' in Christian Tams and James Sloan (eds.), *The Development of International Law by the International Court of Justice* (Oxford University Press, 2013).

Bianchi, Andrea, 'The Role of Non-State Actors in the Globalization of Human Rights: An International Lawyer's Perspective' in Gunther Teubner (ed.), *Global Law without the State* (Dartmouth Gower, 1997).

Bianchi, Andrea, *International Law Theories: An Inquiry into Different Ways of Thinking* (Oxford University Press, 2016).

Bianchi, Andrea, 'On Power and Illusion: The Concept of Transparency in International Law' in Andrea Bianchi and Anne Peters (eds.), *Transparency in International Law* (Cambridge University Press, 2013).

Blake, Michael, 'We Are All Cosmopolitans Now' in Gillian Brock (ed.), *Cosmopolitanism versus Non-Cosmopolitanism: Critiques, Defenses, Reconceptualizations* (Oxford University Press, 2013).

Boisson de Chazournes, Laurence, 'Responsibility to Protect: Reflecting Solidarity?' in Rüdiger Wolfrum and Chie Kojima (eds.), *Solidarity: A Structural Principle of International Law* (Springer, 2010).

Boisson de Chazournes, Laurence, *Fresh Water in International Law* (Oxford University Press, 2013).

Boisson de Chazournes, Laurence and Rudall, Jason, 'Co-operation' in Jorge E. Viñuales (ed.), *The UN Friendly Relations Declaration at 50: An Assessment of the Fundamental Principles of International Law* (Cambridge University Press, 2020).

Brock, Gillian, 'Rethinking the Cosmopolitanism versus Non-Cosmopolitanism Debate: An Introduction' in Gillian Brock (ed.), *Cosmopolitanism versus Non-Cosmopolitanism: Critiques, Defenses, Reconceptualizations* (Oxford University Press, 2013).

Brölmann, Catherine, 'The PCIJ and International Rights of Groups and Individuals' in Christian Tams and Malgosia Fitzmaurice (eds.), *Legacies of the Permanent Court of International Justice* (Martinus Nijhoff, 2013).

Brown, Garrett Wallace, *Grounding Cosmopolitanism: From Kant to the Idea of a Cosmopolitan Constitution* (Edinburgh University Press, 2009).

Brownlie, Ian, *Principles of International Law* (7th ed., Oxford University Press, 2008).

Buchanan, Allen, *Justice, Legitimacy and Self-Determination: Moral Foundations for International Law* (Oxford University Press on Demand, 2004).

Bull, Hedley, *The Anarchical Society: A Study of Order in World Politics* (2nd ed., Columbia University Press, 1977).

Campbell, Tom, *The Left and Rights: A Conceptual Analysis of the Idea of Socialist Rights* (Routledge, 1983).

Caney, Simon, 'Human Rights and Global Climate Change' in Roland Pierik and Werner Wouter (eds.), *Cosmopolitanism in Context: Perspectives from International Law and Political Theory* (Cambridge University Press, 2010).

Capps, Patrick, *Human Dignity and the Foundations of International Law* (Hart, 2009).

Cassese, Antonio, *International Law* (2nd ed., Oxford University Press, 2005).

Cavallar, Georg, *The Rights of Strangers* (Ashgate, 2002).

Chesterman, Simon, *Just War or Just Peace?: Humanitarian Intervention and International Law* (Oxford University Press, 2001).

Christian, Tams, *Enforcing Obligations Erga Omnes in International Law* (Cambridge University Press, 2010).

Clapham, Andrew, *Human Rights Obligations of Non-State Actors* (Oxford University Press, 2006).

Clapham, Andrew, 'Responsibility to Protect: "Some Sort of Commitment"' in Vincent Chetail (ed.), *Conflits, sécurité et coopération: Liber amicorum Victor-Yves Ghebali* (Bruylant, 2007), 169.

Clapham, Andrew, 'Rights and Responsibilities: A Legal Perspective' in Oliver Jutersonke and Keith Krause (eds.), *From Rights to Responsibilities: Rethinking Interventions for Humanitarian Purposes* (Programme for Strategic and International Security Studies, 2006).

Comte, Auguste, *System of Positive Polity, Volume 1: Containing the General View of Positivism & Introductory Principles*, translated by John Henry Bridges (Burt Franklin, 1973).

Condorelli, Luigi and Boisson de Chazournes, Laurence, 'Quelques remarques a propos de l'obligation des Etates de "respecter et faire respecter" le droit international humanitaire "en toutes circonstances"' in Christophe Swinarski (ed.), *Studies and Essays on International Humanitarian Law and Red Cross Principles in Honour of Jean Pictet* (ICRC/Martinus Nijhoff, 1984).

Craven, Matthew, *The International Covenant on Economic, Social and Cultural Rights: A Perspective on Its Development* (Clarendon Press, 1995).

Crisp, Roger, 'Ethics and International Environmental Law' in Samantha Besson and John Tasioulas (eds.), *The Philosophy of International Law* (Oxford University Press, 2010).

Dagan, Hanoch, *Unjust Enrichment: A Study of Private Law and Public Values*, vol. 7 (Cambridge University Press, 1997).

Dann, Philipp, *The Law of Development Cooperation: A Comparative Analysis of the World Bank, the EU and Germany* (Cambridge University Press, 2013).

Dann, Philipp, 'Solidarity and the Law of Development Cooperation' in Rüdiger Wolfrum and Chie Kojima (eds.), *Solidarity: A Structural Principle of International Law* (Springer, 2010).

Dawidowicz, Martin, *Third-Party Countermeasures in International Law* (Cambridge University Press, 2017).

Dawkins, Richard, *The Selfish Gene* (2nd ed., Oxford University Press, 1989).

Delanty, Gerard, *Citizenship in a Global Age* (Open University Press, 2000).

Deng, Francis M., Kimaro, Sadikiel, Lyons, Terrence, Rothchild, Donald and Zartman, William, *Sovereignty as Responsibility: Conflict Management in Africa* (Brookings Institution Press, 1996).

Domingo, Rafael, *The New Global Law* (Cambridge University Press, 2010).

Donagan, Alan, *The Theory of Morality* (University of Chicago Press, 1979).

Donnelly, Jack, *Universal Human Rights in Theory and Practice* (Cornell University Press, 2003).

Dowell-Jones, Mary, *Contextualising the International Covenant on Economic, Social and Cultural Rights: Assessing the Economic Deficit*, vol. 80 (Martinus Nijhoff, 2004), 84.

Dupuy, Pierre-Marie and Viñuales, Jorge E., *International Environmental Law* (2nd ed., Cambridge University Press, 2018).

Dupuy, Pierre-Marie, 'La communauté internationale. Une fiction?' in Nicolas Angelet et al., *Droit du pouvoir, pouvoir du droit: mélanges offerts à Jean Salmón* (Bruylant, 2007).

Ehrlich, Eugen, *Fundamental Principles of the Sociology of Law* (Harvard University Press, 2002).

Finnemore, Martha, 'Constructing Norms of Humanitarian Intervention' in Peter J. Katzenstein (ed.), *The Culture of National Security: Norms and Identity in World Politics* (Columbia University Press, 1996).

Fish, Stanley, *Is There a Text in This Class* (Harvard University Press, 1980).

Flescher, Andrew Michael and Worthen, David, *The Altruistic Species: Scientific, Philosophical, and Religious Perspectives of Human Benevolence* (Templeton Foundation Press, 2007).

Franceschet, Antonio, *Kant and Liberal Internationalism* (Palgrave Macmillan, 1990).

Franck, Thomas, *Fairness in International Law and Institutions* (Clarendon Press, 1995).

Franke, Mark F. N., *Global Limits: Immanuel Kant, International Relations, and Critique of World Politics* (State University of New York Press, 2001).

Friedmann, Wolfgang, *The Changing Structure of International Law* (Columbia University Press, 1964).

Fuller, Lon, *The Morality of Law* (Yale University Press, 1964).

Garrett, Stephen, *Doing Good and Doing Well: An Examination of Humanitarian Intervention* (Praeger, 1999).

Geiß, Robin, 'The Obligation to Respect and to Ensure Respect for the Conventions' in Andrew Clapham, Paola Gaeta and Marco Sassòlli (eds.), *The 1949 Geneva Conventions: A Commentary* (Oxford University Press, 2015).

Giddens, Anthony, *The Consequences of Modernity* (Polity Press, 1990).

Goldsmith, Jack L. and Posner, Eric A., *The Limits of International Law* (Oxford University Press, 2006).

Goodwin-Gill, Guy S., *The Refugee in International Law* (Clarendon Press, 1996).

Gray, Kevin, 'Conflict Diamonds and the WTO: Not the Best Opportunity to be Missed for the Trade-Human Rights Interface' in Thomas Cottier,

Joost Pauwelyn and Elsabeth Bonanomi Burgi (eds.), *Human Rights and International Trade* (Oxford University Press, 2005).

Griffiths, Martin, Roach, Steven C. and Solomon, Scott M., *Fifty Key Thinkers in International Relations* (2nd ed., Routledge, 1999).

Habermas, Jürgen, *Justification and Application, Remarks on Discourse Ethics* (MIT Press, 1993).

Habermas, Jürgen, *Moral Consciousness and Communicative Action* (MIT Press, 1990).

Habermas, Jürgen, 'Postscript to Between Facts and Norms' in Mathieu Deflem (ed.), *Habermas, Modernity and Law* (Sage, 1996).

Heater, Derek, *World Citizenship* (Continuum, 2002).

Held, David, McGrew, Anthony, Goldblatt, David and Perraton, Jonathan, *Global Transformations: Politics, Economic and Culture* (Polity Press, 1999).

Held, David, 'Principles of Cosmopolitan Order' in Gillian Brock and Harry Brighouse (eds.), *The Political Philosophy of Cosmopolitanism* (Oxford University Press, 2009).

Henkin, Louis, *How Nations Behave* (2nd ed., Columbia University Press, 1979).

Herman, Barbara, *Moral Literacy* (Harvard University Press, 2007).

Hey, Ellen, 'Global Environmental Law and Global Institutions: A System Lacking "Good Process"' in Roland Pierik and Werner Wouter (eds.), *Cosmopolitanism in Context: Perspectives from International Law and Political Theory* (Cambridge University Press, 2010).

Higgins, Rosalyn, *Problems and Process: International Law and How We Use It* (Clarendon Press, 1994).

Hinsley, Francis Harry, *Sovereignty* (2nd ed., Cambridge University Press, 1986).

Hobbes, Thomas, *Leviathan* (Richard Tuck ed., Cambridge University Press, 1991).

Hoffe, Otfried, *Kant's Cosmopolitan Theory of Law and Peace* (Cambridge University Press, 2006).

Horkheimer, Max and Adorno, Theodor W., *Dialectic of Enlightenment: Philosophical Fragments* (Gunzelin Scmid Noerr ed., Edmund Jephcott trans., Stanford University Press, 2002).

Ishay, Micheline, *The History of Human Rights* (University of California Press, 2004).

Kant, Immanuel, 'Perpetual Peace: A Philosophical Sketch' in Reiss Hans (ed.), *Kant's Political Writings* (2nd ed., Cambridge University Press, 1991).

Kant, Immanuel, 'To Perpetual Peace: A Philosophical Sketch' (1795) in Ted Humphrey (trans.), *Perpetual Peace and Other Essays* (Hackett Publishing Company, 1983).

Kelman, Mark, *A Guide to Critical Legal Studies* (Harvard University Press, 1987).

Kelsen, Hans and Tucker, Robert W., *Principles of International Law* (Holt, Rinehart and Winston, 1966).

Kennedy, David, *The Dark Sides of Virtue: Reassessing International Humanitarianism* (Princeton University Press, 2005).

Keohane, Robert O. and Nye, Joseph, *Transnational Relations and World Politics* (Harvard University Press, 1972).

Kingsbury, Benedict, 'The International Legal Order' in Peter Cane and Mark Tushnet (eds.), *Oxford Handbook of Legal Studies* (Oxford University Press, 2003).

Klabbers, Jan and Piparinen, Touko (eds.), *Normative Pluralism and International Law: Exploring Global Governance* (Cambridge University Press, 2013).

Knox, John H., 'Diagonal Environmental Rights' in Mark Gibney and Sigrun Skogly (eds.), *Universal Human Rights and Territorial Obligations* (University of Pennsylvania Press, 2010).

Knox, John H., *Diagonal Environmental Rights* (University of Pennsylvania Press, 2010).

Kortmann, Jeroen, *Altruism in Private Law: Liability for Nonfeasance and Negotiorum Gestio* (Oxford University Press, 2005).

Koskenniemi, Martti, *From Apology to Utopia: The Structure of International Legal Argument* (Cambridge University Press, 2006).

Krieg, Andreas, 'National Interests and Altruism in Humanitarian Intervention' in Andreas Krieg (ed.), *Motivations for Humanitarian Intervention* (Springer, 2013).

Künnemann, Rolf, 'Extraterritorial Application of the International Covenant on Economic, Social and Cultural Rights' in Fons Coomans and Menno T. Kamminga (eds.), *Extraterritorial Application of Human Rights Treaties* (Intersentia, 2004).

Langford, Malcolm, Coomans, Fons and Gómez, Isa Felipe, 'Extraterritorial Duties in International Law' in Malcolm Langford, Wouter Vandenhole, Martin Scheinin and Willem van Genugten (eds.), *Global Justice, State Duties: The Extraterritorial Scope of Economic, Social and Cultural Rights in International Law* (Cambridge University Press, 2012).

Lanovoy, Vladyslav, 'Complicity in an Internationally Wrongful Act' in André Nollkaemper and Illias Plakokefalos (eds.), *Principles of Shared Responsibility in International Law* (Cambridge University Press, 2014).

Lauterpacht, Hersch, *International Law and Human Rights* (Stevens and Sons, 1950).

Lauterpacht, Hersch, *The Development of International Law by the International Court* (Cambridge University Press, 1982).

Lauterpacht, Hersch, *The Function of Law in the International Community* (Clarendon Press, 1933).

Lawrence, Peter, *Justice for Future Generations: Climate Change and International Law* (Edward Elgar Publishing, 2014).

Linklater, Andrew, 'Cosmopolitan Harm Conventions' in Steven Vertovec and Robin Cohen (eds.), *Conceiving Cosmopolitanism: Theory, Context and Practice* (Oxford University Press, 2002).

Locke, John, *Second Treatise on Civil Government* (Peter Laslett ed., 3rd ed., Cambridge University Press, 1988).

Luhmann, Niklas, *Law as a Social System* (Oxford University Press, 2004).

Luhmann, Niklas, *Social Systems* (Stanford University Press, 1995).

Macaulay, Jacqueline and Berkowitz, Leonard, *Altruism and Helping Behavior* (Academic Press, 1970).

Mann, Itamar, *Humanity at Sea: Maritime Migration and the Foundations of International Law* (Cambridge University Press, 2016).

McCormack, Tara, 'R2P and the End of the Western Century in Critical Perspectives on R2P' in Phillip Cunliffe (ed.), *Critical Perspectives on the Responsibility to Protect* (Routledge, 2011).

Mégret, Frédéric, 'Where Does the Critique of International Human Rights Stand? An Exploration in 18 Vignettes' in José Maria Beneyto and David Kennedy (eds.), *New Approaches to International Law: The European and the American Experiences* (Springer, 2012).

Meron, Theodor, *The Humanization of International Law* (Martinus Nijhoff, 2006).

Miller, David, *National Responsibility and Global Justice* (Oxford University Press, 2008).

Monroe, Kristen Renwick, *The Heart of Altruism: Perceptions of a Common Humanity* (Princeton University Press, 1996).

Morgenthau, Hans, *Politics among Nations: The Struggle for Power and Peace* (4th ed., Alfred A. Knopf, 1978).

Mower, Glenn, *International Cooperation for Social Justice: Global and Regional Protection of Economic and Social Rights* (Greenwood Press, 1985).

Myrdal, Gunnar, *An American Dilemma* (Harper & Bros, 1944).

Nadakavukaren Schefer, Krista, 'Stopping Trade in Conflict Diamonds: Exploring the Trade and Human Rights Interface with the WTO Waiver for the Kimberley Process' in Thomas Cottier, Joost Pauwelyn and Elisabeth Bürgi Bonanomi (eds.), *Human Rights and International Trade* (Oxford University Press, 2005).

Nagel, Thomas, *The Possibility of Altruism* (Princeton University Press, 1979).

Nagel, Thomas, *The View from Nowhere* (Oxford University Press, 1986).

Neuhold, Hanspeter, 'Common Security: The Litmus Test of International Solidarity' in Rüdiger Wolfrum and Chie Kojima (eds.), *Solidarity: A Structural Principle of International Law* (Springer, 2010).

Nollkaemper, André, '"Failures to Protect" in International Law' in Marc Weller (ed.), *Handbook on the Prohibition of the Use of Force* (Oxford University Press, 2014).

Nussbaum, Martha C., 'Patriotism and Cosmopolitanism' in Joshua Cohen (ed.), *For Love of Country* (Beacon Press, 1996).

Nussbaum, Martha C., *Frontiers of Justice: Disability, Nationality, Species Membership* (Harvard University Press, 2007).

O'Neill, Onora, *Towards Justice and Virtue* (Cambridge University Press, 1996).

Oleschak-Pillai, Rekha, 'Accountability of International Organisations: An Analysis of the World Bank's Inspection Panel' in Jan Wouters, Eva Brems, Stefan Smis and Pierre Schmitt (eds.), *Accountability for Human Rights Violations by International Organisations* (Intersentia, 2010).

Orford, Anne, *International Authority and the Responsibility to Protect* (Cambridge University Press, 2011).

Ost, François, 'Between Order and Disorder: The Game of Law' in Gunther Teubner (ed.), *Autopoietic Law: A New Approach to Law and Society* (De Gruyter, 1988).

Ozinga, James R., *Altruism* (Praeger, 1999).

Peters, Anne, 'The Responsibility to Protect: Spelling out the Hard Legal Consequences for the UN Security Council and Its Members' in Ulrich Fastenrath, Rudolf Geiger, Daniel-Erasmus Khan, Andreas Paulus, Sabine von Schorlemer and Christoph Vedder (eds.), *Bilateralism to Community Interest: Essays in Honour of Judge Bruno Simma* (Oxford University Press, 2011).

Pierik, Roland and Wouter, Werner, 'Cosmopolitanism in Context: An Introduction' in Pierik Roland and Werner Wouter (eds.), *Cosmopolitanism in Context* (Cambridge University Press, 2010).

Pinker, Steven, *The Better Angels of Our Nature: The Decline of Violence in History and Its Causes* (Penguin Books, 2012).

Pogge, Thomas, *World Poverty and Human Rights* (Polity, 2008).

Pogge, Thomas, 'A Universalistic Approach to International Justice' in Giuseppe Zaccaria (ed.), *International Justice and Interpretation* (Lit Verlag, 2002).

Pogge, Thomas, 'Cosmopolitanism and Sovereignty' in Chris Brown (ed.), *Political Restructuring in Europe: Ethical Perspectives* (Routledge, 1992).

Pogge, Thomas, 'Cosmopolitanism' in Robert Goodin and Phillip Pettit (eds.), *A Companion to Contemporary Political Philosophy* (2nd ed., Wiley-Blackwell Publishing, 2007).

Porras, Ileana, 'Liberal Cosmopolitanism or Cosmopolitan Liberalism' in Mortimer Sellers (ed.), *Parochialism, Cosmopolitanism, and the Foundations of International Law* (Cambridge University Press, 2012).

Posner, Eric, *Law and Social Norms* (Harvard University Press, 2000).

Post, Stephen G., Underwood, Lynn G., Schloss, Jeffrey P. and Hurlbut, William B., 'General Introduction' in *Altruism and Altruistic Love: Science, Philosophy, and Religion in Dialogue* (Oxford University Press, 2002).

Puffendorf, Samuel von, *On the Duty of Man and Citizen According to Natural Law* (Cambridge University Press, 1991).

Rajamani, Lavanya, *Differential Treatment in International Environmental Law* (Oxford University Press, 2006).

Ratner, Steven R., *The Thin Justice of International Law: A Moral Reckoning of the Law of Nations* (Oxford University Press, 2014).

Rawls, John, *The Law of Peoples: With 'The Idea of Public Reason Revisited'* (Harvard University Press, 2001).

Raz, Joseph, *The Morality of Freedom* (Clarendon Press,1986).

Redmond, Trevor, *People, States and Hope, Cosmopolitanism and the Future of International Law* (Wolf Legal, 2012).

Romano, Cesare P. R., Alter, Karen J., and Avergerou, Chrisanthi, *The Oxford Handbook of International Adjudication* (Oxford University Press, 2014).

Rorty, Richard, *Contingency, Irony, and Solidarity* (Cambridge University Press, 1989).

Rudall, Jason, *Compensation for Environmental Damage under International Law* (Routledge, 2020).

Rudall, Jason, 'Not Just a Wit But a Cause of Wit in Others: The Influence of Human Rights in International Litigation' in Nikos Skoutaris, Avidan Kent and Jamie Trinidad (eds.), *The Future of International Courts and Tribunals* (Routledge, 2019).

Rushton, Philippe J., *Altruism, Socialization, and Society* (Englewood Cliffs/ Prentice-Hall, 1980).

Salomon, Margot, *Global Responsibility for Human Rights: World Poverty and the Development of International Law* (Oxford University Press, 2007).

Sands, Philippe, *East West Street: On the Origins of Genocide and Crimes against Humanity* (Weidenfeld and Nicolson, 2016).

Schabas, William A., *Genocide in International Law* (Cambridge University Press, 2000).

Scheffler, Samuel, *Boundaries and Allegiances* (Oxford University Press, 2001).

Scheffler, Samuel, *Equality and Tradition: Questions of Value in Moral and Political Theory* (Oxford University Press, 2010).

Schwartz, Mortimer et al., *Problems in Legal Ethics (American Casebook Series)* (8th ed., Thomson West, 2007).

Sellers, Mortimer N. S., *Parochialism, Cosmopolitanism, and the Foundations of International Law* (Cambridge University Press, 2012).

Sengupta, Arjun, 'Poverty Eradication and Human Rights' in Thomas Pogge (ed.), *Freedom from Poverty as a Human Right* (UNESCO Publishing, 2007).

Sepúlveda, M. Magdalena and Carmona, María Magdalena Sepúlveda, *The Nature of the Obligations under the International Covenant on Economic, Social and Cultural Rights*, vol. 18 (Intersentia, 2003).

Shahabuddeen, Mohamed, *International Criminal Justice at the Yugoslav Tribunal – A Judge's Recollection* (Oxford University Press, 2012).

Shany, Yuval, *Assessing the Effectiveness of International Courts* (Oxford University Press, 2014).

Shapcott, Richard, *International Ethics: A Critical Introduction* (Wiley, 2010).

Shaw, Malcolm, *International Law* (5th ed., Cambridge University Press, 2003).
Shue, Henry, 'Human Rights, Climate Change, and the Trillionth Ton' in Denis G. Arnold (ed.), *The Ethics of Global Climate Change* (Cambridge University Press, 2011).
Simma, Bruno, *From Bilateralism to Community Interest in International Law* (Martinus Nijhoff, 1994).
Singer, Peter, *The Expanding Circle: Ethics, Evolution, and Moral Progress* (Princeton University Press, 2011).
Skogly, Sigrun, *Beyond National Borders: States' Human Rights Obligations in International Cooperation* (Intersentia, 2006).
Skogly, Sigrun and Gibney, Mark, 'Economic Rights and Extraterritorial Obligations' in Shareen Hertel and Lanse Minkler (eds.), *Economic Rights: Conceptual, Measurement and Policy Issues* (Cambridge University Press, 2007).
Slaughter, Anne-Marie, *A New World Order* (Princeton University Press, 2005).
Sloan, James and Hernández, Gleider, 'The Role of the International Court of Justice in the Development of the Institutional Law of the United Nations' in Christian Tams and James Sloan (eds.), *Development of International Law by the International Court of Justice* (Oxford University Press, 2013).
Stout, Lynn, 'Law and Prosocial Behaviour' in Eyal Zamir and Doron Teichman (eds.), *The Oxford Handbook of Behavioural Economics and the Law* (Oxford University Press, 2014).
Stout, Lynn, 'Other-Regarding Preferences and Social Norms' in John N. Drobak (ed.), *Norms and the Law* (Cambridge University Press, 2006).
Tadjbakhsh, Shahrbanou, 'Mahub ul Haq's Human Security Vision: An Unfettered Dream?' in Haq Khadija and Richard Ponzio (eds.), *Pioneering the Human Development* (Oxford University Press, 2008).
Tams, Christian and Sloan, James (eds.), *Development of International Law by the International Court of Justice* (Oxford University Press, 2013).
Teitel, Ruti, *Humanity's Law* (Oxford University Press, 2013).
Tesón, Fernando R., *A Philosophy of International Law* (Westview Press, 1998).
Tesón, Fernando R., *Humanitarian Intervention: An Inquiry into Law and Morality* (Transnational Publications, 1988).
Tomuschat, Christian, *Obligations Arising for States without or against their Will* (Martinus Nijhoff, 1993).
Tomuschat, Christian, *Human Rights: Between Idealism and Realism* (2nd ed., Oxford University Press, 2014).
Trindade, Antônio Augusto Cançado, 'A Century of International Justice and Prospects for the Future' in Andenas Mads and Bjorge Eirik (eds.), *A Farewell to Fragmentation: Reassertion and Convergence in International Law* (Cambridge University Press, 2015).
Tsagourias, Nikolaos K., *Jurisprudence of International Law: The Humanitarian Dimension* (Juris Publishing, 2000).

Vertovec, Steven and Cohen, Robin, 'Introduction: Conceiving Cosmopolitanism' in Steven Vertovec and Robin Cohen (eds.), *Conceiving Cosmopolitanism* (Oxford University Press, 2002).

von Bogdandy, Armin and Venzke, Ingo, 'The Spell of Precedents: Lawmaking by International Courts and Tribunals' in Cesare P. R. Romano, Karen J. Alter and Chrisanthi Avgerou (eds.), *The Oxford Handbook of International Adjudication* (Oxford University Press, 2014).

von Tigerstrom, Barbara, *Human Security and International Law: Prospects and Problems* (Hart Publishing, 2007).

Wabwile, Michael Nyongesa, *Legal Protection of Social and Economic Rights of Children in Developing Countries: Reassessing International Cooperation and Responsibility* (Intersentia, 2010).

Waltz, Kenneth, *Man, the State and War: A Theoretical Analysis* (Columbia University Press, 1959).

Walzer, Michael, *Just and Unjust Wars* (3rd ed., Basic Books, 2000).

Weiler, Joseph and Motoc, Iulia, 'Taking Democracy Seriously: The Normative Challenges to the International Legal System' in Stefan Griller (ed.), *International Economic Governance and Non-Economic Concerns - New Challenges for the International Legal Order* (Springer, 2003).

Wellens, Karel, 'Revisiting Solidarity as a (Re-)Emerging Constitutional Principle: Some Further Reflections' in Rüdiger Wolfrum and Chie Kojima (eds.), *Solidarity: A Structural Principle of International Law* (Springer, 2010).

Weller, Marc, *Handbook of the Use of Force in International Law* (Oxford University Press, 2015).

Wheeler, Nicolas, *Saving Strangers: Humanitarian Intervention in International Society* (Oxford University Press, 2000).

Wilde, Ralph, *The Extraterritorial Application of International Human Rights Law on Civil and Political Rights* (Routledge, 2013).

Young, Iris Marion, *Responsibility for Justice* (Oxford University Press, 2011).

Zimmerman, Andreas, 'The Obligation to Prevent Genocide: Towards a General Responsibility to Protect?' in Ulrich Fastenrath, Rudolf Geiger, Daniel-Erasmus Kahn, Andreas Paulus and Sabine von Schorlemer (eds.), *From Bilateralism to Community Interest: Essays in Honour of Bruno Simma* (Oxford University Press, 2011).

Articles

Abi-Saab, Georges, 'Whither the International Community?' (1998) 9 *European Journal of International Law* 248.

Allain, Jean, 'The *Jus Cogens* Nature of Non-refoulement' (2001) 13(4) *International Journal of Refugee Law* 533.

Alland, Denis, 'Countermeasures of General Interest' (2002) 13(5) *European Journal of International Law* 1211.

Alston, Philip and Quinn, Gerard, 'The Nature and Scope of States Parties' Obligations under the International Covenant on Economic, Social and Cultural Rights' (1987) 9(2) *Human Rights Quarterly* 156.

Alston, Philip, 'The Myopia of the Handmaidens: International Lawyers and Globalization' (1997) 3(8) *European Journal of International Law* 447.

Andreoni, James, 'Impure Altruism and Donations to Public Goods – A Theory of Warm-Glow Giving' (1990) 100(401) *The Economic Journal* 464.

Angelini, Antonella, 'A Trouble Shared is a Trouble Halved: How the Structure of Cooperation Matters for the Engagement of Responsibility in the World Bank Partnership Programmes' (2016) 13(1) *International Organizations Law Review* 171.

Arbour, Louise, 'The Responsibility to Protect as a Duty of Care in International Law and Practice' (2008) 34(3) *Review of International Studies* 445.

Authers, Benjamin and Charlesworth, Hilary, 'The Crisis and the Quotidian' (2013) 44(19) *Netherlands Yearbook of International Law* 38.

Azzam, Fateh, 'The Duty of Third States to Implement and Enforce International Humanitarian Law' (1997) 66(1) *Nordic Journal of International Law* 55.

Badescu, Cristina G. and Bergholm, Linnea, 'The Responsibility to Protect and the Conflict in Darfur: The Big Let-Down' (2009) 40(3) *Security Dialogue* 287.

Bedjaoui, Mohamed, 'Droit au développement et *jus cogens*', *Annuaire de l'AAA, (1984/86)* 54.

Beitz, Charles R., 'International Liberalism and Distributive Justice: A Survey of Recent Thought' (1999) 51(2) *World Politics* 269.

Bellamy, Alex J., 'The Responsibility to Protect-Five Years On' (2010) 24(2) *Ethics & International Affairs* 143.

Benvenisti, Eyal, 'Sovereigns as Trustees of Humanity: On the Accountability of States to Foreign Stakeholders' (2013) 107(2) *American Journal of International Law* 298.

Benzing, Markus, 'Community Interests in the Procedure of International Courts and Tribunals' (2006) 5(3) *Law and Practice of International Courts and Tribunals* 369.

Berman, Paul Schiff, 'From International Law to Law and Globalisation' (2015) 43 (2) *Columbia Journal of Translation Law* 485.

Bianchi, Andrea, 'Ad-hocism and the Rule of Law' (2002) 13(1) *European Journal of International Law* 265.

Bianchi, Andrea, 'Immunity versus Human Rights: The Pinochet Case' (1999) 10 (2) *European Journal of International Law* 237.

Bianchi, Andrea, 'Human Rights and the Magic of *Jus Cogens*' (2008) 19(3) *European Journal of International Law* 194.

Boisson de Chazournes, Laurence and Condorelli, Luigi, 'Common Article 1 of the Geneva Conventions Revisited: Protecting Collective Interests' (2000) 82(837) *International Review of the Red Cross* 67.

Boisson de Chazournes, Laurence, 'Les Ordonnances en Indication de Mesures Conservatoires dans L'affaire Relative à L'application de la Convention pour Law Prevention et la Repression du Crime de Genocide' (1993) 39(1) *Annuaire Français de Droit International* 515.

Boisson de Chazournes, Laurence, 'The EJIL Foreword: Plurality in the Fabric of International Courts and Tribunals: The Threads of a Managerial Approach' (2017) 28(1) *European Journal of International Law* 13.

Brilmayer, Lea and Tesfalidet, Isaias Yemane, 'Third State Obligations and the Enforcement of International Law' (2011–2012) 44(1) *Brigham Young University Journal of International Law and Policy* 1.

Brilmayer, Lea, 'Altruism in the International Environment' (1996) 44(1) *Cleveland State Law Review* 1.

Brunneé, Jutta and Toope, Stephen, 'The Responsibility to Protect and the Use of Force: Building Legality?' (2010) 2(3) *Global Responsibility to Protect* 191.

Buchanan, Ruth and Pahuja, Sundhya, 'Collaboration, Cosmopolitanism and Complicity' (2002) 71(2) *Nordic Journal of International Law* 297.

Caney, Simon, 'Climate Change and the Future: Discounting for Time, Wealth and Risk' (2009) 40(2) *Journal of Social Philosophy* 163.

Cassese, Antonio, 'Ex Iniuria Ius Oritur: Are We Moving Towards International Legitimation of Forcible Humanitarian Countermeasures in the World Community?' (1999) 10(1) *European Journal of International Law* 23.

Cassese, Antonio, 'Forcible Humanitarian Countermeasures in the World Community?' (1999) 10(1) *European Journal of International Law* 23.

Charlesworth, Hilary, 'International Law: A Discipline of Crisis' (2002) 64(3) *Modern Law Review* 377.

Charney, Jonathan I., 'Third State Remedies in International Law' (1989) 10(1) *Michigan Journal of International Law* 57.

Charney, Jonathan I., 'Universal International Law' (1993) 87(4) *American Journal of International Law* 529.

Charnovitz, Steve, Bartels, Lorand, Howse, Robert, Bradle, Jan, Pauwelyn, Joost and Regan, Donald, 'The Appellate Body's GSP Decision' (2004) 2(3) *World Trade Review* 239.

Chimni, B. S., 'Third World Approaches to International Law: A Manifesto' (2006) 8(1) *International Community Law Review* 27.

De Schutter, Olivier, Eide, Abjørn, Khalfan, Ashfaq, Orellana, Marcos, Salomon, Margot and Seiderman, Ian, 'Commentary to the Maastricht Principles on Extraterritorial Obligations of States in the Area of Economic, Social and Cultural Rights' (2012) 34(4) *Human Rights Quarterly* 1096.

Devillard, Alexandre, 'L'obligation de faire respecter le droit international humanitaire: l'article 1 commun aux Conventions de Geneve et leur Premiere Protocol Additionnel, fondement d'une droit international humanitarie de cooperation?' (2007) 20(2) *Revue québécoise de droit international* 75.

Dörmann, Knut and Serralvo, Jose, 'Common Article 1 to the Geneva Conventions and the Obligation to Prevent International Humanitarian Law Violations' (2014) 96 *International Review of the Red Cross* 707.

Dupuy, Pierre-Marie, 'International Law: Torn between Coexistence, Co-operation and Globalization: General Conclusions' (1998) 9 *European Journal of International Law* 278.

Dupuy, Pierre-Marie, 'Reviewing the Difficulties of Codification: On Ago's Classification of Obligations of Means and Obligations of Result in Relation to State Responsibility' (1999) 10(2) *European Journal of International Law* 371.

Engel, Christophe, 'Dictator Games: A Meta Study' (2011) 14(4) *Experimental Economics* 583.

Evans, Gareth, 'The Responsibility to Protect: An Idea Whose Time Has Come . . . And Gone?' (2008) 22(3) *International Relations* 283.

Fehr, Ernst and Schmidt, Klaus M., 'Theories of Fairness and Reciprocity – Evidence and Economic Application' (2000) CESifo Working Paper Series No. 403.

Feichtner, Isabel, 'The Waiver Power of the WTO: Opening the WTO for Political Debate on the Reconciliation of Competing Interests' (2009) 20(3) *European Journal of International Law* 615.

Feldman, Noah, 'Cosmopolitan Law?' (2007) 116(5) *Yale Law Journal* 1022.

Feller, Erika, 'Asylum, Migration and Refugee Protection: Realities, Myths and the Promise of Things to Come' (2006) 18(3–4) *International Journal of Refugee Law* 523.

Feria-Tinta, Monica and Milnes, Simon, 'The Rise of Environmental Law in International Dispute Resolution: Inter-American Court of Human Rights Issues Advisory Opinion on Environment and Human Rights' (2016) 27 *Yearbook of International Environmental Law* 64.

Fleck, Dieter, 'International Accountability for Violations of the *Ius in Bello:* The Impact of the ICRC Study on Customary International Humanitarian Law' (2006) 10–11(2) *Journal of Conflict and Security Law* 179.

Focarelli, Carlo, 'Common Article 1 of the 1949 Geneva Conventions: A Soup Bubble?' (2010) 21(1) *European Journal of International Law* 125.

Frances, Webber, 'The Pinochet Case: The Struggle for the Realisation of Human Rights' (1999) 26(4) *Journal of Law and Society* 523.

Gaja, Giorgio, 'The Position of Individuals in International Law: An ILC Perspective' (2010) 21(1) *European Journal of International Law* 11.

Galston, William A., 'Cosmopolitan Altruism' (1993) 10(1) *Social Philosophy & Policy* 118.

Gathii, James, 'TWAIL: A Brief History of Its Origins, Its Decentralized Network and a Tentative Bibliography' (2011) 3(1) *Trade, Law and Development* 26.

Gattini, Andrea, 'Breach of the Obligation to Prevent and Reparation Thereof in the ICJ's Genocide Judgment' (2007) 18(4) *European Journal of International Law* 695.

Glanville, Luke, 'The Antecedents of "Sovereignty as Responsibility"' (2011) 17(2) *European Journal of International Relations* 233.

Golder, Ben, 'Beyond Redemption? Problematising the Critique of Human Rights in Contemporary International Legal Thought' (2014) 2(1) *London Review of International Law* 77.

Gowlland-Debbas, Vera, 'The Limits of Unilateral Enforcement of Community Objectives in the Framework of UN Peace Maintenance' (2000) 11(2) *European Journal of International Law* 380.

Grossman, Gene M. and Sykes, Alan O., 'A Preference for Development: The Law and Economics of GSP' (2005) 41(4) *World Trade Review* 67.

Habermas, Jürgen, 'The Constitutionalization of International Law and the Legitimation Problems of a Constitution for World Society' (2008) 15(4) *Constellations* 444.

Hakimi, Monica, 'State Bystander Responsibility' (2010) 21(1) *European Journal of International Law* 341.

Hall, Margaux J. and Weiss, David, 'Avoiding Adaptation Apartheid: Climate Change Adaptation and Human Rights Law' (2012) 37 *Yale Journal of International Law* 309.

Harrison, Jeffrey L., 'Egoism, Altruism, and Market Illusions: The Limits of Law and Economics' (1985) 33 *UCLA Law Review* 1309.

Held, David and McGrew, Anthony, 'The End of the Old Order? Globalization and the Prospects for World Order' (1998) 24 *Review of International Studies* 219.

Held, David, 'Law of States, Law of Peoples: Three Models of Sovereignty' (2002) 8 (1) *Legal Theory* 9.

Higgins, Rosalyn, 'Ethics and International Law' (2010) 23(2) *Leiden Journal of International Law* 279.

Higgins, Rosalyn, 'Human Rights in the International Court of Justice' (2007) 20 (4) *Leiden Journal of International Law* 746.

Howse, Robert and Teitel, Ruti, 'Does Humanity-Law Require (or Imply) a Progressive Theory of History? (and Other Questions for Martti Koskenniemi)' (2013) 27 *Temple International and Comparative Law Review* 377.

Jeffries, Vincent, 'Virtue and the Altruistic Personality' (1998) 41(1) *Sociological Perspectives* 151.

Jost, John T., Federico, Christopher M. and Napier, Jaime L., 'Political Ideology: Its Structure, Functions, and Elective Affinities' (2009) 60 *Annual Review of Psychology* 307.

Kalshoven, Frits, 'The Undertaking to Respect and Ensure Respect in All Circumstances: From Tiny Seed to Ripening Fruit' (1999) 2 *Yearbook of International Humanitarian Law* 7.

Kennedy, Duncan, 'Form and Substance in Private Law Adjudication' (1976) 89(8) *Harvard Law Review* 1685.

Kennedy, Duncan, 'The Structure of Blackstone's Commentaries' (1979) 28(2) *Buffalo Law Review* 211.

Kingsbury, Benedict, 'A Grotian Tradition of Theory and Practice: Grotius, Law, and Moral Skepticism in the Thought of Hedley Bull' (1997) 17(4) *Quinnipiac Law Review* 3.

Kingsbury, Benedict, Krisch, Nico and Stewart, Richard, 'Global Administrative Law' (2005) 68(15) *Law & Contemporary Problems* 15.

Koskenniemi, Martti, 'Lauterpacht: The Victorian Tradition in International Law' (1997) 8 *European Journal of International Law* 215.

Koskenniemi, Martti, 'Legal Cosmopolitanism: Tom Franck's Messianic World' (2002) 471 *New York University Journal of International Law and Politics* 471.

Krever, Tor, Lisberger, Carl and Utzscneider, Max, 'Law on the Left: A Conversation with Duncan Kennedy' (2015) 10(1) *Unbound* 1.

Lauterpacht, Hersch, 'The Grotian Tradition in International Law' (1946) 23(1) *British Yearbook of International Law* 1.

Levy, Daniel and Sznaider, Natan, 'The Institutionalization of Cosmopolitan Morality: The Holocaust and Human Right' (2004) 3(2) *Journal of Human Rights* 144.

Linklater, Andrew, 'Citizenship, Humanity, and Cosmopolitan Harm Conventions' (2001) 22(3) *International Political Science Review* 261.

Linklater, Andrew, 'The Evolving Spheres of International Justice' (1999) 75(3) *International Affairs* 480.

Macdonald, Ronald St. J., 'Solidarity in the Practice and Discourse of Public International Law' (1996) 8 *Pace International Law Review* 261.

Marks, Stephen and Cooper, Nicolas, 'The Responsibility to Protect: Watershed or Old Wine in a New Bottle?' (2010) 2(1) *Jindal Global Law Review* 86.

Marlier, Grant and Crawford, Neta C., 'Incomplete and Imperfect Institutionalisation of Empathy and Altruism in the "Responsibility to Protect" Doctrine' (2013) 5(4) *Global Responsibility to Protect* 397.

McCorquodale, Robert and Simons, Penelope, 'Responsibility Beyond Borders: State Responsibility for Extraterritorial Violations by Corporations of International Human Rights Law' (2007) 70(4) *Modern Law Review* 598.

Meron, Theodor, 'Extraterritoriality of Human Rights Treaties' (1995) 89 *American Journal of International Law* 78.

Meron, Theodor, 'Common Rights of Mankind in Gentili, Grotius and Suarez' (1991) 85(1) *American Journal of International Law* 110.

Milanovic, Marco, 'State Responsibility for Genocide: A Follow-Up' (2007) 18 *European Journal of International Law* 670.

Millar, Richard, 'Humanitarian Intervention, Altruism and the Limits of Casuistry' (2000) 28(1) *The Journal of Religious Ethics* 3.

Nollkaemper, André and Jacobs, Dov, 'Shared Responsibility in International Law: A Conceptual Framework' (2013) 34 *Michigan Journal of International Law* 359.

Nussbaum, Martha C., 'Kant and Stoic Cosmopolitanism' (1997) 5(1) *Journal of Political Philosophy* 1.

Oetken, J. Paul, 'Form and Substance in Critical Legal Studies' (1991) 100(7) *The Yale Law Journal* 2209.

Paris, Francesco and Ghei, Nita, 'The Role of Reciprocity in International Law' (2003) 36(1) *Cornell International Law Journal* 93.

Paulus, Andreas L., 'Law and Politics in the Age of Globalization' (2000) 11 *European Journal of International Law* 472.

Pauwleyn, Joost, 'WTO Compassion or Superiority Complex?: What to Make of the WTO Waiver for "Conflict Diamonds"' (2003) 24(4) *Michigan Journal of International Law* 1177.

Peltonen, Hannes, 'Modelling International Collective Responsibility: The Case of Grave Humanitarian Crises' (2010) 36(2) *Review of International Studies* 235.

Peters, Anne, 'Humanity as the A and Ω of Sovereignty' (2009) 20(3) *European Journal of International Law* 513.

Pillai, Priya, 'Expanding the Scope of Provisional Measures under the Genocide Convention' (2020) 79(2) *Cambridge Law Journal* 201.

Pogge, Thomas W., 'Cosmopolitanism and Sovereignty' (1992) 103(1) *Ethics* 49.

Pound, Roscoe, 'A Theory of Judicial Decision for Today' (1923) 36(8) *Harvard Law Review* 558.

Reisman, Michael W., 'Acting before Victims Become Victims: Preventing and Arresting Mass Murder' (2008) 962 *Faculty Scholarship Series.*

Rudall, Jason, 'A Cartography of Cosmopolitanism: Particularising the Universal' (2014) 3(3) *Cambridge Journal of International and Comparative Law* 747.

Rudall, Jason, 'Certain Activities Carried out by Nicaragua in the Border Area (Costa Rica v. Nicaragua) – Compensation Owed by the Republic of Nicaragua to the Republic of Costa Rica' (2018) 112(2) *American Journal of International Law* 288.

Sassòli, Marco, 'State Responsibility for Violations of International Humanitarian Law' (2002) 84(846) *Revue Internationale de la Croix-Rouge/International Review of the Red Cross* 401.

Schachter, Oscar, 'International Law in Theory and Practice: General Course in Public International Law' (1982) 178 *Collected Courses of the Hague Academy of International Law* 333.

Schiff, Berman Paul, 'Review Essay: "Seeing Beyond the Limits of International Law," Goldsmith Jack L. and Posner Eric A., "The Limits of International Law"' (2006) 84 *Texas Law Review* 206.

Schwartz, Shalom, 'Normative Influences on Altruism' (1977) 10 *Advances in Experimental Social Psychology* 221.

Simma, Bruno and Alston, Philip, 'The Sources of Human Rights Law: Custom, Jus Cogens, and General Principles' (1988) 12 *Australian Yearbook of International Law* 82.

Snyder, David, 'The Case of Natural Obligations' (1995) 56(2) *Louisiana Law Review* 423.

Stahn, Carsten, 'Responsibility to Protect: Emerging Norm or Political Rhetoric?' (2007) 101(1) *American Journal of International Law* 99.

Stone, Christopher D., 'Common but Differentiated Responsibilities in International Law' (2004) 98 *American Journal of International Law* 276.

Strauss, Ekkehard, 'A Bird in the Hand is Worth Two in the Bush: On the Assumed Legal Nature of the Responsibility to Protect' (2009) 1(3) *Global Journal on the Responsibility to Protect* 291.

Sypnowich, Christine, 'Law as a Vehicle of Altruism' (1985) 5(2) *Oxford Journal of Legal Studies* 276.

Tesón, Fernando R., 'The Kantian Theory of International Law' (1992) 92(1) *Columbia Law Review* 53.

Torpey, John, 'Making Whole What Has Been Smashed: Reflections on Reparations' (2001) 73(2) *Journal of Modern History* 333.

Trivers, Robert, 'The Evolution of Reciprocal Altruism' (1971) 46(1) *The Quarterly Review of Biology* 35.

Trubek, David M., 'Where the Action Is: Critical Legal Studies and Empiricism' (1984) 36 *Stanford Law Review* 578.

Vandenhole, Wouter, 'Economic, Social and Cultural Rights in the CRC: Is There a Legal Obligation to Cooperate Internationally for Development?' (2009) 17(1) *The International Journal of Children's Rights* 23.

Wabwile, Michael, 'Re-examining States' External Obligations to Implement Economic and Social Rights of Children' (2009) 22(2) *Canadian Journal of Law and Jurisprudence* 407.

Welsh, Jennifer M. and Banda, Maria, 'International Law and the Responsibility to Protect: Clarifying or Expanding States' Responsibilities?' (2010) 2(3) *Global Responsibility to Protect* 213.

Wilde, Ralph, 'Human Rights Beyond Borders at the World Court: The Significance of the International Court of Justice's Jurisprudence on the Extraterritorial Application of International Human Rights Law Treaties' (2013) 12 *Chinese Journal of International Law* 639.

Wilde, Ralph, 'Triggering State Obligations Extraterritorially: The Spatial Test in Certain Human Rights Treaties' (2007) 40(2) *Israel Law Review* 503.

Wolfrum, Rüdiger, 'Solidarity amongst States: An Emerging Structural Principle of International Law' (2010) 49(1) *Dirieto ao desenvolvimento* 57.

Online Sources

Accra Agenda for Action (2008), www.oecd.org/dac/effectiveness/34428351.pdf.

'Altruism', *English Oxford Living Dictionary*, https://en.oxforddictionaries.com/definition/altruism.

'Altruism', *Oxford Dictionaries*, www.oxforddictionaries.com/definition/english/altruism.

Annan, Kofi, 'Two Concepts of Sovereignty 1999', www.un.org/news/ossg/sg/stories/kaecon.html.

Bartelson, Jens, *On the Indivisibility of Sovereignty* (Preprint 2010) VOLUME 2 (2). http://arcade.stanford.edu/rofl/indivisibility-sovereignty.

Benhabib, Seyla, 'Cosmopolitanism and Democracy: From Kant to Habermas,' www.goethe.de/ges/phi/prj/ffs/the/a97/en9507770.htm.

Bernstein, Alyssa, 'Moral Cosmopolitanism', in Chatterjee Deen *et al.* (eds.), *Encyclopaedia of Global Justice* (2012) 711, at 712, 716, www.philosophy.ohiou.edu/PDF/EGJ_Moral%20Cosmopolitanism_Vol-2.pdf.

Bohman, James and Rehg, William, 'Jürgen Habermas', *The Stanford Encyclopedia of Philosophy* (Winter 2011 Edition), Edward N. Zalta (ed.), http://plato.stanford.edu/archives/win2011/entries/habermas/.

Burton, Neel, 'Does True Altruism Exist', *Psychology Today* (27 March 2012), www.psychologytoday.com/blog/hide-and-seek/201203/does-true-altruism-exist.

Clark, David, 'Kosovo Was a Just War, Not an Imperialist Dress Rehearsal', *The Guardian*, (16 April 2009), www.theguardian.com/commentisfree/2009/apr/16/clark-kosovo-war-crimes.

Costa, Karen, 'Meeting the Challenges of a Globalized World: Extraterritorial Obligations in the Field of Human Rights' (October 2010) *H-Human Rights* 1, www.h-net.org/reviews/showrev.php?id=30023.

'David Cameron: UK to Accept "Thousands" More Syrian Refugees', BBC News, www.bbc.com/news/uk-34148913.

'Decision Removes Final Patent Obstacle to Cheap Drug Imports' (30 August 2003), www.wto.org/english/news_e/pres03_e/pr350_e.htm.

Ding, Jeffery, 'An Altruistic Approach to Human Rights Policy', www.drake.edu/media/departmentsoffices/international/nelson/ding.pdf.

Doha Declaration on Financing for Development (United Nations, 2008), www.un.org/esa/ffd/doha/documents/Doha_Declaration_FFD.pdf.

Dreef, Sofie, 'Review: Cosmopolitanism: Ideals and Realities' (2011) 3(4) *Amsterdam Law Forum* 105, http://amsterdamlawforum.org/article/viewFile/242/429.

Evans, Gareth, Interview with Yale Global editor Nayan Chanda (8 April 2011), www.youtube.com/watch?v=akshf67dnAs.

Extraterritorial Obligations Consortium website, www.etoconsortium.org.

Feria-Tinta, Monica and Milnes, Simon, 'The Rise of Environmental Law in International Dispute Resolution: Inter-American Court of Human Rights issues Advisory Opinion on Environment and Human Rights', *EJIL: Talk!* (26 February 2018), www.ejiltalk.org/the-rise-of-environmental-law-in-international-dispute-resolution-inter-american-court-of-human-rights-issues-landmark-advisory-opinion-on-environment-and-human-rights/.

Global Centre for the Responsibility to Protect, 'The Georgia-Russia Crisis and the Responsibility to Protect: Background Note' (19 August 2008), www.globalr2p.org/media/files/the-georgia-russia-crisis-and-the-r2p-background-note.pdf.

Hestermeyer, Holger, 'Reality or Aspiration? Solidarity in International Environmental and World Trade Law', Diversity and Homogeneity, Outcome Paper 2/2012 (Max Planck Institute, 2012), www.mpil.de/ww/de/pub/forschung/forschung_im_detail/projekte/otto_hah.

Hobbes, Thomas, *Leviathan or the Matter, Forme, & Power of a Common-Wealth Ecclesiastical and Civill* (1651), www.gutenberg.org/files/3207/3207-h/3207-h.htm.

Interlaken Declaration of 5 November 2002 on the Kimberley Process Certification Scheme for Rough Diamonds, www.kimberleyprocess.com/documents/basic_core_documents_en.html.

International Commission on Intervention and State Sovereignty, 'The Responsibility to Protect' (December 2001), http://responsibilitytoprotect.org/ICISS%20Report.pdf.

International Law Association website, www.ila-hq.org/en/about_us/index.cfm.

Kant, Immanuel, *Perpetual Peace: A Philosophical Sketch* (1795), www.mtholyoke.edu/acad/intrel/kant/kant1.htm.

King, Martin Luther, 'I've Been to the Mountaintop' (3 April 1968), www.americanrhetoric.com/speeches/mlkivebeentothemountaintop.htm.

Kleingeld, Pauline and Brown, Eric, 'Cosmopolitanism' in Edward N. Zalta (ed.), *The Stanford Encyclopedia of Philosophy* (Fall, 2013), http://plato.stanford.edu/archives/fall2013/entries/cosmopolitanism/.

Legislationonline.org, www.legislationline.org/documents/section/criminal-codes/country/30.

Maastricht Guidelines on Violations of Economic, Social and Cultural Rights 1997, adopted by a group of academic experts meeting in Maastricht from 22–26 January 1997, http://hrlibrary.umn.edu/instree/Maastrichtguidelines_.html.

Maastricht Principles on the Extraterritorial Obligations of States in the Area of Economic, Social and Cultural Rights 2011, www.ilsa.org/jessup/jessup17/Batch%202/Maastricht%20Principles%20on%20Extraterritorial%20Obligations%20of%20States%20in%20the%20Area%20of%20Economic,%20Social%20and%20Cultural%20Rights.pdf.

Millennium Development Goals, www.un.org/millenniumgoals/bkgd.shtml.

Orwell, George, 'Politics and the English Language', *Horizon* (April 1946), www.orwell.ru/library/essays/politics/english/e_polit.

Powderly, Joseph, 'Does "The Lady Doth Protest" Mark the Beginning of Myanmar's Reckoning?', *Justiceinfo.net* (10 December 2019), www.justiceinfo.net/en/justiceinfo-comment-and-debate/opinion/43190-the-lady-doth-protest-beginning-myanmar-reckoning.html.

Stout, Lynn, 'Judges as Altruistic Hierarchs' (2002) *Cornell Law Faculty Publications*, Paper 449, http://scholarship.law.cornell.edu/facpub/449?utm_source=scholarship.law.cornell.edu%2Ffacpub%2F449&utm_medium=PDF&utm_campaign=PDFCoverPages.

INDEX

Printed in the United Kingdom by TJ Clays Ltd.